Implementing Electronic Card Payment Systems

For quite a long time, computer security was a rather narrow field of study that was populated mainly by theoretical computer scientists, electrical engineers, and applied mathematicians. With the proliferation of open systems in general, and of the Internet and the World Wide Web (WWW) in particular, this situation has changed fundamentally. Today, computer and network practitioners are equally interested in computer security, since they require technologies and solutions that can be used to secure applications related to electronic commerce. Against this background, the field of computer security has become very broad and includes many topics of interest. The aim of this series is to publish state-of-the-art, high standard technical books on topics related to computer security. Further information about the series can be found on the WWW at the following URL:

http://www.esecurity.ch/serieseditor.html

Also, if you'd like to contribute to the series by writing a book about a topic related to computer security, feel free to contact either the Commissioning Editor or the Series Editor at Artech House.

Recent Titles in the Artech House Computer Security Series

Rolf Oppliger, Series Editor

Computer Forensics and Privacy, Michael A. Caloyannides

Demystifying the IPsec Puzzle, Sheila Frankel

Developing Secure Distributed Systems with CORBA, Ulrich Lang and Rudolf Schreiner

Implementing Electronic Card Payment Systems, Cristian Radu

Implementing Security for ATM Networks, Thomas Tarman and Edward Witzke

Information Hiding Techniques for Steganography and Digital Watermarking, Stefan Katzenbeisser and Fabien A. P. Petitcolas, editors

Internet and Intranet Security, Second Edition, Rolf Oppliger

Non-repudiation in Electronic Commerce, Jianying Zhou

Secure Messaging with PGP and S/MIME, Rolf Oppliger

Security Fundamentals for E-Commerce, Vesna Hassler

Security Technologies for the World Wide Web, Second Edition, Rolf Oppliger

Software Verification and Validation for Practitioners and Managers, Second Edition, Steven R. Rakitin

For a listing of recent titles in the *Artech House Computing Library*, turn to the back of this book.

Implementing Electronic Card Payment Systems

Cristian Radu

Artech House
Boston • London
www.artechhouse.com

Library of Congress Cataloging-in-Publication Data
Radu, Cristian.
   Implementing electronic card payment systems / Cristian Radu.
      p. cm.—(Artech House computer security series)
   Includes bibliographical references and index.
   ISBN 1-58053-305-1 (alk. paper)
   1. Electronic funds transfers.   2. Credit cards.   3. Debit cards.   4. Payment—Data processing.
   5. Electromagnetic compatibility.   I. Title.   II. Series.
   HG1710 .R33 2003
   658.8'8—dc21   2002033224

British Library Cataloguing in Publication Data
Radu, Cristian
   Implementing electronic card payment systems.—(Artech House computer security series)
   1. Electronic commerce—Security measures   2. Electronic funds transfers   3. Smart cards
   I. Title
   005.8'2
   ISBN   1-58053-305-1

Cover design by Yekaterina Ratner

© 2003 ARTECH HOUSE, INC.
685 Canton Street
Norwood, MA 02062

International Standard Book Number: 2002033224
Library of Congress Catalog Card Number: 1-58053-305-1

10 9 8 7 6 5 4 3 2 1

To Valentina, Cristina, and Matei

Contents

5   EMV™ Certificates   125

6   Debit and Credit with EMV™   147

Acknowledgments

At the end of this work it is a real pleasure for me to thank all the people who helped me during the writing of this book.

During my time with Integri I felt the warm friendship of all my colleagues, whose constructive assistance helped me a lot in working out many technical issues. The support of Frédéric Klopfert and Jan De Meester, directors of the Integri management team, is also highly appreciated. They encouraged me to start this work and they gave me the opportunity to participate in many interesting projects.

For their patient assistance with all my questions related to the elaboration of the final manuscript and for the constant encouragement during the whole project, I acknowledge Ruth Harris and Tim Pitts from Artech House Books.

Last, but definitely not least, I want to thank my wife, Valentina, my daughter Cristina, and my son Matei for their overwhelming love, devotion, and understanding that helped me to finish the work on this book.

CHAPTER

1

Contents

Introduction

There are several payment markets that can be identified, each using specific forms of money. The business-to-consumer (B2C) payment is used in commercial activities where the merchant is paid directly by the consumer for goods or services. This type of payment is also called retail payment. The direct payment between persons is called person-to-person (P2P) or even consumer-to-consumer (C2C). Administration-to-consumer (A2C) payment addresses the payment of taxes toward the government. Finally, the payment intervening between companies buying and those offering products and services is referred to as business-to-business (B2B) payment. A payment instrument refers to a form of money. A payment mechanism or payment method refers to the way a payment instrument is used to complete a payment transaction. Certainly, the range of payment instruments and payment mechanisms for B2C payments is different from the set of instruments available for other types of payments. This book analyzes only electronic payment instruments for B2C payments.

The concrete implementation of these instruments depends on the payment behavior of the consumer, the channels of interaction between the consumer's device and the merchant's device during payment, and the type of devices used to store the electronic payment instrument and to perform the corresponding payment mechanism.

The implementation of payment instruments is dependent on the consumer's payment behavior. Thus, payment instruments are designed to address consumers with credit, debit, or

1

prepaid payment behavior. The value of the transactions performed with credit cards is paid later, at the end of a certain period. When using debit cards, the value of the transactions is paid now, at the moment when a transaction takes place. The prepaid instruments require that the consumers make the provision of funds before engaging any payment transaction. Thus, an electronic purse is a prepaid instrument since the consumer has to transfer money from his or her account kept with the bank in the record of funds kept by the electronic purse in order to be able to pay. We limit the presentation of payment instruments to the range of debit and credit, since at present they show the biggest market potential in the area of retail payments.

The channel of interaction established during the payment between the consumer's device and the merchant's device determines the forms of payment instruments. In a face-to-face payment the consumer and the merchant, represented by their devices, are physically present at the place were the transaction is made. Paying with a magnetic stripe debit card at a point of sale (POS) terminal is a face-to-face payment where the consumer's device is a magnetic stripe card and the merchant's device is the POS terminal equipped with a magnetic stripe reader. In a remote payment both the consumer and the merchant are represented by their devices, which need a telecommunication network to complete the payment protocol, indifferent to their physical location. Using a payment application that runs on the consumer's personal computer (PC) and that communicates with the peer payment application running on the merchant's Web site is a remote payment that relies on the Internet. Remote payment also includes paying for an item at a vending machine with a mobile phone, since the payment protocol involves interaction between the two entities over a wireless communication network, even though the two entities are physically located at the same place. Debit and credit payment cards can be used in both face-to-face and remote interactions (provided that adequate communication channels are available for remote payment). For example, a dual mobile phone handset, which has a supplementary card reader for a chip card, can serve as a personal terminal that allows the consumer to pay with a debit or credit chip card and transport the financial data over wireless communication networks. There are many other types of intelligent platforms that allow for remote chip card payments, provided they are equipped with a chip card reader—namely, personal computers, workstations, personal digital assistants (PDAs), and TV set-top boxes.

We are concerned with two types of devices, both with plastic support, for the implementation of debit cards and credit cards: magnetic stripe cards where the financial information concerning the consumer and the issuer is carried in a magnetic stripe attached on the backside of the card, and chip cards where the information is stored in the permanent memory of a micro-processor chip embedded in the card.

The considerations mentioned above delimit the boundaries of our goal in this book. We will concentrate on the analysis and design of debit and credit payment cards, in both face-to-face and remote interactions, with implementations in magnetic stripe and chip card devices.

The book is logically organized into three major parts that reflect the evolution of debit and credit cards from implementations with magnetic stripe to chip and from face-to-face interaction towards remote interaction. This organization follows the actual trend in the retail financial industry, which spends considerable resources on chip migration and on the use of chip cards from various access devices over different interaction channels.

Part I: Magnetic stripe debit and credit cards

This part includes only Chapter 2. It analyzes debit and credit payment instruments as they are currently implemented with magnetic stripe cards. First we outline the general picture of electronic payment systems, identifying the participant roles and their business interactions. In this context, we concentrate on the magnetic stripe implementation of a debit/credit card and we discus the content of the financial data recorded on its magnetic tracks. Then we analyze the processing performed by the terminal on the financial data captured from the card for completing a transaction carried out at the point of service. We consider the security mechanisms that can be put in place for this type of card, and we identify some of the security threats that make them vulnerable to certain types of attacks. This security analysis aims to show the need of chip migration, which will better enforce the security of the participants in a payment system. Finally, we offer a high level view of the authorization, clearing, and settlement processing, which represent the backbone activity of any payment system that facilitates the business interaction between issuers of the payment cards and the acquirers of payment transactions collected from merchants.

Part II: Chip migration with EMV™

This part includes five chapters. In Chapter 3 we discuss chip migration, which defines the process of changing the implementation of a debit/credit card from magnetic stripe to chip. Two chip migration paths are identified and are analyzed through comparison. The first path is chip migration according to proprietary solutions. These solutions were independently adopted by pioneering payment systems that were willing to use new chip technology to cut down on losses generated by counterfeit and fraudulent transactions. The second path represents a chip migration solution where the interoperability plays a central role in the business model. In this case we discus only the EMV™ chip solution jointly proposed by the three major card associations—namely, Europay, MasterCard, and Visa (EMV™). We have chosen EMV™ since it has become a de facto standard in the area of debit/credit payment systems, considering the important market share held by these three card associations in retail financial services.

Chapter 4 discusses the organization of data according to EMV™. This data organization is common to those chip cards and card applications that claim to be EMV™ compliant regardless of the specific payment method they actually implement. The EMV™ data organization satisfies the issuers' business requirement of accommodating multiple payment applications, which are provided by different payment system operators, in the same chip card. It also satisfies the acquirers' business requirement of running an application selection mechanism in terminals without being aware beforehand of the internal organization of cards. These demands imply the need for a data organization that provides openness and interoperability, and EMV™ offers these features.

Chapter 5 defines the EMV™ certificates that are needed to build the trust relationship between an EMV™ card and the terminal at the point of service.

Chapter 6 details the EMV™ payment method for debit and credit. The aim is to offer a tutorial presentation on the transaction profile of the EMV™ debit and credit payment application. This presentation should allow for an easier understanding of the EMV™ documents by someone who has no time to read the entire specification. The emphasis of the presentation is placed on the analysis of the protocol between the chip card and the terminal, rather than discussing the card and the terminal separately. In this chapter, the functionality of the EMV™ debit and credit payment cards is considered only in a face-to-face interaction.

Chapter 7 focuses on management and organizational issues concerning the EMV™ chip migration. In this context we analyze the impact of chip migration on the roles involved in the implementation of the payment system infrastructure.

Part III: Remote debit and credit with EMV™

This part of the book, consisting of Chapter 8, is concerned with the analysis of the EMV™ Chip Electronic Commerce framework. In this framework, EMV™ chip cards can be used for remote payments, both in the electronic commerce (e-commerce) and mobile commerce (m-commerce) environments. Both types of remote payments build on top of the Secure Electronic Transaction™ (SET) specification, jointly developed by a consortium including MasterCard and Visa. SET is a secure protocol for using credit cards for conducting electronic payments over the Internet. This leverages the EMV™ functionality with the SET payment mechanism to provide the modality of a secure and cost-effective chip card transaction over the Internet.

The presentation order of the payment instruments in these three parts follows a ranking based on their proven business success at the moment, on their potential in conjunction with e-commerce and m-commerce, and on their possible evolution in the industry of retail payments.

In the last decade, credit and debit payment cards proved to be a big commercial success all over the world. Actual implementations with magnetic stripe cards, however, showed vulnerability to fraud, which generates significant financial losses. The migration towards chip cards is seen as a natural technological improvement that offers higher protection against fraud, better decision support at the point of service, and enhanced cardholder verification methods. In the European Union the issuing and acquiring banks that are members of Europay, MasterCard, and Visa card associations are migrating from the magnetic stripe cards to the EMV™ chip solution; the transition period ends on January 1, 2005. It can be expected that member banks of MasterCard and Visa located worldwide will also undergo the EMV™ chip migration path, but probably within a larger transition period.

Within the last few years, payments over the Internet have shown a big increase in number of transactions and value. The dominant payment mechanism at the moment is the transmission of financial data embossed on the front side of credit cards via a secure socket layer (SSL)-enabled browser, which securely communicates with the merchant's server. Whereas the SSL protocol offers confidentiality, authenticity, and integrity of the financial data during its journey from the consumer's browser to the merchant's Web server, it does not provide the non-repudiation security service, which would protect the merchant against a potential denial of the consumer. Once the financial data arrives at the merchant's site, it is stored in clear in the merchant's Web server. This renders the SSL powerless against subsequent attacks that target the financial data on the Web server itself, which is often the case. The use of SET, even though it offers enhanced security features compared to SSL, is still uncertain. One explanation could be that people consider the SET protocols too complex and expensive to process using dedicated software that must be bought by both consumers and merchants, while SSL offers a reasonable level of security to participants without the need to buy supplementary software. A strong business interest of participants already using SSL-enabled browsers and servers for migrating towards SET implementations would have to exist. The ability to use the same EMV™ debit/credit card products used in face-to-face transactions in remote payments over the Internet can increase the interest for SET as secure payment technology. Moreover, the SET infrastructure can be also used for processing financial transaction details captured in mobile payments.

Mobile payment instruments are, at the moment, highly ranked from the point of view of future potential rather than proven business success. It has become commonplace for people to click their mobile phone handsets while walking, driving, or traveling. The financial services industry has recognized this reality and hopes to increase the volume of retail financial operations using the mobile phone handset. This allows the triggering of a payment application based on a virtual card or simply facilitates the use of an EMV™ debit/credit card over public wireless networks.

MasterCard and Visa have made a significant effort in developing the SET and EMV™ specifications, as well as all the corresponding certification procedures for assessing software and hardware devices implementing these specifications. Therefore, it is foreseeable that they will also commercially promote their EMV™ integrated circuit card (ICC) solution as a means for payment for conducting e-commerce and m-commerce transactions over the Internet and mobile networks.

Considering the proposed content of this book, its target audience includes payment system designers, technical and business managers dealing with payment card products, card and terminal developers, as well as test engineers. These categories of specialists could be involved in ongoing projects based on the EMV™, SET, and wallet server technologies in face-to-face and remote payments. Researchers, graduate students, and undergraduate students will find an overall picture of the debit and credit payment instruments actually used in the industry of retail financial services. This can represent a starting point for potential improvements and innovations of payment instruments and payment mechanisms.

PART

I

Magnetic Stripe Debit and Credit Cards

CHAPTER

2

Contents

Payment Card Processing

The last three decades witnessed major advancements in payment technologies. On one hand, the payment infrastructure was created. This infrastructure consists of highly reliable computer networks connecting automatic teller machines (ATMs) and POS terminals with powerful mainframe computers of financial institutions. On the other hand, new carriers of the customer's financial data emerged. The most common are the magnetic stripe cards and ICCs, also known as chip cards. These developments provided the framework for the electronic processing of payment transactions.

This chapter considers only the electronic processing of credit and debit payment cards implemented with magnetic stripes. For those impatient to discover the overall picture, Section 2.1 gives a quick, broad view on payment card processing. This landscape reveals roles of the acquirer, the payment system operator, and the issuer, and Section 2.2 highlights their attributions in the payment card processing. Many actors can play the role of a payment system operator. In many countries, national bank associations have created dedicated companies to run a national payment network. The most reputed actors, however, are the multinational card associations like Visa, MasterCard, American Express, Europay, Diners Club, Discover, and JBC, which provide global coverage of their payment card processing and have boosted the payment card to the status that it enjoys today. Section 2.3 explains the concepts of card association and brand, which are at the core of the card business. Section 2.4 explains the main features of credit and debit cards, highlighting the differences between these two payment card products. Starting with the Section 2.5, we move quickly to more detailed functionality. First, we discuss the content of the financial data that is embossed or printed on a payment card and stored on its magnetic stripe. The possibilities of reading this information at the point of service are also outlined. Section 2.6 describes potential attacks on payment cards, as well as the corresponding security protections available for this type of card. This security analysis highlights the limitations of the magnetic stripe cards, revealing the need for migrating to ICC implementations. Section 2.7 focuses on the processing performed by the terminal. The rest of the chapter deals with what is called the payment system backbone. Its functionality is described in terms of payment messages exchanged between the acquirer, the payment system operator, and the issuer to complete various transactions. The concepts of authorization, clearing, and settlement are explained; these are basic processes carried out by the payment system. It is important to stress that the processing in the payment system backbone does not change drastically for the credit/debit payment transactions carried out with ICC.

2.1   Payment card processing at a glance

We address this section to those impatient to have at a glance the overall picture of payment card processing. We have chosen for this purpose the cash withdrawal transaction at an ATM terminal. As with any quick, general view, the reader can benefit from a fast orientation to the topic of payment card processing, but not all the details will be visible.

The overall picture is split into two parts: Figure 2.1 shows the things people usually see when using a debit card for withdrawing money at an ATM; Figure 2.2 reveals the unseen part of the payment card processing, which is sometimes referred to as the network and back-office processing. The financial institutions, including banks, payment system operators, and card associations, are involved in the completion of this part of the processing for each transaction carried out with a payment card.

On the backside of the debit card used for performing the money withdrawal, there is a magnetic stripe. It contains the financial data related to the cardholder in connection with an account kept with a bank. While passing this card through the magnetic stripe reader of the ATM, the financial data is read by the terminal and stored in its random access memory (RAM).

The cardholder is prompted to type in his or her personal identification number (PIN), which establishes the link between the user at the point of service and the legitimate cardholder. The cardholder is also prompted to

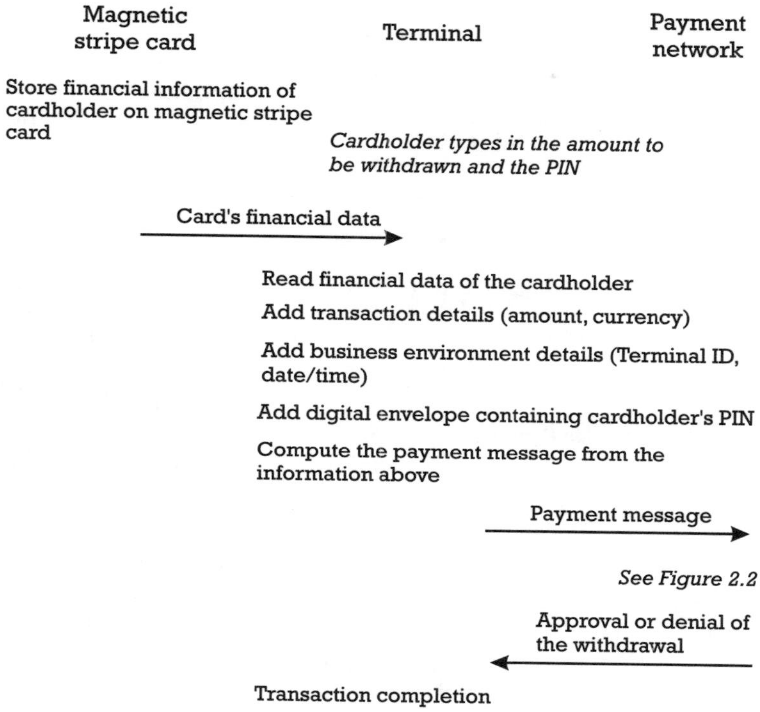

Figure 2.1
Payment card
processing—
things one can
see.

| Magnetic stripe card | Terminal | Payment network |

Store financial information of cardholder on magnetic stripe card

Cardholder types in the amount to be withdrawn and the PIN

Card's financial data →

Read financial data of the cardholder

Add transaction details (amount, currency)

Add business environment details (Terminal ID, date/time)

Add digital envelope containing cardholder's PIN

Compute the payment message from the information above

Payment message →

See Figure 2.2

← Approval or denial of the withdrawal

Transaction completion

type in the amount of cash to withdraw. After capturing this information from the cardholder, the terminal constructs the payment message. It contains the amount of the cash withdrawal combined with other information about the business environment at the point of service. This information includes but is not limited to the currency in which the amount is expressed, the identifier of the terminal, the date and time when the transaction took place, and the current serial number of the transaction performed by the terminal. The payment message also includes a cryptogram of the cardholder's PIN, which is the result of an encryption algorithm applied to the PIN.

At this point the processing performed by the ATM terminal ends, and the long journey of the payment message through the payment network begins. Figure 2.2 schematizes this journey to an oversimplified circuit composed of the acquirer, the payment system operator, and the issuer. It is important to notice that not all transactions at the point of service are directed on-line to the issuer for authorization. It could be that, after capturing the whole information from the card, the terminal has enough information for concluding the transaction off-line. In the case of an ATM money withdrawal, however, the issuer is usually involved on-line in the

Figure 2.2
Network and
back-office
processing of
payment card
transactions.

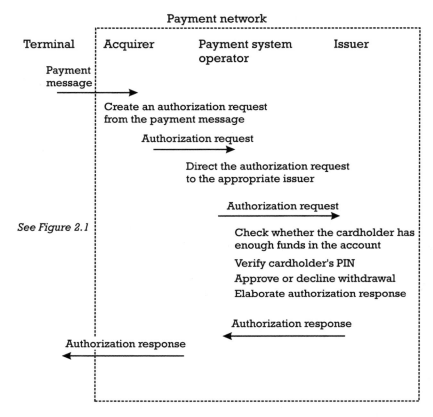

transaction for a better risk management. We will assume this situation for the remainder of this section.

The ATM terminal at the point of service forwards the payment message to the acquirer, which further submits the received message to an intricate electronic processing system. Several cooperating parties (the acquirer, the payment system operator, and the issuer of the payment card) participate in completing this processing. Payment messages are exchanged in real time or compiled in batch files following clearly established protocols. Each payment message conveys certain data elements depending on the scope of the processing. While the message is sent from one party to another, each party performs a predetermined set of transformations on the data elements contained in the message according to their business role in the payment system. The following steps roughly describe the processing.

The acquirer creates the authorization request. To this end, the acquirer adds to the payment message received from the terminal some data elements kept in its terminals database. These data elements include the location of the terminal involved in the withdrawal transaction, the type of terminal at the point of service and its capabilities, and the identification information of the acquirer node that creates the authorization request message. In addition, the acquirer translates the initial PIN cryptogram received from the terminal into a second cryptogram that can be deciphered by the payment system operator's secure module. The acquirer attaches the translated cryptogram to the authorization message.

The acquirer transmits the authorization message to the payment system operator's node in the payment network to which its acquirer host is connected. If the ATM withdrawal occurs in a foreign country, after receiving the authorization message, the payment system operator adds to it the actual exchange rate between the currency of the amount requested at the point of service and the currency used in the home country by the cardholder's issuer. Afterwards, the authorization message is directed to the destination node in the payment system operator's network, which is connected to the issuer host. It could be that the payment system operator performs a third conversion of the cardholder's PIN cryptogram using cryptographic parameters that are accessible to the secure module attached to the issuer host.

The issuer host is the final destination point for the authorization message. Based on the financial data in the authorization message, the account of the cardholder is identified. The cryptogram containing the PIN of the cardholder is deciphered in the secure module of the issuer host. This value is used to compute the PIN image control value, which is compared to a similar witness value stored in the cardholders' database since the personalization of the card. If the two values are equal, the issuer accepts the link between the user of the card at the point of service and the legitimate cardholder. Then, the issuer converts the cash amount in its own currency, using the currency exchange rate indicated by the payment system operator. If after deducting the amount requested in the transaction, the balance of the cardholder account is still higher than a floor limit (which could be either a negative value or zero), the issuer accepts the cash withdrawal transaction. Through an authorization response, the issuer host informs the acquirer about the approval or denial of the transaction. The acquirer instructs the ATM terminal at the point of service either to provide the required cash or to decline the transaction.

2.2   Roles involved in payment card processing

Several parties, also referred to as roles, are involved in the processing of a payment card transaction—namely, the issuer, the cardholder, the merchant, the acquirer, the card association, and the settlement bank. An overview of the payment system, including all these roles, is presented in Figure 2.3.

The issuer is a licensed financial institution or its agent that issues the payment card to the cardholder and is responsible for the provision of responses to authorization requests. The issuer remains unchanged during a transaction. The financial institution can be a bank, also referred to as the issuing bank, that is member of a card association and adopts a payment card product promoted by the card association. The issuer keeps the accounts of cardholders to which they charge bills or directly debit the amounts involved in the financial transactions performed by the cardholders. The issuer guarantees payment for authorized transactions, processing the payment card in accordance with the payment card product regulations and local legislation. The issuer supports the clearing and settlement functions between the cardholder and the acquirer. The issuer host is the computing system that accesses the cardholder accounts database and represents the issuer during the authorization, clearing, and settlement.

The cardholder is a customer of the issuer that uses a payment card in a B2C payment transaction. The cardholder is associated with the primary account number (PAN). The PAN gives enough information for identifying the account of the cardholder to which bills are charged or from which amounts are directly debited and the financial institution that keeps this account.

The card acceptor is the party that accepts a payment card at the point of service, formats the data of the transaction in a payment message, and forwards the payment message to the acquirer. The card acceptor can be a

Figure 2.3
Roles involved in
payment card
processing.

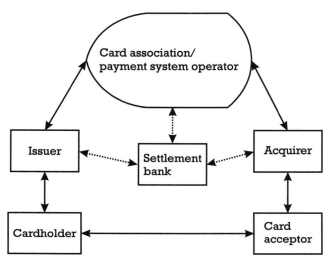

merchant selling goods or services or a branch bank disbursing cash for its customers. A supermarket selling groceries, a vending machine for beverages, a travel agent, or a small café can play the role of the merchant.

The acquirer is a licensed financial institution or its agent that acquires the payment message relating to a transaction from the card acceptor and feeds that data into an interchange system. The acquirer remains unchanged during a transaction. The financial institution can be a bank, also referred to as the acquiring bank, that is a member of a card association and adopts the payment card product designed and operated by that card association. From this perspective, the acquirer intermediates between the card acceptor and the card association, providing the card acceptor with operational support and needed infrastructure for card authorization, clearing, and settlement through the interchange system. The acquirer keeps the accounts of merchants, to whom they credit the amounts involved in the financial transactions performed at their point of service. The acquirer host is the computing system that accesses the merchant accounts database and represents the acquirer during the authorization, clearing, and settlement processes.

The card association is the owner of the payment card product. The card association's members are issuers and acquirers, providing the direct retail financial service for cardholders and merchants. The card association is responsible for running the interchange system that exchanges transaction data between acquirers and issuers during authorization, clearing, and settlement. The interchange system is implemented as a payment network with processor nodes connected to issuer hosts and acquirer hosts.

The settlement institution is a financial institution that holds the accounts of issuers and acquirers that are members of the card association. The settlement institution can be a bank that is subcontracted by the card association. This settlement bank acts on the transaction information provided by the issuers, acquirers, and the card association by transferring the appropriate funds between their accounts.

2.3   Payment card brands

A payment card is a payment instrument that allows bills in payment transactions to be charged to a designated account, which is linked to the card.

A card association or a payment system operator plays the central role in the card business. They have founded payment card brands to promote their payment card products, to establish and enforce rules for their use and acceptance, and to provide networks to connect end-to-end issuing and acquiring financial institutions. The brand signifies acceptance of a payment card with ATMs and POS terminals in shops, restaurants, and hotels, guaranteeing the availability of the payment service anytime and anywhere the logo of the brand is displayed. The logo is represented as a payment card decal that appears in the store window of the merchants accepting the corresponding card product. The decal itself is a representation that the merchant has a relationship with an acquirer, allowing it to accept the payment card brand. Each brand develops the necessary network infrastructure to support its cards, providing the availability of retail financial services for the customer. Some of the most known card associations are Visa [1], MasterCard [2], American Express [3], Europay [4], Diners Club [5], Discover [6], and JBC [7], to name only those reaching a global scale. Some of these card associations, like Visa, MasterCard, and Europay, are built as membership associations of banks, which mutually recognize and guarantee the payments done with their payment cards.

Each card association or payment system operator develops specific card products, addressing credit and debit payment behavior, but also electronic purse or virtual cards. Even in the same category of payment behavior, various card products are marketed. They address groups of people with various financial possibilities, within different categories of age, for ATM or POS services. Card products are designed for either face-to-face interaction or more recently for remote interaction, using the Internet or wireless telecommunication networks. There are card products that can answer both interaction modes simultaneously.

Each payment product implies a payment mechanism that describes the protocol of the payment transaction between the consumer and the merchant, as well as the processing performed by the acquirer, the card association, and the issuer on the payment message generated by this transaction.

2.4   Credit and debit payment cards

The emergence of payment cards was related to credit payment behavior, providing the convenience for consumers not to pay for purchases immediately, but rather pay later. The financial institution—either the card association itself or a member bank—that guarantees the consumer's payment allows for a well-established period of time for making the payment. Usually, for a credit card product all the payments performed between the end of the previous month and the end of the current month are compiled together in a single itemized statement. The consumer has to make a payment in full of the entire debt at the beginning of the next month.

When a bank issues a credit card, it can provide the real credit facility to its customers through revolving credit cards. When such an agreement intervenes between the bank and the customer, only an agreed percentage of the debt has to be paid each month. For the rest of the amount to be reimbursed, the bank applies a certain credit interest rate, which is referred to as the annual percentage rate (APR), which is spread out over a monthly period. When offering revolving credit cards, the financial institution may require the opening and maintaining of a savings account as security for the customer's line of credit, depending upon credit history that, for example, could have suffered some damages following a revenue crash [8, 9]. The revolving credit card with a savings account is sometimes called a secured (revolving credit) card. The possibility of offering revolving credit has to be seen as a customized feature, considering, for example, a temporary financial conjuncture of the customer.

Credit cards allow payments that involve amounts over a certain threshold or even some cash advance. To the basic financial service, the card issuer can add a number of supplementary services like quick credit card replacement, emergency money in case of lost or stolen cards, and juridical assistance in case the customer has disputes using the card.

The amounts involved in transactions performed with debit cards are debited directly from the designated account of the customer as soon as the bank keeping this account is informed of the transaction or at the latest when the clearing is performed.

Debit cards are always linked to the customer's account, enabling customers to immediately access their money. Therefore, having an account is an obligatory condition for debit card issuance. The customer and the issuing bank can set up two types of agreements. In the first setup, the condition of a successful payment is that the amount to be paid is less than the balance of the account. In this case both purchasing and ATM money withdrawal services are possible. In the second setup, the issuing bank accepts that purchase transactions can be still performed even when the balance of the customer's account is less than the amount of the transaction, with the condition that the deficit is not higher than an agreed-upon negative threshold.

2.5 Focusing on the magnetic stripe card

There are several coexisting possibilities for storing financial data on the plastic card:

▸ Data is embossed on the front side of the card and some data items are printed on the back side of the card.

- Data is laser engraved or is printed with indent printing machines, or is even thermal printed and displayed on the front side of the card.

- Data is encoded according to the bar code system and is displayed on the front side of the card.

- Data is encoded and recorded on a single magnetic stripe, which is applied on the back side of the card.

- Data is written in the permanent memory of an integrated circuit embedded in the card.

A payment card is basically a carrier of financial data. The ICC, however, provides active processing power in addition to passive storage facilities. In this chapter the encoding of financial data is explained in the case where data is embossed on the card or is recorded on a magnetic stripe attached to the card. The techniques of encoding financial data in the permanent memory of an ICC are described in Sections 3.3.1 and 3.4.1. The techniques of encoding the financial data according to the bar code system are not presented in this book.

2.5.1   Embossed financial data

Data is embossed on the front side of the card, according to the standard ISO/IEC 7811 [10], and some data items can be printed on the back side of the card.

Among the financial data items embossed on the card is the identification number of the card, which consists of a series of digits used to identify the card issuer and cardholder according to the standard ISO/IEC 7812 [11]. Note that that the identification number of the card is equivalent to the PAN, as introduced in the ISO/IEC 4909 [12]. Therefore, in the remainder of the book we will refer to the PAN whenever the identification number of the card is concerned. The PAN consists of a string of digits, divided into three items: the issuer identification number (IIN), the individual account identification, and a check digit.

- The first digit of the IIN specifies the major industry identifier (MII). It designates the branch of activities in which the issuer of the card is involved. The MII differentiates between cards issued by airline, travel and entertainment, banking and financial, or petroleum companies. The remaining digits of the IIN, which are referred to as the issuer identifier, designate a specific issuer in that branch of activities.

‣ The individual account identification is an individual number assigned by the issuer for the purpose of identifying an individual account related to the cardholder. It encodes the identity of the bank managing the account, in case this bank is not the issuer itself, and the number of the account kept by the cardholder with this bank.

‣ The check digit represents redundancy information computed as a check sum on all the other digits of the PAN.

Besides the PAN, the other data items embossed on the card are the expiration date, representing the year and the month after which the card is no longer valid, and the cardholder's name.

On the front side of the card is the logo of the card association's brand, the logo of the issuing organization, if this is different from the card association, and a hologram, which is an efficient visual method for card authentication.

On the back side of the card, beneath the magnetic stripe, there is a tamper evident band that stores the handwritten signature of the cardholder, which serves for the cardholder's verification. On this tamper-evident band the issuer can print supplementary security data for card authenticity verification. During an on-line validation of the card made by the operator at the point of service, this code is communicated on the telephone line to the issuer's operator, who can assess the authenticity of the card. This process is also referred to as voice referral at the point of service.

The embossed and printed information on the payment cards allows the manual capturing of financial data. Manual capturing is continually decreasing in face-to-face transactions at the point of service. This is determined by three factors:

1. The financial infrastructure of issuers, acquirers, and card associations is rapidly expanding, offering the possibility of electronic processing at the point of service, even in developing countries in Africa, Latin America, Asia, and Eastern Europe.

2. The price of electronic terminals and network connections to acquirers has become affordable even for small retailers.

3. The last (but not least) determinant factor is the liability of parties in case of fraud. The example below illustrates the concept of liability, since the liability policies applied by card associations are too complex to be explained here. In case a fake card was captured manually, the merchant or his acquirer is liable, whenever the issuer can prove

that the corresponding genuine card was carrying a magnetic stripe, which could have avoided the fraud.

However, the manual capturing of financial data is still practiced for the mail order (MO) transactions, as well as e-commerce transactions. In these cases the cardholder fills in the card data in appropriate fields in printed orders or in Hypertext Markup Language (HTML)/Common Gate Interface (CGI) forms, which are then sent to the merchant's mail dispatching center or Web server. Nonautomated capturing of card data is performed by the cardholder when communicating the financial data of the payment card to an operator of the merchant taking the cardholders' orders by telephone—these are telephone order (TO) transactions. Then, the operator manually captures the financial data communicated by the cardholder. In fact, the possibility of manually capturing the card's financial data made the payment cards one of the earliest payment instruments that can be easily used in remote payment transactions. The transactions triggered through mail orders or telephone orders are generically referred to as MO/TO transactions.

2.5.2 Financial data on the magnetic stripe

Data can be encoded and recorded on a single magnetic stripe that is applied on the back side of the card. The details are described in the standard ISO/IEC 7811 [10].

The magnetic stripe can store up to three tracks of recorded data: track 1 and track 2 are read-only magnetic tracks, and track 3 is a read/write magnetic track. The formats of tracks 1 and 2 are specified in the standard ISO/IEC 7813 [13], while the format of track 3 is detailed in the standard ISO/IEC 4909 [12].

The tracks contain extensive financial data about the cardholder, the issuer, as well as the financial parameters that serve in the process of terminal risk management.

2.5.2.1 Track 1 and track 2

Track 1 includes information similar to that embossed on the front side of the card—namely, the PAN, the cardholder's name, and the expiration date—to which some supplementary information is added. This information consists of the service code, the country code (which is included only for certain categories of PAN, the encoding of which is country-dependent), and the discretionary data. A check digit is added at the end of the first track as a verification of the correctness of all information recorded on the track.

The service code gives an indication about the type of business environment in which the card is authorized for use in a financial transaction. It consists of a code of three digits:

▸ The first digit specifies the type of interchange permitted: international, national, or restricted to bilateral agreements between issuers. Besides the interchange information, the encoding of the first digit specifies whether an alternative technology than the magnetic stripe is available on the card for conveying the financial data, like the integrated circuit, for example.

▸ The second digit of the service code specifies the authorization processing indicator associated by the issuer to the card. This indicator decides whether the positive authorization by the issuer or the agent that is acting on its behalf is mandatory for the successful completion of the transaction. Otherwise, it can be that only an off-line checking is acceptable, like the verification as to whether the transaction amount is lower than an agreed upper floor limit.

▸ The third digit indicates the range of services available to the card product and the cardholder verification method required for providing that service. Several examples are: cash only/PIN required, goods and services only, and no restrictions/PIN required.

The discretionary data allows the issuer to enforce some security protections for providing the card authenticity and cardholder verification services. These security protections are implemented with security mechanisms using symmetric cryptographic techniques (see Appendix D, Sections D.5.2 and D.6.1). The rationales related to these security protections will become evident when discussing threats associated with magnetic stripe cards (see Section 2.6). In addition to security protections, discretionary data can include other operational information needed by the issuer for the authorization processing according to its own needs—for example, the starting date that the payment card can be used. Another example is the card sequence number, which is a number that distinguishes between separate cards linked to the same PAN. The discretionary data can also contain a language selection parameter that can instruct the terminal regarding the preferred language of the cardholder when displaying the messages.

Track 2 includes the same information as track 1, except for the card-holder's name. It is important to notice that the length of the discretionary data conveyed by track 2 is smaller than that carried on track 1, while the content of this data is also proprietary to the issuer.

In the case of credit card products, the name of the cardholder is printed on the receipt of the transaction, which is signed at the point of service by the cardholder. Therefore, credit card products designed for international interchange usually encode financial data on track 1, or sometimes on both track 1 and track 2, since the name of the cardholder is stored on track 1. Debit card products designed for international interchange usually encode the financial data on track 2, since the name of the cardholder is not printed on the receipt delivered at the point of service.

2.5.2.2   Track 3

Track 3 includes the PAN, the country code for certain categories of PAN (the encoding of which is country-dependent), and the expiration date. The interchange control parameter indicates whether or not the card can partici-pate in international interchange or not. In case the card cannot be used in international interchange, the interchange control parameter points out whether the card is restricted to national use or can be used within the boundaries of a consortium of card issuers. The type of account (TA) speci-fies whether the account identifier in the PAN is associated to a current account, a savings account, or a credit account. The service restriction (SR) provides for control of interchange and control of debits, credits, and trans-fers applied to the account identifier specified by the PAN.

Track 3 can encode, in addition to the PAN (which designates the princi-pal account of the cardholder), two optional subsidiary account numbers: SAN-1 and SAN-2. These accounts can provide the fallback authorization facility in case authorization is refused in connection with the account pointed by the PAN. Thus, when a debit card aims for authorization and the balance of the account associated with the PAN is smaller than the transac-tion amount, the authorization is not refused. The issuer checks whether the transaction amount can be supported from the balance of the SAN-1 or SAN-2. A separate set of type of account and service restriction parameters characterizes each SAN, in a similar way that the homonym parameters explained above characterize the PAN. The card sequence number encoded on track 3 distinguishes between separate payment cards associated with the same PAN. These cards can be issued concurrently or consecutively. The field is set at original issue or at the renewal of the card following expiration. It is incremented each time an additional or replacement card is issued.

Not only can track 3 be read, but there are also fields that can be updated.

> ▸ The issuer can statically update fields at dedicated terminals. In this case the updating of fields is performed in a separate transaction than a financial transaction.

> ▸ The interchange partners (e.g., acquirers having bilateral agreements with issuers) can dynamically update some of the fields directly at the point of service terminals. In this case the updating is performed inside the current financial transaction.

Track 3 offers the possibility of storing and updating financial parameters that control the cardholder's spending in a period of time. The parameter *cycle length* designates the duration of this period as established by the card issuer (e.g., 1 week or 10 days). The parameter *cycle begin* specifies the beginning of each new cycle period. This field is dynamically updated to the current date whenever the value of the field *cycle begin* plus the value of the field *cycle length* is less than or equal to the current date. The card issuer also establishes the amount authorized per cycle period, which is an upper floor limit for spending during a cycle. At the beginning of the cycle, the *amount remaining this cycle* parameter is dynamically set to the value of the amount authorized per cycle period. Each time a transaction is performed, the *amount remaining this cycle* is dynamically updated to a new value, reflecting the subtraction of the transaction amount. The type of currency, in which the parameters *amount authorized per cycle period* and *amount remaining this cycle* are expressed, is specified on track 3. The currency exponent specifies the number of times the content of the fields *amount authorized per cycle period* or *amount remaining this cycle* must be multiplied by 10 to express a value in the major currency unit of the currency type. For example, an amount of 1,000 Belgian francs can be expressed as the amount 1,000 and the currency exponent 1, or as the amount 100 and the currency exponent 2.

Track 3 offers a set of parameters that can be used for providing security protections:

> ▸ The *personal identification number control* parameters (PINPARAM) and the *retry count* parameter can be used locally at the point of service in connection with the cardholder verification by means of a PIN. The *retry count* parameter can be dynamically updated at the point of service to reflect the outstanding attempts available to enter the PIN

associated with the card. The issuer can also statically update the PINPARAM following a PIN changing procedure started by the cardholder at a dedicated terminal in the branch bank.

▸ The *card security number* is also a parameter on track 3 that can be dynamically updated, providing the possibility to relate the data contained on the magnetic stripe to the physical card. In Section 2.6.4 we present a method for using this field, together with a synchronous value kept in the issuer host, to detect counterfeit cards.

▸ The crypto check digits (CCD) can be dynamically updated on the card. They can provide a means of verifying the integrity of the data elements recorded on track 3 that where dynamically modified during the current transaction.

▸ The *additional data* field can store other data customized according to the card issuer's policies to provide security protections for improving card authenticity and cardholder verification.

▸ The *transaction date*, which is a parameter specifying the date of the last cash dispense transaction, can also be dynamically updated on track 3. This parameter can be used in the terminal risk management process for determining the frequency of cash dispensing required by the cardholder, which could reveal a suspect account activity.

Track 3 offers the possibility of dynamically updating fields on the magnetic stripe right at the point of service, which confers certain advantages concerning the security of the payment card. To this end, only acquirers that have interchanged some cryptographic material with the issuer of the card can legitimately perform the updating. This security feature limits the interoperability of payment products using this track. Therefore, track 3 serves as storage support for proprietary implementations on a national scale or restrained to a group of issuers/acquirers having enforced bilateral business agreements.

Using the storage space on tracks 1, 2, and 3, a payment card can simultaneously accommodate debit/credit applications used both internationally (track 1 and 2) as well as nationally (track 3).

2.6   Threats and security protections

This section analyzes some of the possible threats that can be identified when using the financial data embossed and/or encoded on the magnetic stripe of a payment card. The most well-known attacks resulting from these threats are described, along with possible security countermeasures that can diminish the effects of these attacks. This analysis highlights the limitations of the security mechanisms that can be implemented on a magnetic stripe card. This analysis could make the business case for the migration to ICC, like the EMV™ solution.

2.6.1   Channel protection versus eavesdropping

In the case of payment cards, the threat of eavesdropping or monitoring (see Appendix B) consists of obtaining the financial data, which is either embossed on the card or stored on the magnetic stripe of the card, and/or the confidential cardholder identification information like the PIN.

The financial data can be tapped while it is exchanged between the card and the operator/terminal at the point of service in a face-to-face transaction or when it is sent over communication channels during a remote payment transaction. The attacker can later use this data in a variety of attacks for obtaining material advantages. Below, some of the most frequent eavesdropping scenarios targeting financial data are outlined.

- The simplest eavesdropping attack is the *waiter attack*. The consumer has a magnetic stripe credit card and uses it at a restaurant. While taking the card of the consumer for reading it in the payment terminal, the waiter writes down the financial data embossed on the front side of the card: card's brand and issuer, cardholder's name, PAN, and expiration date.

- A fake ATM or POS terminal under the control of the attacker is used to illegitimately read the financial data encoded on the magnetic stripe of the card. In January 2001, Scotland Yard issued a worldwide warning to hotels, restaurants, and the public to watch out for a tiny electronic device that can be handheld and can read the magnetic stripe of a card in few seconds [14]. The content of the magnetic stripe of up to 50 cards could be simultaneously stored in the permanent memory of the device. The size of a matchbox, these devices were found among the possessions of several waiters working in high-class London restaurants where customers routinely pay with platinum and gold credit cards. In a few hours the content of the device was transferred to the logistic department of a criminal organization that creates the counterfeit magnetic stripe cards (see Section 2.6.4).

▸ In the electronic commerce scenario the waiter attack is performed as follows. Hackers (a term referring to an attacker whose target is an Internet connection or a Web site) are sniffing the transfer between the browser of the consumer and the Web site of the merchant. "Sniffing" is another term for eavesdropping, which is preferred in the Internet literature. A filter runs and isolates cardholders' financial data.

Another target of eavesdropping is capturing the cardholder identification information, like the PIN (see Appendix D, Section D.5). Several possibilities can be envisaged:

▸ The attacker tries to spy over the shoulder, recording with a miniature camera the PIN pad of a terminal.

▸ The attacker captures the PIN while the cardholder is typing it in the PIN pad of a false ATM or other unattended terminal, which is under the control of the attacker.

The eavesdropping of the PIN is an essential step that facilitates the mounting of more complex attacks using stolen or lost cards (as outlined in Section 2.6.2) or counterfeit cards (as presented in Section 2.6.4).

Little can be done to protect against eavesdropping at a point of service. Discretely typing the PIN using the palm as a shield is the simplest protection method. When participating in an electronic commerce transaction over the Internet, the legitimate cardholder can protect his or her financial data against the sniffing of the connection by using either SSL [15] or the transport layer security (TLS) [16], which are integrated in the majority of browsers. Thus, a secure connection is established between the browser of the cardholder and the merchant's server, if this is also SSL/TLS-enabled and operational, which can safeguard the confidentiality of financial data.

In the examples of attacks presented above, the eavesdropping threat was mainly analyzed on the interface between the cardholder and the merchant, which is the most vulnerable. Nevertheless, in case of debit/credit payment cards, the long circuit performed by the authorization request/response sent to the interchange system is also sensitive to eavesdropping. The authorization request/response conveys the financial data of the card together with the (encrypted) PIN of the cardholder, in case the cardholder's verification is performed on-line by the issuer (see Appendix D, Section D.5.2). In this case the wiretapping task of the attacker is more difficult, considering the inaccessibility of the proprietary payment networks, unless the attacker colludes with insiders, managing the nodes traversed by the authorization messages.

2.6.2 Cardholder verification versus impersonation

The cardholder impersonation threat consists of the false association between the consumer undertaking a payment transaction and the authorized owner to whom the payment card was issued.

A dishonest waiter who has abusively captured the information embossed on the front side of a credit card (Section 2.6.1) can impersonate the legitimate cardholder when ordering purchases by phone. Similarly, a hacker who has successfully recorded the financial data associated with a credit card sent over an insecure Internet connection can impersonate the legitimate owner of the card when participating in other electronic commerce transactions. The lack of reliable cardholder verification procedures in these types of transactions facilitates the possibility of fraud.

An attacker who has stolen or found a payment card or has produced a counterfeit card (Section 2.6.4) tries to impersonate the authorized cardholder when attempting to use the card for his convenience. If the stolen card is a credit card, the attacker can use it for making purchases in a shop, exposing him to some risk.

- ▸ When the transaction amount is below the upper floor limit and the service code does not indicate positive authorization by the issuer, then the issuer is not asked on-line for authorization. In this case the attacker must be skilled enough to mimick the legitimate cardholder's signature, which is the common cardholder verification method (see Appendix D, Section D.5.1) used for credit cards presented at an attended POS terminal. The attacker hopes that the shopkeeper makes only a cursory comparison between the forged signature and the witness signature on the back side of the card and that the issuer did not post the stolen card to the blacklist stored in the terminals (if this possibility exists). A blacklist is a database that stores the PAN of all cards that were reported stolen or lost, or which were abused in any other way and about which the issuer is aware.

- ▸ If the attacker aims for higher material returns over the upper floor limit, he faces additional risks. The attacker must rely on the assumption that at the moment when the authorization request is analyzed on-line by the issuer, the cardholder has not realized the theft/loss of the card and has not reported it to the issuer.

If the stolen card is a debit card or a credit card that allows for cash advance, there is a high probability that the attacker will try to impersonate the cardholder at an ATM for money withdrawal. In this case, the common cardholder verification procedure is based on the PIN verification.

- When the attacker has already spied the PIN (Section 2.6.1), the attack is successful if the card has not yet been reported to the issuer as stolen or lost.

- If the attacker did not record the PIN, there is still a small probability that he can guess the PIN (if the cardholder wrote it on the back side of the card, then guessing is not needed). This probability is higher when the number of digits in the PIN is small, the number of permitted wrong attempts is high, and the number of wrong attempts is not stored from one ATM session to another. This is the reason why a PIN is at least four digits, the number of attempts is limited to three, and the number of attempts left is either recorded on the magnetic track 3 or in the cardholder accounts database managed by the issuer. In this case the success probability of guessing is limited to 3×10^{-4}.

The PIN verification method applied to magnetic stripe cards is the PIN image verification method, which is described in Appendix D, Section D.5.2.

In case the issuer host performs the PIN verification, the terminal securely sends the PIN of the cardholder to the issuer host via the interchange system, using a communication channel that provides confidentiality. Upon receipt, the secure module of the issuer host retrieves the PIN from the cryptogram included in the authorization message. It then computes the PIN image control value and compares it against the PIN image stored value, which is kept in the cardholder accounts database. Every time the comparison fails, the counter of available PIN attempts, which is kept in the cardholder's record in the accounts database, is decreased. The counter is reset to the initial value of three attempts only after a successful PIN verification. The value of this counter is persistent from one session to another, such that an attacker cannot make more than three guesses.

If the terminal at the point of service performs the PIN image verification locally, two conditions have to be fulfilled:

1. First, the PIN image stored value is encoded on the magnetic stripe.

    - If only track 1 or track 2 is present on the magnetic stripe, the PIN image stored value can be recorded only during the personalization stage of the card among the items contained in the discretionary data field. This technique is decreasingly used since it prevents deployment of a user-selectable PIN different from the value generated by the issuer during the personalization of the card. This is because track 1 and track 2 cannot be written but just read, and therefore, updating the PIN image stored value computed in connection with a new PIN selected by the cardholder is not possible. For the same reason, there is no possibility of updating the counter of available PIN attempts on track 1 or track 2, which allows an attacker to perform more PIN guesses. For example, after two incorrect PIN submissions, the attacker interrupts the session at the current terminal and withdraws the card. Later, he reinitiates a new session and tries new PIN values either at the same terminal or at another terminal operated off-line.

▸ If track 3 is encoded on the magnetic stripe of the card, local PIN verification is improved. Since track 3 can be written, the cardholder can choose for a different PIN than the one generated by the issuer at the personalization stage. The issuer can statically update the PINPARAM field on track 3 to reflect a new PIN image stored value, following, of course, a PIN changing procedure at a dedicated terminal in the issuer's premises. There is also the possibility of updating the counter of available PIN attempts left, which is stored in the field retry count on track 3. Thus, the number of possible PIN guesses is limited to the initial value of the retry count, which will be reset by the terminal only after a successful PIN verification.

2.   Secondly, the terminal has to be able to compute locally the PIN image control value to be compared against the PIN image stored value read from the magnetic stripe. When the PIN image is computed with a message authentication code (MAC), the acquirer and the issuer must have a bilateral business agreement through which they have exchanged the necessary keys for the computation of the MAC. This limits the interoperability of the payment application, and this is one more reason why track 3 is used for national interchange.

A fraudulent transaction is considered any transaction where the user of the card is not the authorized cardholder. This definition includes all transactions using stolen cards, lost cards, or cards that were sent from the issuer but never received by the intended cardholder (card-not-received cards).

2.6.3   Static authenticator versus modifying financial data

Modifying the content of financial data stored on the magnetic stripe can help an attacker to mislead the authorization process, especially when authorization is carried out locally at the point of service.

Any field of a magnetic track can be a target for the attacker; however, the following attempts are most common:

> • If an attacker has found an expired card that was not destroyed by the cardholder but rather negligently thrown away, he would try to extend the expiration date of this payment card. In this way, he could further bill on behalf of the legitimate cardholder—assuming the account related to the PAN is still active.

> • Let us consider the scenario where the attacker has stolen a payment card but did not succeed in spying the PIN of the cardholder. In this case, the target of the attacker could be to modify the service code such that the PIN verification in connection with a service is not required.

> • If track 3 is encoded on the magnetic stripe, the attacker could try to modify the amount remaining this cycle field to extend the spending limits and the cycle begin parameter to increase the frequency of spending.

To avoid the modification of financial data stored on track 1 or track 2, the issuer computes for each track during the personalization stage a static authenticator using the MAC-based static data authentication (SDA) mechanism (see Appendix D, Section D.6.1). This mechanism provides data authentication for the financial data stored on the magnetic stripe. The effective input data used to compute this MAC value is specific to each issuer. The static authenticator is stored among the items of the discretionary data field and has the same value during the whole lifetime of the card, since data on these tracks cannot be written.

If the magnetic stripe encodes the financial data on track 3, there are data items that can be statically changed by the issuer during the lifetime of the card, when the card is operated at a specialized terminal. One such example is the PIN control parameters field (PINPARAM), which changes after the cardholder chooses a different PIN. Correspondingly, the issuer updates the value of the static authenticator stored on the magnetic stripe each time financial data has changed on the card. The static authenticator can be encoded among the data items in the discretionary data subfield of the additional data field.

There is other financial data on track 3 that can be dynamically changed on the card by the terminal at the point of service, including the cycle begin field, the amount remaining this cycle field, and the transaction date field reflecting the last date when the cash dispense operation was performed. To enforce the authenticity of this data, a supplementary static authenticator can be computed at the point of service, which is dynamically updated in the CCD filed stored on track 3. To this end, each issuer must provide acquires participating in the interchange with appropriate cryptographic material for the computation and verification of the corresponding MAC.

The static authenticators mentioned above are intended for protecting the authenticity of financial data stored on the magnetic stripe. A static authenticator can be also computed for the financial data embossed on the card and printed on the back side of the card. This authenticator is printed in the tamper-resistant band that displays the witness signature of the cardholder. When ordering by phone, the cardholder is required to read the value of this authenticator from the back side of the card in addition to the financial data embossed on the front side of the card. The operator at the merchant's site could further request a specialized service of the acquirer that can assess whether the financial data of the card is authentic or not.

2.6.4   Timeliness versus card counterfeiting

Counterfeiting money has been a threat ever since coins emerged as a means of exchange in commercial transactions. When coins were made of precious metals (such as gold or silver), biting the coin was the way one verified its authenticity. This would work regardless of the authority that issued the coins, since their value was intrinsically covered by the weight of the precious metal. Later coins were made of common metals and their value was guaranteed by an authority that stored a reserve in precious metals, whose value was equivalent to the value of the monetary mass in circulation. In this case, counterfeiting involved the replication of the head and tail artwork embossed on the two faces of a coin, which were the distinctive signs of the authority issuing the coins and guaranteeing their value. As cash evolved to paper banknotes, more and more attention was paid to embedding in their physical structure enough distinctive authenticity shapes (known as watermarks) to make them distinguishable from possible counterfeits.

The proliferation of payment cards has also exposed financial institutions to risk from counterfeiting. Counterfeiting cards is a threat that consists of impersonating the origin of financial data as coming from a genuine card, while in fact an emulator providing the same functionality as the card and cloning the content of its financial and authentication data is used instead. This emulator is referred to as the counterfeit card.

The earliest attempts of card counterfeiting targeted the embossed financial data. The attacker produces a matrix that allows falsifying the artwork on the front and back sides of the card, including the position and dimension of the embossed and printed characters. Through eavesdropping (Section 2.6.1), the attacker obtains a set of financial data that will be embossed on the counterfeit cards. The attacker impersonates the legitimate cardholder (Section 2.6.2) and tries to make a purchase at an attended point of service that has no electronic terminal. To prevent such kinds of attack, a hologram specific to the card association brand, which is easily recognizable by an operator at the point of service, is embedded in the plastic card. This security protection provides a visual means for checking the authenticity of the card at the point of service.

The successful passing of a counterfeit card in a payment transaction is more difficult if the point of service is equipped with an electronic terminal. The attacker has to emulate the magnetic stripe and its content that corresponds to a genuine card. To this end, the attacker collects transaction receipts negligently thrown away by the cardholders. The attacker attempts to reconstruct the content of the financial data stored on the genuine card and to encode it on the fake magnetic stripe. A simple protection against this threat is to avoid printing all the financial data stored on the magnetic stripe on the transaction receipts. Moreover, during the personalization stage of the payment card or even during its lifetime, the issuer computes and stores a static authenticator on the magnetic stripe (Section 2.6.3), which could serve as a cryptographic watermark.

Certainly, this measure becomes inefficient if a fake ATM captures all of the data on the magnetic stripe, including the static authenticator and the CCD field. In this case, the attacker can completely clone the genuine magnetic stripe. If the cardholder does not realize that the ATM was a fake, but only that it was out of service, it can take some time before she notices the damage to her account. The attacker uses the PIN learned by eavesdropping with the corresponding counterfeit card, which reproduces the financial data captured from the matching genuine card, for making ATM money withdrawals.

The presence of track 3 on the magnetic stripe can provide an extra protection against counterfeiting. If the transaction at the point of service is always authorized on-line by the issuer, an efficient timeliness mechanism (see Appendix C, Section C.1) based on random numbers can be implemented. At the personalization time the issuer records a random number in the card security number field on track 3. The same number is recorded in connection with the card in the cardholder accounts database. Every time a transaction is authorized on-line, the card security number is compared against the stored value. If the two values are equal, the issuer host performs the authorization process, otherwise the authorization is aborted, and the card is considered counterfeit. If the authorization process is continued, the issuer host sends back a fresh random number in the authorization response, which is correspondingly updated in the cardholder accounts database. At the point of service the terminal dynamically updates this value in the card security number. If a counterfeit card is produced and operated, the card security number of either the genuine card or of the counterfeit card will lose its synchronization with the value stored in the cardholder accounts database, which will lead the issuer host to blacklist the card. The financial loss is limited to the number of transactions executed with the counterfeit card until the moment the genuine card is used once again. Unfortunately, this kind of protection works only for a payment card that uses track 3.

2.6.5   Merchant attacks and colluding attacks

Merchants can mount themselves or can collude with stronger organizations in some of the attack scenarios described in the previous sections.

Within the category of eavesdropping attacks (like those described in Section 2.6.1), the merchant can mount waiter attacks in face-to-face transactions or can abuse the financial information gathered from customers during electronic commerce transactions and stored in the merchant's Web server. Colluding with a strong criminal organization, the merchant can facilitate attacks using fake or modified terminals, towards tapping both the financial data stored on the cards as well as the PIN of the cardholders. This information would allow the production of counterfeit cards (see Section 2.6.4), which used in combination with the PIN, can grant to the attacker complete control over the cardholder's account.

The merchant can also collude with the attacker in mounting impersonation attacks like that described in Section 2.6.2. When a credit card is stolen, the merchant can facilitate the task of the attacker by not performing the cardholder verification method. The merchant does not compare the signature produced by the attacker with that of the legitimate cardholder, which is recorded on the back side of the card. The merchant can also facilitate the use of counterfeit cards, deliberately skipping all the visual controls of the authentication artwork foreseen on the front side of the card (see Section 2.6.4).

The payment system operator, however, can easily monitor the activity of the merchant. The merchant can be included on a violation list if suspicious activity is detected at his point of service:

- A large percentage of the counterfeit or fraudulent transactions is traced back to his point of service;

- The ratio of the transactions rejected on-line from the total number of on-line authorizations requested to the issuer is high;

- The number of transactions where the financial data is captured manually is high, considering that the point of service is equipped with an electronic terminal;

- The monitoring software of the payment system detects multiple authorization requests linked to the same PAN or multiple authorizations requiring the same amount, regardless of the account to which they are linked;

- A high number of authorization requests are noticed, compared to the average number of authorizations characterizing that point of service.

2.7   Processing at the point of service

Several steps have to be performed at the point of service for the processing of a payment card transaction.

First, an attendant manually captures the financial data embossed on the payment card, or a terminal electronically captures the financial data stored on the magnetic stripe. "Capturing" means both reading the financial data from the payment card (as presented in Sections 2.5.1 and 2.5.2) and formatting a payment message to be forwarded to the acquirer. The following verifications are performed, depending on the type of capturing at the point of service:

- If an operator attends the point of service, the operator checks that the card's brand and the type of card product are accepted at the point of service. The operator visually verifies the card authenticity, based on the hologram embedded in the card, and checks the validity of the card with respect to the expiration date.

- When the point of service is equipped with an electronic terminal, the check digit of the PAN, as well as the check digit of the entire magnetic track that stores the financial data of the card, are verified.

If these verifications do not pass, the authenticity of the card is not accepted or the integrity of the data stored on the magnetic stripe is not validated and the payment transaction is declined. Otherwise, the payment message is formatted. This message includes the financial data read from the card and data elements characterizing the payment transaction at the point of service. Among the data elements featuring the point of service, the following can be included:

- *Business environment data elements:* This group includes the name and location of the point of service, the merchant type, the identifier of the merchant, the identifier of his terminal, local time, and date when the transaction is captured. Since the financial data of the card can be read in several ways (embossed data, magnetic stripe, integrated circuit), a data element must state the actual reading method of the financial data at the point of service as well as the possibilities of the terminal to read financial data. This data element is referred to as the point of service data code in the ISO/IEC 8583 standard [17].

- *Transaction data elements:* This group includes the amount of the transaction and the currency code in which the amount is expressed. It also includes the type of transaction performed in case several transaction types are accepted at the point of service. Several examples of transaction types are payment for goods, payment for goods and cash back, and cash advance using a credit card. The transaction type data element is referred to as the processing code [17].

- *Message identification data element:* This is a kind of serial number that allows the unique identification of a payment message in the system. This data element is referred to as the system trace audit number (STAN) [17].

The attendant, or terminal, at the point of service decides whether the payment transaction can be concluded off-line at the point of service or if an authorization has to be obtained on-line from the card issuer. The corresponding processing is called point of service risk management. The decision of off-line or on-line completion impacts on the further processing of the payment message by the acquirer, which either submits it to a clearing processing or to an authorization processing, respectively. The point of service risk management procedure takes into account the type of payment card product, the business environment at the point of service, and the amount of the transaction when compared against prearranged floor limits.

When the point of service is equipped with an electronic terminal connected to the acquirer network and the service code data element recorded on the magnetic stripe indicates that on-line authorization by the issuer is mandatory, the payment message is forwarded for authorization to the issuer. In this case the card authenticity is verified by the issuer, which assesses the correctness of the static authenticator recorded on the magnetic stripe. If track 3 is used, a supplementary control can be performed against counterfeiting, considering the synchronization of the card security number stored on the track and the corresponding random number stored in the cardholder accounts database in connection with the card. If the PIN verification method is required by the card product, the cardholder types in the PIN in the secure PIN pad of the terminal. The terminal securely sends the encrypted PIN for verification to the issuer, which computes the PIN image control value. Whatever the result of the authorization, the terminal is informed by the issuer host about the acceptance or the rejection of the transaction. Upon a positive authorization by the issuer, and if the cardholder verification method is the handwritten signature, the operator at the point of service requires a handwritten signature of the consumer on the sales receipt. This signature is visually compared against the witness signature of the legitimate cardholder on the back side of the card. This ends the on-line authorization processing of the transaction.

If the payment card product does not require a mandatory on-line authorization by the issuer, the authorization of the transaction can be performed locally. This is usually the case at attended points of service that are not equipped with electronic terminals, or at points of service equipped with electronic terminals that are not permanently connected on-line to the acquirer's network. The local authorization is mainly based on comparing the transaction amount against floor limits available at the point of service—floor limits established by the acquirer. If the transaction amount is less than the lower floor limit, the transaction is rejected since the price of the electronic processing of the payment transaction is considered too high compared to the transaction amount. If the transaction amount is higher than the upper floor limit, the transaction is rejected since the risk at the point of service is considered unacceptable for the acquirer.

PIN image verification can be locally performed as the cardholder verification method at the point of service when two conditions are fulfilled. First, the PIN image stored value parameter is recorded on the magnetic stripe of the card. Second, the terminal has a secure PIN pad, which was loaded by the interchange partners with adequate cryptographic keys for the computation of the PIN image control value, using the MAC generation/verification algorithm. In the same way, the static authenticator and/or the CCD (if using track 3) can be verified locally for assessing the card authenticity if the terminal at the point of service has the necessary cryptographic material to perform the MAC verification algorithm.

If the card encodes the amount remaining this cycle field on track 3, the risk management at the point of service is improved with a rudimentary card risk management component intended for protecting the issuer against cardholders that overspend. The transaction is authorized off-line if the transaction amount is smaller than both the upper floor limit (acquirer's requirement) and the amount remaining this cycle parameter, which specifies the spending limitation as imposed by the issuer.

The payment messages describing the transactions authorized off-line are gathered in the permanent memory of the terminal at the point of service. Periodically, or when the capacity of the permanent memory is exhausted, the payment messages are compiled in batch files, which are forwarded to the acquirer. Periodically, the acquirer transmits these batch files in the interchange system for clearing.

2.8   **Payment network and interchange messages**

Terminals located at various points of service are connected to the acquirer host via the acquirer's network. The formats of (1) the payment messages generated by the terminal at the point of service and forwarded to the acquirer host and (2) the confirmation messages returned by the acquirer host to the terminal are proprietary to the acquirer's network.

In the simplest scenario, the acquirer managing the terminal at the point of service and the issuer of the card involved in the payment transaction are subscribers to the services offered by the same payment system network. This network is the property of a card association or a payment system operator that is responsible for managing the network and for settling funds between the issuer and the acquirer following a payment transaction. Each acquirer host (AH) and issuer host (IH) is connected to separate nodes of the payment network, referred to as the acquirer node (AN) and issuer node (IN), respectively. In order to increase the availability of the issuer's service, an issuer can duplicate the functionality of an IH through a second computer acting as an active reserve. The payment system operator can provide a stand-in processing facility to an issuer, through which the payment system operator can answer to an authorization request on behalf of the issuer in case none of its hosts is available in the authorization process.

In a more complex scenario, the acquirer managing the terminal at the point of service and the issuer of the card involved in the payment transaction are subscribers to the services offered by different payment system networks, which have established mutual supporting agreements. In order to guarantee the compatibility between these two different networks, two gateway nodes, GN1 and GN2 (one on each payment network), must provide the message translation between the two heterogeneous environments. Different rules concerning the definition of the transaction messages and their flow could govern the two interconnected payment networks. A possible topology of a payment network is schematized in Figure 2.4.

In this topology a national payment system operator transacting in one single currency could manage the payment system network, while an international card association transacting in multiple currencies could manage the cooperating payment system network.

2.8.1 Message structure

The acquirers and issuers must exchange messages towards completing authorization, clearing, and settlement processing. Both the acquirer and

Figure 2.4
Payment
network
topology.

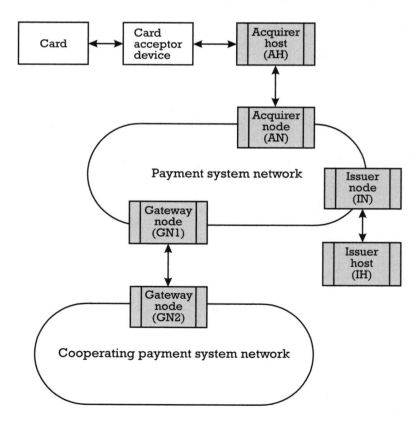

the issuer can play the role of a sender or receiver of a message. In order to facilitate the interconnection between payment system networks that cooperate, the ISO/IEC 8583:1993 standard [17] defines the format of these messages, which have the following structure:

- Message type identifier;

- Bitmap representation, which consists of one or two bitmaps of 64 bits each, giving the index of the data elements that are incorporated in the message;

- A series of data elements, in the order specified in the bitmap representation, which represents the message's body.

The standard defines the dictionary of data elements that can be used in interchange. When a bit is set in the message's bitmap representation, the corresponding data element is included in the message's body. Some data elements are of fixed length. Some other data elements are of variable length, which is specified in a fixed length prefix. The standard, however, does not preclude the use of additional data elements not specified in the dictionary, which could be required by the specific needs of payments system operators for private use.

The message type identifier is a numeric field consisting of four digits. The first digit identifies the message version number as follows:

- 0: messages defined in the previous issue of the standard referred to as the ISO 8583:1987;

- 1: messages defined in the current issue of the standard referred to as the ISO 8583:1993;

- 2–7: reserved for ISO use;

- 8: reserved for national use;

- 9: reserved for private use.

The second digit encodes the message class as follows:

- 0—ISO reserved: Messages in this class are reserved for ISO use.

- 1—authorization: Messages in this class are used for an authorization transaction, which is an approval or guarantee of funds given by the card issuer to the acquirer. Following the authorization, the transaction amount that is approved by the issuer is not immediately billed to the cardholder's account. This is postponed until a financial message, which is sent by the acquirer to the issuer, confirms the completion of that transaction at the point of service, following the authorization.

- 2—financial: Messages in this class perform a financial transaction that directly bills the transaction amount to the cardholder's account.

- 3—file action messages: Messages in this class allow the initiation of a remote control transaction over the file system hosted in a device, like adding, changing, deleting, and replacing a record in a file or adding/deleting a file in the file system. These messages are used to perform the management of blacklists, which contain those cards that were compromised (stolen, abused through overspending, cards with compromised cryptographic material, etc.).

- 4—reversal/chargeback: Reversal transactions are used to undo the effect of a previous authorization or financial transaction. The acquirer triggers a reversal transaction any time the result of an authorization or financial transaction is not received from the issuer in due time, or when the cardholder voluntarily cancels the authorization or financial transaction at the point of service. Chargeback transactions also undo the effect of a previous authorization or financial transaction, but at the initiative of the issuer. The reasons that the issuer can invoke for performing a chargeback transaction include a customer dispute, an infringement of rules concerning the use of a certain type of card product on a specific terminal, the use of an expired card, or an invalid transaction.

- The messages in the classes 5—reconciliation, 6—administrative, 7—fee collection, and 8—network management are not explained in this book, but the interested reader can find their definition in the ISO 8583:1993 standard.

The third digit of the message identifier specifies the context in which the message is used. Three different situations are identified:

- The sender addresses a request message (third digit = 0) to inform the receiver that a transaction is in progress and its response is required to complete it. The receiver evaluates the request and approves or denies it, transmitting back to the sender its decision in a request response message (third digit = 1).

- The sender informs the receiver with an advice message (third digit = 2) about a certain activity that has been completed at the point of service. The receiver is not required to approve or deny the advice, but it has to elaborate an advice response message (third digit = 3), which is sent back to the sender.

- The sender informs the receiver with a notification message (third digit = 4) about a certain activity that has been performed. The notification message requires no response back from the receiver to the sender.

The fourth digit identifies the originator of a transaction and whether the current transaction is a repeat of a previous transaction.

- 0: The acquirer is the transaction originator.

- 1: The acquirer is the originator of the repeated transaction.

- 2: The issuer is the transaction originator.

- 3: The issuer is the originator of the repeated transaction.

- 4: The other role is the transaction originator.

- 5: The other role is the originator of the repeated transaction.

It is important to mention that there are some interdependencies between the last three digits of the message type identifier; for example, a reversal transaction shall use only advice messages (1420/1431 and 1430/1431) or notification messages (1440/1441).

2.8.2   Message flows

The standard also specifies the possible message flows that describe the circumstances when a message shall (or may) be sent, and the relationship between messages. In the remainder of this section we focus on several message flow examples that correspond to typical situations that appear during transaction processing. The message flows depicted in the figures below do not represent the AN, the IN, and the payment system network, but just the acquirer and the issuer.

When a terminal is connected on-line to the acquirer and the amount involved in the transaction is greater than a risk threshold limit, the terminal triggers an authorization transaction. After receiving the appropriate transaction data from the terminal (see Section 2.7), the acquirer performs an authorization phase. If the authorization does not impact the cardholder's account, a subsequent clearing stage follows.

In a dual message network, the authorization phase is performed with an authorization request message (1100). Following the evaluation of this request by IH, the guarantee of funds is approved or denied by the issuer according to the financial situation of the cardholder. The acquirer is informed about the appropriate action through an authorization request response message (1110). Following the authorization, the transaction amount that is approved by the issuer is not immediately billed to the cardholder's account. This is postponed until a separate financial message, which is sent by the acquirer to the issuer, confirms the completion of that transaction at the point of service, following the authorization. This financial message performs the clearing stage. One can distinguish between two possible approaches:

▸ *On-line clearing:* Following the reception of each authorization request response message (1110), the acquirer forms a financial advice message (1220), which bills the transaction amount to the cardholder's account. The issuer informs the acquirer about the result of this operation with a financial advice response message (1230). An overview of the on-line clearing in dual message networks is presented in Figure 2.5.

▸ *Off-line clearing:* Following the reception of each authorization request response message (1110), the acquirer forms a financial notification

Figure 2.5
On-line transaction in a dual message network with on-line clearing.

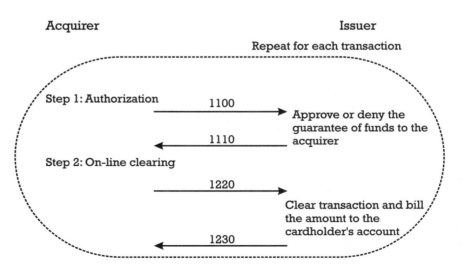

message (1240), which is stored in a clearing batch file. Periodically, this file is forwarded to the issuer, which bills each and every transaction amount of each financial notification message to the appropriate cardholder account. An overview of the off-line clearing in dual message networks for transactions approved on-line is presented in Figure 2.6.

In a single message network, the authorization phase and the clearing phase are simultaneously performed with a financial request message (1200). Following the evaluation of this request by the IH, the guarantee of funds is approved or denied by the issuer according to the financial situation of the cardholder. The acquirer is informed about the appropriate action through a financial request response message (1210). Following the financial authorization, the transaction amount that is approved by the issuer is immediately billed to the cardholder's account. An overview of the financial authorization is given in Figure 2.7.

When a terminal has no on-line connection or the amount involved in the transaction is below a risk threshold limit—which is accepted by both the issuer and the acquirer—the authorization phase can be completed locally between the card and the terminal. In this case the terminal initiates no authorization transaction, and consequently, the acquirer generates

Figure 2.6
On-line transaction in a dual message network with off-line clearing.

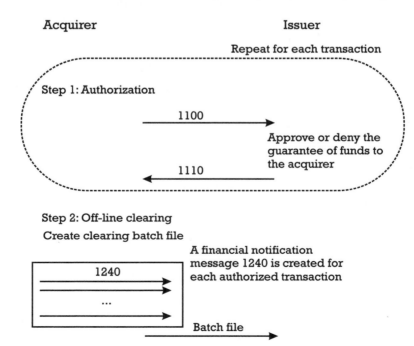

Figure 2.7
On-line
transaction in a
single message
network.

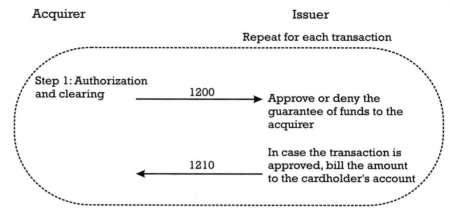

neither an authorization request message (1100) nor a financial request message (1200) for the issuer. After the terminal reports all the transactions it performed off-line during a certain period, the acquirer informs the issuer about the local completion of these transactions at the point of service, during a clearing stage. Two possibilities can be envisaged, depending on the features supported by the payment network:

> A financial advice message (1220) is issued for each transaction that is completed off-line, which allows an on-line clearing of the transactions. Each financial advice response message (1230) informs the acquirer whether the issuer accepted the transfer of liability corresponding to a transaction completed off-line. The corresponding amount involved in the locally authorized transaction is billed to the appropriate cardholder account. This is characteristic of a single message network. The corresponding message flow is schematized in Figure 2.8.

Figure 2.8
Off-line
transaction in a
single message
network with
on-line clearing.

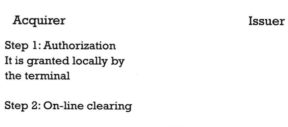

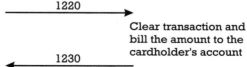

> • In a dual message network, the acquirer firstly informs the issuer with an authorization advice message (1120) about the authorization transaction that was completed off-line at the point of service. In the authorization advice response message (1130), the issuer informs the acquirer whether it accepts or rejects the proposed transfer of financial liability. The acquirer forms a batch file, where it generates a financial notification message (1240) for each transaction accepted by the issuer. During an off-line clearing stage the batch file is forwarded to the issuer, which bills the cardholders involved. The corresponding message flow is schematized in Figure 2.9.

2.9 On-line authorization

On-line authorization is the process through which the IH performs the risk management associated with a transaction carried out at the point of service. On-line authorization provides a better control of the risk for the issuer. The cardholder is better assured against fraudulent use of his or her card. Indeed, in an authorization request message the PIN of the cardholder is included in an encrypted form, which allows its verification by the issuer.

Figure 2.9
Off-line
transaction in a
dual message
network with
off-line clearing.

Acquirer   Issuer

Step 1: Authorization
It is granted locally by the terminal

Step 2: Authorization advice

——————— 1120 ———————▶

Authorize or deny the
transfer of financial liability

◀——————— 1130 ———————

Step 3: Off-line clearing
Create clearing batch file

Clear transaction and
bill the amount to the
cardholder's account

1240

...

Batch file

The benefit to the merchant is that the payment system guarantees its payment for each on-line authorized transaction.

On-line authorization can be triggered for the types of transactions listed below:

> Cash withdrawals at ATM terminals or branch banks, which are performed with either debit or credit cards;

> Payments performed at POS terminals with debit cards;

> Payments performed at POS terminals with credit cards, in case the transaction amount is greater than a floor limit established by the payment system.

In the explanation below we refer to a payment network topology like that described in Figure 2.4. After receiving the demand of on-line authorization from the terminal, the AH checks the completeness and correctness of the transaction data received from the terminal. The AH verifies whether the brand of the card product involved in the transaction is accepted, and whether the service required is appropriate for that brand. If all the verifications are successfully passed, the AH forms an authorization request message (1100) according to the specifications of the payment system network to which is directly connected. This message also includes the identifier of the acquirer. The AH forwards the 1100 message to the AN, which represents the entry point of the AH in the payment system network. The AN verifies whether the 1100 message comes from a member acquirer and whether the data it contains is complete and accurate. If these verifications are passed, the AN uses the issuer identification number (IIN, which is a component of the PAN) for further routing the 1100 message to the adequate destination IN in the payment system network. If the AN knows the IIN, the message is forwarded to the appropriate IN to which the destination IH is connected. Otherwise, the AN forwards the message to the gateway node GN1, which tries to identify the IIN in the cooperating payment system network to which is connected. After performing the appropriate adaptations, the message is forwarded from one payment network to the other, until the destination IH is reached.

The correctness, completeness, and integrity of the 1100 message are verified once it arrives at the IH. If all the controls are passed, the authorization request message is stored in the accounts database. The validity of the PAN and the expiration date of the transacting card are checked. If an encrypted PIN was sent for the cardholder's verification, then the secure module of the IH computes the PIN image control value, which is compared with the PIN image stored value kept in the accounts database for the corresponding PAN. If a debit card is used, the balance of the account is checked for enough funds. If a credit card is used, the issuer checks that the cardholder did not reach the spending limit associated with the card. The guarantee of funds is finally approved or rejected and a response code is included in the authorization request response (1110), giving further details in case the guarantee of funds has been denied.

If the payment network fails to reach the appropriate IN or if the destination IH is not available, then the payment network can stand in for the issuer in elaborating an authorization request response (1110), which is returned to the originating AH. This service can be provided if there is a business agreement between the issuer and the payment system operator and if the issuer has delegated enough approval data to the payment network.

The authorization request response message (1110) is identified with the same reference number as the corresponding authorization request message (1100). The 1110 message is sent back to the terminal over the payment network(s) and the AH. When the card acceptor's terminal receives the approval, cash is disbursed in case of an ATM terminal or the purchase is handed to the cardholder. In case of an attended point of service and if a credit card product was used, a paper slip is printed and the cardholder is required to sign it. The signature on the paper slip is compared against the witness signature on the back of the card for the cardholder's verification. The terminal records the completion of the transaction in order to send it later to the acquirer for clearing. The acquirer records each approved transaction for submitting to the clearing process.

2.10 Clearing and settlement

Clearing is the process initiated by an acquirer through which issuers are informed about the payment transactions performed by their cardholders. These transactions were completed at points of service managed by card acceptors that are the clients of the acquirer. Following the clearing process, the issuer can bill the transaction amounts to the accounts of the appropriate cardholders and can settle its debt with each of the acquirers that accepted its payment cards. Settlement is the process through which funds are exchanged between the members of the payment system(s) for the value of the transaction amounts cleared during a certain period [17].

The payment network topology in Figure 2.4 shows the clearing and settlement process. We assume that a national operator, handling transactions only in the national currency, manages the upper payment system network, while an international card association, able to handle multiple currencies, manages the cooperating payment system network. We also assume for simplicity that both networks support the off-line clearing with dual messages (see Section 2.8.2).

The transaction records stored at the points of service by either POS or ATM terminals are transmitted electronically to the AH. After checking and validating the received transaction records from one terminal, the transaction records database of the card acceptor kept with the AH is appropriately updated. The AH forms a financial notification message (1240) from each valid transaction record. Then it creates a separate clearing batch file with all the 1240 messages having the same IIN.

> ‣ If a clearing batch file gathers transactions, the IIN of which corresponds to an issuer located in the same country as the acquirer and subscribing to the same national payment system network, then the acquirer directly transmits the clearing batch file to the appropriate issuer.

> ‣ If a clearing batch file gathers transactions performed with cards issued by members from other countries than the acquirer but subscribing to the same international payment system network with which the national payment system network cooperates, this file is transmitted over the gateway nodes (GN1, GN2) to the card association. The currencies in which these transactions will be settled are different from the currency in which the transaction amount is expressed at the point of service.

The card association continues the clearing process, collecting the clearing batch files containing transactions in various currencies from the acquirer members. Clearing batch files received from different acquirers in different currencies are sorted according to the IIN of the card, and a separate IIN batch file is compiled for each issuer. Each IIN batch file contains transactions performed with one type of card product, while the transaction amounts are expressed in various currencies. These currencies are different from the billing currency, which is the currency in which the billing of the cardholder account is performed.

The issuer can receive IIN batch files compiled by both card associations and local acquirers. Using the unique transaction reference number retrieved from each financial notification message (1240), the issuer matches each 1240 message received during clearing against the authorization database, containing all the previously accepted or rejected authorization request messages (1100). All the matching records are separately compiled. For each record received from the card association a currency exchange operation is performed from the currency in which the amount at the point of service is expressed to the billing currency agreed by the issuer. The records are sorted according to the PAN corresponding to each cardholder, and a statement file is separately compiled for each cardholder. The issuer knows all the information it needs to settle payment with its customers. The issuer recovers the disbursed amount during the clearing period by billing its cardholders. The total in each statement file, corresponding to a cardholder, is computed. For debit cards, the resulting total amount is debited directly from the cardholder's account kept with the issuer. For credit cards, the total of the statement file is posted to a temporary account linked to the cardholder's account, updating its balance, which is held until the statement billing time. This completes the reimbursement of the issuer.

After the clearing of the transactions carried out in a well-defined time period is performed, *settlement* can be accomplished. The three organizations involved in the processing of a point of service transaction (namely, the card acceptor, the acquirer, and the card association) are reimbursed for their services. The card association computes the financial compensations between issuers and acquirers. The transfer of funds is performed through an international settlement bank, which is designated by the card association and which can handle various currencies. Both acquirers and issuers have an account with this bank.

The settlement process can be schematized as follows. The clearing batch file compiled by the card association containing the transaction data that was submitted for clearing to the issuer with transaction amounts in various currencies is submitted to a currency exchange procedure with currency exchange rates provided by the settlement bank. The amount in each transaction record of the batch file is converted from the card acceptor's currency, which is the local currency at the point of service, to a settlement currency agreed by each issuer. After all the transaction amounts are converted in the issuer's settlement currency, a total is computed that reflects the amount to be debited from the issuer's account kept with the settlement bank. The issuer is notified about the settlement of its debt. The card association repeats this process for each issuer that participated in the clearing.

The card association processes the transaction data file received from each acquirer and computes the total of the transaction amounts of all the records in the file. The resulting value is credited in the acquirer's account kept with the settlement bank. The acquirer is notified about the crediting of its account. The card association repeats this process for each acquirer that participated in the clearing. Each acquirer credits the amount in each card acceptor master file to the corresponding account, which finishes the settlement process.

References

[1] Visa, "Products & Services," http://www.visa.com.

[2] MasterCard, "Our Cards," http://www.vis.com.

[3] American Express, "Cards," http://www.americanexpress.com.

[4] Europay International, "Brands," http://www.europay.com.

[5] Diners Club, "Credit Cards," http://www.dinersclub.com.

[6] Discover Financial Services, http://www.discovercard.com.

[7] Japanese Business Cards, http://www.japanese-business-cards.com.

[8] Federal Trade Commission, "Secured Credit Card Marketing Scams," http://www.ftc.gov, October 1996.

[9] Brobeck, S., "Recent Trends in Bank Credit Card Marketing and Indebtedness," Consumer Federation of America, http://www.abiworld.org, July 1998.

[10] ISO/IEC 7811, "Identification Cards—Recording technique—Part 1: Embossing," "Part 2: Magnetic Stripe," "Part 3: Location of Embossed Characters on ID-1 Card," "Part 4: Location of Read-Only Magnetic Tracks—Track 1 and 2," "Part 5: Location of Read-Write Magnetic Track—Track 3," 1985.

[11] ISO/IEC 7812, "Identification Cards—Numbering System and Registration Procedure for Issuer Identifiers," 1987.

[12] ISO/IEC 4909, "Bank Cards—Magnetic Stripe Data Content for Track 3," 1987.

[13] ISO/IEC 7813, "Identification Cards—Financial Transaction Cards," 1987.

[14] Stern, C., "Micro-Thief That 'Steals' Credit Cards," *Sunday Mirror Magazine*, January 28, 2001.

[15] Freier, A. O., P. Karlton, and P. C. Kocher, *The SSL 3.0 Protocol*, Internet-Draft, November 1996.

[16] Dierks, T., and C. Allen, *The TLS Protocol—Version 1.0*, Internet-Draft, November 1997.

[17] ISO/IEC 8583:1993, "Financial Transaction Card Originated Messages–Interchange Message Specifications," 1995.

PART

II

Chip Migration with EMV™

3

Chip Migration

Payment cards for debit and credit have proven to be a huge business success for the retail financial industry. The magnetic stripe technology is cheap enough to make the cost of cards small. Moreover, the payment network and the terminals at the point of service have been in place for years now. Therefore, there is no further need to invest in infrastructure. Meanwhile, the operation of debit and credit cards increases year after year, both in the number of issued cards and in the geographical coverage. Consequently, profit has increased, so there is no apparent cause for concern.

The first section of this chapter lists several causes of concern that should encourage payment system operators, issuers, and acquirers to consider the migration from magnetic stripe to chip. We believe that this motivation could help a chip solution vendor make his business case when talking to skeptics about switching from the magnetic stripe technology to chip.

The second section reminds the reader of the essentials of chip card technology. In this book the terms ICC and chip card are used interchangeably to refer to one and the same device, which not only stores data in its permanent memory but is also able to process data. Therefore, it would be more accurate to refer to these cards as microprocessor chip cards, to clearly distinguish them from the memory chip cards, which can store data but cannot process it. For the fluency of presentation, however, we will refer to the microprocessor chip cards as simply chip cards or ICCs. In Section 3.2.1 we give an overview of the hardware and software structure of a chip card, as well as the life cycle of the chip card. We then make a diagonal presentation of the ISO/IEC 7816 standard, which dominates the world of ICC with contacts. The emphasis is only on few topics from Part 4 of the ISO/IEC 7816 standard. We briefly review the basics about a card file system and the methods of referencing files (Section 3.2.2). Then, the formats of the commands/responses sent to and returned from the card, as well as the most common commands, are briefly presented (Section 3.2.3). This is the minimum amount of knowledge someone would need to be able to understand the rest of this book. For an extensive introduction to chip card technology, the reader should refer to [1]. At the end of the section, we present the concepts of terminal application and card application, and their interactions in a client server model when performing a transaction (Section 3.2.4).

After these foundations of the ICC technology are revisited, two possible chip migration paths are outlined: closed proprietary payment applications and open interoperable payment applications. We analyze some of the features of a payment application that allows interoperability (Section 3.4). These features contrast with the homologue features of a proprietary application (identified in Section 3.3), and thus emphasize the price one pays for open design and interoperability.

3.1 A business case for chip migration

A cause of concern against keeping in place the magnetic stripe technology is the increase of abuses in magnetic stripe payment cards reported worldwide. Attackers have great insight about the design details of these cards, which helps them to identify security weaknesses that could lead to fraud.

In face-to-face payment transactions, counterfeiting the magnetic stripe has become a dangerous threat [2, 3]. This threat combined with sophisticated methods of monitoring the cardholder's PIN cause significant damages to financial institutions issuing such card products (see Section 2.6).

Card associations and payment system operators are concerned with decreasing the amount of fraud. In this context, the migration of actual payment card products from implementations using the magnetic stripe as a storage medium to a chip is seen as a necessary security improvement. The term "chip" designates the integrated circuit embedded in the plastic card. For the purpose of this book, we consider only those chips that offer protection against probing their resources. A chip providing this feature is referred to as tamper-resistant. The reduction of fraud becomes possible because of several factors:

- It is very hard to clone chip cards, particularly the secret cryptographic parameters they contain, unless the tamper resistance of the chip is overtaken. Even though more and more papers report methods of subverting the tamper resistance of chip cards, the attacks are far too complicated for common attackers to mount.

- Through its processing power, the chip card is actively involved in the risk management at the point of service. The chip card becomes a remote agent of the issuer that is able to correctly intervene in a local authorization process performed at a terminal that is not connected on-line to the payment network. The chip can enforce the proper policies for an optimal trade-off between the availability of the retail financial service provided to the cardholder and the security of the issuer against fraudulent transactions.

- The chip improves the process of determining counterfeit cards, through implementing the card authentication method with dynamic authentication mechanisms. It also provides greater protection of the cardholder against fraudulent transactions through the off-line verification of the PIN in the card, for transactions authorized off-line.

The cost of the chip migration is impressive. Integrated circuit cards are much more expensive to issue than magnetic stripe cards. This entails significant costs for the issuers. New terminals are needed at the point of service, which are equipped with integrated circuit card readers. This entails high costs for the acquirer. The host computers of issuers and acquirers as well as the payment network must be adapted for chip migration.

These economic factors have caused many financial institutions to question whether it is cheaper to continue to support the loss due to fraud or to change the whole infrastructure. This is mainly the case for financial institutions located in developed countries, where the existing payment infrastructure is huge. Moreover, their losses are kept reasonably low, considering that the majority of the transactions, if not all, are authorized on-line, which decreases the risk of fraudulent transactions. In developing countries with large territories, however, where the payment infrastructure is poor, the payment transaction is assessed off-line in the majority of situations. In these cases it makes sense to invest in a chip solution from the beginning, since the security protection is clearly better.

Card associations and/or payment system operators have adopted new operating rules for their chip card products, which has motivated issuers and acquirers to perform the chip migration. Thus, the policy of decreasing the interchange fees for acquirers that do not adapt their terminals to accept chip cards can be a good reason for acquirers to implement the chip technology. At the same time, both issuers and acquirers could be encouraged to adopt the chip, through a right liability policy. This policy could stipulate that issuers and acquirers that have not accomplished the chip migration assume the entire risk in case of fraud when making a transaction with an acquirer/issuer that has performed the chip migration.

There is still another strong reason for chip migration. Instead of thinking in terms of reducing fraud, maybe it is better to think in terms of increasing revenue streams as a consequence of chip migration:

1.   Because of better decision-making by the chip at the point of service, it is possible to improve authorization controls at a lower cost. This means that communication costs related to the on-line authorization of a transaction can be reduced in situations where the card risk management together with the terminal risk management decides that authorization can be granted locally. This improves the efficiency of debit/credit cards in a segment of payments, which were previously judged too small.

2.   Since the chip has computation power, the payment card becomes "smart." Card applications can provide far more flexible financial services and better answer the rapid changes in the retail financial market. The same chip can accommodate several card applications, which provides the multiapplication dimension of the chip cards. This allows issuers to reduce the investment cost per card application and better combine several payment instruments that satisfy different payment behaviors. For example, the same chip card can accommodate a national debit scheme used for domestic payments, an international credit scheme suitable for relatively important payments made while travelling abroad, and a cross-border electronic purse for paying per byte for information on demand bought from Internet providers. Thus, the flexibility of customizing the financial service provided to each cardholder on an individual basis further strengthens the relationship between the cardholder and his or her bank.

3.2   An overview of the chip card technology

This section presents a quick overview of the chip card technology. The functionality of an ICC is based on the standard ISO/IEC 7816, "Identification cards—Integrated circuit(s) card with contacts" [4–7]. First, we look at the hardware and software structure of a chip card. Second, we review the basics about a card file system and the methods of referencing files. Third, the format of the command/response pairs sent to and returned from the card as well as the most common commands are briefly presented. Finally, the concepts of terminal application, card application, and their interaction in a client server model are presented.

3.2.1 Hardware and software structure of chip cards

The chip card is a plastic card that incorporates an integrated circuit, which is a single-chip computer. This computer contains a microprocessor that can access read-only memory (ROM), electrically erasable programmable memory (EEPROM), and RAM. The memory management unit (MMU) controls the access to these memories. The hardware structure of the single-chip computer is shown in Figure 3.1.

Figure 3.1
Hardware
structure of
the single-chip
computer in
the card.

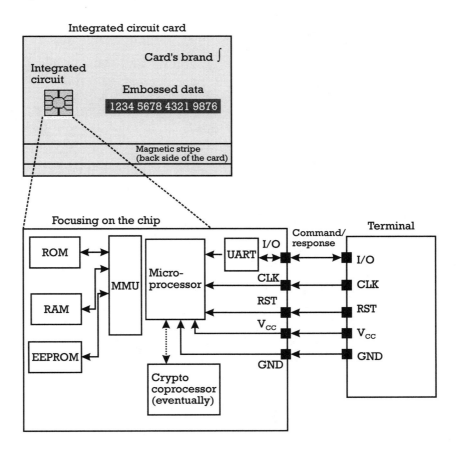

The ROM is masked in the chip and cannot be changed during the whole lifetime of the chip card. The EEPROM permanently stores data that can be read but also modified during the lifetime of the card. The RAM is volatile memory that keeps data needed for the processing performed by the chip's microprocessor during one card session.

The chip is connected to the outside world through five contacts, which are assigned as follows:

> • *I/O:* The chip has only one input/output serial line for communicating with the outside world. The universal asynchronous receiver transmitter (UART) serializes both commands coming from and responses going to the terminal. Among the protocols that can be implemented at the transmission level between the chip card and the terminal, we mention only two protocols known as T = 0 and T = 1 [4], since they are the only transmission protocols accepted by the EMV™ cards.

> • V_{cc} and *GND:* The electrical power for the chip is provided by the terminal on these two contacts.

> • *CLK:* The execution of all the processing in the chip is synchronized with a clock that is received from the terminal.

> • *RST:* This contact receives the electrical reset signal from the terminal, which brings the chip to an initial status (see Section 3.2.4).

The single-chip computer is a slave depending on the terminal, which can be regarded as a master. The chip does not take initiative, but is simply driven by the terminal. Figure 3.2 shows two possible software architectures of a chip card, which can be regarded as a pile of software packages.

The left side of Figure 3.2 shows a proprietary software organization that does not allow for the portability of card applications. It can be seen that the card application makes direct calls to either a proprietary application programming interface (API) or to the card's operating system. Since each ICC producer has its own operating system and its own proprietary API, the card application is not portable from one chip card to another. Every time an issuer changes the chip card producer, the card application has to be rewritten. Regarding the mapping of hardware resources to the software architecture, it must be noted that a large diversity of possibilities exists, depending on the memory capacity allocated for ROM and EEPROM. The operating system and proprietary API are masked in the ROM, whereas the card

Figure 3.2
Two software
architectures
for chip cards.

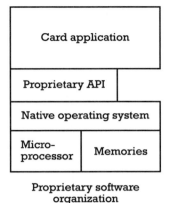

Proprietary software
organization

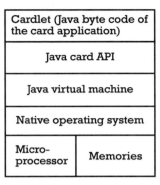

Java card organization

application can reside either in the ROM or in the EEPROM. In the majority of the proprietary card implementations, however, the card application physically resides in the ROM and is logically integrated in the operating system instead of being on top of the operating system. The card file system that contains the data structures needed during the processing performed by the card application is always kept in the EEPROM, since both read and write operations must be available on the permanently stored data.

In the right side of Figure 3.2 the software organization of a Java card [8] is presented. In this software architecture the code of the card application is isolated from specific hardware and operating system libraries through the Java virtual machine (JVM). The JVM interprets the byte code corresponding to the Java source of the card application and translates it into instructions that are executable by the hardware and native operating system. Each chip hardware platform has its own JVM, which allows the card application to be independent of the hardware and the native operating system of the card. One of the big benefits of this platform, which can justify its higher price, is the reduced time to get new applications to the market. They also support the downloading of "cardlets," which is the term sometimes used for the applets downloaded to a chip card, even when the card is already in its utilization stage. Last but not least, the applications written for one chip card can be ported to other chip cards, provided they have the same Java card API, which is actually standardized as Java Card 2.1.1 [9]. Thus, this software organization guarantees the interoperability of card applications written for different chip card platforms.

The actual competitor of the Java card is the MULTOS operating system for chip cards, whose specifications are created by the MAOSCO consortium [10]. Card applications are coded in the MULTOS executable language (MEL), which is an interpreted language that is hardware-independent.

Therefore, similar to the Java card, the MULTOS architecture bases its functionality on a MEL interpreter, which can be regarded as a virtual machine, and an application loader. Generally there is a distinction between off-card and on-card virtual machines. In contrast to the Java card, the MULTOS virtual machine is completely realized on-card. This allows implementing firewalls between the applications, which provides a suitable security level for multiapplication environments. The application loader ensures the possibility of secure loading and deletion of card applications to and from the EEPROM, even during the utilization life stage of the card.

It is important to note that the software configuration and the file system loaded in the card are dependent on the life stage of the chip card. Table 3.1 presents each life stage of the card, along with the most important operations performed by a certain role in that stage.

3.2.2 Card file system and file referencing

The operating system of the chip card manages a file system that stores the data needed by each card application. ISO/IEC 7816-4 [5] supports two categories of files: dedicated files (DFs) and elementary files (EFs). They are organized in a hierarchical tree, with DF as branches and EF as leaves. A typical organization of the card's file system is schematized in Figure 3.3.

3.2.2.1 Master file and dedicated files

The highest DF in the hierarchy, which is the root of the tree, is also called the master file (MF), which is the only mandatory DF in the file organization. In the example presented in Figure 3.3, the MF contains one leaf, the elementary file EF1, and two branches, the dedicated files DF1 and DF2. Data that is used for all the applications in the card (e.g., administrative and general security information such as the ICC serial number, access control keys, card's general PIN, as well as data concerning the management of the card's life cycle) are stored in elementary files at the MF level. This information can be used by the operating system for creating another DF at the MF level.

The dedicated file DF1 contains four leaves. The first three of them (EF11, EF12, and EF13) are working EFs, while EF14 is an internal EF. We will later see the difference between working and internal elementary files. The semantic of the information in DF1 and its elementary files will be explained in Section 3.3. The dedicated file DF2 contains only two leaves, which are the working elementary files EF21 and EF22. Each dedicated file can further contain other hierarchically inferior dedicated files. In Figure 3.3, DF2 contains one subdedicated file DF21.

Table 3.1
The Life Cycle of a Chip Card

Life Stage	Operation	Role Involved
IC fabrication	The integrated chip (IC) is produced, with the operating system in the ROM mask. For a proprietary card, this mask can contain the card application. For a Java card, the ROM contains the Java virtual machine. A unique ICC serial number is assigned to each chip.	IC manufacturer
ICC fabrication	The integrated chip is embedded in the plastic card.	Card manufacturer
Prepersonalization	The file system of the card is created. The data that is specific to the payment system and is common to all chip cards participating in the same scheme is also written during this stage.	Card manufacturer
	For a proprietary card, if the card application is resident in the EEPROM, the application software is loaded. For the Java card all the card applications that are foreseen in the standard configuration of the card are loaded.	
Personalization	The data specific to each cardholder is filled in the appropriate files of the card.	Card issuer
Utilization	The card is operated according to the business goals of each application.	Cardholder
	For Java cards, card applications can be dynamically added in the EEPROM during the utilization stage. The only restriction is that the corresponding byte code originates from an application provider agreed upon by the card issuer and there is enough EEPROM space. Card applications can be also dynamically deleted from the EEPROM, according to the preferences of the cardholder.	
End life	When the validity of the card expires, the card is disaffected by the card issuer, which can for example block the entire card.	Card issuer

A dedicated file can be seen as a container of data belonging to one card application. Several data elements of the card application that are semantically related are stored in the same elementary file. Application control information and cardholder's financial data are stored in the elementary

Figure 3.3
The organization
of the card's file
system.

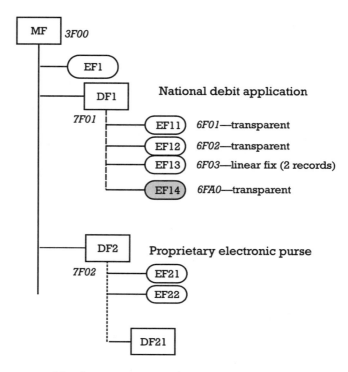

files encompassed in the same DF. Each DF may contain cryptographic keys for implementing various security services, and each may have its own application PIN, which can be used to refine the access control mechanism of a multiapplication card.

The referencing of a DF in the card's file system, which corresponds to the possibility of selecting a card application from the terminal's side, can be performed in two distinct ways:

1.   *Referencing with a fixed file identifier (FID), which consists of 2 bytes (4 hexadecimal digits).* For example, the MF always has the FID equal to 3F00, while DF1 has the FID equal to 7F01 and DF2 has the FID equal to 7F02, and so on. In order to be able to select a card application with its FID, the terminal application must know beforehand the file organization in that card. For example, in order to select DF21 starting from the MF level as the current directory, the terminal must first select DF2 with its FID, and only after this selection is successful can it select DF21 with its corresponding FID.

2.   *Referencing with an application identifier (AID), which consists of up to 16 bytes.* The encoding of the AID is detailed in the ISO/IEC 7816-5 [6].

The AID comprises either the registered application provider identifier (RID), which optionally is concatenated with the proprietary application identifier extension (PIX), or the proprietary application identifier. The referencing of card applications with registered application provider identifiers has the advantage that the terminal does not have to know in advance the FID of the DF that stores the application or its position in the card's file system. Moreover, since the RID is unique worldwide, several applications can be stored in the card with no danger of referencing conflicts.

It will become obvious in Section 3.3 that referencing a DF with its FID is suitable for closed design proprietary card applications. In Section 3.4 we show that the open design interoperable card application uses DF referencing through the AID.

3.2.2.2   EFs

The data elements of a card application are encoded in elementary files. The elementary files of a card application can be further subdivided into working EF and internal EF:

▸ A working EF stores data that is not interpreted by the card application, but rather used by the terminal application exclusively during the execution of a protocol with the card.

▸ An internal EF stores data managed only by the card application for management and control purposes. Cryptographic parameters used for security services provided by the card as well as the cardholder's witness PIN or other cardholder verification codes (CHVs) are stored in internal EFs.

Two referencing methods for elementary files are used:

1. *Referencing with an FID, which consists of 2 bytes (4 hexadecimal digits).* The same FID referencing mechanism as that described for the DF can be also used for the EF. The disadvantage of this referencing mode is that before a file management command can be applied on an EF, the terminal must explicitly select this EF inside the DF corresponding to the card application. Examples of file management operations are the reading of some bytes from a transparent EF or the writing of a record in a linear fixed EF. Another disadvantage is that the terminal must know beforehand the FID of all the elementary

files inside the card application's DF. The advantage of this referencing mode, however, is that the selection of either a DF or EF in the card is done uniformly, which simplifies the card's implementation. This referencing mode of EF is suitable for closed design proprietary card applications (see Section 3.3).

2. *Referencing with a Short File Identifier (SFI), which consists of a number between 1 and 30 that can be encoded on 5 bits.* This referencing method has the advantage that the SFI can be used as a file handler, which can be given as an input parameter to a file management command. This means that there is no need of executing an explicit selection of an EF inside the DF before calling a read/write command from/to an EF. Moreover, the SFI of all the working EFs in the card's application DF can be easily listed in a kind of DF table of contents. This helps the terminal learn by itself the publicly available working EF(s) existing in a DF. Therefore, this referencing method of EFs is preferred in open design interoperable card applications (see Section 3.4).

The structure of an EF depends on its intended use. As explained in ISO/IEC 7816-4 [5] one can distinguish among four basic types of EF structures. Transparent files consist of a sequence of bytes. A linear fixed file consists of a number of records, all having the same length. A linear variable file consists of a number of records, each with a variable length. The cyclic files contain records of fixed length organized in a ring structure. After all the records are written, the oldest entry in the file will be overwritten by the current entry to be stored. Figure 3.4 schematizes the four types of file structures.

The file header of each EF stores information about the type of EF file structure and the size of the file. It also stores the possible actions to be performed on the file (read, write, invalidate, rehabilitate, increase) as well as the access conditions under which a terminal application can perform that action (card's general PIN or application PIN, authentication with a symmetric key, access always permitted or access never permitted).

Figure 3.4
Four types of elementary file data structures.

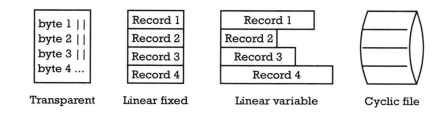

| Transparent | Linear fixed | Linear variable | Cyclic file |

3.2.3 Command and response format

In accordance with the OSI 7-layer model, the information transaction exchanged between the card and the terminal can be divided into three protocol sections:

1. The physical layer protocol (layer 1) corresponds to the electrical signals on the I/O contact of the card.

2. Data transmission protocols (layer 2) correspond to T = 0 and T = 1 protocols [4]. They are both asynchronous, half-duplex protocols. T = 0 is a byte-oriented transmission protocol of the first-generation chip cards when the computing power and the RAM on the chip was limited. It does not allow the transmission of data both in the command and in the response. T = 1 is a block-oriented protocol, which better respects the OSI reference model and allows transmission of data both in the command and in the response. The data is handled in blocks and the error checking is carried out on an entire block of data rather than on 1 byte.

3. Application protocols for command and response data (layer 7). A step in an application protocol consists of sending a command application protocol data unit (C-APDU) from the terminal application to the card application. The latter processes it and sends back the response application protocol data unit (R-APDU) to the terminal application. A schematized picture of a C-APDU/R-APDU pair is given in Figure 3.5.

The C-APDU consists of a mandatory header of 4 bytes and an optional body of a variable length. The header includes the class of instructions to which the command belongs (CLA), the instruction code (INS) determining the command inside of a class, and the parameters of the instruction

Figure 3.5
Command/
response pair
(C-APDU/
R-APDU).

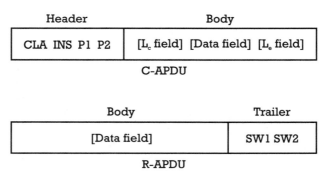

[parameter 1 (P1) and parameter 2 (P2)]. The meaning of these parameters is dependent on the instruction code. The body of the command is optional and may contain the following fields:

- L_c: This field (of 1 or 3 bytes) can contain the number of bytes present in the data field of the command.

- *Data field:* This field (of L_c bytes) contains the string to be sent as input data to the card application.

- L_e: This field (of a variable length up to 3 bytes) can contain the maximum number of bytes expected in the data field of the response returned by the card.

The R-APDU contains a conditional body of variable length L_r that can be less than or equal to L_e. The R-APDU includes the trailer, which is a mandatory field of 2 bytes containing the status words (SW1, SW2). The status words inform the terminal application about the result of executing the command in the card application.

The ISO/IEC 7816-4 [5] standard defines only the basic commands. They can be grouped in file selection, read data, modify/delete data, generate data, compare data, and authenticate through cryptographic functions. In addition to these standardized commands, each card operating system or each card application defines private use commands. For example, the EMV™ debit/credit card application defines its own commands beside those in ISO/7816-4 (e.g., the GET PROCESSING OPTIONS, and GENERATE AC). The commands for the creation and personalization of files in the card's file system and the commands for blocking either an application or the entire card are further examples of private use commands. One can understand why even if chip card operating systems have been implemented according to the ISO/IEC 7816 standard, it does not necessarily mean that they are compatible with each other [11].

3.2.4 Card application and terminal application

The terminal at the point of service is a card acceptor device (CAD) equipped with a chip card reader, which is often referred to as the Interface Device (IFD). The terminal interacts with an ICC according to the client server model.

- A client application runs in the terminal. This client application is referred to as the terminal application.

‣ A server application runs in the ICC. This server application is referred to as the card application.

The terminal application sends commands as a client to the card application, which responds as a server.

To easily explain the processing performed by both the terminal application and the card application, as well as their interaction in the client server model, it is convenient to represent them as algorithmic state machines (ASM). For an ASM the next state depends on the actual state and the event that triggers the transition from one state to another. The state of the ICC consists of a set of data elements and cryptographic parameters. The cryptographic parameters are organized in the card's file system. From this point of view the ICC can be seen as a permanent storage medium. Compared to a magnetic stripe card, which was a passive storage medium, the ICC has computational power provided by its own microprocessor. The event that triggers the transition of the ICC from one state to another is a command with parameters received from the terminal. As a consequence of this transition the ICC performs an action. First, the action consists of updating the value of the data elements and cryptographic parameters stored in the ICC (i.e., the state of the ICC), according to the requirements of the command and the accompanying parameters. Second, the action computes a response that is returned to the terminal. The response can contain the value of one or more data elements stored or computed in the card and a status word, which describes whether or not the command was successfully completed in the card. In case of failure, the status word indicates the source of error. The response received from the card represents the event that triggers the transition of the terminal from one state to another.

The terminal brings the ICC from an initial state S_0 to an operational state S_1 through an electrical reset. The action performed by the card following the reset is to prepare and send back to the terminal an answer to reset (ATR) response, which contains enough information to allow the communication subsystem of the terminal to synchronize with the communication subsystem of the card. Once this initial handshake is performed, the terminal can send C-APDU to and receive R-APDU from the card. The client-server relationship established between the terminal and the card is presented in Figure 3.6.

The set of commands and responses exchanged between the terminal and the ICC in the framework of a transaction is called a transaction profile.

A card application in the ICC contains a set of data elements that can be accessed by the terminal after a successful selection of the application. A data element is the smallest information unit that can be identified by a

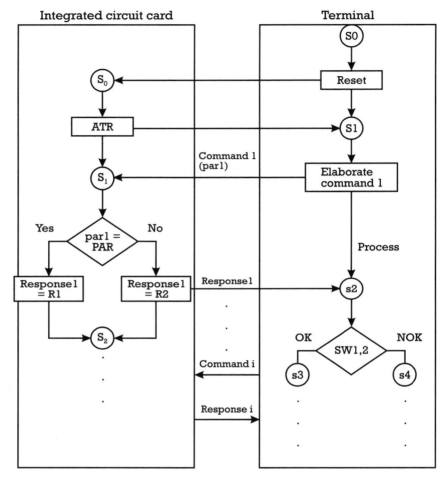

Figure 3.6
Terminal
application and
card application
in a client server
configuration.

name, a description of its logical content, and a format. Data elements are mapped onto data objects, which are encoded according to a certain format (e.g., fixed length format, BER-TLV format, and others).

The terminal application consists of the sequence of commands, which are launched by the terminal to trigger the transition of the card application from one state to another. This determines the processing in the card according to the functionality of the card application. The terminal application also processes the data objects received in the responses from the card and the status words reported at the end of each command.

Several issues are identified in relation to the design of a card and terminal application, indifferent to whether it is a proprietary or interoperable solution:

1. One has to define the encoding of data elements into data objects in the card and the terminal application.

2. The organization of these data objects in a file system stored in the card and the referencing of files in this system must be defined. If several card applications reside in the same card, it is necessary to specify the separation of files corresponding to each application.

3. The set of commands supported by the card and the possible responses elaborated towards the terminal must be also defined.

4. The underlying cryptographic technology used for implementing the necessary security protections in both the card and the terminal must be chosen.

The possible solutions to these issues are restricted to the framework provided by the ISO/IEC 7816. The next two sections show how the aforementioned issues are solved in the case of a proprietary and closed payment application and in the case of an interoperable and open payment application, respectively.

3.3 Proprietary payment application

The approach described in this section outlines an oversimplified proprietary design solution, which can be adopted by payment system operators migrating from magnetic stripe cards to integrated circuit cards. The purpose is to show the shortcoming of this approach, in case open design and interoperability are business requirements.

Let us assume that a payment system operator provides a proprietary payment application, which consists of both a card and a terminal application. It is intended for the purpose of a dedicated business goal—for example, a national debit scheme for POS payments. The proprietary application is completely controlled by the payment system operator, who has designed and specified it according to its business requirements.

The card application is instantiated in chip cards of cardholders who are clients of an issuer. The issuer has established a business agreement for implementing the card application, which is provided by the payment system operator. The issuer has no freedom to customize the card application to its specific business needs. An ICC carrying the proprietary card application is accepted with terminals managed by an acquirer that has also established a business relationship with the payment system operator. The acquirer agrees to implement the terminal application, which is provided by the payment system operator. The acquirer has no freedom in customizing the terminal application specified by the payment system operator.

Let us assume that the card application stores the financial information characterizing the cardholder. This information consists of the following data elements:

- *Application Preferred Name:* This is the name associated with the application running in the card. This name is printed on the display of the POS terminal for informing the cardholder about the application that is currently selected in the card.

- *Application Version Number:* This is the version number of the software implementation of the card application.

- Application Expiration Date: This data element represents the date after which the card application expires.

- *Application PAN:* This is the information that uniquely identifies the account of the cardholder and the issuer that keeps this account.

- *Cardholder Name:* This represents the name of the cardholder to be printed on the sale slip produced at the point of service.

- *Issuer's operator, first number:* This is a telephone number displayed on the man-machine interface of the shopkeeper if the processing at the point of sale performed by the terminal determines that a voice referral is necessary.

- *Issuer's operator, second number:* This is a second telephone number the shopkeeper can call for the voice referral in case the first number is congested.

When the terminal sends an INTERNAL AUTHENTICATE C-APDU, with a body containing a random number and data elements characterizing the business environment at the point of service (amount, terminal ID, date, and time), the card computes a dynamic authenticator on this data. This authenticator is computed with a MAC-based dynamic data authentication (DDA) mechanism, like that presented in Appendix D, Section D.7.1. The card sends an R-APDU, which contains the dynamic authenticator in its body, back to the terminal. More details about the computation by the card of the dynamic authenticator and its verification by the terminal are provided in Section 3.3.4.

3.3.1 Encoding data elements with a fixed format

A convenient and simple method of encoding the data elements can be obtained with a predefined fixed format, where each data element is mapped into a data object consisting of a fixed number of bytes. This number represents the maximal length of the object. If the representation of data is smaller than the maximal length, then data is justified right or left in that field and the remainder of the field is padded accordingly. For the data elements listed above, an example of their encoding is given in Table 3.2.

The definition of data elements can be proprietary to the payment system operator, but it can also be a subset of the interindustry data elements defined in ISO/IEC 7816-6 [7].

The data objects are not explicitly identified in the card application, but they are identified implicitly. This implicit identification is obtained through their location in one elementary file or another of the card's file system, and through their position in that file. This mapping of data objects into the card's file system is totally at the discretion of the payment system operator that decides which data object goes to which elementary file, and in which relative position of that file. A possible mapping is shown in Figure 3.7.

Table 3.2
Encoding with Fixed Format of Data Elements

Name	Format	Length
Application Preferred Name	an 16 (alphanumeric on maximum 16 characters)	16 bytes—maximum. Right justified, left padded with blanks
Application Version Number	b (binary)	2 bytes
Application Expiration Date	n6 (YYMMDD) (numeric on 6 digits, in the order: year, month, day)	3 bytes
Application PAN	cn 19 (numeric on 19 digits)	10 bytes—maximum Right justified, left padded with zeros
Cardholder Name	ans 26	26 bytes—maximum Right justified, left padded with blanks
Issuer's operator, phone number	n16 (numeric on 16 digits)	8 bytes
MAC-based dynamic authenticator	b	8 bytes
Application Transaction Counter	b	2 bytes

Figure 3.7
Mapping of data
objects into the
card's file
system.

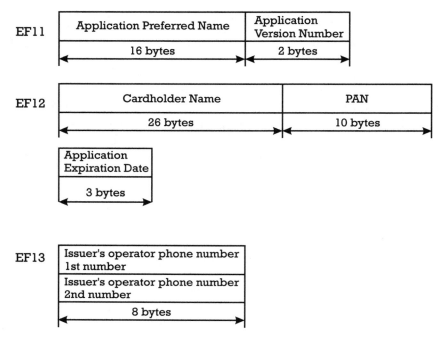

In this example, all the data objects present in the card application are mapped in three elementary files as follows:

1. EF11, which is a transparent file, stores the Application Preferred Name and the Application Version Number in this order. It has a total of 18 bytes, of which the first 16 bytes store the Application Preferred Name and the last 2 bytes store the Application Version Number.

2. EF12, which is also a transparent file, stores the following data objects: the Cardholder Name in the first 26 bytes, the application PAN in the next 10 bytes, and the Application Expiration Date in the last 3 bytes.

3. EF13, which is a linear fixed file, contains two records of the same length. They store the first phone number and the second phone number of the issuer's operator. These are phone numbers where the POS operator can call the issuer if any suspicions appear about the current transaction or cardholder.

3.3.2 Fixed file system organization

The file system of the card hosting the proprietary debit application is outlined in Figure 3.3.

After resetting the card, the current referenced DF is the MF, which represents the default entry in the card file system. The MF in this example has one single EF as a leaf (EF1). This elementary file keeps the ICC serial number, which is a data element that is uniquely assigned by each card manufacturer. There are two DFs that are branches of the MF. Each DF is an entry point to another card application. For example, DF1 is the entry point for the national debit card application, while DF2 is the entry point of a dedicated electronic purse scheme. Note that the payment system operator providing the first application is not necessarily the same as the payment system operator providing the second application.

The DF1 contains four leaves. Three of them are the working elementary files EF11, EF12, and EF13 presented above. The fourth leaf is an internal elementary file EF14, which contains a symmetric key for computing the dynamic authenticator. This key, which is denoted K_d and is unique for each card, is derived from the issuer master key (IMK). The IMK is managed by the issuer for the computation of dynamic authenticators. The key K_d is obtained with the formula $K_d = F_1(IMK)[PAN]$, according to the principles explained in Appendix E, Section E.5. The diversification information *Diversification_Info* consists of the PAN assigned to the cardholder. F_1 is a one-way function, like a MAC based on a 64-bit length block cipher (see Appendix E, Section E.4). The issuer computes the key K_d and writes its value in the EF14 of the DF1 during its personalization stage. The terminal application in the POS, as well as any other agent except the card application itself, have no access to the content of EF14, which should remain secret during the whole lifetime of the card.

The terminal application uniformly references the DF1 and the elementary files EF11, EF12, and EF13, using their FID on 2 bytes. In Figure 3.3 the file identifiers are listed next to each file in the system.

3.3.3 Preestablished command and response formats

In a proprietary payment scheme, the terminal application is aware of the encoding of data elements into data objects, the mapping of data objects into elementary files, and the organization of the dedicated/elementary files in the card. All these design details are fixed beforehand by the payment system operator and are implemented in the same form by all the participants in the system.

Therefore, the format of the commands and responses is fixed. The set of data objects that is transmitted within the body of each C-APDU is always the same. The set of data objects that is returned in the body of each R-APDU is also preestablished.

Moreover, the transaction profile is fixed, since the sequence of commands in the terminal application is predetermined and is not negotiable between the card and terminal. The steps below describe this transaction profile:

- Step 1: The terminal application selects DF1, which contains the debit application.

- Step 2: The terminal selects EF11 and reads its binary content.

- Step 3: It repeats the same sequence of commands for EF12.

- Step 4: It selects the linear fixed file EF13 and reads its two records.

- Step 5: The terminal prepares a message *M1* containing a random number *R*, and some data about the business environment. This business environment data includes the amount of the transaction (which is typed in the terminal's keypad by the POS operator), the identifier of the terminal *TerminalID*, and the time/date when the transaction took place *TimeDate*. The message *M1* is the body of the INTERNAL AUTHENTICATE C-APDU, which is sent to the card. This C-APDU triggers the computation of the MAC-based dynamic authenticator in the card, the value of which is denoted *mac_card*. A more detailed look at the computation performed by the card is postponed to Section 3.3.4. The value *mac_card* together with the Application Transaction Counter (ATC) is returned in the body of the R-APDU. The R-APDU body is always 10 bytes, where the first 8 bytes contain the value of *mac_card* and the last 2 bytes contain the ATC.

In each step of the transaction profile described above, the terminal sends a set of commands and processes the received responses. The processing performed by the terminal on these responses can be described as follows:

- After reading the content of the elementary files EF11, EF12, and EF13, the terminal application identifies the data elements of the card application according to their predetermined position in an elementary file. Thus, the first 16 bytes of EF11 are identified as being the

Application Preferred Name, the next 2 bytes are the Application Version Number, and so on.

▸ The terminal displays the Application Preferred Name to inform the cardholder about the card application that is currently effective. The terminal application performs some checks. For example, the Application Version Number in the card must be equal to the Application Version Number of the terminal application. The Application Expiration Date read from the card must be smaller than the current date in the terminal (card not expired). If all these verifications are passed, the terminal continues processing; otherwise the card session is aborted.

▸ The terminal creates a message $M0$ containing the cardholder's financial information stored in the card. The Cardholder Name, the PAN, and the Application Expiration Date of the card are concatenated in $M0$.

▸ If the transaction amount is less than a threshold limit imposed as a security parameter by the acquirer, the transaction is processed off-line, without the intervention of the IH. Thus, the transaction is accepted if the value of the MAC-based dynamic authenticator produced by the card (mac_card) is correct. More details of this assessment process is postponed until Section 3.3.4. The validity of the dynamic authenticator proves the authenticity of the card and the fact that the card is not counterfeit, which obviously is a big step forward compared to magnetic stripe cards.

▸ When the transaction amount is above a threshold limit, the terminal sends on-line to the IH the financial data captured from the card ($M0$), the data characterizing the business environment of the POS terminal ($M1$), the ATC, and the dynamic authenticator computed by the card mac_card. The IH checks whether the dynamic authenticator is valid or not in the same way that this checking is performed off-line by the terminal. The IH, however, can perform supplementary verifications compared to the off-line case, which increase the security of the authorization process. Thus, the issuer can verify whether the balance of the account indicated by the PAN has enough funds for supporting the transaction. The issuer can also verify whether the card was blacklisted, for reasons of being reported stolen, or having compromised keys, etc. If all these verifications are passed, the issuer informs the POS terminal about the outcome of the authorization, approving or denying the transaction.

3.3.4   Symmetric cryptographic technology

The security protection in the transaction profile described in Section 3.3.3 is deliberately oversimplified. It serves solely for the presentation of concepts related to the choice of an appropriate cryptographic technology for either proprietary or interoperable design solutions.

The only security service foreseen in this transaction profile is card authentication. The MAC-based dynamic data authentication, as explained in Appendix D, Section D.7.1, is the security mechanism implementing this security service.

Since the scheme is proprietary, the payment system operator can easily coordinate the whole key management process for both issuers and acquirers in the framework of symmetric cryptographic techniques.

- Using a secure key distribution channel established in advance, each issuer receives an IMK. The payment system operator derives IMK from its master key (MK). The issuer identifier serves as the diversification information *Diversification_Info* (i.e., $IMK = F_2(MK)$ [*Issuer Identifier*]) (see Appendix E, Section E.5). As it was explained in Section 3.3.2, during the card personalization stage, the issuer uses IMK to produce the key K_d, which is a symmetric key for computing the dynamic authenticator.

- The payment system operator provides acquirers with a security application module (SAM) that stores the MK. The SAM is a tamper-resistant chip, which is not embedded in a plastic card but rather is directly plugged into a specialized connector inside the terminal. Note that since this chip contains the MK, its tamper resistance is an essential assumption for the security of the payment system operator.

In the remainder of the section we concentrate only on step 5 of the transaction profile described in Section 3.3.3. We zoom in on both the processing performed by the card to produce the dynamic authenticator *mac_card* as well as on its verification by the terminal, with the help of its SAM, in case the authorization is granted off-line.

Figure 3.8 outlines the computation of the dynamic authenticator by the card application.

The terminal prepares the C-APDU with a header (CLA, INS, P1, and P2) corresponding to the internal authenticate command. The body of the C-APDU contains the message $M1 = R \parallel amount \parallel TerminalID \parallel TimeDate$. $M1$ is constructed as the concatenation from left to right of the random number R,

Figure 3.8
Computation
of the dynamic
authenticator.

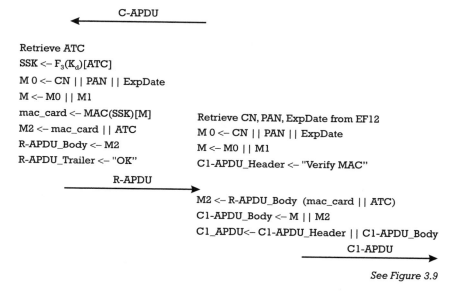

the amount of the transaction *amount*, the identifier of the terminal *TerminalID*, and the time/date when the transaction took place *TimeDate*.

After receiving this C-APDU, the card application performs the following processing:

- Retrieve the current ATC and use it as a diversifier for obtaining the session key SSK from the card's unique key K_d (i.e., $SSK = F_3(K_d)[ATC]$).

- Compute a message $M0 = CN \| PAN \| ExpDate$. This message is the concatenation from left to right of the Cardholder Name (CN), the PAN, and the Application Expiration Date of the card.

- Retrieve the message *M1* from the C-APDU body and construct the message *M* as the concatenation of *M0* and *M1* (i.e., $M = M0 \| M1$).

- Compute the dynamic authenticator as $mac\_card = MAC\,(SSK)\,[M]$.

- Compute the R-APDU body as the $M2 = mac\_card \| ATC$. Return R-APDU.

Figure 3.9 outlines the verification of the dynamic authenticator by the terminal application with the support of the SAM.

After receiving the R-APDU, the terminal can verify off-line the correctness of the dynamic authenticator *mac_card* received from the card, using the SAM. In this case the SAM can be regarded as the issuer's remote agent validating the dynamic authenticator. To this end the terminal constructs *M0* in the same way as the card did, using the data elements CN, the *PAN*, and the Application Expiration Date previously read from the card. The terminal computes the message *M* concatenating *M0* and *M1*. The terminal

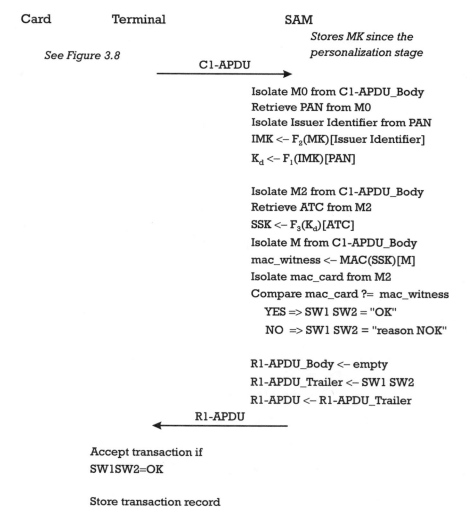

Figure 3.9
Verification of
the dynamic
authenticator.

Card	Terminal	SAM
		Stores MK since the
		personalization stage
	See Figure 3.8	

C1-APDU $\longrightarrow$

Isolate M0 from C1-APDU_Body
Retrieve PAN from M0
Isolate Issuer Identifier from PAN
IMK <– F_2(MK)[Issuer Identifier]
K_d <– F_1(IMK)[PAN]

Isolate M2 from C1-APDU_Body
Retrieve ATC from M2
SSK <– $F_3(K_d)$[ATC]
Isolate M from C1-APDU_Body
mac_witness <– MAC(SSK)[M]
Isolate mac_card from M2
Compare mac_card ?= mac_witness
   YES => SW1 SW2 = "OK"
   NO => SW1 SW2 = "reason NOK"

R1-APDU_Body <– empty
R1-APDU_Trailer <– SW1 SW2
R1-APDU <– R1-APDU_Trailer

$\longleftarrow$ R1-APDU

Accept transaction if
SW1SW2=OK

Store transaction record
containing M and M2 for clearing

prepares another C1-APDU, this time addressed to the SAM. Its header (CLA, INS, P1, and P2) corresponds to the *Verify MAC* command supported by the SAM. The body of this C1-APDU contains the message $M = M0 \parallel M1$ concatenated with the message $M2 = mac\_card \parallel ATC$.

After receiving the C1-APDU, the SAM performs the verification of the dynamic authenticator *mac_card*, following the steps listed below:

- Retrieve the *PAN* from *M0* and isolate the issuer identifier. Use it as a diversifier to obtain the IMK as $IMK = F_2(MK)[Issuer\ Identifier]$, where MK was stored in the SAM since its personalization.

- Using the PAN as a diversifier, derive the unique key of the card K_d, used for the computation of the dynamic authenticator, from the IMK (i.e., $K_d = F_1(IMK)[PAN]$).

- Retrieve the ATC from *M2* and use it as a diversifier for deriving the session key SSK from the unique key of the card K_d (i.e., $SSK = F_3(K_d)[ATC]$).

- Compute the dynamic authenticator as $mac\_witness = \text{MAC (SSK) [M]}$.

- Retrieve the dynamic authenticator *mac_card* computed by the card from *M2* and compare it with the recomputed value *mac_witness*.

- If the two values are equal, position the SW1 and SW2 status words in the trailer of the R1-APDU as OK. Otherwise, position them as NOK. Return R1-APDU.

After receiving the outcome of the dynamic authenticator verification in R1-APDU, the terminal decides whether to approve (SW1SW2="OK") or deny (SW1SW2="NOK") the transaction. The terminal keeps a transaction record (M, M2) in its permanent memory. The record will be sent to the acquirer for the clearing process.

If the terminal decides that the authorization is performed on-line by the IH, the authorization request message (1100) will transport $M = M0 \parallel M1$ concatenated with the message $M2 = mac\_card \parallel ATC$. After receiving these messages, the security module of the IH will perform the same processing for verifying the dynamic authenticator as the processing described for the SAM.

As one can see, in the case of a proprietary payment application, which can authorize off-line transactions involving small amounts, symmetric key cryptographic techniques are appropriate for implementing security mechanisms. In this case the payment system operator controls the whole key management for both issuers and acquirers, which allows an easy and cost-effective operation of symmetric key cryptographic algorithms. The immediate consequence is that the card does not need to implement asymmetric cryptographic algorithms, and therefore, a cryptographic coprocessor for long arithmetic computation is not needed in its hardware architecture (see Appendix D, Section D.1.2). This keeps the price of chip cards low. The use of the SAM in the structure of the terminal allows the off-line verification of the MAC-based dynamic authenticator. The SAM increases the cost of the terminal, which is the price to pay for off-line authorization of transactions involving small amounts. If the payment system operator decides that all the authorizations must be performed on-line, indifferent of the transaction amount, the presence of the SAM in the terminal is no longer needed. In this case, the verification of the dynamic authenticator is directly performed by the issuer, which simplifies the design of the terminal and its cost.

We have argued that the use of symmetric key cryptography is rather cheap for securing proprietary payment schemes, at least from the point of view of issuers. This does not mean, however, that public key cryptographic techniques are ruled out for securing the off-line authorization of transactions in proprietary payment schemes. With the advance of chip technology, it can be foreseen that the emphasis of security computations will shift towards public key enabled chips, which will render unnecessary the presence of a SAM in the hardware structure of a terminal.

3.4   Interoperable payment application

The design principles explained in the previous section are not suitable for interoperability. The following business case for an interoperable payment application is now analyzed.

The proprietary card application described in Section 3.3 is referred to as *C1*. The card hosting *C1* is issued by the issuer *I1* and is accepted at a terminal managed by the acquirer *A1*, running the terminal application *T1*. The whole payment scheme is managed by the payment system operator denoted *O1*.

Assume that a cardholder has an ICC storing a card application *C2*, providing the same functionality as *C1*. However, the issuer *I2* that manages the ICC containing *C2* is not a subscriber of the payment system operator *O1*. The issuer *I2* is a subscriber of the payment system operator *O2*, which did not establish any business agreement with *O1*. The payment system operator *O2* made its own design for the card application *C2* and for the terminal application *T2*. This basically means that:

- The rules of encoding the data elements into data objects adopted in *C2* could be different than the rules adopted in *C1*.

- It could be that the rules of encoding data elements into data objects adopted by both *C1* and *C2* are the same—for example, according to ISO/IEC 7816-6 [7]. There is a high probability, however, that the mapping of data objects in elementary files is different from one card application to the other, since there is no standard that regulates this matter. Then the implicit identification of data objects in the two card applications is different.

- The file organization in *C2* is different than the file organization in *C1*, since the file tree structure and the file identifiers adopted by the file organization in *C2* are probably different than in the file organization adopted by *C1*.

- Both payment applications use interindustry commands as defined in ISO/IEC 7816-4 [5]. Because of the differences, however, in mapping data objects in files and in the file organization, the set of data objects to be transmitted with each command and the set of data objects expected to be received with each response are different from one card application to another. This determines two different transaction profiles for the two payment applications, which finally means two distinct terminal applications *T1* and *T2*.

- It is also possible that the formulas for computing the dynamic authenticator differ from one card application to another, while the cryptographic keys involved in this computation are certainly proprietary to each payment system operator.

In case the acquirer *A1* would like to broaden its financial services to cardholders of the issuer *I2*, then *A1* should establish a separate business relationship with the payment system operator *O2*. Following this agreement, the acquirer *A1* loads in its terminals another distinct terminal application *T2*, which is proprietary to *O2*. Moreover, considering that symmetric cryptographic technology is used, the terminal should be able to accommodate in addition to the security application module *SAM1* used by *T1*, a supplementary security application module *SAM2*, which is exclusively used by *T2*. Another possibility would be to cumulate the security functions and the corresponding cryptographic parameters of both *SAM1* and *SAM2* into one single SAM, with the condition that the payment system operators *O1* and *O2* have established a business relationship in this sense. In practice, this alternative is almost ruled out both by concurrency reasons between operators and for reasons determined by logistic problems related to key management and personalization of the SAM. As more and more system operators propose proprietary payment applications to acquirers, the management of the terminal applications and SAM(s) would become very difficult and the terminal more and more expensive.

A possible solution for interoperability would be that payment system operators create a consortium that specifies coproprietary card and terminal applications, with closed design solutions. As a result, everyone interested in being interoperable with this closed system would adhere to a memorandum of understanding proposed by the initial consortium. This policy, however, is not appropriate for the world of banking and financial services. Payment system operators, issuers, and acquirers would like to independently decide how the payment application would best match their interests.

A consortium comprised of Europay, MasterCard, and Visa (which is referred to as the EMV™ consortium) proposed an interoperable and open solution. In the framework of their solution each payment system operator, issuer, and acquirer can still customize a card/terminal application to its own business needs, providing they respect the basic negotiation mechanisms proposed by the EMV™ specifications. The rest of this section explains the principles of how this can be achieved.

3.4.1 Self-determined encoding of data elements

Instead of adopting a predefined fixed format for encoding data elements into data objects and an implicit identification of these data objects, the solution adopted by the EMV™ is to explicitly identify each data object. This is achieved with a tag, which can be regarded as a unique identification label. The data object has also attached the information about the length of the data element it encodes, such that there is no need of specifying beforehand a fixed length for each data element supported by an application. Thus, a data element is encoded following the tag-length-value (TLV) convention, described in the Basic Encoding Rules (BER) contained in the ISO/IEC 8825 standard [12]. Only the value field of the EMV™ data object actually conveys the useful information, while the tag and length fields convey the identification information. The BER-TLV encoding of the data elements in the card application $C1$ is listed in Table 3.3.

The BER-TLV representation is suitable from the point of view of interoperability. Since every EMV™ data element is completely characterized by the tag and the length fields, the EMV™ terminal application can identify each data element and retrieve the conveyed information in the

Table 3.3
BER-TLV Encoding of Data Elements

Name	Format	Tag	Length
Application Preferred Name	an 1-16	9F12	1–16
Application Version Number	b	9F08	2
Application Expiration Date	n6 (YYMMDD)	5F24	3
Application PAN	cn 19 var. up to 19	5A	Var. up to 10
Cardholder Name	ans 2-26	5F20	2–26
Issuer's operator, phone number	n16	To be defined	8
MAC-based dynamic authenticator (called Application Cryptogram in EMV™)	b	9F26	8
Signed Static Application Data	b	93	The length of the RSA modulus of the issuer (for further details on RSA, see Appendix F)
Signed Dynamic Application Data	b	9F4B	The length of the RSA modulus of the card

value field, indifferent of their "position" in the card (which EF and on which position). Therefore, the EMV™ terminal application has no need to know in advance the structure of the EMV™ files in the ICC to retrieve financial data needed for the completion of a payment transaction. As it will become evident in the next paragraph, it is sufficient that the terminal application knows the references of all the publicly available elementary files of the card application and the indexes of all the retrievable records from these files. The terminal application, however, has no need of previous information about how data is organized in these records. This allows complete freedom for the issuer of the EMV™ cards about the modality of mapping data objects into elementary files. No business relationship has to be established in advance between the issuer of the ICC and the acquirer responsible for the terminal, except that they are members of the same payment system operator/card association. The mapping of data objects in application elementary files (AEF) is illustrated in Figure 3.10.

An elementary file can be regarded as a sack where the data objects can be located in any position. Once the elementary file is read in the terminal,

Figure 3.10
EMV™ mapping
of data objects
in elementary
files.

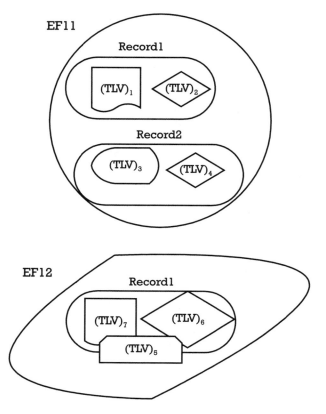

the sack is emptied. The terminal recognizes data objects in the heap according to their tags and not according to their relative position in the elementary file from which they were downloaded.

The price paid for interoperability is a lower efficiency of the BER-TLV
encoding. Every data element needs more bytes for its representation
because of the addition of the tag and length fields besides the actual information conveyed in the value field of the data object.

3.4.2 Customized file system organization

The file system of an EMV™ card is also compatible with ISO/IEC 7816-4
[5]. A possible EMV™ file system is presented in Figure 3.11.

The file system is divided into application definition files (ADF) and
directory definition files (DDF), allowing several card applications to be
simultaneously accommodated in the card. A separate ADF corresponds to
each card application present in the card. An ADF is referenced with an AID
(see Section 3.2.2.1). Each ADF encompasses one or more AEF(s). An AEF

Figure 3.11
File system in
an EMV™ card.

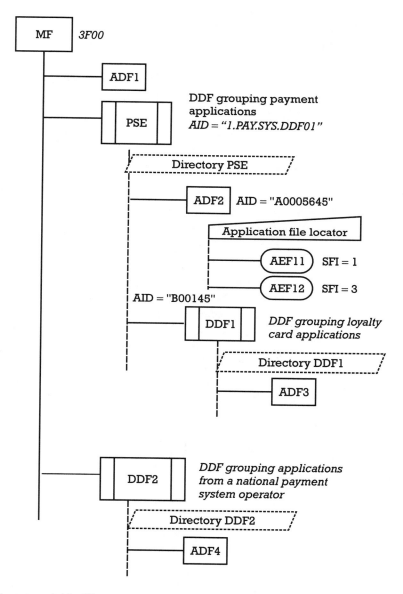

is a linear variable file containing the public information of the card application available to the counterpart terminal application. From this perspective
an ADF can be regarded as an application data container. Inside the ADF
each AEF is referenced with a SFI, which is a number in the range 1 to 30
(see Section 3.2.2.2). The SFI can be used as the handler of the AEF, once
the ADF container is selected and known to the terminal. This handler can
be directly used by the card commands performing file operations.

A DDF encompasses a group of related ADF(s). Each DDF in the card's file system is also referenced with an AID.

- The nature of the applications can be the criteria for grouping the ADF(s) in a DDF. For example, all the payment card applications in an EMV™ card could be gathered in the same DDF. The DDF that groups them is called the payment system environment (PSE) and has a special AID represented by the string 1PAY.SYS.DDF01, which is a reserved AID.

- The ADF(s) can be also grouped according to the payment system operator that proposed them. In the example of Figure 3.11, DDF2 gathers all the payment card applications of a national payment system operator.

A DDF can also include other hierarchical inferior DDF(s). For example, the PSE can further contain a DDF dedicated to loyalty card applications, denoted DDF1 in Figure 3.11. The DDF can be seen as a container of card applications.

The organization of files in an EMV™ card is more flexible, such that the EMV™ terminal is not compelled to know this organization in advance in order to perform a transaction profile. The terminal has to be aware only about the AID of the DDF applications containers in the card and of the ADF data containers that are not included under a DDF. Thus, the acquirer has to set up in the terminal a list of all the acceptable applications (ADFs) or of all the acceptable groups of applications (DDFs).

- Once the selection of a DDF applications container is performed, the terminal can find the table of contents of the DDF. This table of contents is organized in a directory file, containing as entry points the AID of all ADF data containers and the AID of all the other hierarchical inferior DDF applications containers. For example, the directory file at the level of the PSE contains the AID of ADF2 and DDF1, and the directory file at the level of DDF1 contains the AID of ADF3. By reading a directory file, the terminal is able to learn the file organization in that DDF.

- Whenever the terminal has selected an ADF container, it is further able to read another table of contents, which this time lists the AEF(s) that are publicly readable from a card application. This table of contents is referred to as an Application File Locator (AFL).

3.4.3   Variable formats for commands and responses

In an EMV™ setup the card application and the terminal application can be designed by different roles, within the limits established by the EMV™ specifications. The roles do not have to agree in advance on the list of meaningful data objects to be transmitted from the terminal application to the card application within a command. These data objects are needed by the card to perform its processing. This means that the set of data objects to be transmitted within a command can be different from one card application to another.

Therefore, the card must instruct the terminal about the data objects acceptable to be transmitted in a command. To this end the card application sends to the terminal application a data object list (DOL). This contains the list of all the tag-length identifiers of the data objects to be included by the terminal application in a command body.

For each command accepting a variable data input, the EMV™ specifications have defined a separate type of DOL, which is transmitted to the terminal application before the invocation of the command. The list of items (TL)1, (TL)2, (TL)3, ... included in each DOL type contains compulsory data objects specified by the EMV™ specifications and also chosen data objects of each issuer. The DOL(s) are personalized in the card application by the issuer before the card is operated during the utilization life stage.

The terminal uses the tag-length identifiers (TL) of the data objects in the DOL to retrieve the corresponding objects from its application heap. The data objects in the heap correspond to the current business environment: *amount*, *TerminalID*, *Time/Date*, and so on. The terminal retains the field value of the data objects identified in the DOL and concatenates them in a byte string, which is given as a data input to the corresponding command. The mechanism is depicted in Figure 3.12.

Moreover, the transaction profile is also variable, since the sequence of commands depends on the capabilities of the card concerning the implementation of some basic security mechanisms. Included among these mechanisms are the card authentication method (CAM), the cardholder verification method (CVM), and the decision as to whether the terminal performs risk analysis or if everything must be judged on-line by the issuer.

The Application Interchange Profile (AIP) is the data element stored in the card since the personalization, which instructs the terminal concerning the acceptable sequence of commands from the card's viewpoint.

3.4.4   Asymmetric cryptographic support

In the beginning of Section 3.4 we saw that implementing the off-line card authentication service using symmetric cryptographic techniques requires

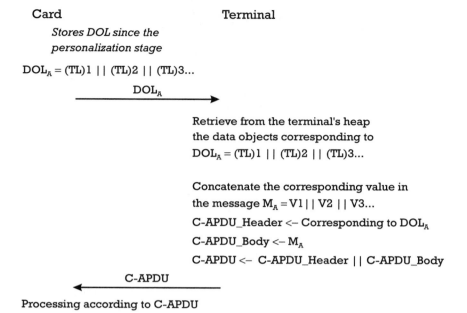

Figure 3.12
Variable
command data
input with DOL
mechanism.

each payment system operator to provide the acquirer with a dedicated SAM. This impacts negatively on the complexity of the terminal and of the key management process.

Openness of design and interoperability imply the use of asymmetric cryptographic techniques for implementing the off-line card authentication service. Thus, in order to prove the authenticity of the financial data personalized in the card, as well as the fact that the card is genuine, instead of using the MAC-based DDA mechanism, one has to use the digital signature–based DDA mechanism, as presented in Appendix D, Section D.7.2. In this case there is no need for the distribution of sensitive secret cryptographic parameters by the payment system operator, which is a considerable advantage. Correspondingly, the hardware structure of the terminal is simplified, as is the key management overhead. The chip card, however, must be able to produce a digital signature, which requires an RSA operation in the case of EMV™ chips. Therefore, the hardware structure of the chip includes a cryptographic coprocessor for speeding up the computations performed by the card (see Appendix D, Section D.1.2). Moreover, there is need for more EEPROM space in the chip card to keep the private key used for signature generation as well as of the corresponding public key with the accompanying issuer certificate to be forwarded to the terminal for signature verification. These extra facilities are expensive both in terms of computation power and permanent storage space. They significantly increase the cost of the chip card supporting asymmetric cryptography when compared to the chip card supporting only symmetric cryptography. When considering also that the latter card is several times more expensive than the magnetic stripe card, we can see that the former card is around 10 times more expensive than a magnetic stripe card. One can also understand a card manager's reluctance in asking the issuer's administration board for a dollar amount with an added zero at the end (read $1,000,000 instead of $100,000) for paying for the chip migration. As one can see, in relative terms the effort of the issuer increases spectacularly.

The normal reaction of the issuer's administration board would be to cut it in half. In the given circumstances, the card manager remembers past experiences with magnetic stripe cards. In that case the card authentication service was implemented with a MAC-based static data authentication (SDA) mechanism (see Section 2.5.3 and Appendix D, Section D.6.1). The issuer computes the static authenticator and writes it on the magnetic track during the personalization stage. Since the static authenticator in this case is computed with symmetric cryptographic techniques, the same limitations on openness and interoperability would be encountered as explained in the beginning of Section 3.4. Consequently, the EMV™ proposes the cheap solution that mirrors somehow the security protection with static authenticator but in an interoperable way. The issuer can compute this time a static authenticator using the signature-based SDA mechanism (see Appendix D, Section D.6.2). In this case the chip card would compute nothing (no need for a coprocessor) but only store some more bytes corresponding to the signature-based static authenticator. However, the security is also drastically reduced if the EMV™ transaction is concluded off-line and no on-line support is demanded from the issuer. The static authenticator would prove the authenticity of the financial data personalized in the card but would provide no protection against counterfeit. There is the impression that cloning the public information of the chip is more difficult than cloning the magnetic stripe. Cloning this public information, however, is still feasible for a hacker appropriately equipped (more details on this attack in Section 7.7.4).

Thus, while spending $400,000 for chip cards supporting symmetric cryptography on top of the costs of magnetic stripe implementation, the issuer loses the benefit of high security against counterfeit in small value transactions concluded off-line. Moreover, the issuer will not be able to implement the asymmetric enciphered PIN cardholder verification method (see Appendix D, Section D.5.5). This method would improve the security of the cardholder's PIN at the point of service, which is a very sensitive asset. Finally, the issuer is not able to implement on a multiapplication chip card other "heavy" cryptography card applications, like the interoperable electronic purse CEPS, electronic brokerage, and electronic administration applications for tax paying. Thus, it appears more and more that it is better for chip migration to be done with support of asymmetric cryptographic techniques.

It is also important to note that the payment system operator escaped from the burden of organizing symmetric key generation and distribution processes, but it must operate a public key infrastructure instead. This is an equally difficult task, if not even more difficult. The operator, however, is motivated by the same hope of being able to diversify its services towards its subscribers.

References

[1]   Rankl, W., and W. Effing, *Smart Card Handbook*, Chichester, England: John Wiley and Sons, 1997.

[2]   Chan, E, "Fraud, a Common Virus in Asia," *Cards Now*, March/April 2001.

[3]   Stern, C., "Micro-Thief That 'Steals' Credit Cards," *Sunday Mirror Magazine*, January 28, 2001.

[4]   ISO/IEC 7816-3, "Identification Cards—Integrated Circuit(s) Cards with Contacts—Part 3: Electronic Signals and Transmission Protocols," 1997.

[5]   ISO/IEC 7816-4, "Identification Cards—Integrated Circuit(s) Cards with Contacts—Part 4: Interindustry Commands for Interchange," 1995.

[6]   ISO/IEC 7816-5, "Identification Cards—Integrated Circuit(s) Cards with Contacts—Part 5: Numbering System and Registration Procedure for Application Identifiers," 1994.

[7]   ISO/IEC 7816-6, "Identification Cards—Integrated Circuit(s) Cards with Contacts—Part 4: Interindustry Data Elements," 1996.

[8]   Hassler, V., et al., *Java Card for E-Payment Applications*, Norwood, MA: Artech House, 2002.

[9]   Sun, Java Card 2.1.1, Platform specifications, http://java.sun.com/products/javacard.

[10] Maosco Ltd., *Multos Overview*, http://www.multos.com/multpres.ihtml.

[11] Vedder, K., and F. Weikmann, "Smart Cards—Requirements, Properties, and Applications," in B. Preneel and V. Rijmen (eds.), *State of the Art in Applied Cryptography*, Springer LNCS 1528, 1998, pp. 307–331.

[12] ISO/IEC 8825, "Information Technology—Open Systems Interconnection—Specification of Basic Encoding Rules for Abstract Syntax Notation One (ASN.1)," 1990.

Contents

EMV™ Compliant Data Organization

The actual trend in the industry of electronic payment systems is the use of chip cards that simultaneously accommodate several payment products. Issuers are interested in providing their clients with a comprehensive package of payment products, which cover all their payment preferences. For example, an issuer could be interested in a chip card that can accommodate three payment applications:

▸ A debit product, which allows the direct use of money from an account;

▸ A credit product for important spending at home or abroad;

▸ An electronic purse that allows for small payments and even for micropayments like buying information on demand in an electronic commerce scenario.

Thus, the business requirement of issuers is the possibility of accommodating multiple payment applications in the same chip card. Different payment system operators could operate these applications. The business requirement of acquirers is the possibility of implementing application selection mechanisms in terminals without being aware beforehand of the internal organization of cards. These business requirements imply the need of a data organization that provides openness and interoperability. In Section 3.4 we identified several features that can accomplish both openness and interoperability:

- ▸ Possibility of self-determined encoding of data elements in data objects;

- ▸ A customized and flexible file system organization;

- ▸ Variable formats for command and response APDUs.

We also saw that the EMV™ chip card technology offers the appropriate data organization principles needed to support these features. This technology is described in the *EMV Integrated Circuit Card Specifications for Payment Systems*, which we shortly refer to as the EMV™ specifications. The EMV™ data organization is common to all those chip cards and card applications that claim to be EMV™ compliant, regardless of the specific payment method they actually implement.

This chapter focuses on the EMV™ compliant data organization. It contains four sections. Section 4.1 briefly describes the documents that compose the EMV™ specifications. Section 4.2 outlines the encoding of the EMV™ data elements, explaining the BER-TLV encoding scheme. Section 4.3 presents the file types in an EMV™ card. Section 4.4 presents two application selection mechanisms proposed by the EMV™ specifications.

4.1   Organization of the EMV™ specifications

This section presents the set of documents (Book 1 to Book 4) that form the specification known as the *EMV 2000—Integrated Circuit Card Specification for Payment Systems* [1–4]. This set of documents replaces the set of documents referred to as the *EMV '96—Integrated Circuit Card (Terminal, Application) Specification for Payment Systems* [5–7]. The *EMV '96* was effective until December 2000 and served as the technical reference for implementations performed before this date. For the reader who is already familiar with the documents comprising the *EMV '96*, we provide a mapping of their content into the new set of documents that form the *EMV 2000*.

For a better understanding of the documents composing the EMV 2000 specification, the reader is referred to Figure 4.1. In this figure we outline the generic EMV™ communication protocol stack, which describes the interaction between the ICC and the terminal and between the terminal and the AH. We also show the user interfaces of the terminal towards the cardholder and the attendant.

The *EMV 2000* consists of the following documents:

Book 1: Application Independent ICC to Terminal Interface Requirements [1].
This document is divided into two parts:

Figure 4.1 The EMV™ protocol stack and its mapping to *EMV 2000.*

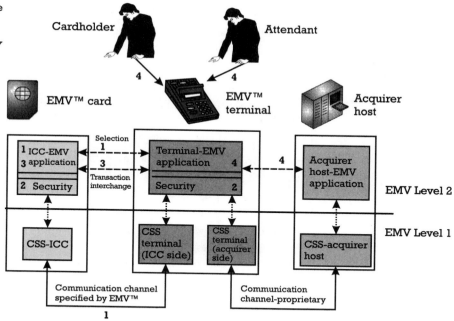

1- *Book 1: Application Independent ICC to Terminal Interface Requirements*
2- *Book 2: Security and Key Management*
3- *Book 3: Application Specification*
4- *Book 4: Cardholder, Attendant and Acquirer Interface Requirements*
CSS = Communication subsystem

> ▸ *Part I—Electromechanical Characteristics, Logical Interface, and Transmission Protocols.* This part contains the specification of the communication subsystem of the ICC and of the terminal, referred to in Figure 4.1 as the CSS-ICC and CSS Terminal (ICC side), respectively. It describes the electromechanical interface between the ICC and the terminal, specifying both the mechanical and electrical characteristics of the ICC and of the terminal. It also describes the answer-to-reset (ATR) of the card, the physical transportation of characters, the transmission protocols T = 0 and T = 1, and the description of a card session. This part of the specification is a reconsideration of Part I (with the same title) of the *EMV '96—Integrated Circuit Card Specification for Payment Systems* [5]. This part of the specification is said to be application independent since it presents a layer beneath the application layer. Often people refer to this part of the specification as the EMV Level 1. It is important to mention that the communication subsystem between the ICC and the terminal is not analyzed in this book.

‣ *Part II—Files, Commands, and Application Selection.* This part contains the specification of the EMV™ application selection mechanism and of the data structures, files, and commands needed for implementing this mechanism. The EMV™ application selection mechanism allows a terminal to select an application that claims to be EMV™ compliant in a multiapplication ICC. Such an application conforms to the EMV™ specification only from the point of view of the selection mechanism. Otherwise, the selected application can implement payment protocols other than the EMV™ credit/debit (e.g., an electronic purse conforming to CEPS [8], or a proprietary electronic purse scheme). For this reason this part of the specification is also labeled as application independent, even though it specifies data structures, files, and commands at the application level of the EMV™ protocol stack. This part of Book 1 is a reconsideration of the EMV™ application selection mechanism from "Part III—Application Selection" of the *EMV '96—Integrated Circuit Card Specification for Payment Systems* [5]. Concerning the data structures, files, and commands used for application selection, these were previously presented in "Part II—Data Elements and Commands" of the same *EMV '96—Integrated Circuit Card Specification for Payment Systems* [5].

Book 2: Security and Key Management [2].   This document presents a detailed specification of the security mechanisms in the ICC and terminal:

‣ SDA and dynamic data authentication (DDA) based on digital signatures. The principles of these mechanisms are explained in Appendix D, Sections D.6.2 and D.7.2, respectively.

‣ PIN encipherment. This mechanism is outlined in Appendix D, Section D.5.5.

‣ Secure messaging for integrity and authentication. This mechanism is presented in Appendix D, Section D.2.2. The session key is obtained through a key derivation algorithm, whose principle is explained in Appendix E, Section E.5.

‣ Secure messaging for confidentiality. We present this mechanism in Appendix D, Section D.1.1.

The topics mentioned above are reconsidered from "Part IV—Security Aspects" of the *EMV '96—Integrated Circuit Card Specification for Payment Systems* [5].

Certification Authority Public Key Management Principles and Policies is a new topic introduced in *EMV 2000, Book 2*. The topic *Terminal Security and Key Management Requirements* can also be considered as newly introduced in *EMV 2000, Book 2*. We make this statement since the terminal security was just briefly mentioned in "Section 4—Security Requirements," in *Part I—General Requirements* of the *EMV '96—Integrated Circuit Card Terminal Specification for Payment Systems* [6].

Book 3: Application Specification [3]   This document is divided into two parts:

▸ *Part I—Data Elements and Commands.* This contains the data structures, files, and commands needed for the implementation of the financial transaction interchange that describes an EMV™ debit and credit payment application. The material in this part reconsiders "Part II—Data Elements and Commands," of the *EMV '96—Integrated Circuit Card Specification for Payment Systems* [5].

▸ *Part II—Debit and Credit Application Specification.* This contains the specification of the financial transaction interchange that describes an EMV™ debit and credit payment application. This interchange is characterized by a transaction flow, obtained through the chaining of transaction processing functions (e.g., initiate application processing, read application data, off-line data authentication, etc.). The material in this part reconsiders the *EMV '96—Integrated Circuit Card Application Specification for Payment Systems* [7].

Book 4: Cardholder, Attendant, and Acquirer Interface Requirements [4]   This document reconsiders the content of the *EMV™ '96—Integrated Circuit Card Terminal Specification for Payment Systems* [6]. It is divided into three parts:

▸ *Part I—General Requirements.* This part contains the acceptable terminal types and their capabilities, the generic functional requirements of the terminal, and its physical characteristics.

▸ *Part II—Software Architecture.* This part presents the software architecture of an EMV™ terminal as well as the software and data management procedures that are needed.

▸ *Part III—Cardholder, Attendant, and Acquirer Interface.* This contains the specification of the functionality needed by the man-machine interface to interact with the terminal attendant and cardholder. The interface between the terminal and the AH is also presented in this part.

4.2 EMV™ data elements

An EMV™ debit/credit payment application in the ICC consists of a set of data elements that can be accessed by the terminal after a successful selection of the application. A data element is the smallest information unit that can be identified by a name, a description of its logical content, and a format.

Data elements are mapped onto data objects, which are BER-TLV encoded, as defined in the ISO/IEC 8825 standard [9]. Each data object consists of three fields: a tag, a length, and a value. Section 3.4 explained that the BER-TLV encoding is appropriate when interoperability is a requirement.

When the value field of a data object consists of one single data element, it is called a primitive data object. When the value field of a data object recursively encapsulates one or more other data objects, it is called a constructed data object. Figure 4.2 shows the recursive representation of the value field of the constructed data objects.

The tag uniquely identifies a data object within the environment of an EMV™ application. Although the BER-TLV encoding rules specify that the tag can be represented on 1, 2, or more than 2 bytes, the tags currently used

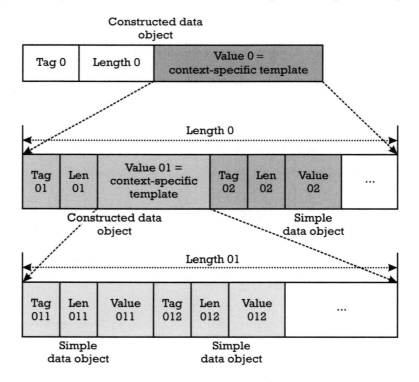

Figure 4.2
Recursive
representation
of constructed
data objects.

in *EMV 2000* are represented on either 1 or 2 bytes. Different tags are assigned to primitive data objects and constructed data objects, with a specific meaning in the application environment. The tag field encodes a class, a type, and a number.

1. The first byte of the tag specifies the following:

   ▸ The class, using the bits b8 and b7 (details about the tag's class are presented in Book 3 [3], Annex B1.1):

      ▸ 00—*universal class*;

      ▸ 01—*application class*, including templates defined in *EMV 2000* and ISO 7816;

      ▸ 10—*context specific class*, including primitive data objects defined in *EMV 2000* and specific data objects defined by an EMV™ payment system operator;

      ▸ 11—*private class*, containing primitive and constructed data objects at the discretion of the issuer of an EMV™ application in the ICC.

   ▸ The type, using the bit b6:

      ▸ 0—primitive data object;

      ▸ 1—constructed data object.

   ▸ The tag number, using the bits b5, b4, b3, b2, and b1. These five bits can encode a tag number in the range of 0 to 30. When the value of these five bits is 31 (all bits on 1) the tag number is continued in the second byte of the tag, in the range of 31 to 127.

2. The second byte of the tag encodes tag numbers that are greater than or equal to 31 (all bits 0) or less than or equal to 127 (01111111). Bit 8 of the second byte is 0 in case the tag number is less than or equal to 127, and is 1 in case a third byte is needed for encoding a tag number greater than or equal to 128.

The length field of a BER-TLV encoded data object specifies the number of bytes needed to represent the value field of the data object.

- When the length of the value field is less than or equal to 127, the length field is encoded on one single byte with b8 = 0.

- When the length of the value field is greater than 128, b8 = 1 in the first byte, while the remaining bits b7...b1 in the first byte encode the number of bytes needed for the representation of the length. A length in the range of 128 to 255 needs a second byte, while a length in the range of 256 to 65,535 needs also a third byte.

The data elements accepted by the *EMV 2000* specification are divided in two classes:

1. Data elements that may be used for application selection, as presented in Book 1 [1], Annex B, Table B-1;

2. Data elements that may be used for EMV™ debit/credit financial transaction interchange, as presented in Book 3 [3], Annex A, Table A-1.

The complete specification of an EMV™ data element in any of the aforementioned tables contains the following items:

- *Name:* This specifies a unique identifier attached to a data element in the *EMV 2000* specifications (e.g., Application Cryptogram).

- *Description:* This specifies a brief description of the data element in the context of the *EMV 2000* specifications (e.g., "Cryptogram returned by the ICC in the response of the GENERATE AC command").

- *Format:* This specifies the encoding rule of the value field. Several encoding rules can be mentioned:

  - `n nbr:` numeric type on a number of digits equal to `nbr`;

  - `n 6 YYMMDD:` numeric type with a date content (year, month, day);

  - `an nbr:` alphanumeric type on a number of characters equal to `nbr`;

  - `b:` binary value. In the case of the application cryptogram, the format is binary.

- *Template:* A data object, primitive or constructed, can be further encapsulated in a context-specific template. Thus, this field describes whether or not the current data element is encapsulated in a certain template.

▸ *Source:* This specifies the device (namely, the ICC, the terminal, or the IH) that is concerned with the current data element (e.g., the ICC stores the application cryptogram).

▸ *Tag:* This uniquely identifies the data element in the EMV™ environment.

▸ *Length:* This determines the length of the value field of a data object.

EMV™ data elements either mapped to primitive or constructed BER-TLV encoded data objects can be grouped in record templates. One or several record templates that are semantically related can be further grouped in an AEF (see Section 3.4.2). The mapping of EMV™ data objects in record templates and their collection in AEFs are left at the discretion of the issuer.

4.3 EMV™ file system

The file organization in an EMV™ ICC is derived from the ISO/IEC 7816-4 [10] and is described both in Part II of Book 1 [1] and in Part I of Book 3 [3] of the *EMV 2000* specifications. Figure 3.11 already presented a high level view of the EMV™ file system. We focus now on details concerning the data structures associated with EMV™ files. The terminal sees the EMV™ file system as a tree structure, having either ADF(s) or DDF(s) as branches.

4.3.1 ADFs

Logically, an ADF (as introduced in Section 3.4.2 and illustrated in Figure 3.11) encapsulates all the data files related to a card application. These data files are referred to as AEF(s) (see Section 3.4.1). Since an ADF is the entry point to one or several AEF(s) related to only one card application, it can be considered that an ADF ensures the separation between card applications.

Structurally, an ADF represents a DF as defined in the ISO/IEC 7816-4 [10], whose content consists of a File Control Information (FCI) Template, identified with the tag 6F. This template is context specific, and when it refers to an ADF it contains data objects as presented in Figure 4.3 (according to Table 40 in Book 1 [1]).

Figure 4.3
FCI of an ADF.

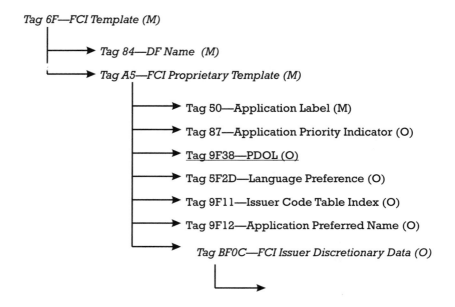

Tag 6F—FCI Template (M)

Tag 84—DF Name (M)

Tag A5—FCI Proprietary Template (M)

Tag 50—Application Label (M)

Tag 87—Application Priority Indicator (O)

Tag 9F38—PDOL (O)

Tag 5F2D—Language Preference (O)

Tag 9F11—Issuer Code Table Index (O)

Tag 9F12—Application Preferred Name (O)

Tag BF0C—FCI Issuer Discretionary Data (O)

In this figure, a data element marked M is mandatory for inclusion in the template, while a data element marked O may be optionally included in the template.

4.3.1.1   The meaning of data elements in the FCI of the ADF

The subsequent paragraphs explain the meaning of the data elements encoded in the FCI of an ADF.

DF Name (tag 84)   This mandatory data element represented on 5 to 16 bytes in a binary format stores the name of the DF that organizes the ADF. The terminal uses this element for referencing by the DF name the ADF (see Section 3.2.2).

The value of the DF name field can be the AID of the payment application contained in that ADF. The structure of the AID is defined in the ISO 7816-5 [11] as follows:

- A RID on 5 bytes, unique to an application provider and assigned by a specialized agency, which guarantees the uniqueness of the RID;

- The PIX, which is an optional field of up to 11 bytes assigned by the application provider to distinguish among several of its card application products. The PIX is unique only with respect to a RID and need not be unique across different RID(s).

Application Label (tag 50)   This is a mandatory data element encoded as an alphanumeric string of 1 to 16 characters, which represents a name related with the AID of the card application in the ADF. It is defined in ISO 7816-5 [11]. The card application provider specifies the Application Label for displaying it at the man-machine interface of the terminal at the point of service. The Application Label is usually the trademark of the payment product.

Application Preferred Name (tag 9F12)   This is an optional data element encoded as an alphanumeric string of 1 to 16 characters, which can provide a supplementary name for qualifying the card application in the ADF at the man-machine interface. For the same Application Label corresponding to a trademark belonging to a card association, different alphanumeric strings could be attached depending on a preferred alphabet used by the card issuer in a certain country.

Issuer Code Table Index (tag 9F11)   This is an optional data element indicating the code table of an alphabet (according to ISO 8859 [12]) used for displaying the characters in the alphanumeric string Application Preferred Name. If the tag 9F12 is present in the FCI, then tag 9F11 should be also present.

Language Preference (tag 5F2D)   This is an optional data element encoded as one to four alphanumeric strings of two characters each, indicating to the terminal a list of one to four language codes. Each language code is encoded according to ISO 639 [13]. These codes indicate the languages and their priority that the terminal should use at the man-machine interface for displaying messages to the cardholder.

Application Priority Indicator (tag 87)   This is an optional data element encoded binary on 1 byte that indicates the priority given by the issuer (eventually tacking into account the cardholder's payment behavior) to the card application in this ADF compared to other card applications stored in the same card in other ADF(s). This priority indicator helps the terminal to establish the order of preference of card applications when displaying them at the terminal. This lets the cardholder choose the means of payment for a transaction according to its payment behavior.

The priority rank granted to the card application is specified in the bits b4 to b1. The value 1 indicates the highest priority, while 15 indicates the lowest priority. A value of 0 indicates that the ADF has no priority assigned. The bits b7 to b5 are RFU. Bit b8 specifies whether the explicit confirmation of the cardholder is needed for the selection of the card application in that ADF (b8 = 1) or not (b8 = 0).

Processing Options Data Object List (tag 9F38)   The Processing Options Data Object List (PDOL) is an optional data element of the type DOL. The principles of working with a DOL were explained in Section 3.4.3.

The PDOL contains the list of tag-length identifiers of those data elements that the card application (contained in the ADF) would need to obtain from the terminal. These data elements help the card application to figure out its optimal behavior with respect to the business environment present at the point of service.

For example, the PDOL could include the tag-length identifiers of the Amount, Authorized (Binary) (tag 81) and Terminal Type (tag 9F35) data elements for optimally choosing the AIP that is returned in the response to the GET PROCESSING OPTIONS command (the details will follow in Chapter 6). In this case, the PDOL in the File Control Information (FCI) Template can be encoded as outlined in Figure 4.4.

An example of a rationale performed by the card based on the content of the data elements required in the PDOL and received from the terminal can be resumed as follows. If Amount, Authorized is below a floor limit and the Terminal Type is "Unattended, Offline Only, Controlled by the Financial Institution" then the AIP should state the inclusion of at least "Offline static data authentication is supported" card authentication in the transaction's profile.

FCI Issuer Discretionary Data (tag BF0C)   This is an optional template that can store some data elements specifically defined by the issuer. For example, a

Figure 4.4
Example of
a PDOL
encoding.

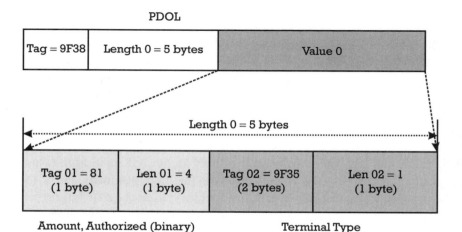

Amount, Authorized (binary)   Terminal Type

data element in this template could be a key identifier of a secret key present in the card application. This key can be used by a specialized terminal of the issuer for authenticating to the card. This specialized terminal allows administrative card management operations. After correct authentication, the specialized terminal obtains the administrator rights for updating sensitive data files in the card application.

Other examples of data elements that can be contained in this template are data elements specifying the manufacturing environment (like the identifier of the card manufacturer), the type of integrated circuit used in the card, the version of the ROM mask, and the version of the operating system.

4.3.1.2 ADF and direct application selection service

The selection of an ADF allows access to the logical structure of a card application hosted in that ADF. Following its selection, the ADF returns the FCI template to the terminal.

Considering the application selection service, an EMV™ card in a multi-application environment shall be able to respond positively to a direct application selection performed by a SELECT command specifying the AID as the file name.

The C-APDU of the SELECT command is given in Table 4.1 (according to Table 35 in Book 1 [1]).

The data field returned in the R-APDU of the SELECT command contains the FCI of the ADF (as schematized in Figure 4.3) and the status words SW1 SW2 = 9000, if the command executed successfully.

4.3.1.3 More on partial name selection

The support of the ICC for partial name selection is optional in EMV™, but if it is supported the rules to be observed are listed in Section 7.3.5 of Book 1 [1]. To explain the partial name selection mechanism we refer to the example presented in Figure 4.5.

In this example the file structure of an EMV™ card contains three ADF files, hosting different card applications coming from the same application provider. Three different application identifiers AID1, AID2, and AID3 represent the DF name field in the FCI of ADF1, ADF2, and ADF3, respectively. They have in common the first 5 bytes, which represent the RID of the application provider, but each of the AID is qualified with a different PIX. Thus, the values of the AID(s) are AID1 = RID ∥ PIX1, AID1 = RID ∥ PIX2, and AID3 = RID ∥ PIX3. The terminal does not know the AID of all the card applications proposed by that application provider, but it knows its RID. In order to retrieve from the card all the card applications of the application provider, the terminal and the card perform the following steps:

Table 4.1
C-APDU of the SELECT Command

Code	Value
CLA	*00* (Interindustry command as defined in ISO 7816-4 [10])
INS	*A4*
P1	*Reference control parameter* (according to Table 36 in Book 1 [1])
	It accepts only one single value, 04, corresponding to "select by name" (i.e., referencing by the DF name according to the ISO/IEC 7816-4 [10])
P2	*Selection options* (According to Table 37 in Book 1 [1])
	b8 to *b3* are RFU
	b2 b1 = 00h = *first or only occurrence*—mandatory selection option
	$\qquad$ = 10h = *next occurrence*—optional, available only in case the EMV card supports partial name selection. When supported, successive sending of the SELECT command with the same value of the File Name shall select ADF(s) whose names (in the DF Name field of FCI) start with the identifier in the File Name.
Lc	*05h–10h*
Data	*File Name*
	The file name field is a DF name, possibly right truncated:
	When the file name is a complete DF Name of the ADF, the SELECT command performs complete name selection;
	When the file name is only the beginning of the DF Name of the ADF (i.e., the file name is the DF Name right truncated to at least 5 bytes) the SELECT command performs partial name selection.
Le	*00*

> ▸ *Step 1:* The terminal sends a SELECT command to the ICC with file name = RID and P2 = 00h, which means "First occurrence." The parameter Lc = 5, since the RID has 5 bytes. After receiving the command, if the ICC supports the partial name selection mechanism, it will send back the response containing SW1SW2 = 9000 and the FCI of ADF1. From this FCI the terminal can find out the complete application identifier AID1 of the first card application. The card internally marks the ADF1 as "already selected."

> ▸ *Step 2:* The terminal repeats the previous SELECT command, with the same file name but with a different P2, which is set now to the value 02h, which means "Next occurrence." After receiving the command, the card selects a different DF file matching the partial name RID. This file is ADF2. The terminal learns the AID2 of the second card application. The card internally marks ADF2 as "already selected."

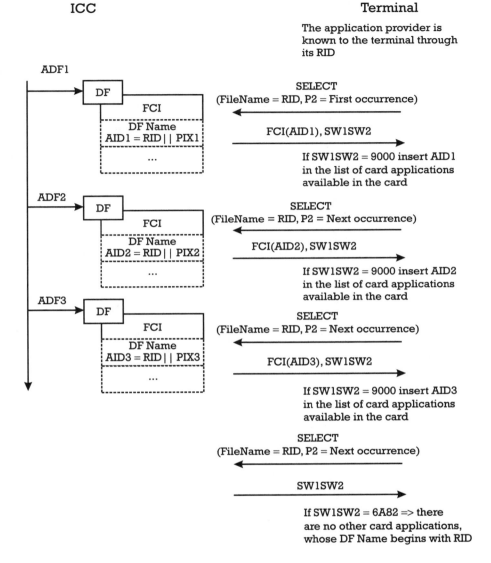

Figure 4.5
Partial name
selection
mechanism.

▸ *Step 3:* The terminal repeats the previous SELECT command, with the same file name and with the same P2 ("Next occurrence"). After receiving the command, the card selects a different DF file than in the previous two steps matching the partial name RID. This file is ADF3, since the other two ADF(s) have already been marked as selected. The terminal learns the AID3 of the last card application. The card internally marks ADF3 as "already selected."

▸ *Step 4:* Since the terminal does not know how many different AID(s) exist related to the application provider and how many of the corresponding card applications are personalized in the ICC, it will send once more the SELECT command with the same parameters as in Step 3. This time the card checks the partial name with all the ADF(s), but since they have been already marked as selected, the card shall send only SW1SW2 = 6A82 (file not found). These status words will inform the terminal not to issue a new SELECT command with the same file name.

The direct application selection service and the partial name selection mechanism are the basis of the application selection procedure presented in Section 4.4.2.

4.3.2 AEFs

The AEF(s) (as introduced in Section 3.4.1 and illustrated in Figure 3.11) are the effective containers of the data elements needed by a card application hosted in an ADF. An AEF is mapped to an elementary file (EF) as defined in ISO 7816-4 [10] and is never used as an entry point to another file.

After an ADF is selected, all the AEF(s) encapsulated in that ADF can be referenced through their SFI (see also Section 3.2.2). Any AEF within a given card application is referred by an SFI in the range of 1 to 30. The SFI shall be unique within a card application.

4.3.2.1 AEF with SFI in the range of 1 to 10

The AEF(s) addressed with an SFI in the range of 1 to 10 contain only data elements not interpreted by the card application in its internal processing (i.e., data to be used by the terminal exclusively). From this point of view an AEF in this range can be seen as a working EF. The content of these AEF(s) must be readable unconditionally by the terminal, and for updating they have access conditions to be fulfilled by an administrator of the card issuer from a specialized terminal.

The structure of an AEF in this range can be assimilated with a linear fix file or linear variable file (see Section 3.2.2) containing one or multiple records, each addressed by a record number. Each record is coded as a constructed data object referred to as the AEF Data Template with tag 70, which is an EMV™ proprietary tag. The length field of the AEF Data Template indicates the total length of the data objects encapsulated in the template. This length would be no bigger than 251 bytes. For interoperability reasons, the AEF Data Template shall encapsulate in its value field only data objects accepted by the EMV™ debit/credit application, as defined in Book 3 [3], Annex A, Table A-1. The mapping of these EMV™ data objects in AEF Data Templates and the grouping of these templates in AEF(s) are left to the discretion of the issuer.

The SFI can be used as a file handler in the READ RECORD commands. These commands allow the terminal at the point of service to read the public content of the AEF(s) in the selected ADF.

The C-APDU of the READ RECORD command is given in Table 4.2 (according to Table 33 in Book 1 [1] and Table I-21 in Book 3 [3]).

The data field returned in the R-APDU of a successfully executed READ RECORD command contains the record that is actually read from the AEF, which is encoded within an AEF Data Template. The R-APDU also returns the status words SW1 SW2 = 9000 if the command is successfully executed.

For the purpose of an EMV™ debit/credit card application that conforms to Book 3 [3], there is another data element that should be attached to an ADF beside the FCI. This data element is called the AFL (tag 94), providing a list of all the AEF(s) accessible to the terminal, indicating for each AEF its location (SFI) and the range of records in that AEF that are relevant for a given application. More details on the AFL will be provided in Section 6.2.3.

4.3.2.2 AEF with SFI in the range of 11 to 20 and 21 to 30

AEF(s) with a SFI in the range of 11 to 20 are reserved for grouping proprietary data elements of an EMV™ debit/credit application as specified by the individual payment system operators developing an EMV™ payment card product. Application elementary files with a SFI in the range of 21 to 30 are

Table 4.2
C-APDU of the READ RECORD Command

Code	Value
CLA	*00* (Interindustry command as defined in ISO 7816-4 [10])
INS	*B2*
P1	*Record number*
P2	*Reference control parameter* (according to Table 34 in Book 1 [1] and Table I-22 in Book 3 [3])
	b8 – b4 (5 bits): it encodes the SFI of the AEF whose record, with the number indicated in P1, must be read
	b3 b2 b1 = 100: it indicates that P1 has the meaning of a record number
Lc	*Not present*
Data	*Not present*
Le	*00*

reserved for grouping proprietary data elements of an EMV™ debit/credit application, which are defined by the issuer for its own needs.

4.3.2.3 AEF storing the directory file of a DDF or PSE

While an AEF as presented above can be seen as a data container for EMV™ card applications, it can also store a directory file. In this case the AEF encodes the directory entries of a DDF or of a PSE. All the details related to a DDF, a PSE, and their directory structure implemented as an AEF are provided in Sections 4.3.3 and 4.3.4 below.

4.3.3 Directory definition files

Logically, a DDF (as introduced in Section 3.4.2 and illustrated in Figure 3.11) provides an entry point to one or more ADF(s) and to one or more hierarchically inferior DDF(s). To this end the DDF introduces a directory, which lists a separate entry for each ADF and (hierarchically inferior) DDF to which the current DDF offers access.

4.3.3.1 Directory file, directory entry, and directory structure

The implementation of a directory is performed with a directory file. The directory file is an AEF referenced with an SFI in the range of 1 to 10 containing one or several records. Each record is encoded as an AEF Data Template (see Section 4.3.2). Remember that an AEF attached to an ADF may contain any data objects accepted by the EMV™ debit/credit application, as defined in Book 3 [3], Annex A, Table A-1. In opposition, an AEF Data Template in a directory file encapsulates in its value field just one or more application templates (tag 61), according to ISO/IEC 7816-5 [11]. In its turn, each Application Template encodes only one directory entry for either an ADF or a DDF.

The encoding of a directory entry is different for an ADF than for a DDF:

> ‣ According to Table 43 in Book 1 [1], an ADF directory entry contains two mandatory data elements. The first element is the ADF name (tag 4F), encoded on 5 to 16 bytes in binary format, which contains the AID of the card application stored in the corresponding ADF. The second element is the Application Label of the card application stored in the ADF. The meaning of this data element was explained in Section 4.3.1. Optionally, the ADF directory entry may encapsulate the Application Preferred Name and the Application Priority Indicator, which were also introduced in Section 4.3.1.

▸ According to Table 42 in Book 1 [1], a DDF directory entry contains the mandatory data element DDF Name (tag 9D) encoded on 5 to 16 bytes in binary format.

Both the ADF directory entry and the DDF directory entry can incorporate a *Directory Discretionary Template* (tag 73), which may encode some proprietary data objects meaningful for the organization managing the ADF or DDF.

Figure 4.6 exemplifies an AEF Data Template of a directory file, which introduces two ADF(s) and one hierarchically inferior DDF.

The directory structure of a DDF consists of its own directory and the directories introduced by all the hierarchically inferior DDF(s) to which this DDF offers access.

4.3.3.2 FCI of a DDF

Structurally, a DDF represents a DF as defined in the ISO/IEC 7816-4 [10], whose content consists of an FCI template. This template is context specific, and when it refers to a DDF, it contains data objects as presented in Figure 4.7 (according to Table 39 in Book1 [1]).

Some explanations of the data elements in the FCI of the DDF are provided below.

Figure 4.6
Example of an AEF Data Template in a directory file.

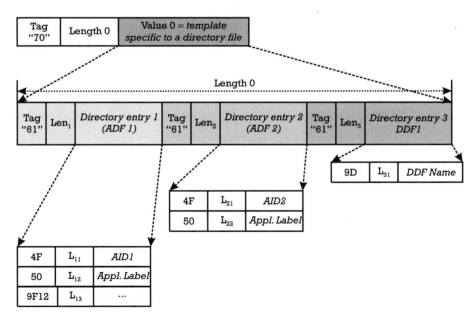

Figure 4.7
FCI of a DDF.

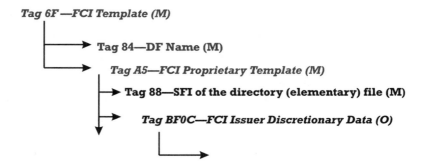

Tag 6F —FCI Template (M)

Tag 84—DF Name (M)

Tag A5—FCI Proprietary Template (M)

Tag 88—SFI of the directory (elementary) file (M)

Tag BF0C—FCI Issuer Discretionary Data (O)

- The FCI of the DDF includes the DF Name field. This mandatory data element is represented on 5 to 16 bytes in binary format and stores the name of the DF that organizes the DDF.

- Since the DDF introduces a directory file implemented in an AEF, the FCI of the DDF must include the SFI reference of this directory file. This SFI reference is mapped to the data element SFI of the directory elementary file, with tag 88. This element is encoded binary on 1 byte with the three high-order bits set to zero.

- Optionally, the FCI of the DDF may also include the FCI Issuer Discretionary Data template, which encapsulates one or more additional private data elements from the application provider that manages the applications grouped under the DDF, from the card issuer, or from the IC card supplier.

The terminal uses the DF Name element for referencing by the DF name the DDF (see Section 3.2.2). This can be achieved with a SELECT command as introduced in Section 4.3.1. In case of complete name selection, the file name parameter of the SELECT command is the complete DF Name, while in case of partial name selection the file name is the DF Name right truncated to at least 5 bytes. The response of the SELECT command provides the FCI of the DDF, with the complete DF Name and the SFI of the AEF that stores the directory file.

4.3.3.3 Directory structure and indirect application selection service

The directory structure allows the implementation of the *indirect application selection service*. Through this service the terminal can learn by itself all card applications and groups of card applications to which the DDF offers access. The condition is that the terminal knows only the reference to this DDF.

Assume that a DDF introduces a directory file, implemented as an AEF with SFI = 2. This directory file contains only one record, encapsulating the

AEF Data Template that was exemplified in Figure 4.6. Admit also that the DF name of the DDF is encoded as an ASCII string "DDFName." The terminal, which knows only the DF name of the DDF, can implement the indirect application selection service with the following sequence of commands:

▸ *Step 1:* The terminal sends a SELECT command to the ICC with file name = "DDFName" and P2 = 00h, which means "First occurrence." The parameter Lc = 7, since the file name can be encoded on 7 bytes using the ASCII representation. After receiving the command, the ICC will send back the response containing SW1SW2 = 9000 and the FCI of the DDF. From this FCI the terminal can find out the SFI of the directory file introduced by the DDF, which is 2.

▸ *Step 2:* The terminal sends a READ RECORD command to the ICC with P1 = 1 (indicating the first record) and P2 = 14h (the SFI = 2 is encoded as 00010 in the leftmost 5 bits of P2, and 100 in the rightmost 3 bits of P2). The card returns the response containing the status words SW1SW2 = 9000 and the AEF Data Template exemplified in Figure 4.6.

▸ *Step 3:* The terminal once again sends a READ RECORD command to the ICC, since it does not know how many records are encoded in the directory file. The command is sent with P1 = 2 (indicating the second record) and P2 = 14h. The card returns the response containing only the status words SW1SW2 = 6A83, "Wrong parameters(s) P1 P2; record not found." Thus, the terminal knows that the directory file was composed of one single record.

▸ *Step 4:* The terminal parses the AEF Data Template in three distinct application templates (under the tag 61), each containing a distinct directory entry.

  ▸ The first and the second application templates are ADF directory entries, since they start with tag 4F. When parsing the first directory entry, the terminal can learn the AID of the first card application introduced by the DDF (namely AID1), its application name, and even the application preferred name. However, there is no Application Priority Indicator attached to this first application. Parsing the second entry, the terminal learns the AID of the second card application introduced by the DDF (namely AID2), as well as its Application Label. The terminal has now enough information to perform the selection of any of these two applications.

‣ The third Application Template is a DDF directory entry, since it starts with a tag 9D. The terminal learns the DDF name of the only hierarchically inferior DDF introduced by the current DDF, which can be assumed to be the identifier "DDF1Name."

‣ *Step 5:* The terminal sends a SELECT command to the ICC with file name = "DDF1Name" and P2 = 00h, which means "First occurrence." The parameter Lc = 8, since the identifier can be encoded on 8 bytes using the ASCII representation. After receiving the command, the ICC will send back the response containing SW1SW2 = 9000 and the FCI of the DDF1. From this FCI the terminal can find out the SFI of the directory file introduced by the DDF1. From now on the terminal can appropriately repeat the sequence consisting of step 2 to step 4 to recursively construct the whole directory structure of the initial DDF.

The protocol above is outlined in Figure 4.8.

The directory structure and its use for the indirect application selection service are the basis of the application selection procedure presented in Section 4.4.1.

4.3.4   Payment system environment

Logically, a PSE is a DDF, whose DF name is given the value 1PAY.SYS.DDF01. The PSE represents a predefined entry point to a set of payment card applications or groups of payment card applications. An application provider, who can be a payment system operator or a card association, can manage a group. The presence of the PSE in the ICC is optional, but when it is present it should comply with the rules stated in Section 8.2.2 of Book 1 [1].

As with any DDF, the PSE is mapped onto a DF in the ICC, which could or could not be the master file (MF). When the PSE is organized in the MF, the multiapplication ICC can be considered as a payment dedicated ICC. If the PSE is organized in a DF under the MF, the ICC can store card applications outside the PSE. These card applications can provide different functionality than payment.

The content of the PSE consists of an FCI template. This template is context specific, and when it refers to a PSE, it contains data objects as presented in Figure 4.9 (according to Table 38 in Book 1 [1]).

Figure 4.8
Directory
structure
and indirect
application
selection
service.

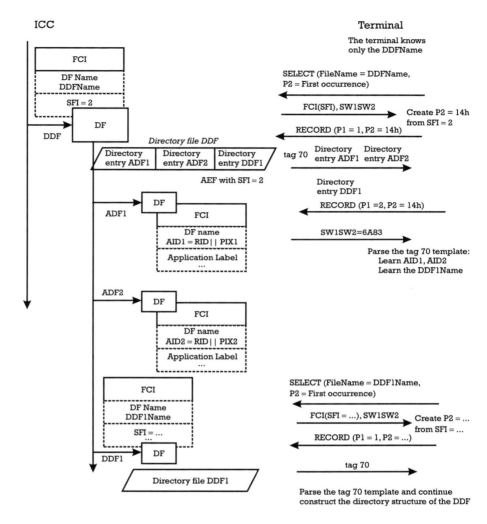

Some explanations on the data elements in the FCI of the PSE are provided below.

- The FCI of the PSE includes the DF name field, which has the predefined value 1PAY.SYS.DDF01.

- Since the PSE introduces the payment system directory file, also referred to as the DIR file, its FCI must include the SFI reference of this directory file. This SFI reference is encoded in the same way as explained for a DDF.

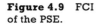
Figure 4.9 FCI
of the PSE.

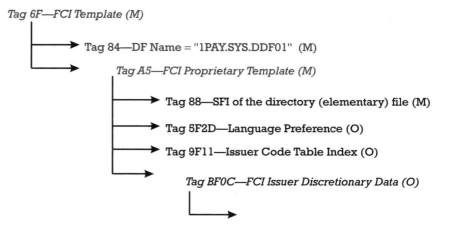

Tag 6F—FCI Template (M)

    Tag 84—DF Name = "1PAY.SYS.DDF01" (M)

    Tag A5—FCI Proprietary Template (M)

        Tag 88—SFI of the directory (elementary) file (M)

        Tag 5F2D—Language Preference (O)

        Tag 9F11—Issuer Code Table Index (O)

        Tag BF0C—FCI Issuer Discretionary Data (O)

- The FCI of the PSE may optionally include the Language Preference and the Issuer Code Table Index, with the same meaning as that explained in connection with an ADF. When these elements are present in the FCI of the PSE, they should also exist in the FCI of each ADF encompassed in the PSE, and they should have the same value. This is because the terminal could use these elements from either location. When the terminal implements the indirect application selection service, it will read these elements from the FCI of the PSE; when using the direct application selection service, it will read these elements from the FCI of the ADF directly selected.

- Optionally, the FCI of the PSE may also include the FCI Issuer Discretionary Data template, with a similar meaning as for a DDF.

The terminal uses the identifier 1PAY.SYS.DDF01 for referencing by the DF name the PSE. This can be achieved with a SELECT command as introduced in Section 4.3.1 with complete name selection. Thus, the file name parameter of the SELECT command is the identifier 1PAY.SYS.DDF01 and P2 is set to "First or only occurrence." The response of the SELECT command provides the FCI of the PSE, with the SFI of the AEF that stores the DIR file.

The directory structure of the PSE consists of the DIR file at the PSE level and all the additional directory files introduced by DDF(s), which are subordinated to the PSE.

The ADF and DDF directory entries in the DIR file correspond to ADF(s) and DDF(s) that are formatted according to Book 1 [1]. An application defined by an ADF, which is mentioned in the DIR file, might be an EMV™ debit/credit payment application according to Book 3 [3]. However, there could be ADF(s) that define payment applications implementing payment methods other than EMV™ debit/credit (e.g., an electronic purse with CEPS, or a loyalty scheme).

The directory structure of the PSE will include only those payment card applications that the issuer wants to be visible in an interoperable environment. Thus, there could be card applications whose ADF is not included in any directory file in the directory structure, and which could be selected only by a proprietary terminal that is aware about their existence in the ICC card.

4.4 EMV™ application selection

In order to support the multiapplication business requirement, the terminal should implement appropriate procedures for card application selection. To this end the acquirer that manages the terminal shall maintain a list of the card applications supported by the terminal and their AID(s). This list is determined by the business relationships existing between the acquirer and various national and international payment system operators and card associations proposing payment card applications.

Only a limited number of the card applications accepted by the terminal are implemented in the ICC present at the point of service. Thus, the terminal must determine which of the card applications in its list the ICC currently supports. This process consists of building the candidate list.

‣ Section 4.4.1 introduces a procedure of building the candidate list when both the ICC and the terminal implement the indirect application selection service (as described in Section 4.3.3.3). To this end, the ICC must implement the PSE and the terminal must be able to interpret the payment system directory file (DIR file) of the PSE and to construct the corresponding directory structure of the PSE. From this directory structure the terminal obtains the complete list of card applications in the PSE, which the issuer of the card wants to be visible in an interoperable environment. In order to obtain the candidate list, the terminal compares the card applications in its list of supported applications with the list of card applications existing in the PSE. Thus, the terminal applies for each AID in its list of supported applications the matching criterion explained below.

‣ In case either the ICC or the terminal does not support indirect application selection, the candidate list is built according to the procedure described in Section 4.4.2. In this case the terminal will try each AID it knows from its list of supported applications through direct application selection against the ICC (as described in Section 4.3.1.2). All the card applications responding positively to this inquiry will be inserted in the candidate list if their DF name fulfills the matching criterion against the AID (tag 9F06) in the list of supported applications kept by the terminal.

Building the candidate list with any of the two aforementioned procedures needs a matching criterion between the AID (tag 9F06) of a card application as known to the terminal and the DF name (tag 84)/AID (tag 4F) of a card application as reported by the ICC.

> • *Complete name matching:* In this case, the terminal supports the ICC application only if the DF name/AID of the card application as reported by the ICC has the same length and value as the AID of the card application in the list of supported applications stored in the terminal. Since each AID in the file system of the ICC is unique, for each AID in the list of supported applications there is at most one matching ADF in the ICC, whose FCI will be copied in the candidate list.

> • *Partial name matching:* In this case, the terminal supports the ICC application only if the DF name/AID of the card application as reported by the ICC begins with the entire AID of the card application in the list of supported applications stored in the terminal. This allows the ICC to have multiple ADF(s) matching the terminal application by adding unique information to the DF name used by each of the ADF(s). If the card has only one ADF matching the terminal AID, it should identify the DF name of that ADF with the exact AID known to the terminal. If the ICC has multiple ADF(s) supported by a single terminal AID, three conditions must be simultaneously fulfilled:

> 1. The ICC must support partial name selection.

> 2. All of the matching DF name/AID in the ICC must be distinguished by adding unique data to the PIX;

> 3. None of the ICC's DF name/AID shall be of the same length as the AID in the terminal.

For each of the AID(s) within the list of applications supported by the terminal, the terminal shall keep in the data element Application Selection Indicator an indication of which matching criterion to use.

To better illustrate the concept of matching criteria, we assume the list of supported applications in the terminal proposed in Table 4.3.

If the list of card applications existing in the PSE of the card is given in the first column of Table 4.4, then the other two columns determine which of these applications are recorded in the candidate list built by the terminal and for which rationale.

Table 4.3
List of Supported Applications in the Terminal

AID in the Terminal	Application Selection Indicator
A0034	Partial name matching
A0045123	Complete name matching
A0012121113	Complete name matching
A1001	Partial name matching
A00B2	Partial name matching
A00A1	Partial name matching
A101010101	Complete name matching

Table 4.4
Example of Applying Matching Criteria for a Given List of Card Applications Existing in the PSE

DF Name/AID in the Card	Presence in the Candidate List	Rationale
A0034A1	Yes	—
A0034A2	Yes	Both these DF Name/AID data elements in the card begin with and have a different length from the AID = A0034 known to the terminal. The terminal supports partial name matching and the card supports partial name selection
A0012121113	Yes	The DF Name/AID in the card has the same length and value with the AID in the terminal, which supports complete name matching
A26798	No	There is no AID in the terminal matching the DF Name/AID in the card neither completely nor partially
A00B2A	No	This DF Name/AID in the card cannot be recorded in the candidate list because the card has only one ADF whose DF Name/AID partially matches the terminal's AID = A00B2, which supports partial name matching

4.4.1 Building the candidate list from the PSE

If the terminal implements the indirect application selection service it can easily build the candidate list from the directory structure of the PSE, if the PSE is implemented in the ICC. This directory structure can be built with an algorithm similar to that already described in Section 4.3.3.3. This algorithm is presented below and is overtaken from Section 8.3.2 of Book 1 [1].

‣ *Step 1:* Determine the existence of PSE in the card. The terminal issues a SELECT command using file name = 1PAY.SYS.DDF01, P2 = 00h ("First and only occurrence"), and Lc = 0Eh.

  ‣ If SW1SW2 = 6A81 ("Wrong parameters P1 P2; function not supported"), this means that either the card is blocked or it does not support the SELECT command with referencing by the DF Name. In this case the terminal aborts the card session.

  ‣ If SW1SW2 = 6A82 ("Wrong parameters P1 P2; file not found"), this means that there is no PSE implemented in the card. The direct application selection as presented in Section 4.4.2 should be run instead.

  ‣ If SW1SW2 = 6283 ("State of the nonvolatile memory unchanged; selected file invalidated"), this means that there is a PSE in the card but it is blocked. The direct application selection as presented in Section 4.4.2 should be run instead.

  ‣ If SW1SW2 = 9000, the terminal reads from the FCI of the PSE (returned in the response to the SELECT command beside SW1SW2) the SFI of the payment system directory file (DIR file) of the PSE.

‣ *Step 2:* The terminal reads all the records in the DIR file with the READ RECORD command, beginning with record number 1 and continuing with successive record numbers until the card returns SW1 SW2 = 6A83 ("Wrong parameter(s) P1 P2; record not found"). The details of this operation are similar to those described in steps 2 and 3 in Section 4.3.3.3. If the card returns SW1 SW2 = 6A83 in response to a READ RECORD for record number 1, no directory entries exist in the DIR file, and step 5 (below) applies. For each record of the DIR file, the terminal begins with the first directory entry and processes each entry in turn as described in steps 3 to 5 below.

- *Step 3:* If the directory entry corresponds to an ADF, and its AID (tag 4F) fulfills the matching criterion of any AID in the list of supported applications kept in the terminal, the AID of the card application joins the candidate list for the final application selection procedure.

- *Step 4:* If the directory entry corresponds to a DDF, the terminal selects that DDF using the DDF name (tag 9D) from the directory entry. Using the SFI of the directory file introduced by this DDF (read from the FCI of the selected DDF), the terminal reads the directory file of the current DDF and processes it in the same way as the DIR file of the PSE (steps 2 through 5). After finishing the processing of all the directory entries in the hierarchically inferior directory file, the terminal resumes the processing of the previously interrupted directory file one level higher.

- *Step 5:* When the terminal exhausts all the directory entries in the DIR file of the PSE, all the ADF(s) that are visible in an interoperable environment have been determined. The search and the candidate list are complete. The terminal continues with the final application selection procedure.

This procedure of building the candidate list is recommended whenever the number of EMV™ compliant applications in the list of supported applications kept in the terminal is large and there is a PSE present in the ICC card.

4.4.2   Building the candidate list directly

The method of building the candidate list presented in this section overtakes the algorithm introduced in Section 8.3.3 of Book 1 [1]. This method is used when the terminal does not implement indirect application selection. This is the case when the list of supported applications kept by the terminal is small. Otherwise, the method is used whenever the terminal has an empty candidate list following the indirect application selection procedure based on the PSE.

The following steps describe the algorithm of building the candidate list through direct application selection:

- *Step 1:* The terminal issues a SELECT command using as the value for the file name parameter the first AID in the list of supported applications.

- *Step 2:* If the SELECT command fails because the card is blocked or the card does not support the command (SW1 SW2 = 6A81), the terminal terminates the card session. If the SELECT command reports that the application is blocked (SW1 SW2 = 6283) the FCI of the selected ADF is not added to the candidate list. The terminal proceeds to step 5. If the SELECT command reports any other SW1 SW2 different than 6A81, 6283, and 9000, the terminal proceeds to step 5. Otherwise, the terminal continues with step 3.

• *Step 3:* If the SELECT command is successful (SW1 SW2 = 9000), the terminal compares the DF name returned in the FCI of the selected ADF with the current AID in the list of supported applications. If the two identifiers are identical, continue with step 4; otherwise continue with step 6.

• *Step 4:* The terminal adds to the candidate list the current AID regardless of its application status indicator. The candidate list must also store, besides the AID, the Application Priority Indicator of the matching application. Thus, the terminal can arrange the applications in the candidate list in the order preferred by the issuer. If the terminal displays the candidate list to allow the cardholder to make his or her choice, other data elements in the FCI of the eligible ADF (the Application Label, the Application Preferred Name) have to be saved in the candidate list.

• *Step 5:* The terminal issues a new SELECT command using as file name the next AID in its list of supported applications and returns to step 2. If there are no other AID(s) left in the list of supported applications, the terminal starts the final application selection procedure as described in Section 4.4.3.

• *Step 6:* This step is reached when the DF name of the selected ADF begins with the current AID in the list of supported applications in the terminal and is longer than this AID.

   • When the application selection indicator corresponding to the current AID is set to "Complete name matching," the terminal does not add the FCI of the selected ADF to the candidate list. The processing continues with step 7.

   • When the application selection indicator corresponding to the current AID is set to "Partial name matching," the terminal adds the FCI of the selected ADF to the candidate list only if SW1SW2 = 9000. The processing continues with step 7.

‣ *Step 7:* The terminal issues a new SELECT command, with the same file name but with P2 set to 02h ("Next occurrence"). The terminal returns to step 2.

4.4.3   Final application selection

‣ *Step 1:* If there are no mutually supported applications, the terminal ends the card session.

‣ *Step 2:* If there is only one mutually supported application, the terminal checks the bit b8 of the Application Priority Indicator:

   ‣ If b8 = 0, the terminal selects the application.

   ‣ If b8 = 1, the terminal requires confirmation by the cardholder. The application is selected if the cardholder approves. If the terminal requires confirmation and the cardholder does not approve, the terminal ends the card session.

‣ *Step 3:* If there are several applications mutually supported by the card and the terminal, there are two possibilities:

   ‣ The terminal may offer a selection possibility to the cardholder. Processing continues with step 4.

   ‣ The terminal makes the selection itself. Processing continues with step 5.

‣ *Step 4:* If a list is presented to the cardholder, it shall be in a priority sequence, with the application having the highest priority listed first. If there is no priority sequence specified in the card, the list should be displayed in the order in which the applications were encountered in the card, unless the terminal has its own preferred order. The same applies whenever duplicate priorities are assigned to multiple applications or individual entries are missing the Application Priority Indicator. This means that the terminal may use its own preferred order for displaying these applications, or the terminal may display the duplicate priority applications or nonprioritized applications in the order encountered in the card.

▸ *Step 5:* The terminal may select the application without the assistance of the cardholder. In this case, the terminal shall select the highest priority application from the candidate list of mutually supported applications. If the terminal does not provide the possibility for confirming the selected application, applications prohibiting such a selection (b8 = 1 in the Application Priority Indicator) shall be excluded from possible selection. The terminal sends the SELECT command with the value of the file name parameter identical to the AID corresponding to the card application chosen in the candidate list.

References

[1] EMVCo, *EMV 2000 Integrated Circuit Card Specification for Payment Systems, BOOK 1—Application Independent ICC to Terminal Interface Requirements,* Version 4.0, December 2000, http://www.emvco.com/specifications.cfm.

[2] EMVCo, *EMV 2000 Integrated Circuit Card Specification for Payment Systems, BOOK 2—Security and Key Management,* Version 4.0, December 2000, http://www.emvco.com/specifications.cfm.

[3] EMVCo, *EMV 2000 Integrated Circuit Card Specification for Payment Systems, BOOK 3—Application Specification,* Version 4.0, December 2000, http://www.emvco.com/specifications.cfm.

[4] EMVCo, *EMV 2000 Integrated Circuit Card Specification for Payment Systems, BOOK 4—Cardholder, Attendant, and Acquirer Interface Requirements,* Version 4.0, December 2000, http://www.emvco.com/specifications.cfm.

[5] EMVCo, *EMV '96 Integrated Circuit Card Specification for Payment Systems,* Version 3.1.1, May 31, 1998, http://www.emvco.com/specifications.cfm.

[6] EMVCo, *EMV '96 Integrated Circuit Card Terminal Specification for Payment Systems,* Version 3.1.1, May 31, 1998, http://www.emvco.com/specifications.cfm.

[7] EMVCo, *EMV '96 Integrated Circuit Card Application Specification for Payment Systems,* Version 3.1.1, May 31, 1998, http://www.emvco.com/specifications.cfm.

[8] CEPSCo, *Common Electronic Purse Specification, Functional Requirements,* Version 6.3, September 1999, http://www.cepsco.com/.

[9] ISO/IEC 8825, "Information Technology—Open Systems Interconnection—Specification of Basic Encoding Rules for Abstract Syntax Notation One (ASN.1)," 1990.

[10] ISO/IEC 7816-4, "Identification Cards—Integrated Circuit(s) Cards with Contacts—Part 4: Inter-Industry Commands for Interchange," 1995.

[11] ISO/IEC 7816-5, "Identification Cards—Integrated Circuit(s) Cards with Contacts—Part 5: Numbering System and Registration Procedure for Application Identifiers," 1994.

[12] ISO/IEC 8859-8, "8-Bit Single-Byte Coded Graphic Character Sets Latin/Hebrew Alphabet," 1999.

[13] ISO/IEC 639, "Code for the Representation of Names of Languages," 1988.

EMV™ Certificates

There are two types of certificates considered by the EMV™ specifications, which we generically call the EMV™ certificates:

▸ *EMV™ public key certificates:* The certificates in this category prove the temporal link, until a certain expiration date, between the public key of an entity and its identity. The entity public key is the object to be certified. It consists of the entity public key modulus and the entity public key exponent.

▸ *Signed Static Application Data:* This is a certificate provided by an issuer concerning the authenticity of the application data personalized in an ICC. It is intended to prove that the content of financial data in the card did not change since the card was issued.

The presentation in this chapter concentrates on the specific issues related to EMV™ certificates and does not cover the general framework of certification. The reader interested in a more comprehensive discussion about certificates can consult Appendix D, Section D.4, in this book.

5.1 Certification mechanism and algorithm

In the EMV™ environment, a certifier is the organization that produces an EMV™ certificate using an asymmetric

125

mechanism, consisting of a digital signature scheme providing message recovery, as stated in Annex A2.1 in Book 2 [1]. In Appendix D, Section D.3.2, of this book the reader can find a brief review of this mechanism.

It is important to note that in Annex B.2 in Book 2 [1] the only cryptographic algorithm approved at the moment in the *EMV 2000* specifications to implement an asymmetric mechanism is the RSA algorithm.

Then, without restraining the generality, someone can say that the certifier runs an RSA scheme, where the mapping of its parameters according to the EMV™ terminology is the following (see also Appendix F in this book):

- The modulus, denoted in the RSA context n, represents the certifier public key modulus data object in the EMV™ context.

- The public exponent, denoted in the RSA context e, represents the certifier public key exponent data object in the EMV™ context. Note that the certifier public key consists of the certifier public key modulus and the certifier public key exponent, which in the RSA context represents the public key (n, e). It is used by anyone that verifies the certificate.

- The secret exponent, denoted in the RSA context d, could be assimilated with a certifier secret key exponent data object, which is not explicitly defined in the EMV™ context. Note that the certifier private key consists of the certifier public key modulus and the certifier secret key exponent, which in the RSA context represents the private key (n, d). The certifier uses the certifier private key to generate the signature representing the certificate.

5.2 Public key certificate for RSA scheme

In its turn, the entity requiring an EMV™ public key certificate also runs an RSA scheme, regardless of whether it is used for digitally signing information (see Appendix D, Section D.3) or for creating a digital envelope that encrypts a PIN using the asymmetric encryption mechanism (see Appendix D, Sections D.1.2 and D.5.5).

Correspondingly, the parameters entity public key modulus and entity public key exponent submitted for certification correspond to the modulus n and the public exponent e, respectively, of an RSA scheme. For this reason the Public Key Algorithm Indicator—which is an item in the certificate specifying the type of algorithm that uses the certified parameters—is set at the moment to a unique value 01h corresponding to the RSA algorithm.

The entity private *signing* key, which is denoted (n_S, d_S) in the RSA context, can be used for generating a digital signature on a message. Everyone having the corresponding entity public *verification* key, which is denoted (n_S, e_S) in the RSA context, and (part of) the message that is signed can verify the correctness of the signature.

The entity can use the entity private *decryption* key, which is denoted (n_E, d_E) in the RSA context, to decrypt any digital envelope computed with the corresponding entity public *encryption* key, which is denoted (n_E, e_E) in the RSA context.

Note that when the storage space of the entity allows it, an entity keeps separate key pairs (private key/public key) for signing and encrypting [i.e., $((n_S, d_S)/(n_S, e_S))$ and $((n_E, d_E)/(n_E, e_E))$, respectively].

5.3 Entities and certifiers

In the *EMV 2000* specifications there are two types of entities requiring certificates on their public keys: the issuer of a card containing an EMV™ debit/credit application and the ICC.

5.3.1 Issuer requires a public key certificate

When the issuer is the entity that requires an EMV™ public key certificate, the material to be certified is the issuer public key, which consists of the issuer public key modulus, denoted n_I with the byte-length N_I, and the Issuer Public Key Exponent (tag 9F32), denoted e_I. The corresponding certificate is referred to as the Issuer Public Key Certificate (tag 90). The actual upper limitation on N_I is 248 bytes, while the value of e_I can be either 3 or $2^{16} + 1$. In this case, the certificate format, which is an item of the certificate content that distinguishes among several types of certificate formats, is set to 02h.

In this case the certifier is named the Certification Authority (CA), which runs an RSA digital signature scheme with recovery (see Appendix F, Section F.3). This scheme is parameterized with the certification authority public key modulus, denoted n_{CA} with the byte-length N_{CA}, the certification authority public key exponent, denoted e_{CA}, and the certification authority secret key exponent, denoted d_{CA}. The actual upper limitation on N_{CA} is 248 bytes, while the value of e_{CA} can be either 3 or $2^{16} + 1$. Moreover, the relationship between N_I and N_{CA} has to be $N_I \leq N_{CA}$.

A card association or a payment system operator proposing an EMV™ debit/credit application can play the role of the CA.

5.3.2 ICC requires a public key certificate

When the ICC is the entity that requires an EMV™ public key certificate, the material to be certified can be:

- The ICC public key modulus, denoted n_{IC} with the byte-length N_{IC}, and the ICC Public Key Exponent (tag 9F47), denoted e_{IC}. The ICC public key consists of the pair ICC public key modulus and ICC Public Key Exponent. The corresponding certificate is referred to as the ICC Public Key Certificate (tag 9F46). The actual limitation on N_{IC} is 248 bytes, while the value of e_{IC} can be either 3 or $2^{16} + 1$. In this case, the certificate format is set to 04h. The associated RSA scheme is used by the card for digitally signing information that includes at least a random number received from the terminal. This is performed with the corresponding ICC private key, consisting of the pair ICC public key modulus n_{IC} and the ICC secret key exponent d_{IC}.

- The ICC PIN encipherment public key modulus, denoted n_{PE} with the byte-length N_{PE}, and the ICC PIN Encipherment Public Key Exponent (tag 9F2E), denoted e_{PE}. The ICC PIN encipherment public key consists of the pair ICC PIN encipherment public key modulus and ICC PIN Encipherment Public Key Exponent. The corresponding certificate is referred to as the ICC PIN Encipherment Public Key Certificate (tag 9F2D). The actual upper limitation on N_{PE} is 248 bytes, while the value of e_{PE} can be either 3 or $2^{16} + 1$. In this case, the certificate format is set also to 04h. The terminal uses the ICC PIN encipherment public key (n_{PE}, e_{PE}) for creating a digital envelope that includes the cardholder's PIN, which is sent encrypted for local verification in the card. The card uses the corresponding ICC PIN encipherment private key (n_{PE}, d_{PE}), for decrypting the digital envelope. The parameter d_{PE} is referred to as the ICC PIN encipherment secret key exponent.

In this case the certifier is the card's issuer, which runs an RSA digital signature scheme with recovery (see Appendix F, Section F.3). The scheme is parameterized with the issuer public key modulus (n_I), the Issuer Public Key Exponent (e_I), and the issuer secret key exponent, denoted d_I. The issuer private key, which consists of the issuer public key modulus and the issuer secret key exponent $(n_I,\ d_I)$, is used for signing the certificates for the ICC. Note that N_I, N_{IC}, and N_{PE}, should respect the relations $N_{IC} \le N_I$ and $N_{PE} \le N_I$.

5.4 Entity public key remainder

Before giving any details about the splitting of the entity public keys that are certified using a digital signature scheme with recovery, we make the following remark. In the *EMV 2000* specifications, through an abuse of notation, the term "entity public key" refers only to the entity public key modulus. Therefore, in order to keep consistent with the EMV™ notations, and at the same time to make clear that it is the modulus part of an entity's public key we are talking about, we refer to it with the notation "entity public key (modulus)."

It is important to note that since the entity public key certificate is produced using a digital signature with recovery, the message $M = M_R \parallel M'$ to be signed has to be split in two parts (see Appendix D, Section D.3.2):

1. A part M_R that can be recovered from the signature, which can be the complete message if its length is small enough (see Table 5.1) compared to the length of the modulus of the underlying RSA scheme;

2. A part M' that has to be sent separately to the verifier for the verification of the signature.

Correspondingly, any issuer, ICC, or ICC PIN encipherment public key (modulus) submitted to certification can be conventionally split in two parts. The first part referred to as the *leftmost digits of the public key (modulus)* can be recovered from the certificate, while the second part, which is referred to as the Public Key (modulus) Remainder, must be sent separately for the verification of the certificate. Table 5.1 summarizes this splitting for issuer, ICC, and ICC PIN encipherment public key (modulus).

5.5 EMV™ certification chains

The EMV™ certification chain is presented in Figure 5.1.

The CA public key consists of the pair CA public key modulus and the CA public key exponent. This public key has to be stored in all the terminals that verify certificates originating from this CA, either directly or through the EMV™ certification chain.

Table 5.1
Splitting of the Entity Public Key (Modulus)

Name of the Modulus	Part Recovered from the Certificate	Part Sent Separately from the Certificate
Issuer public key (modulus): n_I	If $N_I \leq N_{CA} - 36$, then the entire n_I can be recovered from the certificate. Otherwise, only the $N_{CA} - 36$ most significant bytes of the issuer public key (modulus) can be recovered from the certificate	If $N_I > N_{CA} - 36$, some part of the n_I, which is referred to as the Issuer Public Key (modulus) Remainder (tag 92), cannot be recovered from the certificate. It represents a separate item to be transmitted to the verifier
ICC public key (modulus): n_{IC}	If $N_{IC} \leq N_I - 42$, then the entire n_{IC} can be recovered from the certificate. Otherwise, only the $N_I - 42$ most significant bytes of the ICC public key (modulus) can be recovered from the certificate	If $N_{IC} > N_I - 42$, some part of the n_{IC}, which is referred to as the ICC Public Key (modulus) Remainder (tag 9F48), cannot be recovered from the certificate, and represents a separate item to be transmitted to the verifier
ICC PIN encipherment public key (modulus): n_{PE}	If $N_{PE} \leq N_I - 42$, then the entire n_{PE} can be recovered from the certificate. Otherwise, only the $N_I - 42$ most significant bytes of the ICC PIN encipherment public key (modulus) can be recovered from the certificate	If $N_{PE} > N_I - 42$, some part of the n_{PE}, referred to as the ICC PIN Encipherment Public Key (modulus) Remainder (tag 9F2F) cannot be recovered from the certificate, and represents a separate item to be transmitted to the verifier

Figure 5.1
EMV™
certification
chain.

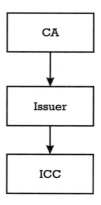

There is no higher instance that can certify on this primary public key, and therefore, special precautions have to be taken for its authenticity and management as explained in Section 10 of Book 2 [1].

Furthermore, when an acquirer decides to participate in several EMV™ payment schemes, the terminal at the point of service has to store a database that keeps one record for each of the operational public keys of each CA accepted by the acquirer. A possible organization of this database is presented in Table 5.2. In this database a record corresponding to a CA public key is identified with two items:

1.   The RID of the application accepting this CA;

2.   An index allocated by the card association or payment system opera-tor playing the role of the CA to each of its CA public keys, which could be operational at a certain moment. This index is kept in the terminal in the data object with tag 9F22.

The record corresponding to a CA contains the modulus (n_{CA}) and the public exponent (e_{CA}) of each CA public key, as well as the algorithm indica-tor, which determines the type of algorithm that is used in conjunction with the CA public key for the verification of a certificate. In the example presented in Table 5.2, the certification authority CA1 has two operational CA public keys that are versioned with two different indexes, index 1 and index 2, respectively.

If a terminal needs to verify the Issuer Public Key Certificate received from a card to recover the corresponding issuer public key, the terminal also needs to receive the CA public key index (tag 8F) from the card.

Using this index, the terminal identifies in the CA public keys database the appropriate public key of the CA that shall be used for checking the Issuer Public Key Certificate. When this certificate verifies correctly, the ter-minal can obtain the issuer public key (issuer public key modulus and Issuer Public Key Exponent).

▸ The terminal can use the issuer public key for verifying the authentic-ity of the certificate on the data personalized in the card by the issuer, which is referred to as the Signed Static Application Data (see Section 5.9). The terminal verifies this certificate in the case of off-line static data authentication (see Section 6.4.2).

▸ Otherwise, the recovered issuer public key can be further used for verifying either an ICC Public Key Certificate or an ICC PIN

Table 5.2
Terminal Database of the CA Public Keys Accepted by the Acquirer

RID	CA Public Key Index (tag 9F22)	Algorithm Indicator	CA Public Key Modulus—n_{CA}	CA Public Key Exponent—e_{CA}
RID 1	CA1 index 1	AlgInd11	CA1 public key (modulus) 1	CA1 public key exponent 1
RID 1	CA1 index 2	AlgInd12	CA1 public key (modulus) 2	CA1 public key exponent 2
RID 2	CA2 index 1	AlgInd21	CA2 public key (modulus) 1	CA2 public key exponent 1
...	...	...	...	...
RID n	CAn index 1	AlgInd$n$	CAn public key (modulus) 1	CAn public key exponent 1

Encipherment Public Key Certificate, which represents the second level of certificates in the EMV™ certification chain.

Once the ICC Public Key Certificate verifies correctly, the terminal can recover the ICC public key modulus and the ICC Public Key Exponent. Using this public key the terminal can verify any signature produced by the card with this key, which is the case of the off-line DDA (see Section 6.4.3).

If the ICC PIN Encipherment Public Key Certificate verifies correctly, the terminal can recover the ICC PIN encipherment public key modulus and the ICC PIN Encipherment Public Key Exponent. Using this public key, the terminal can produce a digital envelope and encrypt the PIN of the cardholder. Only the card can decrypt this digital envelope with the corresponding private key (see Section 6.6.5).

5.6   Issuing EMV™ public key certificates

The EMV™ public key certificates are issued with a digital signature scheme giving message recovery based on the RSA algorithm. This scheme is described in Appendix F, Section F.3.1 (case 2) of this book. Therefore, in this section we refer to the notations introduced in the aforementioned appendix.

5.6.1   Data items included in the certificate

Let us denote with $M = M_R \,\|\, M'$ the entity public key data to be signed by the certifier. The length of this data is L, and the byte-length of the certifier public key (modulus) is N. The entity can be the issuer (if the certifier is the CA) or the entity can be the ICC or the ICC PIN encipherment (if the certifier is the issuer).

Then the part M_R of the message M that is recoverable from the entity public key certificate consists of $N - 22$ bytes, containing the following data items (which summarizes the content of Tables 1, 6, 7, and 19 in Book 2 [1]):

> • *Field 1—Certificate Format (1 byte):* This item distinguishes among several possible certificate formats corresponding to the Issuer Public Key Certificate (02h), or ICC/ICC PIN Encipherment Public Key Certificate (04h).

‣ *Field 2—Entity Identifier:* This item identifies the entity that owns the public key certificate. Its format depends on the entity requiring the certificate:

  ‣ *Issuer Identification Number—IIN (4 bytes):* This represents the leftmost 3 to 8 digits from the PAN (padded to the right with the hexadecimal digit F), in case the issuer is the entity requiring a certificate signed by the CA;

  ‣ *Application PAN (8 bytes):* This is padded to the right with the hexadecimal digit F till the bound of 8 bytes, in case the ICC is the entity requiring a certificate signed by the issuer.

‣ *Field 3—Certificate Expiration Date (2 bytes):* This date in the format MMYY indicates the date after which the certificate is no longer valid.

‣ *Field 4—Certificate Serial Number (3 bytes):* This data item with binary representation specifies a unique number associated with the certificate. This number is assigned by the CA in the case of an Issuer Public Key Certificate, or by the issuer in the case of an ICC/ICC PIN Encipherment Public Key Certificate.

‣ *Field 5—Hash Algorithm Indicator (1 byte):* This identifies the hash algorithm used to produce the hash code H. This value is used in step 1 of the algorithm described in Appendix F, Section F.3.1 (case 2). At the moment, SHA-1 is the hash algorithm recommended by the *EMV 2000* specifications in Annex B3.1 of Book 2 [1]. Thus, the value of the hash algorithm indicator is set to 01h.

‣ *Field 6—Entity Public Key Algorithm Indicator (1 byte):* This indicates the type of public key algorithm used by an entity in conjunction with the public key contained in this certificate. At the moment this indicator is set to 01h, indicating an RSA algorithm.

‣ *Field 7—Entity Public Key Length (1 byte):* This indicates the length in bytes of the entity public key (modulus) that is currently certified. This length is denoted N_I, N_{IC}, or N_{PE}, depending whether the entity is the issuer, ICC, or ICC PIN encipherment, respectively.

‣ *Field 8—Entity Public Key Exponent Length (1 byte):* This indicates the length in bytes of the entity Public Key Exponent that is currently certified. This length is either 1 or 3, depending whether the exponent is 3 or $2^{16} + 1$, respectively.

• *Field 9—Entity Public Key or Leftmost Digits of the Entity Public Key:* The field is of variable length depending on the type of entity:

  • When the entity is the issuer, the length of this field is $N_{CA} - 36$. If $N_I \leq N_{CA} - 36$, this field consists of the full issuer public key modulus, padded to the right with $N_{CA} - 36 - N_I$ bytes of value BBh. If $N_I > N_{CA} - 36$, this field consists of the $N_{CA} - 36$ most significant bytes of the issuer public key modulus.

  • When the entity is the ICC (for signing), the length of this field is $N_I - 42$. If $N_{IC} \leq N_I - 42$, this field consists of the full ICC public key modulus, padded to the right with $N_I - 42 - N_{IC}$ bytes of value BBh. If $N_{IC} > N_I - 42$, this field consists of the $N_I - 42$ most significant bytes of the ICC public key modulus.

  • When the entity is the ICC PIN encipherment, the length of this field is $N_I - 42$. If $N_{PE} \leq N_I - 42$, this field consists of the full ICC PIN encipherment public key modulus, padded to the right with $N_I - 42 - N_{PE}$ bytes of value BBh. If $N_{PE} > N_I - 42$, this field consists of the $N_{PE} - 42$ most significant bytes of the ICC PIN encipherment public key modulus.

The part M' of the message M (entity public key data) that has to be separately transmitted for certificate verification has variable length, containing the following data items (which summarizes the content of Tables 1, 6, 7, and 19 in Book 2 [1]):

• *Field 10—Entity Public Key Remainder:* This is a field of variable length depending on the type of entity as follows:

  • When the entity is the issuer, the length is either 0 or $N_I - N_{CA} + 36$. This field is only present if $N_I > N_{CA} - 36$, and consists of the $N_I - N_{CA} + 36$ least significant bytes of the issuer public key modulus.

  • When the entity is the ICC (for signing), the length is either 0 or $N_{IC} - N_I + 42$. This field is only present if $N_{IC} > N_I - 42$, and consists of the $N_{IC} - N_I + 42$ least significant bytes of the ICC public key modulus.

  • When the entity is the ICC PIN encipherment, the length is either 0 or $N_{PE} - N_I + 42$. This field is only present if $N_{PE} > N_I - 42$, and consists of the $N_{PE} - N_I + 42$ least significant bytes of the ICC PIN encipherment public key modulus.

> *Field 11—Entity Public Key Exponent:* This is a field of length 1 or 3 bytes, depending whether the exponent is 3 or $2^{16} + 1$.

> *Field 12—Static Data to Be Authenticated:* This is a field of variable length, which is present only in the ICC public key data to be signed by the issuer [i.e., when the entity is the ICC (for signing)].

5.6.2   Generating the public key certificate

In order to generate the Issuer Public Key Certificate, the CA applies the algorithm described in Appendix F, Section F.3.1 (case 2), on the issuer public key data (as described in Section 5.6.1 where the entity is the issuer) with the following RSA parameters: $n_s = n_{CA}$ and $d_s = d_{CA}$.

> The Issuer Public Key Certificate, of length N_{CA}, is generated every time an issuer adopts the EMV™ debit/credit application supervised by a CA. Subsequently, this certificate is regenerated every time the CA public key changes.

> The Issuer Public Key Certificate is loaded during the personalization of every card managed by the issuer, which supports off-line data authentication (Section 6.4) and/or enciphered PIN verification by the card (Section 6.6.5).

In order to obtain the ICC Public Key Certificate, of length N_I, the issuer applies the algorithm described in Appendix F, Section F.3.1 (case 2), on the ICC public key data (as described in Section 5.6.1 where the entity is the ICC) with the following RSA parameters: $n_s = n_I$ and $d_s = d_I$. The issuer generates the ICC Public Key Certificate for each card that supports off-line DDA (Section 6.4.3). This certificate is loaded in the card during its personalization stage.

In order to obtain the ICC PIN Encipherment Public Key Certificate, of length N_I, the issuer applies the algorithm described in Appendix F, Section F.3.1 (case 2), on the ICC PIN encipherment public key data (as described in Section 5.6.1 where the entity is the ICC PIN encipherment). The issuer uses the following RSA parameters: $n_s = n_I$ and $d_s = d_I$. The issuer generates the ICC PIN Encipherment Public Key Certificate for each card that supports enciphered PIN verification by the card (Section 6.6.5). This certificate is loaded in the card during its personalization stage.

5.7 Verifying EMV™ public key certificates

This section presents the verification procedure of the Issuer Public Key Certificate in Section 5.7.1 and the verification procedure of the ICC Public Key Certificate in Section 5.7.2. Note that the verification procedure of an ICC PIN Encipherment Public Key Certificate is identical with the verification procedure of the ICC Public Key Certificate, and consequently it is not separately detailed.

5.7.1 Verification of the Issuer Public Key Certificate

The following steps describe the procedure of verifying the Issuer Public Key Certificate. The verifier of the certificate is a terminal at the point of service, and the certificate together with some other data needed for the certificate verification are received from the EMV™ card.

- Step 1: Verify that the length of the Issuer Public Key Certificate (tag 90) data object is N_{CA}.

- Step 2: Apply the signature verification/recovery algorithm in Appendix F, Section F.3.2 (case 2), where S is the value field of the Issuer Public Key Certificate, $n_s = n_{CA}$, and $e_s = e_{CA}$. The length N of the modulus is N_{CA}.

- Step 3: The data that is recovered X is parsed as $X = B \parallel M_R \parallel H \parallel E$. The following processing is performed on these items:

  1. Check that E (last byte of X), which is the recovered data trailer, equals BCh.

  2. Check that B (first byte of X), which is the recovered data header, equals 6Ah.

  3. Consider the M_R as the next $N_{CA} - 22$ bytes after B. Parse M_R according to the nine fields identified in Section 5.6.1.

  4. Check that the certificate format read in field 1 of M_R is 02h.

  5. Create message M' as the concatenation from left to right of the value fields of the Issuer Public Key Remainder (tag 92), if this

data object is present in the card, and of the is Issuer Public Key Exponent (tag 9F32).

6. Create the message M, representing the issuer public key data, as the concatenation from left to right of the recovered part M_R and of the constructed part M' (i.e., $M = M_R \parallel M'$).

7. Read the hash algorithm indicator from field 5 of M_R. Note that at the moment this value is 01h, corresponding to the SHA-1 algorithm, the only approved hash algorithm in the *EMV 2000* specifications (see Annex B3.1 in Book 2 [1]).

8. Use the indicated hash algorithm to compute the hash code h of M.

9. Check that h equals the hash result H, which represents the last 20 bytes in X before E.

If any of the verifications mentioned above failed, the verification of the Issuer Public Key Certificate has failed.

▸ Step 4: Check the consistency of some fields in the recovered part M_R of the issuer public key data.

1. Check that the IIN read from the 4 bytes of field 2, after stripping of the possible padding with the hexadecimal digit F, corresponds to the leftmost 3 to 8 digits of the card's PAN as captured by the terminal.

2. Check that the certificate is not expired. To this end, check that the current date is earlier or equal to the last day of the month MM specified in field 3, certificate expiration date.

3. If the terminal manages a revocation list of issuer public key certificates associated with a CA, check that the certificate serial number read from field 4 is not blacklisted in this revocation list. If the certificate is blacklisted, set up the bit 5, "Card appears on terminal exception file," of byte 1 of the TVR register (see Section 6.2.1).

4. Check that the public key algorithm specified in the Issuer Public Key Algorithm Indicator read from field 6 is among the algorithms known by the terminal. Note that at the moment this indicator has the value 01h corresponding to the RSA algorithm, which is

the only approved asymmetric algorithm in the *EMV 2000* specifications (according to Annex B2.1 in Book 2 [1]).

If any of the verifications mentioned above failed, the verification of the Issuer Public Key Certificate has failed.

▶ Step 5: If all the verifications were valid, the terminal accepts the authenticity of the issuer public key. It consists of the issuer public key modulus n_I and the Issuer Public Key Exponent e_I (tag 9F32).

The issuer public key length N_I read from field 7 of M_R gives the actual length of n_I.

- ▶ If $N_{CA} - 36 - N_I > 0$, remove the $N_{CA} - 36 - N_I$ padding bytes BBh from the rightmost side of field 9 of M_R. The byte string that is obtained represents n_I.

- ▶ If $N_I > N_{CA} - 36$, concatenate from left to right field 9 of M_R and the value field of the Issuer Public Key Remainder (tag 92). The byte string that is obtained represents n_I.

5.7.2 Verification of the ICC Public Key Certificate

The following steps describe the procedure of verifying the ICC Public Key Certificate. The verifier of the certificate is a terminal at the point of service, and the certificate together with some other data needed for the certificate verification are received from the EMV™ card.

▶ Step 1: Verify that the length of the ICC Public Key Certificate (tag 90) data object is N_I.

▶ Step 2: Apply the signature verification/recovery algorithm in Appendix F, Section F.3.2 (case 2), where S is the value field of the ICC Public Key Certificate, $n_s = n_I$, and $e_s = e_I$. The length N of the modulus is N_I.

The data that is recovered X is parsed as $X = B \parallel M_R \parallel H \parallel E$. The following processing is performed on these items:

1. Check that E (last byte of X), which is the recovered data trailer, equals BCh.

2. Check that B (first byte of X), which is the recovered data header, equals 6Ah.

3. Consider M_R as the next $N_I - 22$ bytes after B. Parse M_R according to the nine fields identified in Section 5.6.1.

4. Check that the certificate format read in field 1 of M_R is 04h.

5. Create message M' as the concatenation from left to right of the value fields of the ICC Public Key Remainder (tag 9F48), if this data object is present in the card, of the ICC Public Key Exponent (tag 9F47), and the Static Data to Be Authenticated byte string. The details of formatting this byte string are given in Section 5.8.1.

6. Create the message M, representing the ICC public key data, as the concatenation from left to right of the recovered part M_R and of the computed part M' (i.e., $M = M_R \parallel M'$).

7. Read the hash algorithm indicator from field 5 of M_R. Note that at the moment this value is 01h, corresponding to the SHA-1 algorithm, the only approved hash algorithm in the *EMV 2000* specifications (see Annex B3.1 in Book 2 [1]).

8. Use the indicated hash algorithm to compute the hash code h of M.

9. Check that h equals the hash result H, which represents the last 20 bytes in X before E.

If any of the verifications mentioned above failed, the verification of the ICC Public Key Certificate has failed.

▸ Step 3: Check the consistency of some fields in the recovered part M_R of the issuer public key data.

1. Check that the PAN recovered from field 2 of M_R corresponds to the PAN of the card as captured by the terminal.

2. Check that the certificate is not expired. To this end, check that the current date is earlier or equal to the last day of the month specified in field 3, certificate expiration date.

3. Check that the public key algorithm specified in the Issuer Public Key Algorithm Indicator read from field 6 is among the algorithms known by the terminal. Note that at the moment this indicator has the value 01h corresponding to the RSA algorithm, which is

the only approved asymmetric algorithm in the *EMV 2000* specifications (according to Annex B2.1 in Book 2 [1]).

If any of the verifications mentioned above failed, the verification of
the ICC Public Key Certificate has failed.

> • Step 4: If all the verifications were valid, the terminal accepts the
> authenticity of the ICC public key. It consists of the ICC public key
> modulus n_{IC}, and the ICC Public Key Exponent (tag 9F47) e_{IC}.
>
> The ICC public key length N_{IC}, read from field 7 of M_R gives the
> actual length of n_{IC}.
>
> > • If $N_I - 42 - N_{IC} > 0$, remove the $N_I - 42 - N_{IC}$ padding bytes BBh from
> > the rightmost side of field 9 of M_R. The byte string that is obtained rep-
> > resents n_{IC}.
> >
> > • If $N_{IC} > N_I - 42$, concatenate from left to right field 9 of M_R and the
> > value field of the ICC Public Key Remainder (tag 9F48). The byte
> > string that is obtained represents n_{IC}.

The terminal stores the ICC public key (n_{IC}, e_{IC}) for the current session.

5.8 Issuing signed static application data

The issuer decides which are the data objects of the card application whose
authenticity it would like to protect during the utilization stage of the card.
Beside the mandatory data objects in the card application, as presented in
Section 6.3.2, the issuer may authenticate some other data objects:

> • Application Version Number (tag 9F08);
>
> • Application Usage Control (tag 9F07);
>
> • Application Currency Code (tag 9F42) and Application Currency Expo-
> nent (tag 9F44);
>
> • Application PAN Sequence Number (tag 5F34);
>
> • Track 2 Equivalent Data (tag 57);
>
> • Cardholder Name (tag 5F20);

‣ Issuer Action Code—Default/Denial/On-line (tag 9F0D, tag 9F0E, and tag 9F0F, respectively).

The issuer further decides the mapping of the data objects into records. These records are further mapped into various AEF(s), together with records that may not need to be authenticated. Based on this mapping, the issuer establishes the AFL, which also has to be written in the card. The issuer may also decide that other publicly readable data objects from the card that are not readable from the records may be individually considered for authentication. If this is the case, the issuer defines the Static Data Authentication Tag List, which is created in the card as a data object with tag 9F4A and included in one of the records. Each entry in this list consists of a tag representing a data object in the card. The length of the data object is not included in the entry, which makes the Static Data Authentication Tag List have a different structure than the DOL (see Section 3.4.3). In the *EMV '96* specifications there were no restrictions imposed concerning the data elements to be included in this list; the *EMV 2000* specifications require that when this list exists in the card application it shall include only the tag of the AIP. An intuitive presentation of the AFL and AIP was explained in Sections 3.4.2 and 3.4.3, respectively.

To authenticate the data objects of the card, the issuer performs the following two steps. First, it creates the Static Data to Be Authenticated byte string (Section 5.8.2). Second, it signs this byte string together with other items to generate the Signed Static Application Data (Section 5.8.3). The records to be included in the Static Data to Be Authenticated are listed in the AFL, whose meaning and interpretation is presented in Section 5.8.1.

5.8.1 AFL

The AFL (with tag 94), gives the table of contents of the publicly available information provided by the card application (see also Section 3.4.2). It identifies the AEF(s) and their corresponding records to be used by the terminal for the processing of an EMV™ debit/credit transaction. For each AEF, the AFL also indicates which of the AEF's records are appended to the Static Data to Be Authenticated byte string to be certified by the issuer. The terminal can only read the AEF(s) indicated in the AFL.

The AFL is a list of AEF(s) file entries, each consisting of 4 bytes, the meaning of which is presented below (according to Section 6.2 in Book 3 [2]):

- The first byte encodes in the 5 most significant bits the SFI of the AEF. The least significant 3 bits in this byte are set to 0.

- The second byte encodes the number of the first (or the only) record to be read from the AEF. This number, which is also referred to as *the first record number*, shall never be 0.

- The third byte encodes the number of the last record to be read from the AEF. This number, which is also referred to as *the last record number*, can be greater than or equal to the number in the second byte. In the former case the terminal must read all the records of that AEF referred to with numbers between the first record number and the last record number. In the latter case only the record referred to with the first record number shall be read from the AEF.

- The fourth byte indicates the number of records in that AEF, starting from the first record number, which shall be considered by the terminal in the off-line data authentication processing. This number can be 0 when no records of the actual file are considered for the off-line data authentication. When this number is not zero, the sum of the first record number and the number in the fourth byte minus one is referred to as *the last authenticated record number*.

5.8.2 Creating the Static Data to Be Authenticated

First, the terminal adds to the Static Data to Be Authenticated byte string (which initially is empty) the records of the AEF(s) publicly readable by the terminal (with the SFI in the range of 1–30) and which are indicated in the AFL.

To this end the terminal performs the following processing:

- For each entry Fi, $i = 1, ..., n$ in the AFL = $F1 \parallel F2 \parallel ... \parallel Fn$, check the fourth byte of Fi. When its value is zero none of the records of the current AEF are considered for authentication. The terminal increments the counter i to consider the next AEF indicated in the AFL.

- When the value of the fourth byte of Fi is not zero, the terminal considers l equal to the first record number, as indicated in the second byte of Fi. The terminal also computes L as the sum of the second and the fourth byte of the AFL entry Fi minus one, which represents the last authenticated record number. For each record Rij with a number j such that $l \leq j \leq L$ the terminal concatenates this record to the right most position of Static Data to Be Authenticated (i.e., Static Data to Be Authenticated = Static Data to Be Authenticated || *Rij*).

› If the SFI, which is read from the first byte of *Fi*, is in the range of 1 to 10, then the record tag (70) and the record length are not included in *Rij*.

› If the SFI is in the range of 11 to 30, then the record tag (70) and the record length are included in *Rij*.

Second, to the rightmost position of the Static Data to Be Authenticated byte string, the issuer concatenates the value fields of all the data objects indicated in the Static Data Authentication Tag List. The elements of this list are submitted to processing from left to right. Each element of the list consists of a tag that refers to a simple data object resident in the card, which was not included in any record mentioned for authentication in the AFL. This data object must be defined for interoperability for financial transaction interchange. Note that in the *EMV 2000* specifications (Section 6.3 in Book 3 [2]), it is compulsory that when the Static Data Authentication Tag List exists in the card, it will contain only one tag, corresponding to the AIP data object (tag 82). Note that this restriction did not exist with the *EMV '96* specification. In fact, this requires a higher discipline from the issuer in organizing the data objects needed for authentication in contiguous records of the AEF.

5.8.3 Generate the Signed Static Application Data

The issuer, playing the role of the certifier, applies the digital signature scheme that provides message recovery implemented with the RSA algorithm, as described in Appendix F, Section F.3.1 (case 2). This algorithm is applied on the message $M = M_R \| M'$ with the RSA parameters $n_s = n_I$ and $d_s = d_I$ to obtain a signature, which is referred to as the Signed Static Application Data.

The message $M = M_R \| M'$ is referred to as the static application data to be signed by the issuer (see Table 2 in Book 2 [1]). The part M' consists of the Static Data to Be Authenticated byte string, which is constructed as shown in Section 5.8.2. The part M_R consists of four fields:

› *Field 1—Signed Data Format (1 byte):* This has the fix value 03h.

› *Field 2—Hash Algorithm Indicator (1 byte):* This identifies the hash algorithm used to produce the hash code *H*. This value is used in step 1 of the algorithm described in Appendix F, Section F.3.1 (case 2). At the moment, SHA-1 is the hash algorithm recommended by the *EMV 2000* specifications in Annex B3.1 of Book 2 [1]. Thus, the value of the hash algorithm indicator is set to 01h.

- *Field 3—Data Authentication Code (2 bytes):* This represents a code assigned by the issuer, which can be a part (the most significant 2 bytes, for example) of a cryptogram, and which is unique for each card. This cryptogram can be a MAC computed by the issuer on the PAN associated with the card. The MAC is computed with a key diversified for each card from a unique master key of the issuer assigned for the data authentication codes calculation. When receiving this data element in an authorization request sent on-line or even in a payment capture message during the clearing, the issuer can check the correctness of the code. Assuming that the terminal did not find out this data element from the execution of another EMV™ transaction with the same card, the issuer increases its confidence that the terminal indeed verified the Signed Static Application Data in order to obtain the value of this code. Otherwise, a terminal, which is not able to check an RSA signature, could falsely claim that it performed the off-line static data authentication when in fact it did not do it.

- *Field 4—Pad Pattern:* This contains a number of $N_I - 26$ bytes of value BBh, where N_I is the number of bytes of the modulus n_I.

5.9   Verifying the Signed Static Application Data

The following steps describe the procedure followed by an EMV™ terminal for verifying the Signed Static Application Data stored in an EMV™ card since its personalization.

- Step 1: Verify that the length of the Signed Static Application Data (tag 90) data object is N_I.

- Step 2: Apply the signature verification/recovery algorithm in Appendix F, Section F.3.2 (case 2), where S is the Signed Static Application Data, $n_s = n_I$ and $e_s = e_I$. The length N of the modulus is N_I.

   The data that is recovered X is parsed as $X = B \parallel M_R \parallel H \parallel E$. The following processing is performed on these items:

1. Check that E (last byte of X), which is the recovered data trailer, equals BCh.

2. Check that B (first byte of X), which is the recovered data header, equals 6Ah.

3. Consider the M_R as the next $N_I - 22$ bytes after B. Parse M_R according to the four fields identified in Section 5.8.3.

4. Check that the signed data format read in field 1 of M_R is 03h.

5. Set up the value of the message M' to the value represented by the Static Data to Be Authenticated byte string, as currently computed in Section 5.8.2.

6. Create the message M, representing the static application data to be signed by the issuer, as the concatenation from left to right of the recovered part M_R and of the computed part M' (i.e., $M = M_R \parallel M'$).

7. Read the hash algorithm indicator from field 2 of M_R. Note that at the moment this value is 01h, corresponding to the SHA-1 algorithm, the only approved hash algorithm in the *EMV 2000* specifications (see Annex B3.1 in Book 2 [1]).

8. Use the indicated hash algorithm to compute the hash code h of M.

9. Check that h equals the hash result H, which represents the last 20 bytes in X before E.

If any of the verifications mentioned above failed, the verification of the Signed Static Application Data fails. The terminal rejects the authenticity of the financial data stored in the EMV™ card.

References

[1]   EMVCo, *EMV 2000 Integrated Circuit Card Specification for Payment Systems, BOOK 2—Security and Key Management*, Version 4.0, December 2000.

[2]   EMVCo, *EMV 2000 Integrated Circuit Card Specification for Payment Systems, BOOK 3—Application Specification*, Version 4.0, December 2000.

Debit and Credit with EMV™

The goal of this chapter is to offer a tutorial presentation on the transaction profile of the EMV™ debit and credit payment application. This presentation should allow someone who has no time to read the entire specification to more easily understand the EMV™ payment method. It should be regarded as accompanying material that helps the reader get accustomed with this payment technology as quickly as possible. The chapter *does not aim to replace the specifications*, which should always be kept as the ultimate reference for any details. The presentation emphasizes the analysis of the protocol between the ICC and the terminal, rather than discussing the card and the terminal separately.

The remainder of the chapter is organized as follows. In Section 6.1 we give a high level description of the transaction flow for EMV™ debit/credit payment applications. Starting with Section 6.2, we describe in considerable detail the messages exchanged between the chip card and the terminal during each stage, the processing performed by the card, and the processing performed by the terminal. Matching the EMV™ transaction stages to the chapter sections is as follows: initiate application processing (Section 6.2), read application data (Section 6.3), card authentication (Section 6.4), processing restrictions (Section 6.5), cardholder verification (Section 6.6), and terminal risk management (Section 6.7). Section 6.8, corresponding to the terminal action analysis stage, considers the possible actions proposed by the terminal concerning the finalization of an EMV™ transaction at the point of service. Section 6.9 analyzes the on-line processing and issuer authentication stage. Section 6.10 describes the prescriptions of the EMV™ standard concerning the possibility of updating financial data in the card application through the issuer script mechanism after the card enters its utilization life stage.

6.1 Overview of the EMV™ debit/credit transaction

In this section we give an overall picture of the interchange between the ICC and the terminal (Figure 6.1) and between the terminal and the IH (Figure 6.2) in order to complete the protocol of an EMV™ debit/credit payment application. The reader can compare the processing in these two diagrams with the processing performed for the magnetic stripe cards, as schematized in Figures 2.1 and 2.2 (see Section 2.1). It can be noticed that the complexity of the protocol between the card and the terminal increases in the case of an EMV™ transaction, while the processing performed by the payment network and back-office is comparable.

We refer now to Figure 6.1. All the processing described below is performed if the EMV™ debit/credit application is correctly selected during the application selection mechanism (see Section 4.4).

First, the terminal performs the initiate application processing function. The terminal informs the ICC about the business environment at the point of service, which helps the card tuning its strategy according to the conditions of the current transaction. The card provides a roadmap on its public AEF(s) in the AFL (see Section 3.4.2), and a profile of the transaction interchange in the AIP (see Section 3.4.3).

Based on the information contained in the AFL, the terminal is able to perform the read application data function. With this function all the public information contained in the AEF(s) attached to the EMV™ debit/credit card application is read by the terminal. After reading the content of the card, the terminal decides whether it has all the necessary data objects to continue the transaction.

Then, depending on the information contained in the AIP, the terminal decides whether off-line data authentication must be performed to enforce the card authentication security service. If the answer is positive, the terminal determines whether off-line SDA (see Appendix D, Section D.6.2) or off-line DDA (see Appendix D, Section D.7.2) is the cryptographic mechanism to be used for implementing this security service.

Furthermore, the terminal performs the processing restrictions function, which evaluates whether the ICC is entitled to ask for a certain financial service at the point of service (cash withdrawal, payment at a POS). If the

Figure 6.1
Interchange
between the
ICC and the
terminal for
an EMV™
debit/credit
transaction.

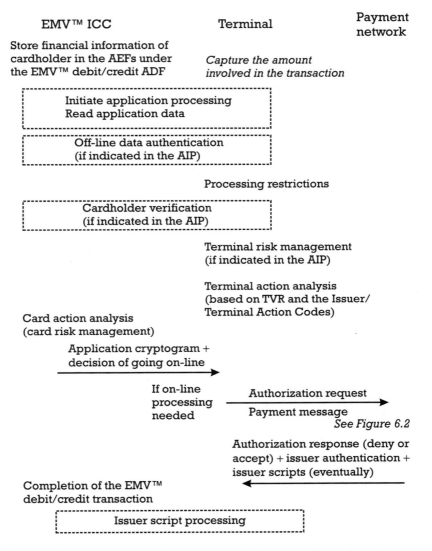

EMV™ ICC   Terminal   **Payment network**

Store financial information of
cardholder in the AEFs under   *Capture the amount*
the EMV™ debit/credit ADF   *involved in the transaction*

Initiate application processing
Read application data

Off-line data authentication
(if indicated in the AIP)

Processing restrictions

Cardholder verification
(if indicated in the AIP)

Terminal risk management
(if indicated in the AIP)

Terminal action analysis
(based on TVR and the Issuer/
Terminal Action Codes)

Card action analysis
(card risk management)

Application cryptogram +
decision of going on-line

If on-line   Authorization request
processing
needed   Payment message
                         See Figure 6.2

Authorization response (deny or
accept) + issuer authentication +
issuer scripts (eventually)

Completion of the EMV™
debit/credit transaction

Issuer script processing

card is eligible for the kind of service required in the allowed environment
(domestic or international), then the transaction interchange is continued
or otherwise is aborted.

The terminal performs the cardholder verification stage if the ICC has
proposed this function in the AIP. If this function is supported by the card
application, the terminal determines a cardholder verification method that
is mutually supported by the ICC and the terminal. Then, using this method,
the terminal and the card establish the link between the user of the card and
the legitimate cardholder.

The terminal also performs the terminal risk management function. This function allows the terminal to establish (from the point of view of the acquirer) whether the amount involved in the transaction is between some acceptable lower and upper floors. The terminal may also decide whether the transaction should be forwarded on-line following a large number of transactions that were completed off-line by the card.

At this stage of the processing, the terminal has a set of results from the completion of the previous functions. These results are accumulated in a 5-byte register called the Terminal Verification Results (TVR). The terminal compares this witness register against the Issuer Action Codes and the terminal action codes, which indicate the action to be performed by the terminal in case one stage in the transaction interchange did not complete as expected. Following this analysis, which is called the terminal action analysis, the terminal either denies or accepts the transaction. In the latter case, the terminal has the choice of completing the transaction locally (off-line) if no major risks are detected, or it can ask for the on-line assistance of the issuer. In either case, the card application is required to produce an application cryptogram, or even a digital signature, which will serve the dual purpose of authenticating on-line the card to the issuer or acting as a non-repudiation proof of the card's participation in a certain transaction.

The ICC performs its own risk management procedure, according to the security policy of the issuer, within the function called card action analysis. Following the card risk management, the ICC could agree with the type of transaction finalization proposed by the terminal or it could ask for another type of finalization. For example, instead of accepting the off-line completion of the transaction, the card may ask the terminal to perform an on-line authorization request to the issuer. After performing the card action analysis, the decision about the off-line or on-line completion of the EMV™ debit/credit transaction is taken.

In case the terminal must contact the issuer on-line, the payment network has to perform its part of processing, as schematized in Figure 6.2.

The processing is similar to that performed in the case of magnetic stripe cards, with the observation that the payment message sent to the acquirer contains the supplementary information gathered by the terminal from the card during the processing explained in Figure 6.1. After receiving this information, the issuer can better assess whether the card is genuine or not, since the Application Cryptogram produced by the card is "fresh" for every new transaction. The authorization response that is sent back by the IH allows the terminal and the ICC either to deny or to accept the transaction, according to the indication transmitted by the issuer. To this end, the issuer

Figure 6.2
Payment
network
processing of
an EMV™
debit/credit
transaction.

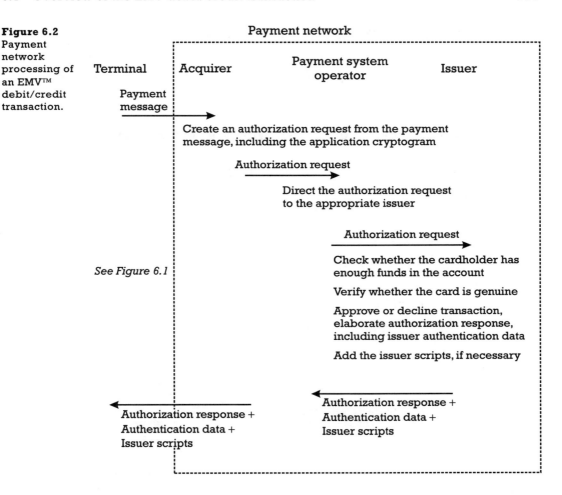

must authenticate itself to the ICC, such that the ICC trusts that the finalization decision for the current EMV™ debit/credit transaction comes from the genuine IH.

It is important to note that the authorization response may also contain a sequence of commands to be transmitted by the terminal to the card, which were requested by the issuer. This is the issuer script processing function, through which the issuer can update the card application's parameters in the ICC during its lifetime, after the personalization stage is completed. In order to perform the issuer script processing, the authentication of the issuer must have been successful, such that the ICC can trust that the genuine issuer sends this sequence of commands through the terminal at the point of service.

6.2   Initiate application processing

After the terminal has completed the final selection of the EMV™ application in the card, it initiates the EMV™ transaction flow, during the initiate application processing stage (see Figure 6.3).

6.2.1   TVR and TSI—two witnesses of terminal processing

First, the terminal resets (bit set on 0) all the bits in the two status registers kept by the terminal—namely, the TVR (see Section 6.1) and the Transaction Status Information (TSI). This operation marks up the initialization of the EMV™ debit/credit transaction in the terminal.

The TVR is a register encoded on 5 bytes, as detailed in Annex C.5 in Book 3 [1]. Each byte of the TVR witnesses the results of the processing performed by the terminal during one of the following stages of the EMV™ debit/credit transaction:

- Off-line data authentication (byte 1);

- Processing restrictions (byte 2);

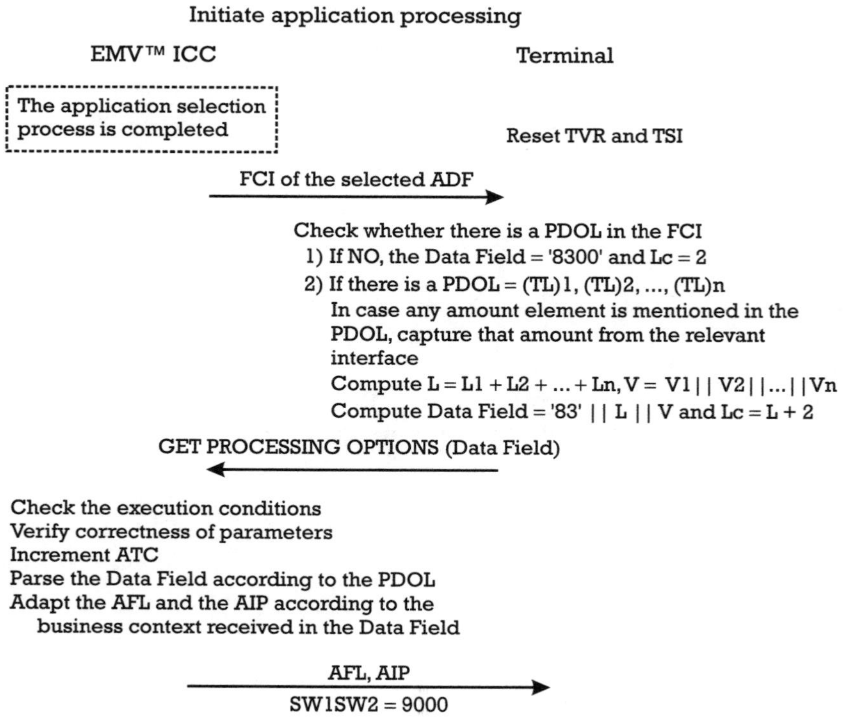

Figure 6.3
Initiate
application
processing.

Initiate application processing

EMV™ ICC   Terminal

```
---------------------------------
: The application selection      :
: process is completed           :        Reset TVR and TSI
---------------------------------
```

FCI of the selected ADF
————————————————————▶

Check whether there is a PDOL in the FCI
1) If NO, the Data Field = '8300' and Lc = 2
2) If there is a PDOL = (TL)1, (TL)2, ..., (TL)n
   In case any amount element is mentioned in the
   PDOL, capture that amount from the relevant
   interface
   Compute $L = L1 + L2 + ... + Ln, V = V1||V2||...||Vn$
   Compute Data Field = '83' || L || V and Lc = L + 2

GET PROCESSING OPTIONS (Data Field)
◀————————————————————

Check the execution conditions
Verify correctness of parameters
Increment ATC
Parse the Data Field according to the PDOL
Adapt the AFL and the AIP according to the
   business context received in the Data Field

AFL, AIP
————————————————————▶
SW1SW2 = 9000

> ⟩ Cardholder verification (byte 3);

> ⟩ Terminal risk management (byte 4);

> ⟩ Issuer authentication/issuer scripts processing (byte 5).

The TSI is encoded on 2 bytes, as detailed in Annex C.6 in Book 3 [1]. At the moment only 6 bits in the first byte of the TSI are used, while the rest are reserved for future use (RFU). Each of these 6 bits witnesses whether the terminal performed (bit positioned on 1) or did not perform (bit positioned on 0) any of the following stages of the EMV™ debit/credit transaction:

> ⟩ Bit 8: Off-line data authentication;

> ⟩ Bit 7: Cardholder verification;

> ⟩ Bit 6: Issuer authentication;

> ⟩ Bit 4: Terminal risk management;

> ⟩ Bit 3: Issuer script processing.

Bit 6 of the TSI witnesses whether the card performed the card risk management or not.

6.2.2 **PDOL and** GET PROCESSING OPTIONS

The terminal informs the ICC that the processing of a new EMV™ transaction begins with a GET PROCESSING OPTIONS command. The C-APDU of this command is summarized in Table 6.1 (according to Table I-17 in Book 3 [1]).

Table 6.1
C-APDU of the GET PROCESSING OPTIONS

Code	Value
CLA	*80* (proprietary to the EMV™ specification)
INS	*A8*
P1	*00* (all other values are RFU)
P2	*00* (all other values are RFU)
Lc	*Variable* (the length of the data field, encoded as a simple TLV)
Data	*Tag '83'* ‖ *Length* ‖ *Byte String* (containing the concatenation of the value fields of the data objects indicated by the card in the PDOL)
Le	*00*

The byte string contains the concatenation of the value fields of those data objects in the terminal that were indicated by the card application in the PDOL. This object is encoded with the tag 9F38 and is optional. The terminal obtains the PDOL, when it is personalized in the card application, from the FCI of the ADF hosting the selected EMV™ debit/credit card application (see Section 4.3.1).

> ‣ When the PDOL is not included in the FCI, the card will always initiate the processing of the EMV™ card application in a standard way, without considering the business environment existent at the point of service. Correspondingly, the response of the card to the GET PROCESSING OPTIONS command will be always the same. In this case the data field of the command will include the data object with tag 83 and the length equal to zero (see Figure 6.3).

> ‣ When the PDOL is included in the FCI it contains the list of identifiers (tag, length) of some data objects, which the card needs from the terminal in order to appropriately adapt its response to the GET PROCESSING OPTIONS command. These data objects could be those describing the business environment at the point of service like the Terminal Type (tag 9F35), Terminal Capabilities (9F33), Terminal Country Code (9F1A), or the Merchant Category Code (9F15). The data field of the command will include the data object with tag 83 and the length equal to the total length of the byte string.

The issuer decides upon the content of the PDOL, which is stored in the card since the personalization stage, as well as upon the processing performed by the card on the corresponding objects received from the terminal.

6.2.3 AIP and AFL

In the case of a successful processing of the C-APDU, the card application is initialized for a new EMV™ debit/credit transaction. Thus, the content of the Application Transaction Counter (ATC) is incremented, and the content of both the AIP and the AFL is adapted according to the business environment at the point of service. The ATC is initially zero, when the card is new, and is incremented by each and every new transaction performed by the card application. The card application returns to the terminal a response R-APDU.

The R-APDU returned by the card to the GET PROCESSING OPTIONS command includes, beside the status words SW1SW2 = 9000, two data objects: the AIP and the AFL. The meaning and content of these two data objects are described below.

The AIP (tag 82) consists of 2 bytes, of which the second byte is RFU, while the first byte encodes the stages of the EMV™ debit/credit transaction flow and the corresponding application functions that are actually supported by the card. The meaning of the bits in the first byte is presented in Table 6.2 (according to Annex C.1 in Book 3 [1]).

The AFL (tag 94) gives the table of contents of the publicly available information provided by the card application. It identifies the AEF(s) and their corresponding records to be used by the terminal for the processing of an EMV™ debit/credit transaction. The terminal can only read the AEF(s) indicated in the AFL.

The AFL is a list of AEF(s) file entries, each consisting of 4 bytes, the meaning of which was explained in Section 5.8.1.

- The first byte encodes the SFI of the AEF.

- The second byte encodes the first record number of the AEF.

- The third byte encodes the last record number of the AEF, which can be greater than or equal to the first record number.

- The fourth byte indicates the number of records in that AEF, starting from the first record number, that shall be considered by the terminal in the off-line data authentication processing.

Table 6.2
AIP, Byte 1

Bit 8	RFU
Bit 7	Indicates whether the off-line SDA is supported: 0—not supported; 1—supported (the same convention apply for the bits 6, 5, and 2 in the AIP)
Bit 6	Indicates whether the off-line DDA is supported
Bit 5	Indicates whether the cardholder verification is supported
Bit 4	Indicates whether the card requires the terminal to perform the terminal risk management stage (bit 4 = 1) or not (bit 4 = 0).
Bit 3	Indicates whether the card supports the issuer authentication through a separate EXTERNAL AUTHENTICATE command (bit 3 = 1) or through the second GENERATE AC command (bit 3 = 0).
Bit 2	Indicates whether the card supports combined off-line DDA and GENERATE AC.
Bit 1	RFU

After receiving the AIP, the terminal will be able to configure the appropriate sequence of commands to be sent to the card, according to the possibilities of the card. The AFL will allow the terminal to retrieve all the public information from the card (see Section 6.3) that is needed for the completion of the EMV™ debit/credit transaction.

6.3 Read application data

During the read application data stage, which immediately follows the initiate application processing, the terminal proceeds to the reading according to the AFL of the publicly available information from the card. While obtaining the data objects available in the card, the terminal checks whether all the mandatory data objects are present. The processing performed by both the card and the terminal during the read application data stage is schematized in Figure 6.4.

6.3.1 AFL processing

First, the terminal processes sequentially the entries of the AFL = $F1 \parallel F2 \parallel ... \parallel Fn$, according to the algorithm listed below.

- Step 1: For each 4-byte entry Fi in the AFL, $i = 1,..., n$, repeat the sequence of steps described below.

- Step 2: Set up the parameter P2, reference control parameter, of the READ RECORD (Section 4.3.2.1) command with the SFI value read from the first byte of Fi, representing the reference of the current AEF.

- Step 3: Check whether the Fi is correctly formatted according to the principles explained in Section 5.8.1. If there is an inconsistency, abort the processing of the current transaction.

  Set up the RecordCounter counter to the value of the first record number of the AEF, read in the second byte of the Fi. Set up LastRecordNumber to the value of the last record number of the AEF, obtained from the third byte of Fi.

- Step 4: Set up the parameter P1, record number, of the READ RECORD command to the value of the RecordCounter counter. Issue the command READ RECORD to the card.

Figure 6.4
Read
application
data.

Read application data

EMV™ ICC   Terminal

Store financial information of
cardholder in the AEFs under
the EMV™ debit/credit ADF

AFL available since the initiate
application processing, which must be
successfully completed before the
read application data

Read the content of the AEF(s)
according to the AFL = F1 || F2 ||...|| Fn

Repeatedly execute with i = 1, ..., n

P2 (reference control parameter) =
SFI read from the 1st byte of *Fi*

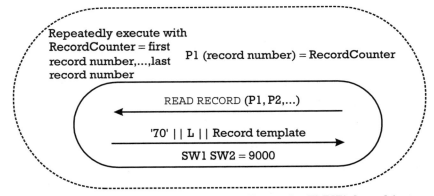

Repeatedly execute with
RecordCounter = first
record number,...,last   P1 (record number) = RecordCounter
record number

READ RECORD (P1, P2,...)

'70' || L || Record template

SW1 SW2 = 9000

Create the EMV™ data objects
heap and compile the static data
to be authenticated byte string
from the received Record
templates

▶ Step 5: If the R-APDU received from the card reports SW1SW2 = 9000,
parse the AEF Data Template with tag 70 received in the R-APDU.
Store all the data objects obtained from the card and check their consistency according to the rules explained in Section 6.3.2.

 If the consistency rules regarding the data obtained from the card
are not observed, the terminal will abort the processing.

▶ Step 6: If LastRecordNumber is greater than the RecordCounter, increment this counter and go back to step 4. Otherwise, continue with
Step 7.

▶ Step 7: If the current AEF file entry *Fi* is not the last one, consider the following AEF entry with index *i* + 1, and go back to step 2. Otherwise, the processing of the read application data is finished.

6.3.2 Consistency rules for the data objects

While dispatching each AEF Data Template received from the card, the terminal creates two data structures: the EMV™ data objects heap and the static data to be authenticated (see Section 5.8.1).

The EMV™ data objects heap is a data structure that stores all the primitive data objects dispatched from the AEF Data Templates. Every time a new primitive data object is added to the heap, the terminal observes the following rules:

▶ A data object with an unknown tag is not included in the heap.

▶ All known data objects, regardless of whether their presence in the card is mandatory or optional, are included in the heap.

▶ The presence of redundant data objects is not allowed in the heap. The terminal will abort the processing of the current transaction immediately if a collision of two data objects with the same tag is detected.

When the read application data processing ends, the terminal verifies the presence of the mandatory data objects in the EMV™ data objects heap. The presence of the following data objects is mandatory (according to Table II-2 in Book 3 [1]):

▶ Application Expiration Date (tag 5F24);

▶ Application Primary Account Number (PAN, tag 5A);

▶ Card risk management data object list 1 (CDOL1, tag 8C);

▶ Card risk management data object list 2 (CDOL2, tag 8D).

The terminal also verifies whether other data objects that are mandatory only in the context of a certain AIP are present in the card or not. These data objects are those needed for:

- Supporting cardholder verification (bit 5 = 1 in the first byte of AIP)—
  the terminal must verify the presence in the card of the Cardholder
  Verification Method (CVM) List (tag 8E).

- Supporting off-line SDA (bit 7 = 1 in the first byte of AIP)—Section 6.4.2
  gives the list of the data objects required by the terminal along with
  specific verification details. This checking is performed only after the
  terminal decides upon the execution of the SDA, as explained in
  Section 6.4.1.

- Supporting off-line DDA (bit 6 = 1 in the first byte of AIP)—
  Section 6.4.3 introduces the list of the data objects required by the
  terminal along with specific verification details. This checking is performed only after the terminal decides upon the execution of the
  DDA, as explained in Section 6.4.1.

Note that if the card supports off-line data authentication (either SDA or
DDA), the data objects CA public key index (tag 8F) and Issuer Public Key
Certificate (tag 90) should be located in the first record referred by the AFL.
This recommendation is only ruled out by a payment product restriction. It
is also a good practice for all the other data involved in the off-line data
authentication stage to be returned by the card as soon as possible. This
allows a multithread terminal to start the verification of the EMV™ public
key certificates (Section 5.7) and of the Signed Static Application Data (tag
93) certificate (Section 5.9) in parallel with other processing.

The static data to be authenticated (as denoted in the last row of Table 2
in Book 2 [2]) is a byte string that gathers the following data items:

- All the records of the AEF(s) that are referred to in the AFL, and
  which are involved in the process of off-line data authentication;

- Other data objects whose authenticity is required by the issuer but
  which are not stored in any of the records mentioned in the AFL.
  These data objects, if they exist, are listed in the Static Data Authentication Tag List (tag 90), which is an optional data object in the card.

Note that the Static Data to Be Authenticated byte string is formed by all
the EMV™ terminals that are not "on-line only" (see Section 6.4.1), according to the rules indicated in Section 5.8.2. This byte string is considered both
in the off-line SDA as well as in the off-line DDA. The static data to be
authenticated is computed while the concerned records are read from the

card, in order to allow multithread terminals to perform off-line data
authentication in parallel with other processing.

6.4   Off-line data authentication

The processing performed by the terminal in this stage determines whether
both the terminal and the card support the off-line data authentication
stage. In the affirmative case the terminal chooses what kind of off-line data
authentication will be performed (i.e., off-line SDA, off-line DDA, or off-line
DDA combined with Application Cryptogram generation).

- In case off-line SDA is performed, the terminal assesses the authenticity of the data personalized in the card by the issuer.

- When off-line DDA is performed, the terminal can determine whether
  the card is genuine or not and whether the data personalized in the card
  has altered since the personalization.

- When the off-line DDA is combined with the Application Cryptogram
  generation, the signature produced by the card can include transaction data, which should be already available in the terminal at this
  stage. This signature, which can be locally verified by the terminal,
  can be used as a non-repudiation proof in case the cardholder would
  later deny the transaction at the point of service. This signature also
  proves the authenticity of the data personalized in the card and the
  fact that the card is genuine.

6.4.1   Selection of the off-line authentication mechanism

A terminal that is "on-line only," which has the Terminal Type (tag 9F35)
with values of 11h, 21h, 14h, 24h, and 34h (according to Annex A.1 in
Book 4 [3]), will skip the off-line data authentication stage. In this case, the
EMV™ transaction is always directed on-line to the issuer, which performs
the card authentication.

A terminal that can process an EMV™ transaction off-line will determine
whether off-line data authentication is to be performed and what kind of
data authentication mechanism will be applied. To this end the terminal will
analyze the third byte (security capability) of the Terminal Capabilities (tag
9F33) data object in the terminal and the first byte of the AIP obtained from
the card (tag 82). Since only these 2 bytes are considered, the description of

the processing refers only to the bit number and the data object (either Terminal Capabilities or AIP), while the byte number is implicit.

Note that the terminal can perform the processing described in the algorithm presented below immediately after the execution of the GET PROCESSING OPTIONS, when the AIP is available.

Choice 1   If the card does not support the off-line data authentication stage (i.e., bit 7, bit 6, and bit 2 are set to 0 in the AIP), the terminal skips the off-line data authentication stage. In this case, bit 8 in byte 1 of the TVR, "Off-line data authentication was not performed," is set to 1. This bit is also set by any terminal that is "on-line only."

Choice 2   The terminal shall perform the combined dynamic data authentication/Application Cryptogram generation if the following conditions are simultaneously fulfilled:

- The card supports the combined dynamic data authentication/Application Cryptogram generation (AIP, bit 2 = 1);

- The terminal supports the combined dynamic data authentication/ Application Cryptogram generation (Terminal Capabilities, bit 5 = 1)

In case the combined dynamic data authentication/Application Cryptogram generation is chosen, the terminal verifies whether all the data objects required by the terminal for the off-line DDA, as explained in Section 6.4.3, are present. The terminal, however, does not perform the processing related to the off-line DDA itself. The terminal processes the other stages of the EMV™ transaction flow, which need to be completed before the terminal action analysis stage can be performed.

Choice 3   The terminal shall perform the off-line DDA if the following conditions are simultaneously fulfilled:

- The card supports off-line DDA (AIP, bit 6 = 1);

- The terminal supports the off-line DDA (Terminal Capabilities, bit 7 = 1);

- Either the card or the terminal (or both) does not support the combined dynamic data authentication/Application Cryptogram generation (i.e., AIP, bit 2 = 0; and/or Terminal Capabilities, bit 5 = 0).

In this case the terminal shall perform the off-line DDA processing as explained in Section 6.4.3.

Choice 4   The terminal shall perform the off-line SDA if the following conditions are simultaneously fulfilled:

- The card supports off-line SDA (AIP, bit 7 = 1);

- The terminal supports off-line SDA (Terminal Capabilities, bit 8 = 1);

- Either the card or the terminal (or both) does not support off-line DDA (AIP, bit 6 = 0; and/or Terminal Capabilities, bit 7 = 0);

- Either the card or the terminal (or both) does not support combined dynamic data authentication/Application Cryptogram generation (AIP, bit 2 = 0; and/or Terminal Capabilities, bit 5 = 0).

In this case the terminal shall perform the off-line SDA processing as explained in Section 6.4.2.

6.4.2   Off-line SDA

The off-line SDA requires two separate stages (as shown in Figure 6.5):

1. During the personalization stage of the card, the issuer computes the Signed Static Application Data certificate, according to the algorithm described in Section 5.8.3. Note that using the terminology adopted in Appendix D, Section D.6.2, the Signed Static Application Data certificate corresponds to the static authenticator *Static_Auth*. This certificate is a signature created with the issuer private key (N_I, d_I) on the static data to be authenticated (referred to as the *financial_data* in Appendix D, Section D.6.2) in the card, which is formed according to Section 5.8.2. The issuer first proves knowledge of the appropriate credentials for obtaining writing rights in the card. Then, the issuer loads into the card the signed static application data, which is stored as the data object with tag 93, together with the certificate of the CA on the issuer public key (N_I, e_I), referred to as the issuer public key certificate.

2. During the utilization stage, when the off-line SDA is required by the EMV™ transaction profile, the card submits to the terminal the data objects it needs to first verify the authenticity of the issuer public key.

Figure 6.5
Overview of
the off-line
SDA.

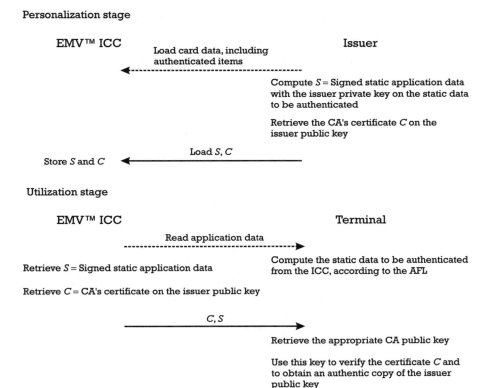

Personalization stage

EMV™ ICC   Issuer

Load card data, including
authenticated items

Compute S = Signed static application data
with the issuer private key on the static data
to be authenticated

Retrieve the CA's certificate C on the
issuer public key

Load S, C

Store S and C

Utilization stage

EMV™ ICC   Terminal

Read application data

Compute the static data to be authenticated
from the ICC, according to the AFL

Retrieve S = Signed static application data

Retrieve C = CA's certificate on the issuer public key

C, S

Retrieve the appropriate CA public key

Use this key to verify the certificate C and
to obtain an authentic copy of the issuer
public key

Use the issuer public key to verify S and to
assess that data in the card did not change
since personalization

If the authenticity of this key verifies correctly, the terminal can use
it to check the authenticity of the signed static application data. If the
verification passes, the terminal agrees on the authenticity of the
financial data stored in the card.

The processing needed to verify the authenticity of the data in the card is
carried out completely by the terminal, while the card only stores those data
objects needed for completing this verification.

Stage 1   The terminal verifies the existence of the following objects in the
EMV™ data objects heap:

‣ Certification Authority Public Key Index (tag 8F);

‣ Issuer Public Key Certificate (tag 90);

- Issuer Public Key Remainder (tag 92), which is present only in certain conditions (see Section 5.4);

- Issuer Public Key Exponent (tag 9F32);

- Signed Static Application Data (tag 93).

If any of the objects mentioned above are not present in the card (except for tag 92), set up bit 6, "ICC data missing," of byte 1 of the TVR and consider that SDA has failed.

Stage 2   The terminal constructs the Static Data to Be Authenticated byte string. Note that for a multithread terminal this processing can be started since the read application data is performed, in parallel with the AFL processing, as described in Section 5.8.2. To this end, the terminal first considers the records indicated for authentication of all the AEF(s) registered in the AFL. Second, after all the records are read from the card and the EMV™ data objects heap is constructed, the terminal considers the data objects indicated in the Static Data Authentication Tag List to be concatenated at the end of the Static Data to Be Authenticated byte string.

If the terminal fails to process any of the records considered for authentication in the AFL, static data authentication has failed.

Stage 3   The terminal verifies the authenticity of the Issuer Public Key Certificate and recovers the issuer public key (n_I, e_I), following the algorithm presented in Section 5.7.1.

The terminal uses the Certification Authority Public Key Index (tag 8F) together with the RID to retrieve the CA public key (n_{CA}, e_{CA}) from the appropriate record of the terminal database of CA public keys (see Table 5.2 in Section 5.5). The RID is obtained from the AID (DF Name, tag 84) returned in the FCI of the currently selected ADF, which contains the EMV™ debit/credit application. The length of the modulus n_{CA} is N_{CA}.

If the verification of the Issuer Public Key Certificate does not pass, then the SDA has failed.

If the terminal manages a revocation list associated with the CA, which contains all the compromised issuer public key certificates, the terminal checks that the certificate serial number corresponding to the current Issuer Public Key Certificate is not blacklisted in this revocation list. If the certificate is blacklisted then the terminal sets up bit 5, "Card appears on terminal exception file," of byte 1 of the TVR register. In this case also, it is considered that the SDA has failed.

Stage 4   The terminal verifies the authenticity of the data objects personalized in the card by checking the authenticity of the Signed Static Application Data certificate received from the card with the authentic copy of the issuer public key (n_i, e_i) obtained in stage 3. This verification is performed according to the algorithm presented in Section 5.9.

If the verification of the Signed Static Application Data certificate fails, the SDA has failed.

Otherwise, the SDA processing is considered successful. The terminal stores the data authentication code, representing field 3 in the recovered part M_R of the static application data to be signed by the issuer (see Section 5.8.3), in the value field of a data object with tag 9F45 and length equal to 2 bytes.

If the terminal decides that SDA has failed in any of the four stages described above, the rest of the processing involved in the SDA stage from that point on is skipped.

‣ The terminal will set bit 8, "Off-line data authentication was performed," in byte 1 of the TSI register.

‣ The terminal will also set bit 7, "Off-line static data authentication failed," in byte 1 of the TVR register.

6.4.3 Off-line DDA

The off-line DDA guarantees the authenticity of the data personalized in the card by the issuer, as well as that of the card itself. This is possible because the card has processing power and can actively compute an asymmetric cryptogram on an Unpredictable Number coming from the terminal. A genuine card is able to produce a correct cryptogram for each new unpredictable number. When the terminal assesses off-line the correctness of this cryptogram, it accepts that the card is genuine. This is true with overwhelming probability, unless a powerful attacker has broken the tamper resistance of the chip to read the private key of the card or has solved the "heavy" mathematical problem on which relies the computation of the asymmetric cryptogram. This is a big step forward when compared with cards implemented with magnetic stripe or SDA-only EMV™ cards. The asymmetric cryptogram computed by the card consists of a digital signature produced on data received from the terminal with the ICC private key. In order to verify this signature, the terminal has to obtain an authentic copy of the corresponding ICC public key, which is recovered traversing the EMV™ certification chain CA/issuer/ICC public key (see Figure 5.1 in Section 5.5). It is important to note that the terminal has similar requirements in terms of computation power as in the case of off-line SDA. However, the card has to be able to compute an RSA operation, which requires the presence of a cryptographic coprocessor in the architecture of the card (see Section 3.4.4 and Appendix D, Section D.1.2). Correspondingly, the price of the card increases. The actual ratio between the price of an EMV™ chip card with and without cryptographic coprocessor may vary in the range 1.25 of to 2. This ratio depends on whether a card producer offers "on-the-shelf" EMV™ cards with coprocessors or rather the developing price for this type of card is shared with the issuer. In the latter case, the bigger the number of ordered cards, the lower the aforementioned ratio. We can expect that this ratio will decrease over the next 5 years, proportionally with the increase of the chip's CPU computation power. At the limit, one can expect that this ratio will become 1, when the CPU will incorporate numerical units for long arithmetic.

This section will first outline the DDA mechanism implemented with digital signatures. Second, the processing performed by the terminal to verify the authenticity of the ICC public key based on traversing the EMV™ certification chain consisting of the Issuer Public Key Certificate and the ICC Public Key Certificate is described. Next, the processing performed by the card for computing the digital signature on the data objects sent by the terminal is presented. Finally, how the terminal assesses the correctness of the digital signature generated by the card is explained.

6.4.3.1 Overview of the DDA

As can be seen in Figure 6.6, the off-line DDA requires two separate stages:

1.   During the personalization stage the issuer loads the Issuer Public Key Certificate in the card. The issuer also generates the pair ICC private key/ICC public key and produces the ICC Public Key Certificate with the issuer private key (Section 5.6). The issuer loads in the card both the ICC private key (using a confidential channel) and the ICC Public Key Certificate.

     Note that the card could generate the pair ICC private key/ICC public key by itself and forward only the ICC public key for certification to the issuer's personalization terminal (using an authentic channel). In this case, the issuer will compute only the ICC Public Key Certificate for downloading it in the card. The generation of the RSA key pairs by the chip card itself would better enforce the non-repudiation security service during an EMV™ transaction, with no supplementary costs related to the chip card.

Figure 6.6
Overview of
the off-line
DDA.

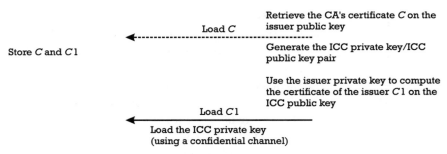

Personalization stage

EMV™ ICC   Issuer

Retrieve the CA's certificate C on the
Load C issuer public key

Store C and $C1$ Generate the ICC private key/ICC
public key pair

Use the issuer private key to compute
the certificate of the issuer $C1$ on the
ICC public key

Load $C1$

Load the ICC private key
(using a confidential channel)

Store the ICC private key in an internal secret file

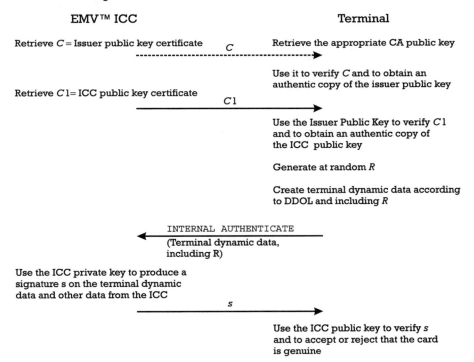

Utilization stage

EMV™ ICC   Terminal

Retrieve C = Issuer public key certificate C Retrieve the appropriate CA public key

Use it to verify C and to obtain an
authentic copy of the issuer public key

Retrieve $C1$= ICC public key certificate $C1$

Use the Issuer Public Key to verify $C1$
and to obtain an authentic copy of
the ICC public key

Generate at random R

Create terminal dynamic data according
to DDOL and including R

INTERNAL AUTHENTICATE
(Terminal dynamic data,
including R)

Use the ICC private key to produce a
signature s on the terminal dynamic
data and other data from the ICC s

Use the ICC public key to verify s
and to accept or reject that the card
is genuine

2.   During the utilization stage the card supplies both the Issuer Public
Key Certificate and the ICC Public Key Certificate to the terminal.
The terminal verifies the authenticity of the Issuer Public Key Cer-
tificate with the corresponding CA public key and retrieves an

authentic copy of the issuer public key (Section 5.7.1). Using this copy, the terminal can verify the authenticity of the ICC Public Key Certificate and the authenticity of the data personalized in the card by the issuer. If all the verifications are successful, the terminal recovers an authentic copy of the ICC public key (Section 5.7.2). The terminal asks the card with an INTERNAL AUTHENTICATE command to produce a digital signature on a byte string constructed from data objects in the terminal. This byte string is formatted according to the indications of the Dynamic Data Authentication Data Object List (DDOL) provided by the card. For implementing the DDA, the DDOL must include the Unpredictable Number (tag 9F37) data object, which is a random number generated by the terminal for each new EMV™ session. After receiving the INTERNAL AUTHENTICATE command with the byte string from the terminal, the card produces a digital signature on this byte string as well as on other data from the card. This signature is referred to in the card as the Signed Dynamic Application Data object with tag 9F4B. The card sends this signature back to the terminal, which will verify it with the authentic copy of the ICC public key. If the verification passes, the terminal accepts that the card is genuine.

6.4.3.2 Verifying the authenticity of the card data and ICC public key

First, the terminal verifies the authenticity of the data personalized in the card and of the ICC public key traversing the EMV™ certification chain composed of the Issuer Public Key Certificate and the ICC Public Key Certificate. This processing is carried out completely by the terminal, while the card only conveys those data objects needed for completing this verification.

Stage 1   The terminal verifies the existence of the following objects in the EMV™ data objects heap:

- All the data objects needed by the terminal for performing the off-line SDA (stage 1 in Section 6.4.2), except for the Signed Static Application Data (tag 93);

- ICC Public Key Certificate (tag 9F46);

- ICC Public Key Remainder (tag 9F48), which is present only in certain conditions (Section 5.4);

- ICC Public Key Exponent (tag 9F47).

If any of the objects mentioned above are not present in the card (except for tag 9F48 and tag 9F49), set up bit 6, "ICC data missing," in byte 1 of the TVR and consider that DDA has failed.

Note that if the terminal does not identify the DDOL (tag gF49) in the EMV™ data objects heap, the terminal should use a default DDOL personalized in the EMV™ terminal application by the acquirer. If the default DDOL is also missing, the DDA has failed.

Stage 2   The terminal constructs the static data to be authenticated byte string as it was described in Section 5.8.2. If the static authentication tag list contains any tags other than those accepted (note that there are some differences between the *EMV '96* and the *EMV 2000* specifications), DDA has failed.

Stage 3   The terminal verifies the authenticity of the Issuer Public Key Certificate (tag 90) and recovers the issuer public key (n_I, e_I) according to the algorithm described in Section 5.7.1.

Stage 4   The terminal verifies the authenticity of the ICC Public Key Certificate (tag 9F46) received from the card with the authentic copy of the issuer public key, (n_I, e_I), which was obtained in stage 3. N_I denotes the length of the modulus n_I.

If any of the verifications mentioned above failed, DDA has failed.

The terminal stores the ICC public key (n_{IC}, e_{IC}) to subsequently verify the Signed Dynamic Application Data produced by the card. The terminal proceeds with the next stage.

Stage 5   The terminal initiates the computation of the Signed Dynamic Application Data in the card with an INTERNAL AUTHENTICATE command.

▸ Step 1: The terminal generates a random number of 4 bytes, the value of which is assigned to the Unpredictable Number data object (tag 9F37). Its role is to guarantee the uniqueness of the digital signature computed by the card, countering potential replay attacks.

▸ Step 2: The terminal creates the terminal dynamic data byte string, concatenating the value fields of all the data objects whose tag-length identifiers are listed in the DDOL. The DDOL should contain at least the tag-length identifier of the unpredictable number, but may also include the identifiers of other data objects from the terminal like the Terminal Identification (tag 9F1C), Terminal Country Code (tag 9F1A), and (tag 9A).

> ‣ If the DDOL received from the card does not have the identifier of the Unpredictable Number among its identifiers, the DDA has failed.

> ‣ If the card did not send the DDOL, the terminal must use the default DDOL. The terminal must check that the tag-length identifier of the Unpredictable Number is among the items listed in the default DDOL. If this is not the case, the DDA has failed.

‣ Step 3: The terminal creates the C-APDU corresponding to the INTERNAL AUTHENTICATE command. This C-APDU is summarized in Table 6.3 (according to Table I-19 in Book 3 [1]).

The control parameter P1 encodes the reference of the algorithm for computing the signed dynamic application data, from the terminal's viewpoint. The actual value accepted for P1 is 00, which means that no information on the algorithm is given through P1. At present, the algorithm used by the card for generating the Signed Dynamic Application Data is the RSA algorithm. After formatting the C-APDU of the INTERNAL AUTHENTICATE command, the terminal sends it to the card.

Note that if the combined dynamic data authentication/Application Cryptogram generation is chosen for implementing the off-line data authentication service (choice 2 in Section 6.4.1), all the processing described above is performed except for step 3 in stage 5. In this case, the terminal does not send a separate INTERNAL AUTHENTICATE command to the card.

6.4.3.3 Signature generation by the ICC

Before computing the signature, the card checks that the parameters P1 and P2 of the INTERNAL AUTHENTICATE command are equal to 00. It then

Table 6.3
The C-APDU Corresponding to INTERNAL AUTHENTICATE

Code	Value
CLA	*00* (interindustry command)
INS	*88*
P1	00
P2	*00*
Lc	*Variable* (the length of the concatenated value fields of the data objects listed in the DDOL or default DDOL)
Data	Terminal dynamic data—this is the byte string containing the concatenation of the value fields of the data objects indicated by the card in the DDOL
Le	*00*

checks that the issuer did not previously block the currently selected application through a post-script command. The card also checks that in the current session the execution of the GET PROCESSING OPTIONS command was successfully performed and no other INTERNAL AUTHENTICATE C-APDU was sent to the card. Otherwise the card returns SW1SW2 = 6985, "Command not allowed; conditions of use not satisfied" (see Table I-4 in Book 3 [1]).

Then the card computes the ICC Dynamic Number (tag 9F4C). This is a time-variant parameter generated by the card. When receiving this parameter in an authorization request sent on-line or even in a payment capture message during the clearing, the issuer can check the freshness of this parameter. Thus, the issuer verifies whether the terminal performed the DDA stage or not, when this is required by the EMV™ transaction profile. The parameter can be a sequence number incremented each time the INTERNAL AUTHENTICATE command is sent to the card, for which the issuer keeps a synchronous counter in the IH. The parameter can also be a symmetric cryptogram, which is unique for each card and for each transaction. This cryptogram can be a MAC computed by the card on the ATC, which is incremented at every transaction. This MAC is computed with a unique key diversified for each card from a unique master key of the issuer assigned for the purpose of computing the ICC Dynamic Number.

Note that the issuer could have required that the terminal send the entire Signed Dynamic Application Data to the IH for verification. But this could overload the authorization request message with N_{IC} bytes, which can amount to 248 bytes instead of the 3 to 9 bytes needed by the ICC Dynamic Number. When non-repudiation is not a security feature required by the issuer, the use of the ICC Dynamic Number is more economical.

The ICC applies the digital signature scheme giving message recovery implemented with the RSA algorithm, as described in Appendix F, Section F.3.1 (case 2). This algorithm is applied on the message $M = M_R \| M'$ with the RSA parameters $n_s = n_{IC}$ and $d_s = d_{IC}$ to obtain a signature S, which is referred to as the signed dynamic application data, stored in the card with the tag 9F4B.

The message $M = M_R \| M'$ is referred to as the dynamic application data to be signed (see Table 11 in Book 2 [2]).

> • The part M' consists of the terminal dynamic data byte string, as received in the INTERNAL AUTHENTICATE command from the terminal.

‣ The part M_R consists of five fields:

1. Field 1—signed data format (1 byte): it has the fix value 05h.

2. Field 2—hash algorithm indicator (1 byte): it identifies the hash algorithm used to produce the hash code H. This value is used in step 1 of the algorithm described in Appendix F, Section F.3.1 (case 2). At the moment, SHA-1 is the hash algorithm recommended by the *EMV™2000* specifications in Annex B3.1 of Book 2 [2]. Thus, the value of the hash algorithm indicator is set to 01h.

3. Field 3—ICC dynamic data length (1 byte): It specifies the byte-length L_{DD} of the ICC dynamic data in field 4. This parameter has to satisfy the relation $0 \le L_{DD} \le N_{IC} - 25$.

4. Field 4—ICC dynamic data (L_{DD} bytes): It consists of L_{DD} bytes, of which the leftmost byte encodes the length of the ICC Dynamic Number (between 2 and 8 bytes), and the following 2 to 8 bytes represent the ICC Dynamic Number. The rest of the ICC dynamic data, until L_{DD} bytes, can be used by each issuer in a proprietary manner.

5. Field 5—pad pattern: It contains a number of $N_{IC} - L_{DD} - 25$ bytes of value BBh.

After the successful completion of this computation, the card sets up an internal flag to mark that DDA was completed. The card can elaborate the R-APDU to be returned to the terminal in two formats:

1. Response Message Template Format 1: This is a primitive data object with tag 80 whose length is N_{IC}. The value field of this data object contains *only* the value field of the signed dynamic authentication data.

2. Response Message Template Format 2: This is a constructed data object with tag 77, which may include several data objects encoded in a BER-TLV format, but which will always contain the signed dynamic authentication data. The other data objects, when they are included, are proprietary to each issuer.

The R-APDU includes at the rightmost position the status words SW1SW2 = 9000.

6.4.3.4   Verifying the signed dynamic authentication data in the terminal

After receiving the signed dynamic authentication data in the R-APDU returned by the card to the INTERNAL AUTHENTICATE command, the terminal verifies its authenticity.

- Step 1: Verify that the length of the Signed Dynamic Application Data is N_{IC}.

- Step 2: Apply the signature verification/recovery algorithm in Appendix F, Section F.3.2 (case 2), where S is the signed dynamic application data, $n_s = n_{IC}$, and $e_s = e_{IC}$. The length N of the modulus is N_{IC}.

   The data that is recovered X is parsed as $X = B \parallel M_R \parallel H \parallel E$. The following processing is performed on these items:

   1. Check that E (last byte of X), which is the recovered data trailer, equals BCh.

   2. Check that B (first byte of X), which is the recovered data header, equals 6Ah.

   3. Consider M_R as the next $N_{IC} - 22$ bytes after B. Parse M_R according to the five fields identified in Section 6.4.3.4.

   4. Check that the signed data format read in field 1 of M_R is 05h.

   5. Set up the value of the message M' to the value represented by the terminal dynamic data. This is the byte string containing the concatenation of the value fields of the data objects indicated by the card in the DDOL. This byte string was already computed for including it in the data field of the INTERNAL AUTHENTICATE C-APDU (Section 6.4.3.2, stage 5).

   6. Create the message M, representing the dynamic application data to be signed (see Table 11 in Book 2 [2]), as the concatenation from left to right of the recovered part M_R and of the computed part M' (i.e., $M = M_R \parallel M'$).

   7. Read the hash algorithm indicator from field 2 of M_R. Note that at the moment this value is 01h, corresponding to the SHA-1 algorithm, the only approved hash algorithm in the *EMV 2000* specifications (see Annex B3.1 in Book 2 [2]).

   8. Use the indicated hash algorithm to compute the hash code h of M.

9.   Check that *h* equals the hash result *H*, which represents the last 20 bytes in *X* before *E*.

If any of the verifications mentioned above fail, DDA has failed.

If the terminal decides that DDA has failed in any of the stages and steps described above, the rest of the processing from that point on is skipped. The terminal sets bit 8, "Off-line data authentication was performed," in byte 1 of the TSI register. The terminal will also set bit 4, "Off-line dynamic data authentication failed," in byte 1 of the TVR register.

Otherwise, the DDA processing is considered successful. The terminal constructs the ICC Dynamic Number data object with tag 9F4C, the length field of which equals the first byte of field 4 (see Section 6.4.3.4). The subsequent bytes in field 4, which is indicated in the first byte of field 4, are saved as the value field of the data object with tag 9F4C.

6.5   Processing restrictions

The terminal carries out this stage by itself. The card is only a carrier of the information involved in the processing. The aim of the processing restrictions is to determine the degree of compatibility between the EMV™ debit/credit application in the card and in the terminal, and to make any necessary adjustments, including the rejection of the transaction. This stage can be performed any time after the completion of the read application data stage and before the completion of the terminal action analysis stage.

Three criteria are considered for judging the compatibility of the card application and the terminal application:

1.   Application Version Number;

2.   Application usage control;

3.   Application effective/expiration dates checking.

6.5.1   Application Version Number

The payment system assigns version numbers on 2 bytes to both the card application [in the Application Version Number (tag 9F08) data object stored in the card] and to the terminal application [in the Application Version Number (tag 9F09) data object stored in the terminal]. The encoding of these numbers is proprietary to the payment system.

The terminal establishes the compatibility of version numbers as follows:

‣ Search for the data object with tag 9F08 in the EMV™ data objects heap.

‣ If the object is not found, assume by default that the card and terminal application versions are compatible. Continue processing as indicated in Section 6.5.2.

‣ Otherwise, compare the value fields of the data objects with tag 9F08 and with tag 9F09.

  ‣ If these values are different, set to 1 the bit 8, "ICC and terminal have different versions," in byte 2 of the TVR.

  ‣ Continue processing as indicated in Section 6.5.2.

6.5.2 Application usage control

The issuer encodes the restrictions concerning the geographic usage and services allowed for the EMV™ card application in the Application Usage Control data object (tag 9F07). This data object is not mandatory to be personalized in the card. The meaning of the bits in the Application Usage Control is presented below:

‣ Bit 8 = 1, Byte 1: Valid for domestic cash transactions;

‣ Bit 7 = 1, Byte 1: Valid for international cash transactions;

‣ Bit 6 = 1, Byte 1: Valid for domestic goods;

‣ Bit 5 = 1, Byte 1: Valid for international goods;

‣ Bit 4 = 1, Byte 1: Valid for domestic services;

‣ Bit 3 = 1, Byte 1: Valid for international services;

‣ Bit 2 = 1, Byte 1: Valid at ATMs;

‣ Bit 1 = 1, Byte 1: Valid at terminals other than ATMs;

‣ Bit 8 = 1, Byte 2: Domestic cashback allowed;

‣ Bit 7 = 1, Byte 2: International cashback allowed;

‣ Bit 6 ÷ Bit 1, Byte 2: RFU.

A cashback transaction is a combination of a purchase transaction of goods or services and a cash transaction, for which the total amount that must be authorized with the issuer is the sum between the Amount, Authorized and the Amount, Other. The Amount, Authorized represents the amount due for the goods or services, while the Amount, Other refers to the amount of cash that the cardholder would like to withdraw directly from the store attendant.

To perform the verification of the geographical usage and service restrictions, the terminal needs the following data objects:

- Terminal Type (tag 9F35 in the terminal): This encodes in 1 byte the category of the terminal, which depends on three features:

  1. Environment: attended/unattended (by an operator at the point of service);

  2. Communication: on-line-only/off-line with on-line capability/ off-line-only;

  3. Operation control: financial institution/merchant/cardholder.

  Note that the encoding of the Terminal Type is provided in the Annex A1 of Book 4 [3].

- Additional Terminal Capabilities (tag 9F40 in the terminal): This encodes on 5 bytes the data input and output capabilities of the terminal (see Annex A3 in Book 4 [3]). The first 2 bytes of its value field indicate the Transaction Type capability, which indicates the transaction type a terminal can support: cash, goods, services, inquiry, transfer, payment, and administrative.

  Note that the two data objects described above are used to discriminate between ATM and non-ATM terminals, as follows:

  - A terminal is an ATM terminal if the value field of the Terminal Type is 14h, 15h, or 16h, and bit 8 ("Cash"), of byte 1 of the Additional Terminal Capabilities is set to 1 (i.e., the terminal has the cash disbursement capability).

  - Any other terminal that does not respect the aforementioned condition is not an ATM terminal.

▶ Transaction Type (tag 9C in the terminal): This indicates the type of financial transaction that is actually accepted by the terminal application. The first two digits of the processing code data element (i.e., cash transaction, purchase of goods, and purchase of services), according to ISO: 8583:1993 [4], represents the transaction type. The value field of this data objects is denoted V1 in the remainder of this section.

▶ Issuer Country Code (tag 5F28 in the card): This indicates on 2 bytes the country code of the issuer, according to the ISO 3166 [5]. The value field of this data object is denoted V2 in the remainder of this section.

▶ Terminal Country Code (tag 9F1A in the terminal): This indicates on 2 bytes the country code of the terminal, according to the ISO 3166 [5]. The value field of this data objects is denoted V3 in the remainder of this section.

▶ Amount, Other [tag 9F04 (binary format), tag 9F03 (numeric format) in the terminal]: This indicates a secondary amount associated with a purchase of goods or purchase of services transaction, representing a cashback amount.

The algorithm that performs the verification of the geographical usage and service restrictions is given below.

```
If Application Usage Control (AUC) is present in the EMV heap
    If Terminal Type = ATM Terminal
        Check that bit 2 ("Valid at ATMs") equals 1 in byte
        1 of the AUC.
    If Terminal Type ≠ ATM Terminal
        Check that bit 1 ("Valid at terminals other than
        ATMs") equals 1 in byte 1 of the AUC.
    If Issuer Country Code is present in the EMV heap
        If V1 = "Cash Transaction" (01 = Debits/Cash, 17-19
        = Debits/Cash advance with credit cards)
            If V2 = V3
                Check that bit 8 ("Valid for domestic cash
                transactions") equals 1 in byte 1 of the AUC.
            If V2 ≠ V3
                Check that bit 7 ("Valid for international
                cash transactions") equals 1 in byte 1 of the
                AUC.
        If V1 = "Purchase of Goods" (00 = Debits/Goods and
        Services)
```

```
If V2 = V3
    Check that bit 6 ("Valid for domestic goods")
    equals 1 in byte 1 of the AUC.
If V2 ≠ V3
    Check that bit 5 ("Valid for international
    goods") equals 1 in byte 1 of the AUC.
If V1 = "Purchase of services" (00 = Debits/Goods and
Services)
    If V2 = V3
        Check that bit 4 ("Valid for domestic
        services") equals 1 in byte 1 of the AUC.
    If V2 ≠ V3
        Check that bit 3 ("Valid for international
        services") equals 1 in byte 1 of the AUC.
If V1 = "Purchase of goods/services" (00 = Debits/
Goods and Services) and Amount, Other is present in
the EMV data objects heap
    If V2 = V3
        Check that bit 8 ("Domestic cashback allowed")
        equals 1 in byte 2 of the AUC.
    If V2 ≠ V3
        Check that bit 7 ("International cashback
        allowed") equals 1 in byte 2 of the AUC.
```

If any of the verifications specified above fail, set to 1 bit 5, "Requested service not allowed for card product," in byte 2 of the TVR. Continue processing as indicated in Section 6.5.3.

6.5.3   Application effective/expiration dates checking

If the terminal retrieves the Application Effective Date (tag 5F25) from the EMV™ heap, it checks whether the current date is greater than or equal to the application effective date. If not, the terminal sets to 1 bit 6, "Application not yet effective," in byte 2 of the TVR.

If the terminal retrieves the Application Expiration Date (tag 5F24) from the EMV™ heap, it checks whether the current date is less than or equal to the Application Expiration Date. If not, the terminal sets to 1 bit 7, "Expired application," in byte 2 of the TVR.

6.6   Cardholder verification

The cardholder verification stage allows the terminal to verify the link between the person at the point of service and the eligible cardholder to whom the application in the card was issued. This stage can be performed any time after the completion of the read application data stage and before finalizing the terminal action analysis stage.

6.6.1 Cardholder verification methods in EMV™

The EMV™ standard accepts several CVMs, which are discussed below. A method number on 6 bits, which is indicated in parentheses, is associated with each CVM, according to Annex C.3, in Book 3 [1].

- *No CVM required* (011111b): This method consists of accepting without proof that the person at the point of service is that to whom the card was issued. For example, at a point of service for paying a highway toll, an operator will capture the card data without requiring the card-holder verification. This is mainly for providing the convenience of the service and the fluency of the traffic in the conditions when the transaction amount is low.

- *Fail CVM processing* (000000b): The card uses this method to force a CVM failure in the terminal. This can lead the terminal to force an on-line connection to the issuer, which could further analyze the card status and apply exceptional risk management policies.

- *Signature (paper)* (011110b): This CVM, explained in Appendix D, Section D.5.1, can be applied for credit card products at a point of service that is attended by an operator. The method consists of comparing the signature produced by the card user on the sales slip against the witness signature of the cardholder written on the back side of the card. The EMV™ preserved this method, since in some countries the legislation requires a handwritten signature as a proof of the cardholder's participation in a transaction.

- *Enciphered PIN verified on-line* (000010b): This method is common for debit and credit card products used in unattended environments, when they are implemented with the magnetic stripe technology. The EMV™ also accepts this method for chip-based card products. The cardholder types his or her PIN in the terminal's PIN pad. The terminal encrypts it using a symmetric encryption mechanism. The IH receives this cryptogram, decrypts it in a secure module, which computes a PIN image control value that is compared against a witness value kept in the cardholder database, referred to as the PIN image stored value. Details of this CVM are presented in Appendix D, Section D.5.2. One reason for keeping this CVM for EMV™ chip products could be that there are issuers that do not trust the transmission in clear of the cardholder's PIN on the interface between the terminal and the chip card. The terminal implementing this CVM has to be equipped with an on-line PIN pad, which is a tamper resistant device that ensures that the PIN of the cardholder never leaves the PIN pad in clear, but just in an encrypted form.

- *Plaintext PIN verification performed by ICC* (000001b): This is a cost-effective cardholder verification method, which is specific for chip card products. The terminal captures the PIN from the user and sends it in clear to the chip card. The chip compares the value received with a witness value stored in its permanent memory since the personalization stage. The method is described in Appendix D, Section D.5.3. Issuers that do not consider the threat of eavesdropping on the interface terminal-card prefer this method to on-line enciphered PIN since implementing it is cheaper and it allows the off-line completion of an EMV™ transaction at an unattended terminal. The terminal implementing this CVM has to be equipped with an off-line PIN pad, which is a tamper resistant device such that capturing the PIN of the cardholder on the interface card-terminal is difficult.

  Note that EMV™ supports a combined cardholder verification method, which is referred to as the *plaintext PIN verification performed by ICC and signature (paper)* (000011b).

- *Enciphered PIN verification performed by ICC* (000100b): This is an expensive cardholder verification method, which is applicable for chip card products able to perform RSA operations. The terminal captures the PIN from the user and sends it encrypted in an RSA envelope to the chip card. The chip decrypts the envelope, retrieves the PIN in clear, and compares the retrieved value with a witness value stored in its permanent memory since the personalization stage. The method is described in Appendix D, Section D.5.5. Issuers that would like to complete transactions off-line and that consider the threat of eavesdropping on the interface terminal-card implement this method. The terminal implementing this CVM has to be equipped with an off-line PIN pad.

  Note that EMV™ supports a combined cardholder verification method, which is referred to as *enciphered PIN verification performed by ICC and signature (paper)* (000101b).

‣ There are some method numbers that are reserved for further use:

   ‣ 000110–011101: method numbers to be assigned by EMV™, for example, for biometrics (see Appendix D, Section D.5.6);

   ‣ 100000–101111: method numbers to be assigned by the individual payment systems—a possible candidate is a one-time password scheme (see Appendix D, Section D.7.3);

   ‣ 110000–111110: method numbers to be assigned by individual issuers.

6.6.2 Data objects involved in cardholder verification

The Cardholder Verification Method List (CVM List) is a data object with tag 8E, which is stored in the card application since its personalization. It contains two amount fields, which are referred to as X and Y, and a list of all the cardholder verification rules accepted by the card. The meaning of these components is described below.

Both the first (X) and second (Y) amount fields are encoded with an implicit decimal point on 4 bytes in a binary format. They are expressed in the same currency, whose type is encoded in the Application Currency Code data object with tag 9F42 stored in the card. X and Y represent two threshold values established by the issuer, which determine whether the terminal should apply a certain CVM or not. This decision depends on the relationship between the amount involved in the current transaction, which is stored in the terminal in the Amount, Authorized data object (tag 81), and X, Y (see also the CVM condition codes below).

A Cardholder Verification Rule (CVR) consists of 2 bytes: the first indicates the type of CVM to be used, while the second specifies in which condition this CVM will be applied.

The first byte, referred to as the Cardholder Verification Method Code (CVM Code), is encoded as follows:

‣ Bit 8: This is RFU.

‣ Bit 7: This instructs the terminal whether to continue the cardholder verification stage if the CVM fails.

   ‣ 0: The terminal finishes the cardholder verification stage when the current method fails.

▸ 1: The terminal is instructed to consider the next method in the list of CVR when the current method fails.

▸ Bit 6, …, bit 1 (the rightmost 6 bits of the CV Code): These bits represent the method number, as defined in Section 6.6.1, indicating which is the CVM that must be applied.

The second byte, referred to as the Cardholder Verification Method Condition Code (CVM Condition Code), indicates the condition to be respected for applying the CVM whose code is specified in the first byte:

▸ 00h: The CVM can be always applied.

▸ 01h: The CVM is applied for all the transactions where cash or cashback is involved (e.g., ATM cash withdrawal, cashback from an attended POS).

▸ 02h: The CVM is applied for all the transactions that do not involve cash or cashback (e.g., POS payment).

▸ 03h: The CVM is applied only in case the terminal is adequately equipped. For example, the plaintext PIN verification performed by ICC is a CVM that can be executed only on a terminal equipped with an off-line PIN pad.

▸ 04h–05h: These values are RFU.

▸ 06h–09h: The CVM is applied when the Transaction Currency Code (tag 5F2A in the terminal) of the Amount, Authorized is the same as the Application Currency Code (tag 9F42 in the ICC) and the value of this amount is:

▸ Under the X value (06h);

▸ Over the X value (07h);

▸ Under the Y value (08h);

▸ Over the Y value (09h).

The issuer specifies the values of the threshold amounts X and Y in the first tow fields of 4 bytes of the CVM List.

▸ 0Ah ÷ 7Fh: This range of values is RFU.

> 80h–FFh: This range of values is reserved for encoding condition codes required by individual payment systems.

Thus, one can see that the CVM List stored in the card application indicates to the terminal the types of CVM supported by the card, the conditions in which each CVM should be applied, and their preferred order.

In its turn the terminal supports all the CVMs indicated in the second byte of the Terminal Capabilities (tag 9F33) (see Annex A2 in Book 4 [3]):

> Bit 8 = 1: *"Plaintext PIN for ICC verification"* is supported.

> Bit 7 = 1: *"Enciphered PIN for on-line verification"* is supported.

> Bit 6 = 1: *"Signature (paper)"* is supported. For this method the terminal shall be an attended terminal, with Terminal Type (tag 9F35) = x1h, x2h, or x3h with $x = 1$ or $x = 2$. The terminal shall support a printer, which is indicated in Additional Terminal Capabilities (tag 9F40), byte 4 "Terminal Data Output Capability," bit 8 = 1: "Print, attendant" (see Annex A3 in Book 4 [3]).

> Bit 5 = 1: *"Enciphered PIN for off-line verification"* is supported.

> Bit 4 – Bit 1: RFU.

In addition, the terminal shall recognize the CVM codes for "No CVM required" and "Fail CVM processing," which may be present in the card's CVM List.

The terminal will register the result of the last CVM that was performed in the cardholder verification method results (CVM Results, tag 9F34), whose encoding is given below (according to Annex A4 in Book 4 [3]):

> Byte 1 and 2: These indicate the CVR of the last CVM performed as indicated in the CVM List.

> Byte 3: This indicates the result of the last CVM performed as known to the terminal:

>> 00h = Unknown (e.g., for signature);

>> 01h = Failed (e.g., for off-line PIN);

>> 02h = Successful (e.g., for off-line PIN).

6.6.3 Common processing performed by the terminal

Whenever bit 5, "Cardholder verification is supported," in byte 1 of the AIP is set, the terminal performs the cardholder verification stage. This section presents the actions performed by the terminal regardless of the type of CVM.

The terminal checks whether the CVM List (tag 8E) is present in the EMV™ heap of the terminal.

> • If the CVM List is not present terminate cardholder verification without setting bit 7, "Cardholder verification was performed," in byte 1 of the TSI. The terminal shall set byte 1 of the CVM Results to "No CVM performed" (3Fh).

> • Else process each CVR in the order it appears in the CVM List. Finish the stage either when a CVM is successful or when there are no more CVR rules in the CVM List.

For each CVR, the processing is described below:

1. Verify the CVM Condition Code (the second byte of the CVR):

    > • Check that the terminal understands the CVM Condition Code. It could be that the EMV™ application in the card is a more recent version than the counterpart application in the terminal. Therefore, it could be that the terminal does not yet know how to interpret a condition whose code is known to the card.

    > • Check that all the data elements involved for the verification of that condition are present in the terminal. For example, the evaluation of a condition that involves the thresholds X and Y needs the presence of the Application Currency Code (tag 9F42).

    > • Verify that the business environment at the point of service for the current transaction respects the condition expressed in this CVR.

    If any of the verifications mentioned above fails, then do:

    If the current CVR is the last in the CVM List:

    > • Set bit 8, "Cardholder verification was not successful," in byte 3 of the TVR.

- The terminal shall set byte 1 of the CVM Results to "No CVM performed" (3Fh).

- Terminate the cardholder verification stage.

- Else consider the next CVR, and restart from step 1.

Else continue with verifying the CVM code in the first byte of the CVR, as detailed below in step 2.

2. Verify that the method number (the rightmost 6 bits) in the CVM code is one of those accepted by EMV™ (see Section 6.6.2) or is otherwise understood by the terminal, as specified by a particular payment system or issuer.

The terminal shall set bytes 1 and 2 of the CVM Results with the method code and condition code of the current CVM rule interpreted from the CVM List.

If the method number in the CVM code is "No CVM required" (011111b) and if the terminal supports "No CVM required," it shall set byte 3 of the CVM Results to "successful." Terminate the cardholder verification stage.

If the method number in the CVM Code is "Fail CVM processing," the terminal shall set byte 3 of the CVM Results to "failed." Terminate the cardholder verification stage.

If the method number in the CVM code is not known and, correspondingly, the terminal does not understand the CVM, then do:

The terminal shall set the third byte of the CVM Results to "failed."

If the CVM condition code is known and correctly satisfied:
- Set bit 7, "Unrecognized CVM," in byte 3 of the TVR.

- If the current CVR is the last in the CVM List:

  - Set bit 8, "Cardholder verification was not successful," in byte 3 of the TVR.

  - Terminate the cardholder verification stage.

  Else consider the next CVR, and restart from step 1.

Else perform the CVM whose code is indicated. Refer to Section 6.6.4 for off-line PIN processing and to Section 6.6.6 for on-line PIN processing.

If the terminal successfully completes the CVM:

- Set bit 7, "Cardholder verification was performed," in byte 1 of the TSI.

- Terminate the cardholder verification stage.

Else (the CVM processing failed)

- If bit 7 of the CVM Code is 0:

  - Set bit 8, "Cardholder verification was not successful," in byte 3 of the TVR.

  - Terminate the cardholder verification stage.

  Else (bit 7 of the CVM Code is 1):

    - If CVR is the last entry in the CVM List

      Set bit 8, "Cardholder verification was not successful," in byte 3 of the TVR.

      Terminate the cardholder verification stage.

  - Else consider the next CVR entry in the CVM List, and continue with step 1.

6.6.4 Off-line PIN processing

The processing described in this section applies for the following CVM(s):

- "Plaintext PIN verification performed by ICC" (000001b);

- "Enciphered PIN verification performed by ICC" (000100b).

First, we discuss two concepts used in the processing performed by the terminal.

- *Off-line PIN support:* A terminal that does not support off-line PIN is a terminal that supports neither off-line plaintext PIN verification nor off-line enciphered PIN verification (see bit 8 and bit 5 in the second byte of the Terminal Capabilities). If either of these two types of verification is supported then the terminal supports off-line PIN.

▸ *Bypassing PIN entry:* There are situations when a new cardholder or a cardholder that is not used with PIN verification is unable to insert the PIN. Then, three situations can be envisaged:

1. Terminate the transaction.

2. Submit PIN-like numbers until the PIN Try Counter kept in the card is exhausted.

3. Bypass the PIN entry processing either at the initiative of the merchant or of the cardholder. Force the transaction to go on-line and inform the issuer of the circumstances. The issuer could decide based on some risk management procedure whether to authorize the transaction without a PIN.

From the point of view of service availability for the cardholder, the third approach is probably better.

The processing performed by the terminal is described below.

If the terminal does not support off-line PIN:

Set bit 5, "PIN entry required and PIN pad not present or not working," in byte 3 of the TVR.

Else

If PIN pad is malfunctioning

Set bit 5, "PIN entry required and PIN pad not present or not working," in byte 3 of the TVR.

Else

If either the merchant or the cardholder bypass the PIN processing

▸ Set bit 4, "PIN entry required, PIN pad present, but PIN was not entered," in byte 3 of the TVR.

▸ The CVM is considered unsuccessful, the CVM Results is not set, and the next CVR in the CVM List is treated.

In case the terminal supports off-line PIN, the PIN pad works correctly, and the cardholder does not bypass the PIN, the processing performed by the terminal is the following. Issue the GET DATA command to the card, with the C-APDU presented in Table 6.4 (according to Table I-16 in Book 3 [1]). This command is used to retrieve the PIN Try Counter primitive data object from the card. This object is not encapsulated in any record within the current application.

The data field of the corresponding R-APDU contains the PIN Try Counter, including its tag 9F17 and its length. When the value of this counter is zero, there are no more PIN trials left.

If SW1 SW2 = 9000 and PIN Try Counter is zero then the following processing is performed:

> • The terminal should not allow off-line PIN entry.

> • The terminal shall set bit 6, "PIN try limit exceeded" in the third byte of the TVR.

> • The terminal shall not display any specific message regarding the status of the PIN.

> • The terminal shall not set the CVM Results.

> • The terminal shall continue cardholder verification processing in accordance with the card's CVM List.

If either SW1SW2 ≠ 9000 or SW1SW2 = 9000 and PIN Try Counter is different than zero, then the following processing is performed:

> • The terminal prompts for PIN entry, displaying "Enter PIN." The PIN can contain between 4 to 12 BCD digits.

> • The PIN is formatted as a 16 nibbles (8 bytes) PIN block as follows:

   C N P P P P P/F P/F P/F P/F P/F P/F P/F P/F F F

   where:

Table 6.4
The C-APDU Corresponding to GET DATA Command

Code	Value
CLA	*80* (EMV™ specific command)
INS	*CA*
P1 P2	9F17 (value corresponding to the PIN Try Counter primitive data object)
Lc	Not present
Data	Not present
Le	*00*

- C = Control field (0010b);

- N = PIN length expressed as a 4-bit binary number (0100b–1100b);

- P = PIN digit (0000b–1001b);

- P/F = PIN/filler, which is determined by the PIN length N;

- F = Filler (1111b).

- If the method number (the rightmost bits of the CVM Code) indicates "Enciphered PIN verification performed by ICC" (000100b) then issue a GET CHALLENGE command. The C-APDU of this command is presented in Table 6.5 (it conforms to the Table I-15 in Book 3 [1]) .

In case of successful execution the card returns the R-APDU containing a random sequence of 8 bytes and SW1SW2 = 9000. The terminal stores this sequence in the value field of the Unpredictable Number data object (tag 9F37). The terminal uses this Unpredictable Number to insure the uniqueness of each RSA digital envelope containing a PIN. This security mechanism impedes an attacker from successfully impersonating the legitimate cardholder by simply replying a previously sent RSA digital envelope or determining the PIN from an RSA digital envelope through a dictionary attack.

- Issue a VERIFY command, which allows the chip card to compare the PIN typed in by the cardholder with a witness value stored in the chip card. Prepare the C-APDU of the VERIFY command as indicated in Table 6.6 (from Table I-24 in Book 3 [1]).

- In case the CVM is "Plaintext PIN verification performed by ICC" (000001b), the data field of the C-APDU is represented by the PIN block of 8 bytes as described above.

Table 6.5
C-APDU of the GET CHALLENGE **Command**

Code	Value
CLA	*00* (interindustry command)
INS	*84*
P1 P2	00 00
Lc	Not present
Data	Not present
Le	*00*

Table 6.6
C-APDU of the VERIFY Command

Code	Value
CLA	*00* (interindustry command)
INS	*20*
P1	00
P2	Qualifier of the reference PIN data:
	00: as defined in ISO/IEC 7816-4
	80: plaintext PIN, formatted as defined above
	88: enciphered PIN, formatted as defined in Section 6.6.5
	81–87 and 89–8B: RFU for the EMV™
	8C–8F: RFU for the individual payment systems
	90–9F: RFU for the issuer
Lc	Variable, depending on P2
Data	Transaction PIN data
Le	*00*

> ‣ In case the CVM is "Enciphered PIN verification performed by ICC" (000100b), the data field of the C-APDU is the RSA digital envelope carrying the cardholder's PIN. This field has N_{PE} bytes, corresponding to the byte length of the modulus in the ICC PIN encipherment public key. Details of producing the RSA digital envelope and the computations carried out by the card to retrieve the PIN from this envelope are detailed in Section 6.6.5.

After retrieving the PIN received in the command either directly or in the RSA digital envelope, the card compares this value with a witness PIN stored in its permanent memory since the personalization. Every time this comparison fails, the number of possible PIN trials stored in the PIN Try Counter is decreased. The status words SW1SW2 are positioned to 6983 or 6984, in case the PIN Try Counter was zero at the moment the VERIFY command was issued. Otherwise, the card answers the code SW1SW2 = 63Cx, where x indicates the remaining number of possible PIN trials, which could also be zero in case PIN Try Counter is zero.

The terminal receives the R-APDU from the card corresponding to the VERIFY command. This R-APDU consists of the status words SW1SW2, which allows the terminal to assess the completion of the required off-line PIN verification in the card:

‣ If SW1SW2 = 6983, 6984, or 63C0, the off-line PIN verification failed. The terminal sets bit 6, "PIN try limit exceeded," in byte 3 of the TVR.

‣ If SW1SW2 = 63C1 or 63C2, the off-line PIN verification failed but there is still one or, respectively, two possible attempts of off-line PIN verification. The terminal points the cardholder for typing in a PIN and the processing restarts.

‣ If SW1 SW2 = 9000, the off-line PIN verification is considered successful.

6.6.5 RSA digital envelope carrying the PIN

Figure 6.7 outlines the CVM "Enciphered PIN verification performed by ICC" (000100b) (see Appendix D, Section D.5.5, for more details). The main advantage of this CVM is that an attacker loses any opportunity to eavesdrop the cardholder's PIN on the interface between the ICC and the terminal, since the PIN is wrapped in an RSA digital envelope.

During the personalization stage, the issuer generates the pair ICC PIN encipherment private key/ICC PIN encipherment public key and produces the ICC PIN Encipherment Public Key Certificate with the issuer private key. The issuing of this certificate is described in Section 5.6. The issuer loads both the ICC PIN encipherment private key (using a confidential channel) and the ICC PIN Encipherment Public Key Certificate in the card. Note, in order to save EEPROM space in the card, the ICC private/public key pair could be used instead of the ICC PIN encipherment private/public key pair to perform the unwrapping/wrapping of the RSA envelopes. It is important to mention, however, that whenever the card has enough EEPROM space, the best security practice is to keep separate key pairs for signature generation/verification and for unwrapping/wrapping RSA digital envelopes.

During a transaction that selected the "Enciphered PIN verification performed by ICC" as CVM the terminal verifies the existence in the EMV™ data objects heap of the following objects:

‣ All the data objects needed by the terminal for performing the off-line static data authentication, except for the Signed Static Application Data (tag 93);

‣ ICC PIN Encipherment Public Key Certificate (tag 9F2D);

Figure 6.7
Overview of
the enciphered
PIN verification
performed by
ICC.

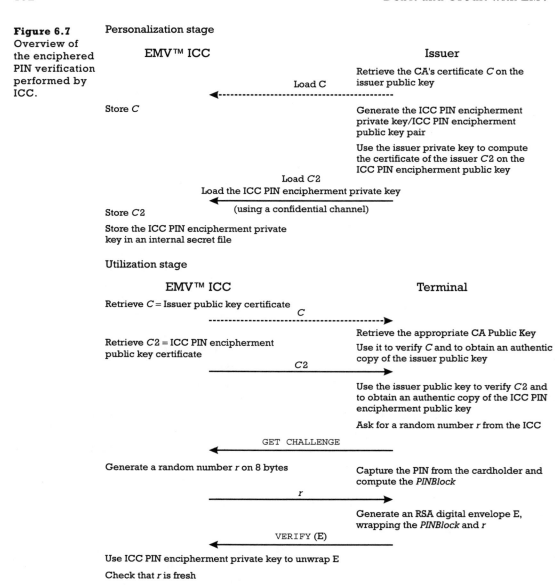

Personalization stage

EMV™ ICC   Issuer

Retrieve the CA's certificate *C* on the
Load C   issuer public key

Store *C*

Generate the ICC PIN encipherment
private key/ICC PIN encipherment
public key pair

Use the issuer private key to compute
the certificate of the issuer *C*2 on the
ICC PIN encipherment public key

Load *C*2
Load the ICC PIN encipherment private key

Store *C*2   (using a confidential channel)

Store the ICC PIN encipherment private
key in an internal secret file

Utilization stage

EMV™ ICC   Terminal

Retrieve *C* = Issuer public key certificate
                                              C

Retrieve *C*2 = ICC PIN encipherment   Retrieve the appropriate CA Public Key
public key certificate   Use it to verify *C* and to obtain an authentic
                                              copy of the issuer public key
                                *C*2

Use the issuer public key to verify *C*2 and
to obtain an authentic copy of the ICC PIN
encipherment public key

Ask for a random number *r* from the ICC

GET CHALLENGE

Generate a random number *r* on 8 bytes
                                             Capture the PIN from the cardholder and
                                             compute the *PINBlock*
                                r

Generate an RSA digital envelope E,
wrapping the *PINBlock* and *r*

VERIFY (E)

Use ICC PIN encipherment private key to unwrap E

Check that *r* is fresh

Compute the PIN from the received PINBlock
and compare it against the witness PIN stored
in the ICC
                              SW1SW2

Accept that Cardholder is legitimate in
case SW1SW2 = 9000

‣ ICC PIN Encipherment Public Key Remainder (tag 9F2F), which is present only when $N_{PE} > N_I - 42$;

▸ ICC PIN Encipherment Public Key Exponent (tag 9F2E).

If the terminal cannot retrieve the last three data objects, it searches for the following three data objects:

▸ ICC Public Key Certificate (tag 9F46);

▸ ICC Public Key Remainder (tag 9F48), which is present only when $N_{IC} > N_I - 42$;

▸ ICC Public Key Exponent (tag 9F47).

If both sets of data objects mentioned above are missing, the enciphered PIN verification performed by ICC fails.

If the first set of data objects is present, the terminal obtains an authentic copy of the ICC PIN encipherment public key (n_{PE}, e_{PE}) applying the same algorithm as that described for obtaining the ICC public key (see Section 5.7.2).

The terminal creates a message M of N_{PE} (or N_{IC}) bytes from the following items:

▸ Data header: 1 byte with value 7Fh;

▸ PIN block: 8 bytes;

▸ ICC unpredictable number: the value field of 8 bytes of the data object with tag 9F37, obtained from the ICC with a GET CHALLENGE command (see Table 6.5);

▸ Random pad pattern: a string of $N_{PE} - 17$ (or $N_{IC} - 17$) bytes generated at random by the terminal.

The RSA digital envelope is obtained through a public RSA operation (see Appendix F, Section F.2) on M with the modulus n_{PE} and the public exponent e_{PE}.

After receiving the C-APDU of the VERIFY command with P2 = 88, the card retrieves the RSA digital envelope E from the data field. The card applies a secret RSA operation (see Appendix F, Section F.2) on this digital envelope with the modulus n_{PE} and the secret exponent d_{PE}, where (n_{PE}, d_{PE}) represents the ICC PIN encipherment private key. The result of this operation is denoted M'.

The card performs the following verifications:

- The first byte of M' must be equal to the data header with value 7Fh.

- Recover the 8 bytes of the ICC unpredictable number, starting with the 10th byte of M'. Check that these 8 bytes correspond to the sequence of random bytes generated by the card and returned in the R-APDU of the GET CHALLENGE command.

- Recover the PIN block of 8 bytes starting from the second position of M' and retrieve the PIN. Check this value against the witness value stored in the card.

If all the verifications mentioned above are passed, the enciphered PIN verification is considered successful.

6.6.6   On-line PIN processing

The processing described in this section applies to the CVM "Enciphered PIN verified on-line" (000010b). The processing performed by the terminal is described below.

If the terminal does not support on-line PIN (see bit 7 in the second byte of the Terminal Capabilities):

Set bit 5, "PIN entry required and PIN pad not present or not working," in byte 3 of the TVR.

Else

If PIN pad is malfunctioning:

Set bit 5, "PIN entry required and PIN pad not present or not working," in byte 3 of the TVR.

Else

If either the merchant or the cardholder bypass the PIN processing:

- Set bit 4, "PIN entry required, PIN pad present, but PIN was not entered," in byte 3 of the TVR.

- The CVM is considered unsuccessful, the CVM Results is not set, and the next CVR in the CVM List is treated.

Else (on-line PIN is successfully entered):

Set bit 3, "On-line PIN entered," in byte 3 of the TVR.

The cardholder verification is complete and successful.

6.7 Terminal risk management

Including the terminal risk management stage in the EMV™ transaction flow protects the issuer, acquirer, and payment system against fraud, through several security measures: floor limit checking, random transaction selection, and velocity checking.

The processing in this stage can be performed any time after the read application data stage and before issuing the first GENERATE AC command. The results of the terminal risk management are recorded in the fourth byte of the TVR register.

This stage is included in the EMV™ transaction flow only in case bit 4, "Terminal risk management is to be performed," in the first byte of the AIP is set to 1. Otherwise, the terminal skips the processing implied by any of the three aforementioned security mechanisms.

Regardless of the coding of the card's AIP, concerning support of terminal risk management, a terminal may support an exception file (black list) per application. When this file exists, the terminal verifies that the Application PAN and, optionally, the Application PAN Sequence Number of the card involved in the current transaction cannot be found in the exception file.

If a match is found in the exception file, the terminal shall set to 1 bit 5, "Card appears in exception file," in byte 1 of the TVR.

After completing the processing in the terminal risk management stage, the terminal sets to 1 bit 4, "Terminal risk management was performed," in byte 1 of the TSI register.

6.7.1 Terminal floor limit

An effective security measure against attempts to overspend is to check that the amount involved in a transaction does not exceed a floor limit established by the acquirer, referred to as the Terminal Floor Limit.

However, if the cardholder colludes with the shopkeeper, an amount over the floor limit needed to buy one expensive item can be split into two distinct amounts below the floor limit, which are authorized in two separate transactions with the same card at the same terminal. This kind of threat is called a split sale.

If the acquirer is willing to provide security protection against split sales, the terminal has to have enough storage space to accommodate a transaction log like that presented in Table 6.7.

The processing performed by the terminal for each new EMV™ transaction is described by the following actions.

1. Use the Application PAN and optionally the Application PAN Sequence Number of the card involved in the current transaction to search for an existing record in the transaction log.

2. If there is such a record, add the value of the Amount, Authorized field in the current transaction (Amount 2) with the Amount, Authorized field in the most recent transaction (Amount 1) with the same Application PAN/PAN sequence number. The cumulated value of the two transactions represents the total.

   If the value of total is greater than or equal to the value field of the Terminal Floor Limit data object with tag 9F1B in the terminal, then set bit 8, "Transaction exceeds floor limit," in byte 4 of the TVR.

   Record the new transaction (e.g., at index 1,000) within the transaction log and end the processing.

3. In case there is no such record in the transaction log, or the terminal does not keep a transaction log, the terminal checks whether the value of the Amount, Authorized in the current transaction is greater than or equal to the value field of the Terminal Floor Limit.

   If this is true, the terminal sets bit 8, "Transaction exceeds floor limit," in byte 4 of the TVR.

6.7.2 Random transaction selection

This security mechanism ensures that low-value transactions, which are usually authorized off-line by the terminal, go from time to time to the

Table 6.7
Transaction Log as a Security Protection Against Split Sales

	Application PAN	Amount, Authorized	Application PAN Sequence Number	Transaction Date
Transaction 1	PAN1	Amount 1	PAN Seq1	05/10/2001
Transaction 2	...	...	...	...
...	...	...	...	...
Transaction 1,000	PAN1	Amount 2	PAN Seq1	05/10/2001
...	...	...	...	...

issuer for on-line authorization. This security mechanism can be implemented in terminals that are not "off-line-only." This mechanism protects against threats that cannot be detected in an off-line environment. The terminal chooses which low-value transaction is recommended for on-line authorization according to a selection function.

In order to implement such a function, the terminal associates a random transaction number in the range of 1 to 99 to each new EMV™ transaction processed by the terminal.

A simple selection function can be implemented as a step function. To this end, the acquirer specifies a new parameter, in addition to the Terminal Floor Limit parameter, called the target percentage to be used for random selection, or simply the target percentage. This parameter is chosen in the range of 0 to 99. In its turn the selection function is implemented as follows:

- For any transaction having the value of Amount, Authorized below the terminal flow limit and with a random transaction number smaller than or equal to the target percentage, the terminal selects the transaction for on-line authorization by the issuer.

- For any transaction having the value of Amount, Authorized greater than or equal to the terminal flow limit, indifferent of the value of the random transaction number, the terminal selects the transaction for on-line authorization by the issuer.

The higher the value of the target percentage, the higher the probability that a small value transaction with Amount, Authorized below the Terminal Floor Limit is selected for on-line authorization.

A more fine-tuned decision about the random transaction selection can be obtained with a biased selection function, where the value of the target percentage parameter can be biased by the value of the transaction amount towards an increased transaction target percentage parameter. This selection function is graphically described in Figure 6.8. To implement it, the acquirer needs to specify two additional parameters:

- *Threshold value for biased random selection:* This is a threshold amount, simply referred to as the threshold value, which can be zero or a positive number smaller than the Terminal Floor Limit. For any transaction amount bigger than this threshold, the biased selection mechanism becomes effective.

- *Maximum target percentage to be used for biased random selection:* This parameter, simply referred to as the maximum target percentage is

Figure 6.8
Biased selection
function for
on-line
authorization.

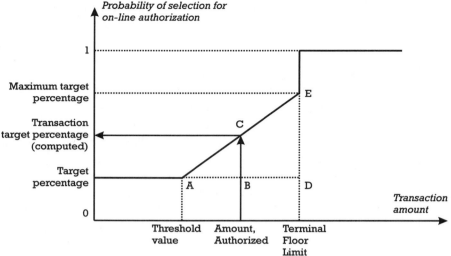

also in the range of 0 to 99 but is at least as high as the target percentage. This parameter represents the desired percentage of transactions with Amount, Authorized just below the Terminal Floor Limit that will be selected by this selection algorithm.

The value of the transaction target percentage is computed for each new EMV™ transaction as a linear interpolation between the target percentage and the maximum target percentage, depending on the position of the Amount, Authorized between the threshold value and the Terminal Floor Limit.

Indeed, from Figure 6.8 one can see that from the equivalence of the triangles *ABC* and *ADE*, one can write the relation: CB/ED = BA/DA. Therefore CB = ED * (BA/DA). Considering that CB = Transaction Target Percentage – Target Percentage, ED = Maximum Target Percentage – Target Percentage, BA = Amount, Authorized – Threshold Value, and DA = Terminal Floor Limit – Threshold Value, then the transaction target percentage is computed as:

Transaction Target Percentage = Target Percentage + (Maximum Target Percentage – Target Percentage) * [(Amount, Authorized – Threshold Value)/(Terminal Floor Limit – Threshold Value)]

The biased selection function is implemented as follows:

▸ For any transaction having the value of Amount, Authorized below the threshold value and with a random transaction number smaller than or equal to the target percentage the terminal selects the transaction for on-line authorization by the issuer.

▸ For any transaction having the Amount, Authorized greater than or equal to the threshold value and smaller than the Terminal Floor Limit and with a random transaction number smaller than or equal to the computed transaction target percentage, the terminal selects the transaction for on-line authorization by the issuer.

▸ For any transaction having the value of Amount, Authorized greater than or equal to the terminal flow limit, indifferent of the value of the random transaction number, the terminal selects the transaction for on-line authorization by the issuer.

If the terminal selects a typical off-line transaction for on-line authorization by the issuer through the (step or biased) selection function, the terminal sets bit 5, "Transaction selected randomly for on-line processing," in byte 4 of the TVR.

6.7.3   Velocity checking

This security mechanism requires that after a card performs a certain number of consecutive off-line transactions, the number of which is specified by the issuer in the parameter *Lower Consecutive Off-line Limit* (tag 9F14 in the ICC), the terminal at the point of service selects the current transaction for on-line authorization.

If for any reason the terminal is not able to go on-line for authorization, transactions may be still completed off-line until a second limit is reached —a limit established by the issuer in the parameter *Upper Consecutive Off-line Limit (tag 9F23 in the ICC)*.

In case the number of consecutive off-line transactions is greater than this upper limit, the recommendation of the issuer might be to reject any transaction that cannot be completed on-line. Once a transaction has been completed on-line with a successful authentication of the issuer, the counting of the number of transactions processed off-line can restart, so that transactions can again be performed off-line until the Lower Consecutive Off-line Limit is reached again.

This measure impedes a cardholder from overspending by simply participating in a large number of low-value transactions concluded off-line.

In order to implement this security mechanism, the two parameters (Lower Consecutive Off-line Limit and Upper Consecutive Off-line Limit) have to be personalized in the card by the issuer. The card must also support the internal management of the following two data objects:

‣ ATC: This is stored in the data object with tag 9F36. This transaction counter managed by each application is incremented every time the card application participates in a new EMV™ session.

‣ Last on-line ATC Register: This is stored in the data object with tag 9F13 in the card. This register is set to the value of the ATC corresponding to the last transaction that was sent on-line for authorization.

The card has to implement the GET DATA command (see Table 6.4). Using this command, the terminal can retrieve both the ATC, in case the value of P1P2 in the C-APDU is set to 9F36, and the last on-line ATC Register in case the value of P1P2 in the C-APDU is set to 9F13. The terminal can compute the number of consecutive off-line transactions as the difference between the ATC and the last on-line ATC Register.

The terminal performs the velocity checking according to the following algorithm:

1. Retrieve from the EMV™ data objects heap the parameters Lower Consecutive Off-line Limit (tag 9F14) and Upper Consecutive Off-line Limit (tag 9F23). If one of these data objects is not present, skip the processing below.

2. Issue the GET DATA command with P1P2 = 9F36 to retrieve the ATC from the card, and the GET DATA command with P1P2 = 9F13, to retrieve the last on-line ATC Register from the card.

    If the status words SW1SW2 returned by any of the two commands are different than 9000, then make the following settings and finish the velocity checking:

   ‣ Set to 1 bit 7, "Lower Consecutive Off-line Limit exceeded," in byte 4 of the TVR.

   ‣ Set to 1 bit 6, "Upper Consecutive Off-line Limit exceeded," in byte 4 of the TVR.

   ‣ Set to 0 bit 4, "New card," in byte 2 of the TVR.

3. Compute the number of consecutive off-line transactions as the difference between the ATC and the last on-line ATC Register.

4.   If the number of consecutive off-line transactions is greater than the Lower Consecutive Off-line Limit, then set to 1 bit 7, "Lower Consecutive Off-line Limit exceeded," in byte 4 of the TVR.

5.   If the number of consecutive off-line transactions is greater than the upper consecutive off-line limit, then set to 1 bit 6, "Upper Consecutive Off-line Limit exceeded," in byte 4 of the TVR.

6.   Check whether the last on-line ATC Register is zero. If this is the case, set to 1 bit 4, "New card," in byte 2 of the TVR.

6.8   Terminal action analysis

In the terminal action analysis stage, the terminal evaluates the results of the processing performed during the current EMV™ transaction and decides whether the transaction should be approved off-line, transmitted on-line to be authorized by the issuer, or declined off-line.

This evaluation is performed after the terminal risk management has been completed, after the transaction data is entered by the cardholder/merchant, and prior to the first use of the GENERATE AC command. However, if the processing in any EMV™ stage results in the setting of 1 bit in the TVR, the terminal can immediately trigger the terminal action analysis to determine whether the transaction should be rejected off-line based upon the issuer's and/or the acquirer's security policies. This can spare subsequent computational effort of the terminal, since the transaction would finally be rejected.

6.8.1   Action codes and security policies

The evaluation of the terminal processing consists of interpreting the content of the TVR against two sets of registers, which are referred to as the Issuer Action Codes and the terminal action codes. Each set contains three registers, which are referred to with the set name and one of the following suffixes: denial, on-line, and default. Each set of registers encodes the security policies considered by the issuer and by the acquirer in case 1 bit in the TVR is 1, determining the action to be performed by the terminal.

The set of registers that encodes the security policies of the issuer is as follows:

▸ *Issuer Action Code-Denial* (tag 9F0E in the card): This register specifies the issuer's conditions that cause the denial of a transaction without attempting to go on-line. If this register is not personalized in the card, the terminal considers, by default, that all the bits are set to 0.

▸ *Issuer Action Code-On-line* (tag 9F0F): This register specifies the issuer's conditions that cause a transaction to be transmitted on-line. If this register is not personalized, the terminal considers by default that all the bits are set to 1.

▸ *Issuer Action Code-Default* (tag 9F0D): This register specifies the issuer's conditions that cause a transaction to be rejected if it might have been approved on-line but the terminal is unable to transmit the transaction on-line. If this register is not personalized, the terminal considers, by default, that all the bits are set to 1.

The bits in these registers are set according to the security policies established by the issuer concerning the action to be taken in case a failure appears during the EMV™ processing. Let us discuss the following examples.

Example 1: Assume that the security policy of the issuer states that:

If off-line SDA fails (which is reflected in bit 7 of byte 1 of the TVR set to 1), *the transaction should be transmitted on-line to the issuer.*
　　If the terminal is off-line only or the on-line connection with the issuer cannot be established, then the transaction must be declined.

In this case, bit 7 of byte 1 in the three action code registers of the issuer should be encoded as follows:

▸ 0 in the Issuer Action Code-Denial, which means that the transaction should not be declined off-line when off-line SDA fails;

▸ 1 in the Issuer Action Code-On-line, which means that the transaction should be directed on-line when off-line SDA fails;

▸ 1 in the Issuer Action Code-Default, which means that in case the transaction cannot be directed on-line to the issuer, the terminal should decline the transaction.

Example 2: Assume that the security policy of the issuer states that:

If cardholder verification was not successful (which is reflected in bit 8 of byte 3 of the TVR set to 1), *the transaction should be declined off-line without attempting to transmit the transaction on-line to the issuer.*

In this case bit 8 of byte 3 in the Issuer Action Code-Denial should be set to 1, while the value of the same bit in the other two registers does not matter.

The set of registers that encodes the security policies of the acquirer is as follows:

> *Terminal Action Code-Denial:* This register specifies the acquirer's conditions that cause the denial of a transaction without attempting to go on-line. If the acquirer specifies no value for this register, the terminal considers by default that all the bits are set to 0.

> *Terminal Action Code-On-Line:* This register specifies the acquirer's conditions that cause a transaction to be transmitted on-line.

> *Terminal Action Code-Default:* This register specifies the acquirer's conditions that cause a transaction to be rejected if it might have been approved on-line, but the terminal is unable to transmit the transaction on-line.

If the last two registers are not personalized, the terminal considers, by default, that all their bits are set to 0. It is strongly recommended, however, that at least the following bits in the first byte of the last two registers be set to 1 by the acquirer:

> Bit 8: Off-line data authentication was not performed.

> Bit 7: Off-line SDA failed.

> Bit 4: Off-line DDA failed.

6.8.2   The terminal proposes and the card disposes

The evaluation of the processing performed during the current EMV™ transaction, according to the content of the TVR and of the issuer/terminal action codes sets, leads the terminal to make a decision concerning the finalization of the EMV™ transaction. The terminal may propose one of the following actions through the first issuance of the GENERATE AC command:

> *Transaction approved:* The card is required to produce a transaction certificate (TC) when the terminal appreciates that there are no risks (according to the security policies adopted by the issuer/acquirer) and recommends the approval of the EMV™ transaction off-line.

▸ *On-line authorization requested:* The card is required to produce an authorization request cryptogram (ARQC) when the terminal recommends that the intervention of the issuer is necessary to decide upon the approval or denial of the EMV™ transaction.

▸ *Transaction declined:* The card is required to produce an application authentication cryptogram (AAC) when the terminal decides that the business risks are unacceptable and the transaction must be declined off-line.

After the first GENERATE AC command is received by the card with a proposal of finalization from the terminal, the card risk management may accept the terminal's recommendation or may override the terminal's decision to a lower decision level. The hierarchy of the decision levels (from highest to lowest) is TC, ARQC, AAC. In addition to these three levels known to the terminal, the card knows a supplementary decision level, according to which a referral is requested by the card for the finalization of the EMV™ transaction through an application authorization referral (AAR) cryptogram. This decision level is situated between the ARQC and the AAC.

Note that Application Cryptogram (AC) generically refers to any of the four types of cryptograms: TC, ARQC, AAR, or AAC.

The following three situations may appear:

1. If the terminal proposes the highest decision level (i.e., TC), the card risk management may either accept it or require a lower decision level, namely ARQC, AAR, or AAC.

2. If the terminal proposes an ARQC, the card may either accept it or request for a lower decision level, which can be either AAR or AAC.

3. If the terminal proposes an AAC, the card accepts it because there is no lower decision level that can override the AAC.

If the card responds with a decision level higher than that proposed by the terminal, this indicates a logic error in the card. When this error appears after the first issuance of the GENERATE AC command, the terminal shall terminate the EMV™ transaction.

6.8.3 Off-line denial of a transaction

For each bit in the TVR with value 1, the terminal checks the corresponding bit in the Issuer Action Code–Denial and Terminal Action Code–Denial.

Together, these two registers specify the conditions that determine the denial of a transaction without attempting to go on-line. If the corresponding bit in either of the two action code registers is set to 1, the terminal decides to reject the transaction according to the indication of either the issuer or the acquirer. The transaction is declined off-line.

In this case the terminal issues a GENERATE AC command, requiring the card to produce an AAC on the data related to the transaction at the point of service. To this end, the reference control parameter, which is P1 in the C-APDU, is set to 00h (see Section 6.8.6 for the significance of the C-APDU of the GENERATE AC).

After receiving this command, the card produces the requested AAC, since this is the lowest decision level. Consequently, bits 8 and 7 are set to 0 in the Cryptogram Information Data, returned in the R-APDU of the GENERATE AC command, encoding the AAC.

The AAC returned by the card indicates:

‣ A rejection of the transaction due to unacceptable business risks;

‣ A restriction that disallows the use of the card in certain business environments. This is the case when the use of a card is not compatible with certain merchant categories, or there is an incompatibility resulting from processing restrictions related to the AUC (see Section 6.5.2).

The card may optionally distinguish between these cases and may return appropriate codes in the least significant 3 bits (bit 3, bit 2, and bit 1), referred to as reason/advice/referral code of the Cryptogram Information Data:

‣ 000—no information given;

‣ 001—service not allowed;

‣ 010—PIN try limit exceeded;

‣ 011—issuer authentication failed (available for the second GENERATE AC);

‣ XXX—other values RFU.

Correspondingly, the terminal application may choose adequate messages to inform the cardholder about the rejection of the transaction.

In certain exceptional cases, like the situation when the PIN try limit is exceeded, the issuer may wish that the card asks the terminal to form and send an advice request message (1220 in the ISO 8583 notation; see Section 2.8.2). This advice request message is sent separately from either an authorization request or a clearing message. In this case the card positions bit 4 in the Cryptogram Information Data to 1, which means "advice (message) required."

When the AAC is forwarded to the issuer, it proves that the card was present during the denied transaction.

6.8.4 On-line transmission of a transaction

If the terminal is "off-line-only" (with Terminal Type in the set of values 13, 23, 16, 26, 36), the analysis described in this section is meaningless.

For "on-line-only" or "off-line with on-line capability" terminals, if the terminal does not reject the transaction off-line, the terminal action analysis continues with the evaluation of the bits in the TVR with respect to the pair of registers Issuer Action Code–On-line and Terminal Action Code–On-line. Together, these two registers specify the conditions that cause a transaction to be completed on-line.

For each bit in the TVR with value 1, the terminal checks the corresponding bits in the Issuer Action Code–On-line and Terminal Action Code–On-line. If the corresponding bit in either of these two action code registers is set to 1, the terminal shall require the on-line completion of the transaction processing.

In this case the terminal issues a GENERATE AC command, requiring the card to produce an ARQC on the data related to the transaction at the point of service. To this end the reference control parameter, P1 in the C-APDU, has bit 8 and bit 7 set to 1 and 0, respectively (see Section 6.8.6). The terminal may explicitly ask for a combined DDA/AC generation, in case the combined off-line DDA and GENERATE AC is indicated in bit 2 of the AIP and the terminal also supports combined DDA/AC generation (Section 6.4.1). In this case, bit 6 in the reference control parameter, P1 in the C-APDU, is set to 1. In case CDOL1 includes the tag 9F33, corresponding to the terminal capabilities, the card can determine by itself whether the combined DDA/AC generation should be performed, indifferent of the value of bit 6 in the reference control parameter (see also Section 6.8.6.1).

After receiving this command, the card risk management decides whether the terminal's ARQC decision is acceptable or this decision should be overridden with one of the lower decision levels, either AAR (referral) or AAC (rejection).

First, if the card risk management decides to reject the transaction, then the AAC is returned. Consequently, the Cryptogram Information Data in the R-APDU encodes the AAC as detailed in Section 6.8.3. This concludes the EMV™ processing.

Second, if the card decides to ask for a referral, then the AAR is returned. Consequently, the Cryptogram Information Data in the R-APDU encodes the AAR as follows: bit 8 = 1, bit 7 = 1, bit 4 = 0 (no advice request message is required). Bit 3 through bit 1 indicate the reason why the referral was required.

The terminal application chooses, based on some proprietary policies of the payment system, how to further process the AAR.

After receiving the AAR, the terminal could provide by itself an Authorization Response Code (tag 8A), based, for example, on the referral reason of the card. According to Annex A6 in Book 4 [3], this code can have one of the following meanings:

- Off-line approved (Y1)/Off-line declined (Z1);

- Approval (after card-initiated referral) (Y2)/Decline (after card-initiated referral) (Z2);

- Unable to go on-line, off-line approved (Y3)/Unable to go on-line, off-line decline (Z3).

The terminal proceeds to the issuance of a second GENERATE AC, requiring either TC (codes Y1, Y2, or Y3) or AAC (codes Z1, Z2, or Z3), which will conclude the transaction. Note that the Authorization Response Code is a data item included in the CDOL2 (see Section 6.8.6.1).

Otherwise, the terminal could use the AAR as an ARQC and go on-line to get further advice from the issuer on whether to authorize the transaction.

Third, if the card agrees with the terminal's decision level, then the ARQC is returned. Consequently, the Cryptogram Information Data in the R-APDU encodes the ARQC as 80h (bit 8, bit 7 = 10, bit 6 = 0, bit 5–bit 1 = 0). The on-line processing of the ARQC is described in Section 6.9.

6.8.5 Default action in a transaction

The terminal action analysis uses the registers Issuer Action Code-Default and Terminal Action Code-default to determine whether to reject or approve off-line an EMV™ transaction as follows:

- If the bit in the Issuer Action Code-Default or the terminal action code-default and the corresponding bit in the TVR are both set to 1, the transaction shall be denied.

- Otherwise, the transaction shall be approved.

This processing is performed in the following two cases:

1. The terminal is an off-line terminal and the transaction was not already rejected based on the content of the Issuer Action Code-Denial and Terminal Action Code-Denial registers (Section 6.8.3). In this case the contents of the Issuer Action Code–On-line and Terminal Action Code–On-line are meaningless. Consequently, the Terminal issues a first GENERATE AC asking for either TC (in case the analysis above indicated approval) or AAC (in case the analysis above indicated denial). This will conclude the EMV™ transaction.

2. The terminal has decided to transmit the transaction for on-line authorization, but the terminal was unable to go on-line (e.g., after sending the authorization request message 1100 to the issuer, the terminal does not receive the authorization response message 1110 in due time). In this case the terminal has already issued a first GENERATE AC with ARQC, and it obtained the ARQC from the card. Consequently, the terminal issues a second GENERATE AC asking for either TC (approval) or AAC (denial). In the former case, the terminal sets the Authorization Response Code to the value "Unable to go on-line, off-line approved" (Y3), while in the latter case, the terminal sets the Authorization Response Code to "Unable to go on-line, off-line decline" (Z3). Note that the Authorization Response Code is included in the CDOL2 (see Section 6.8.6.1). This shall conclude the EMV™ transaction.

In case the terminal recommends approval (TC), the Cryptogram Information Data returned in the R-APDU may be either the TC (approval) or AAC (denial). The choice depends on whether the card risk management agrees with the proposal of the terminal or overrides it with the only lower decision level acceptable in this case, which is AAC. Note that ARQC or AAR decision levels are ruled out since either the terminal is off-line or the R-APDU corresponds to a second GENERATE AC, for which the only acceptable decision levels can be TC or AAC.

In case the terminal recommends denial (AAC), the Cryptogram Information Data returned in the R-APDU must be AAC.

6.8.6 Compute Application Cryptogram with GENERATE AC

The C-APDU of the GENERATE AC command is given in Table 6.8.

Table 6.8
C-APDU of the GENERATE AC **Command**

Code	Value
CLA	*80* (EMV™ specific command)
INS	*AE*
P1	*Reference control parameter:*
	Bit 8 and bit 7: 00—AAC, 01—TC, 10—ARQC, 11—RFU
	Bit 6: 0—combined DDA/AC generation not explicitly requested
	1—combined DDA/AC generation requested
	Bit 5 to bit 1: RFU
P2	00
Lc	*Variable:* equal to the length of the data field
Data	*Transaction related data:* byte string formed with the value fields of the data objects listed in the CDOL1 (in the first issuance) or CDOL2 (in the second issuance)
Le	*00*

6.8.6.1   Transaction related data according to CDOL1/CDOL2

The card specifies in the Card Risk Management Data Object List 1 (CDOL1) the set of data objects from the business environment of the terminal that it needs for processing the first GENERATE AC. CDOL1 is mandatory in the card and is stored with the tag 8C. The card also specifies in the Card Risk Management Data Object List 2 (CDOL2) the set of data objects it needs from the terminal for processing the second GENERATE AC. CDOL2 is mandatory in the card and is stored with the tag 8D (see Section 6.3.2).

The data field of the C-APDU contains the data related to the transaction, which is formed as a raw byte string (which is not TLV encoded) concatenating the value fields of the data objects mentioned either in CDOL1 or in CDOL2. The card uses the data related to the transaction for the following purposes:

- Performing the card risk management processing;

- Determining whether the combined DDA/AC should be performed, even when not explicitly required in bit 6 of the reference control parameter, P1 of the C-APDU;

- Serving as input data for generating the appropriate cryptogram (TC, ARQC, AAR, or AAC) that serves as evidence of a card's participation in a particular EMV™ transaction.

The terminal shall build the data related to the transaction immediately before calling the GENERATE AC command, guaranteeing that the value fields of the data objects in the terminal represent the current values. Note also that even when the same data object is listed both in the CDOL1 and CDOL2, its value field included in the data related to the transaction could be different for the first and second GENERATE AC, since the terminal has continued its processing. This continuation of the processing could have changed the value of certain data objects (e.g., the TVR).

The list of data objects in the CDOL1/CDOL2 must include the tag-length reference of a random number generated by the terminal—Unpredictable Number (tag 9F37')—which guarantees that the evidence produced by the card cannot be replied by an attacker.

If the CDOL1 includes the tag 9F33 corresponding to the Terminal Capabilities, the card can determine by itself whether the combined DDA/AC generation should be performed or not, indifferent of the value of bit 6 in the reference control parameter, P1 in the C-APDU. Otherwise, the terminal must explicitly require the combined DDA/AC generation, setting bit 6 to 1 in the reference control parameter.

The tag-length references of some data objects are included in both the CDOL1 and CDOL2. These data objects indicate the business conditions of the transaction at the point of service:

- Amount, Authorized (Numeric) (tag 9F02);

- Amount, Other (Numeric) (tag 9F03);

- Transaction Currency Code (tag 5F2A);

- Transaction Date (tag 9A);

- Transaction Type (tag 9C);

- Terminal Country Code (tag 9F1A);

- Terminal Type (tag 9F35).

There could exist data objects in the terminal's business environment that are not directly involved in the card risk management but which must be considered for generating the application cryptogram. If this is the case, the issuer specifies their tag-length references in the Transaction Certificate Data Object List (TDOL), with tag 97 in the card. The terminal forms a byte string concatenating the value fields of the objects referenced in the TDOL and computes the hash code of this string (see Appendix D, Section D.2.1). This hash code is stored in the value field of the TC Hash Value data object with tag 98 in the terminal. In order to consider the computed hash code in the generation of the application cryptogram, the ICC must include the tag-length reference of the TC Hash Value among the items listed in the CDOL1/CDOL2.

The CDOL1/CDOL2 also include the tag-length references of the data objects that keep the results of the processing performed by the terminal:

• Terminal Verification Results (tag 95);

• Data Authentication Code (tag 9F4C), proving the completion by the terminal of the SDA (see stage 4 in Section 6.4.2);

• ICC Dynamic Number (tag 9F45), proving the completion by the terminal of the DDA (see Section 6.4.3.4)

The tag-length references of some other data objects are included only in the CDOL1, if these objects have a specific interest for the issuer. They include the data objects Amount in Reference Currency (tag 9F3A), and Transaction Reference Currency Code (tag 9F3C), which are used in a currency conversion procedure, if supported by the terminal.

The Issuer Authentication Data (tag 91) is received from the issuer in the authorization response message 1110. The issuer sends this message after receiving and processing an on-line authorization with ARQC in an authorization request message 1100 (Section 6.9.2). The CDOL2 may include the tag-length reference of the Issuer Authentication Data. The CDOL2 may also include the tag-length reference of the data object with tag 8A, Authorization Response Code. This code can be generated by the issuer, in case an ARQC was successfully sent on-line for authorization to the issuer and the corresponding response came back to the terminal, or by the terminal, in case the transaction is not authorized on-line (see also Section 6.8.4).

6.8.6.2 Application Cryptogram computation

After receiving the C-APDU of the GENERATE AC command, the card performs the card risk management procedure (see Section 7.10) to determine whether it agrees with the decision level proposed by the terminal. As a result, the card establishes the type of Application Cryptogram that it will generate (i.e., TC, ARQC, AAR, or AAC). The card sets the Cryptogram Information Data, which is the object in the card with tag 9F27, according to the type of Application Cryptogram it decides to compute.

In the next step the card generates the application cryptogram, which is the result of a cryptographic transformation performed with a cryptographic parameter that is uniquely linked to the ATC and/or the Application PAN of the card. This transformation is performed on a byte string referred to as a transaction claim, which includes the data objects related to the transaction at the point of service and a random number generated by the terminal. This Application Cryptogram can be regarded as the evidence produced by the card concerning its participation, as a delegate of the issuer, in the current transaction. One can recognize that this security mechanism corresponds to a dynamic authentication of the card (see Appendix D, Section D.7). Implicitly, this means that when producing the application cryptogram, the card dynamically authenticates itself, allowing a verifier to assess whether this is a genuine card or a counterfeit card. In other words, someone can say that there is an indissoluble link between the generation of the Application Cryptogram by the card and its dynamic authentication. The question is to whom the card dynamically authenticates. Or, in other words, which is the entity that can verify the validity of the dynamic authentication performed by the card, through assessing the correctness of the application cryptogram?

> *Case 1:* When the transformation used by the card is a symmetric cryptographic algorithm, the Application Cryptogram is computed as a MAC with a session secret key SK_{AC}. In this case the dynamic authentication of the card is performed with a MAC-based DDA (see Appendix D, Section D.7.1). The issuer of the card is the only entity that can verify the application cryptogram.

> *Case 2:* When the transformation used by the card is an asymmetric cryptographic algorithm, the Application Cryptogram is computed as a digital signature with the ICC private key (see Section 6.4.3). In this case the dynamic authentication of the card is performed with a digital signature–based DDA (see Appendix D, Section D.7.2). Anyone with an authentic copy of the ICC public key, and in particular the terminal at the point of service, can verify the application cryptogram. In Section 6.6 of Book 2 [2] of the *EMV 2000* specifications, this is called the combined dynamic data authentication/Application Cryptogram generation. This can be performed only during the first issuance of the GENERATE AC command and only when the card was requested for a TC or an ARQC.

In the remainder of this section, we describe the processing performed by the card for the computation of the Application Cryptogram in each of the two cases identified above.

Case 1   First, we explain the personalization of the appropriate keys in the card for the computation of the application cryptogram. The IH uses a tamper-resistant cryptographic module containing the issuer master key for Application Cryptogram (IMK_{AC}). The state of the art in cryptography requires that this master key be at least a double-length triple DES key (see Appendix E, Section E.3). When a card is issued, the IH uses the account iden- tification data linked to this card as a diversification information to derive a unique key per card (see Appendix E, Section E.5). The account identification data consists of the Application PAN and the Application PAN Sequence Number, which identifies the current card among several cards that may be linked to the same PAN (see Annex A1.4 in Book 2 [2]). This derived key is referred to as the ICC Application Cryptogram master key (MK_{AC}), which is also a double-length triple DES key (see Section 8.1.2 in Book 2 [2]). The issuer stores MK_{AC} in the ICC.

When the card receives the GENERATE AC command during its utiliza- tion stage, it derives an Application Cryptogram session key (SSK_{AC}) as a double-length triple DES key from the MK_{AC}, using the ATC as diversifica- tion information (see Annex A1.3 in Book 2 [2]). This session key is used to produce the Application Cryptogram with a MAC based on a 64 bit- length block cipher (see Appendix E, Section E.4) applied on the transaction claim.

The transaction claim is a byte string formed as the concatenation of the following data items:

- The value fields of some data objects received from the terminal in the transaction-related data field included in the C-APDU of the GENERATE AC command: Amount Authorized, Amount Other, Transaction Currency Code, transaction date, transaction type, Termi- nal Country Code, TVR, and unpredictable number;

- The value fields of some data objects in the card, describing the con- text of the EMV™ transaction from the viewpoint of the card: the AIP, the ATC, and the card risk management verification results (see Section 7.10).

The Application Cryptogram consists of 8 bytes if it is produced with a DES-based MAC with the symmetric session key SSK_{AC}.

The data field of the R-APDU returned by the GENERATE AC command consists of a BER-TLV data object. The encoding of this data object shall be according to one of the following two formats.

Format 1   The data object can be a primitive data object with a tag equal to 80. Its value field consists of the concatenation without delimiters (tag and length) of the value fields of the following data objects:

> Cryptogram Information Data—mandatory. The meaning of the bits in this data elements was explained in Sections 6.8.3 to 6.8.5;

> Application Transaction Counter (ATC)—mandatory;

> Application Cryptogram (AC)—mandatory;

> Issuer Application Data (IAD)—optional, formed according to the issuer preferences. It may include a key indicator and an algorithm version number to uniquely specify a certain version of the IMK_{AC}, if there are different key versions for time-variant key values, and a certain version of the MAC/derivation algorithms used in the card. The IAD may also include the witness values of the SDA or DDA processing by the terminal (i.e., the Data Authentication Code or the ICC Dynamic Number). In order to motivate certain decisions taken by the card, the issuer may decide to include the card risk management verification results in the IAD.

This format is suitable if the answer of the GENERATE AC has a preestablished format known in advance to the terminal application.

Format 2   The data object that is returned in the response message is a constructed data object with a tag equal to 77. Its value field may contain several BER-TLV encoded objects, but shall always include the Cryptogram Information Data (tag 9F27), the ATC (tag 9F36), and the Application Cryptogram computed by the ICC (tag 9F26).

This format is suitable if the answer of the GENERATE AC has no preestablished format.

Case 2   When the card receives the GENERATE AC command, it uses the ICC private key (n_{IC}, d_{IC}) to produce the signed dynamic application data. The procedure used to compute this signature is the same as that described in Section 6.4.3.3, with the following modifications:

> The leftmost 12 to 18 bytes of field 4, ICC dynamic data, in the M_R part of the dynamic application data to be signed, contains the following data items:

- ICC Dynamic Number length—1 byte;

- ICC Dynamic Number—2 to 8 bytes;

- Cryptogram Information Data—1 byte (supplementary item compared with the simple DDA);

- TC or ARQC—8 bytes (supplementary item compared with the simple DDA).

- The part M' of the dynamic application data to be signed consists only of the Unpredictable Number generated by the terminal (in the framework of the simple DDA, the part M' consists of the whole terminal dynamic data byte string, which includes the unpredictable number).

As one can see, the TC or ARQC is part of field 4. This means that the ICC must first compute the Application Cryptogram on the transaction claim. To this end the ICC computes the MAC based on a 64 bit-length block cipher with the symmetric session key SSK_{AC}, as explained in Case 1.

The data field of the R-APDU returned by the GENERATE AC command consists of a BER-TLV data object encoded according to format 2 in case the card risk management of the card decides to return a TC or ARQC.

Format 2   The data object that is returned in the response message is a constructed data object with a tag equal to 77. The value field may contain several BER-TLV coded objects, but shall always include the Cryptogram Information Data (tag 9F27), the ATC (tag 9F36), and the Signed Dynamic Application Data computed by the ICC (tag 9F4B).

If the card risk management of the card decides to answer with an AAC (rejection) to the combined DDA/AC request, the R-APDU is a BER-TLV data object, encoded either according to format 1 or 2. In either case the R-APDU includes at least the following data objects: Cryptogram Information Data, ATC, and the AAC.

6.8.6.3 Application Cryptogram verification
We have stated that the Application Cryptogram produced by the ICC can serve as evidence of a card's participation in an EMV™ transaction.

- If the GENERATE AC returns an ARQC, this is sent in an authorization request message 1100 to the IH. If the verification of the ARQC passes, the IH has proof that the card used at the point of service is genuine.

Thus, the ARQC serves as the on-line card authentication, which guarantees that no fake card is authorized in the system. This is a significant advance when compared to the debit/credit cards implemented with magnetic stripe.

- If the GENERATE AC returns a TC, this enters in a clearing message 1240, based on which the acquirer claims the Amount, Authorized in the EMV™ transaction from the issuer (see Section 2.10). If the verification of the TC received in the clearing message passes, the issuer knows that its card produced the TC that participated in the transaction. The issuer agrees to pay back the money to the acquirer. However, if the cardholder denies his or her participation in a transaction, the issuer cannot legally prove that the TC evidence is correct, since only the tamper-resistant cryptographic module of the IH can verify this evidence.

- In case the GENERATE AC returns an AAC with the reason code 010, "PIN try limit exceed," in bits 3 to bit 1 of the Cryptogram Information Data, the ICC may require the terminal to generate an advice message 1220 (bit 4 = 1 in the Cryptogram Information Data). This advice message informs the IH about the exceeding of the PIN try limit in the card, and the AAC serves as evidence to this fact.

The IH uses a tamper resistant cryptographic module containing the IMK_{AC} (see Section 6.8.6.2, Case 1). Based on the account identification data of the ICC, the cryptographic module derives the MK_{AC} corresponding to the ICC according to Annex A1.4 in Book 2 [2]. Using this key specific to each card, the cryptographic module computes the session key SSK_{AC} as a leaf in a keys-tree built starting from the MK_{AC} at the root of this tree and using the ATC, which uniquely identifies the EMV™ transaction. This session key is used to produce a MAC based on a 64 bit-length block cipher like DES applied on the transaction claim. This verification MAC is compared against the received application cryptogram, and if the two values are equal, the Application Cryptogram is accepted as valid evidence.

The verification algorithm explained above can be executed in the cryptographic module of the IH provided that the 1100, 1240, 1340, and 1220 messages include the following data items:

- Application Cryptogram (ARQC, TC, or AAC);

- Account identification data of the card (PAN and PAN Sequence Number);

▸ ATC and the Unpredictable Number;

▸ All the data objects necessary to reproduce the transaction claim.

If the ICC performs a combined DDA/AC generation, the terminal can verify off-line that the card is genuine by verifying the correctness of the Signed Dynamic Application Data returned in the R-APDU of the GENERATE AC command.

To this end the terminal first obtains an authentic copy of the ICC public key (n_{IC}, e_{IC}), applying the procedure described in Section 6.4.3.2. Using this key, the terminal verifies the Signed Dynamic Application Data by applying a slightly modified version of the processing described in Section 6.4.3.4. The entire procedure can be found in Section 6.6.2 of Book 2 [2]. If the verification passes, the terminal accepts the fact that the card is genuine. If, however, the Signed Dynamic Application Data is stored (e.g., by the payment system operator), the issuer would have a supplementary possibility to prove in a court of law the participation of an EMV™ card in a certain transaction. This facility, however, has significant costs in terms of storage space, and should be utilized only for transactions involving important values of the parameter Amount, Authorized.

6.9 On-line processing and issuer authentication

During the EMV™ transaction processing, the terminal may send an authorization request message (1100) to the acquirer because of at least one of the following reasons:

▸ The terminal is an "on-line-only" type, which requires always the authorization of the issuer.

▸ The attendant explicitly triggers the authorization request message, since there are some suspicions about the cardholder at the point of service.

▸ The terminal risk management stage has chosen the current transaction at random for on-line authorization. The terminal could reach the same decision following the velocity checking, which revealed a high number of transactions that were performed off-line.

▸ The terminal requires on-line authorization following the terminal action analysis stage, when the TVR was compared against the terminal/Issuer Action Code–On-line. The terminal issues the first

GENERATE AC command with the reference control parameter (P1) set up to ARQC. The card analyzes the proposal of the terminal according to its own card risk management procedure, which reflects the security and availability policies of the issuer, and agrees with an on-line authorization by the issuer.

‣ The terminal requires off-line completion following the terminal action analysis. The terminal issues the first GENERATE AC command with the reference control parameter (P1) set up to TC. The card analyzes the proposal of the terminal according to its own card risk management procedure and decreases the decision level proposed by the terminal from TC to ARQC.

Whenever the card answers with an ARQC in the Cryptogram Information Data, the terminal starts up the on-line processing function. This means that the card and the terminal judged the current transaction outside the limits of risk for an off-line completion, as defined by the issuer, payment system, and acquirer. Therefore, the issuer is required to analyze the actual EMV™ transaction at the point of service, based on the information it receives from the terminal and the account information it stores in the IH in connection with the card. This guarantees that the issuer can review the conditions of the transaction and can approve or reject it.

6.9.1 Authorization request and response with chip data

The terminal generates an authorization request message 1100. The data fields included in this message are those explained in Section 2.9 for the processing of transactions using magnetic stripe cards. In addition, the authorization request message includes the field ICC system-related data, corresponding to bit 55 in the bitmap (see Section 2.8.1) of the data elements present in the 1100 message, according to ISO 8583:1993. This field contains all the data objects from the point of service, which allows the IH to verify the correctness of the ARQC produced by the card. Among these data objects one can mention:

‣ Application Cryptogram (ARQC);

‣ Account identification data of the card (PAN and PAN Sequence Number);

‣ ATC and the unpredictable number;

- Issuer Application Data (IAD), which may include the key indicator and the algorithm version number to uniquely specify a certain version of the IMK_{AC} and of the MAC algorithm used to compute the ARQC in the card. The IAD may also include the witness values of the SDA or DDA processing by the terminal (i.e., the Data Authentication Code or the ICC Dynamic Number, respectively). In addition, the card risk management verification results can also be included in the IAD.

- All the data objects necessary to reproduce the transaction claim.

After receiving the authorization request message 1100, the IH first verifies that the card at the point of service is genuine. To this end, the cryptographic module of the IH must verify the correctness of the ARQC, according to the following steps:

- Use the key indicator present in the IAD to retrieve the correct version of the IMK_{AC}.

- Use the account identification data to derive the key MK_{AC} corresponding to the card participating in the transaction.

- Derive the actual session key SSK_{AC} from MK_{AC}, using the ATC as diversifier information in the keys-tree.

- Use the algorithm version number in the IAD to call the same algorithm for the computation of the MAC as that used in the card.

- Use SSK_{AC} to produce a MAC on the same data objects that were considered by the card in the transaction claim.

- Compare the computed MAC against the ARQC received in the authorization request message 1100. If the two values are equal, the ARQC is accepted as valid evidence that the card at the point of service is authentic and genuine.

The IH identifies the cardholder's account using the account identification data received in the authorization request message. The account information kept in connection with the card, including the history of the most recent transactions, allows the issuer to run an improved risk management procedure. The IH can perform additional verifications that are not possible at the point of service. Thus, the issuer can identify transactions performed with cards that were reported stolen, or that have already spent the limit of the account balance. Correspondingly, the issuer may approve or reject the transaction, indicating also the reason of the rejection.

The issuer prepares the Issuer Authentication Data with tag 91, which consists of two items: the authorization response cryptogram (ARPC) on 8 bytes, and the Authorization Response Code (ARC) on 2 bytes.

The cryptographic module of the IH computes the ARPC as a triple DES cryptogram in ECB mode on the result of an XOR operation between the ARQC and the ARC padded at right with 6 bytes 00h. The ARQC is the value received in the 1100 message and serves as a challenge for countering replay attacks. This cryptogram is produced with the same session key SSK_{AC}, which was already produced by the cryptographic module of the IH, since the verification of the ARQC. The ARPC allows the card to authenticate the issuer and to check that the Authorization Response Code represents the decision of the issuer concerning the finalization of the current EMV™ transaction.

The issuer may also consider the status of the EMV™ transaction, as the terminal reports it in the TVR and as the card reports it in the card risk management verification results, which was a data object included in the IAD. These two data objects are recommended for inclusion in the authorization request message. Interpreting this status information of the EMV™ transaction or considering some other post-issuance management operations, the issuer may decide whether it is necessary to correct the operation of the card. Examples of such corrections include:

> The extension of an expiration date, which would allow a cardholder who forgot to renew his or her card to operate, for a limited period of time, with an expired card;

> The unblocking of an application, following a PIN try limit exceeded;

> The modification of some parameters of the card risk management, like amount spending limits per day, per week, or per month, depending on the cardholder's availability of funds in the corresponding account;

> The updating of some cryptographic parameters, which are periodically changed for security reasons.

All of these corrections decided by the IH are translated in a sequence of post-issuance commands, which are encapsulated in the so-called Issuer Script Template 1 with tag 71 or in the Issuer Script Template 2 with tag 72.

After all this processing, the IH creates the authorization response message 1110. This message includes the data fields already mentioned in Section 2.9, in connection with the processing of transactions carried out with magnetic stripe cards. In addition, the authorization response message optionally includes the ICC system-related data field, corresponding to bit 55 in the bitmap of the data elements present in the 1110 message [4]. When the issuer authentication is performed, this field contains the Issuer Authentication Data, which consists of the ARPC and the ARC. When post-issuance management of the ICC is needed, the issuer includes in this field the Issuer Script Template 1 or the Issuer Script Template 2.

If the terminal does not receive the authorization response message, or it receives it too late, or with an invalid syntax, then the terminal shall process the transaction as being unable to go on-line (see Section 6.8.5).

If the authorization response message is received by the terminal but it does not contain the Issuer Authentication Data, the terminal shall not execute the EXTERNAL AUTHENTICATE command and shall set bit 5, "Issuer authentication was performed," in the TSI to 0. Otherwise, the card performs the issuer authentication as explained below.

6.9.2 Issuer Authentication

If the Issuer Authentication Data (tag 91) is received in the authorization response message 1110, the terminal checks the content of bit 3, "Issuer Authentication is supported," in the AIP.

When this bit is set to 1, the card supports issuer authentication through the EXTERNAL AUTHENTICATE command. In this case, the terminal prepares the C-APDU corresponding to this command according to Table 6.9.

The terminal may send this command only once in a transaction. The ICC should return the SW1SW2 = 6985 in the R-APDU, if this restriction is not respected. Regardless of the status words in the R-APDU, the terminal

Table 6.9
C-APDU of the EXTERNAL AUTHENTICATE **Command**

Code	Value
CLA	*00* (interindustry command)
INS	*82*
P1	00
P2	00
Lc	8 to 16 bytes
Data	*Issuer Authentication Data*—mandatory first 8 bytes contains the ARPC, while the following 1 to 8 bytes, if any, have a proprietary structure. Usually, when the ARC is considered in the computation of the ARPC, the bytes 9 and 10 include the ARC
Le	Not present

shall set to 1 bit 5, "Issuer authentication was performed," in the TSI. In case the SW1SW2 are different than 9000, the terminal shall set bit 7, "Issuer authentication was unsuccessful," in byte 5 of the TVR.

When bit 3, "Issuer Authentication is supported," in the AIP is set to 0, the card may combine the issuer authentication with the second GENERATE AC command. In this case, the issuer should have listed the data object Issuer Authentication Data (tag 91) in the CDOL2.

Regardless of whether EXTERNAL AUTHENTICATE or GENERATE AC is used to perform issuer authentication, the processing performed by the card is the same. The ICC decrypts the ARPC with the session key SSK_{AC}, which was previously derived for the computation of the ARQC. After performing the XOR operation with the value of the ARQC, the ARC can be obtained from the leftmost 2 bytes of the result. This computed value of the ARC is compared against the value received in the Issuer Authentication Data. If the two values are identical, the issuer authentication has passed.

6.10   Issuer scripts

It was mentioned in Section 6.9.1 that the authorization response message 1110 received from the IH can include post-issuance commands to be delivered to the ICC via the terminal. These commands are not relevant for the current EMV™ transaction, but they are used for updating the application data in the card during its utilization lifetime, or for switching an application in the card or even the entire card between the "unblocked" and "blocked" states. EMV™ does not make any provisions for updating the application code in the card. The format of the post-issuance commands can be proprietary to the issuer. They are not meaningful for the terminal, which should only dispatch them from the authorization response message and send them sequentially to the ICC that has to be updated.

6.10.1   Processing of issuer script templates

The IH can group the post-issuance commands in two types of templates:

1.   Issuer Script Template 1 (tag 71) groups proprietary post-issuance commands to be transmitted to the ICC *before* sending the 2nd GENERATE AC to the ICC.

2.   Issuer Script Template 2 (tag 72) groups proprietary post-issuance commands to be transmitted to the ICC after sending the second GENERATE AC to the ICC.

Each issuer script template, regardless of whether it is of the type 1 or type 2, can include the following data objects:

- Issuer Script Identifier (tag 9F18), which is represented on 4 bytes in binary format. This identifier is optional and is not interpreted by the terminal. The Issuer Script Identifier allows the issuer to distinguish among several issuer script templates that can be included in the same authorization response message.

- Issuer Script Command APDU (tag 86) has a variable number of bytes depending on the type of the C-APDU to be sent to the card. Several Issuer Script Command APDU(s) can be included in an issuer script template.

The issuer can send more than one issuer script template in the same authorization response message. The only restriction is that the total length of the issuer script templates is less than or equal to 128 bytes.

After the reception of the authorization response message, the terminal processes each issuer script template in the sequence it appears in field 55 of the authorization response message. For each template the terminal performs the following processing:

- Create a new data structure issuer script results of 5 bytes (see Appendix A5 in Book 4 [3]), which will store the results concerning the processing of the commands contained in the current issuer script template. Add this data structure at the end of a byte string containing the data structures corresponding to other templates that were already processed.

- Reset the command counter that keeps the number of Issuer Script Command APDU(s) identified in the current issuer script template.

- Parse the value field of the current template.

  - Check whether the Issuer Script Identifier (tag 9F18) is present. In the affirmative case, copy the value field of this data object into bytes 2 to 5 in the issuer script results. The Issuer Script Identifier is meaningful to the issuer when interpreting the issuer script results reported by the terminal after sending of the post-issuance commands to the ICC.

  - Create a first-in-first-out stack (FIFO), where each element contains the value field of one Issuer Script Command APDU data object (tag

86) separated from the value field of the template. Each new element added in the stack increments the command counter.

- The processing sequence described below is performed before the second GENERATE AC, if the current template was identified with tag 71, or after the second GENERATE AC, in case the current template was identified with tag 72. Repeat the following steps a number of times equal to the command counter:

  - Pop the C-APDU kept in the current element of the FIFO stack indicated by the stack pointer.

  - Deliver this C-APDU to the ICC.

  - Examine only the status word SW1 in the R-APDU delivered by the ICC.

  - If SW1 indicates normal processing (SW1 = 90) or warning (SW1 = 62 or 63), the processing continues with the next Issuer Script Command APDU stored in the stack. If the command counter indicates that this is the first C-APDU that is processed, set to 1 bit 3, "Script processing was performed," in byte 1 of the TSI.

  - If SW1 indicates an error condition, the processing does not continue with other C-APDU(s) in the stack. The terminal shall set the first nibble of the first byte in the issuer script results to 1, "Script processing failed." The terminal shall write the sequence number of the Issuer Script Command APDU that reported the error in the second nibble of the first byte in the issuer script results. This sequence number equals the value of the command counter, when less than E, or otherwise the sequence number is set to F. The terminal sets to 1 bit 6, "Script processing failed before final GENERATE AC," in the byte 5 of the TVR, if the current template is encoded with tag 71. The terminal sets to 1 bit 5, "Script processing failed after final GENERATE AC," in byte 5 of the TVR, if the current template is encoded with tag 72.

- When the processing of the entire sequence of Issuer Script Command APDU(s) is successfully performed, the terminal sets up the first nibble of the first byte in the issuer script results to 2, "Script processing successful." The terminal shall write the value 0 in the second nibble of the first byte in the issuer script results.

6.10.2 Post-Issuance Commands

The post-issuance commands can be divided into two groups:

1. Commands that change the status of an application or of the entire card, including APPLICATION BLOCK, APPLICATION UNBLOCK, and CARD BLOCK (see Sections 2.5.1, 2.5.2, and 2.5.3 in Book 3 [1]);

2. Commands that change the values of some internal parameters, like the status of a PIN, of some cryptographic keys, or a PIN value, or the values of the data elements associated with the EMV™ application that participates in the card risk management processing. This category includes the EMV™ post-issuance command PIN CHANGE/UNBLOCK (see Section 2.5.10 in Book 3 [1]). Payment systems and issuers may define supplementary commands tailored to their specific needs.

The post-issuance commands use secure messaging:

▸ The integrity and authenticity of the issuer is achieved using a MAC.

▸ The confidentiality of cryptographic keys or of a PIN value to be updated in the EMV™ application is achieved through symmetric key encryption.

References

[1] EMVCo, *EMV 2000 Integrated Circuit Card Specification for Payment Systems, BOOK 3—Application Specification*, Version 4.0, December 2000, http://www.emvco.com/specifications.cfm.

[2] EMVCo, *EMV 2000 Integrated Circuit Card Specification for Payment Systems, BOOK 2—Security and Key Management*, Version 4.0, December 2000, http://www.emvco.com/specifications.cfm.

[3] EMVCo, *EMV 2000 Integrated Circuit Card Specification for Payment Systems, BOOK 4—Cardholder, Attendant, and Acquirer Interface Requirements*, Version 4.0, December 2000, http://www.emvco.com/specifications.cfm.

[4] ISO/IEC 8583:1993, "Financial Transaction Card Originated Messages—Interchange Message Specifications," 1995.

[5] ISO/IEC 3166, "Codes for the Representation of Names of Countries," 1997.

EMV™ Chip Migration Issues

There are many aspects that advocate for the migration from magnetic stripe–based payment systems towards EMV™ chip solutions:

‣ Increased security of the EMV™ CAMs, both in on-line and off-line operation, due to the implementation of dynamic authentication mechanisms using the computational power of the EMV™ chip;

‣ Support for off-line PIN verification at the attended point of service, instead of either on-line PIN verification or handwritten signatures, using the tamper-resistance storage offered by the chip card;

‣ Increased data storage capacity and security of the chip when compared with a magnetic stripe;

‣ The possibility of EMV™ chip cards to accommodate multiple applications at the same time, and to offer supplementary services other than those related to effecting payments.

Consequently, there is a good expectation that payment system operators and their clients, both issuers and acquirers, are going to adopt this technology on a large scale.

While the previous chapter concentrated on presenting the technical aspects related to the EMV™ standard, this chapter focuses on management and organizational issues concerning the EMV™ chip migration. In this context we analyze the impact of the chip migration on the roles involved in the implementation of the payment system infrastructure—namely, the payment system operator, the issuer, and the acquirer. We identify the responsibilities of each role and we summarize the actions to be taken for accomplishing these responsibilities. The main task of the payment system operator is to provide the adequate payment network that supports the EMV™ transactions. The payment system must also define an appropriate regulatory framework that establishes the requirements that must be fulfilled by issuers and acquirers to connect to this network. The main responsibility of the issuer is to design the appropriate EMV™ chip cards and to implement the authorization rules in its host computer, following the minimum requirements stated in the payment system's regulatory framework. The task of the acquirer is to adapt his terminals to support the EMV™ chip transaction at the point of service, and its network to convey the supplementary chip related data from the point of service to the issuer, via the payment system's network, and vice-versa. Note that throughout this chapter the term "chip" designates an EMV™ chip, unless otherwise explicitly stated.

The chapter is organized as follows. Section 7.1 outlines the definition of an EMV™ regulatory framework and its impact on the issuers and acquires participating in the EMV™ payment system. Starting with Section 7.2, we focus on some ICC design issues. First, we present the process of defining ICC specifications by issuers, observing the boundaries established by the EMV™ regulatory framework. Section 7.3 presents criteria for choosing an ICC chip platform. Section 7.4 identifies a number of principles concerning the design of multiapplication cards. Section 7.5 outlines the issuer's business case for an EMV™ debit/credit card application. Section 7.6 presents a design example of adaptive initialization of the application processing. Section 7.7 discusses the choice of the CAM methods, and Section 7.8 outlines the choice of CVM methods, according to the type of payment service supported by a certain EMV™ card application. Section 7.9 outlines the definition of the processing restrictions of a card application. Finally, Section 7.10 analyzes card risk management, which is an essential component of the trade-off between security and availability of the payment service during the processing of a transaction.

7.1   EMV™ regulatory framework

From the point of view of the payment system operator providing financial services to both acquirers and issuers, the impact of the EMV™ chip migration refers to:

- The modification of the network's node computers connecting issuers and acquirers to the payment network and of the processing performed by these nodes such that supplementary chip related data elements could be transported in the authorization/financial/advice messages (see Section 2.8);

- The modification of the gateway node computers, providing message translation between the payment system network run by the current operator and the payment networks run by other payment operators that have business agreements with the current payment operator;

- The definition of a regulatory framework that establishes the EMV™ chip migration path for both issuers and acquirers using the services provided by the payment system.

This regulatory framework establishes the business objectives, functional requirements, and security politics, which facilitate the adoption of the EMV™ chip technology. Issuers and acquirers migrating to EMV™ use this framework to define their own business case in terms of controlling risk and reducing fraud while increasing the availability of the financial service for the cardholder and reducing the costs of the transactions through off-line completion.

7.1.1 Business objectives

First, the payment system operator defines the types of payment services supported by his network (e.g., ATM cash dispensing, POS payments, electronic purse loading, loyalty schemes support).

Second, the payment system operator defines the processing features available for the chip support, which are offered to both acquirers and issuers to implement a certain type of service. Some of these processing features are listed below, ordered according to their increasing complexity:

1. Identification of the transactions carried out at an EMV™-enabled terminal, which is a terminal that can read an EMV™ chip card and complete the associated transaction profile. This identification is possible regardless of the actual method used at the point of service to capture the financial data of the card;

2. Identification of the transactions carried out with an EMV™ chip card at an EMV™-enabled terminal;

3. Support of off-line PIN verification as CVM at the point of service;

4. Support of the chip-related data in the authorization and financial messages, allowing on-line dynamic CAM and issuer script processing;

5. Support of off-line authorization below floor limits through subsequent clearing messages/transactions;

6. Support of post-processing advice messages concerning the allowable number of PIN tries exceeded and the result of the issuer script processing.

Note that not all the services need all the aforementioned processing features. For example, a POS payment service needs processing feature 5 listed above, since local authorization below floor limits is supported. However, an ATM service that authorizes all the money withdrawal transactions on-line does not need it.

Third, the payment system operator redefines its interchange fee strategy to take into account the following two factors:

1. The influence of the chip-related data's size in interchange messages;

2. The promotion of stimulating interchange fees during the process of the chip migration, for the early acceptance of the EMV™ chip technology by acquirers and issuers.

The first factor reflects the modification of the amount of data exchanged between acquirer and issuer in case a transaction is completed with the chip. Chip transactions may determine the increase of the data interchange. Indeed, data interchange increases whenever data related to the on-line dynamic CAM is sent from the acquirer to the issuer in the authorization request message and whenever issuer authentication data and issuer scripts are sent from the issuer to the acquirer in the authorization response message. The amount of data exchanged between the acquirer and the issuer can decrease in chip transactions in case the CVM at the point of service is modified from on-line PIN verification to off-line PIN verification. It is also important to notice that the chip transactions may determine additional messages to be exchanged between the issuer and the acquirer, which can also result in the increase of the data interchange.

The second factor implies the reduction of the interchange fees for acquirers, whenever they cannot prove that a transaction was completed at an EMV™-enabled terminal. In order to obtain the highest exchange fee for a transaction, the acquirer must adapt his terminals to be EMV™ compatible. The acquirer must also upgrade its network to support at least the first three processing features listed above, allowing mainly the identification of all the transactions initiated at an EMV™-compatible terminal.

7.1.2 Functional requirements

A flexible way to define the regulatory framework consists of specifying a minimal set of functional requirements, concerning both issuers' chip cards and acquires' terminals (accepting chip cards).

> • *Minimal card requirements:* This is an issuers' concern when designing the layout of the card files and the functions that must be implemented in the EMV™ chip cards. These minimal card requirements determine the appropriate level of security and availability with respect to financial transactions like cash withdrawal, payments for goods and services at POS terminals, and anticipated payments for incremental amounts (phone calls, fuel stations) at various types of terminals (on-line, off-line, off-line with on-line capability). Issuers claiming the compliance of their chip cards with the minimal card requirements must pass a card type approval [1], which is a procedure defined by each individual payment system. Independent certification laboratories appointed by the payment system operator perform the type approval process. The minimal card requirements impact the definition of the ICC specification by the issuer, as it will be presented in Section 7.2.

> • *Minimal terminal requirements:* This is an acquirers' concern when adapting the terminals to EMV™ compatibility. The acquirer has to install new terminals or upgrade the existing ones such that the Terminal Type approval levels 1 [2] and 2 [3] are obtained. Note that EMVCo elaborates upon these approval procedures for terminals. EMVCo is an organization formed by Europay International, MasterCard International, and Visa International to manage, maintain, and enhance the EMV™ Integrated Circuit Card Specifications. In addition, EMVCo organizes and coordinates the EMV™ level 1 and level 2 type approval activities. Certification laboratories assigned by EMVCo perform these approval processes. When referring to the generic EMV™ communication protocol stack described in Figure 4.1, *EMV level 1* compatibility means the adaptation of the terminals'

communication subsystem, while *EMV level 2* compatibility means the adaptation of the software at the application level to support the EMV™ selection mechanism, the debit/credit transaction flow, and security aspects. EMV level 1 is concerned with the adaptation of both the communication protocol and the corresponding hardware (from the viewpoint of the electrical signals and of the mechanical aspects). A terminal certified EMV level 1 allows the correct communication with the EMV™ card, after the ATR sequence.

Besides the minimal card requirements that must be observed for the issuance of chip cards, the impact of the EMV™ chip migration on issuers is reflected also in the adaptation of the processing performed by the IH. The IH has to be able to correctly evaluate the authorization/financial requests, which include chip-related data, and to provide adequate responses. The requests are received from terminals that accept the EMV™ card application proposed by the issuer, while the responses are elaborated by the IH and sent back to the terminal.

Moreover, the issuer must comply to fallback requirements, which state that an EMV™ chip card must be issued with a magnetic stripe for storing the financial data of the cardholder. The magnetic stripe should allow the completion of a transaction in case the chip fails [4].

From the point of view of the acquirer, the implementation of an EMV™ payment system means both the adaptation of terminals towards EMV™ compatibility, according to the minimal terminal requirements, and the adaptation of the acquirer network. The network of the acquirer connects EMV™ terminals in the field with the AH, and the latter with the AN provided by the payment system operator as an entry point in its payment network. The acquirer network can be adapted in two separate stages, with an increasing degree of complexity.

In the first stage, the network can be modified for partial chip support only, meaning that the messages received from the terminals carry enough data elements that allow:

- Identifying the possibilities of the terminal regarding what kind of data capturing it is able to perform, including the possibility of reading an EMV™ chip;

- Identifying the actual method of data capturing, including the reading of the chip, as used by the terminal in the current transaction;

- Identifying the result of an off-line PIN cardholder verification method.

An acquirer providing partial chip support fulfills the criteria of the payment system operator for obtaining the highest interchange fee, as explained in Section 7.1.1.

In the second stage, the acquirer's network can be completed for full chip support, which also allows:

▸ The support of ICC-related data in the authorization/financial request and response, which allows on-line CAM, issuer authentication, and issuer script processing;

▸ The support of off-line CAM in transactions involving amounts below floor limits, with the processing of subsequent financial advice messages for clearing.

▸ Post-processing advice messages on allowable number of PIN tries (off-line PIN validation), issuer authentication result, and issuer script results.

Note that the acquirer can directly adapt his network for the full chip support. The main stimulus for the full chip support is the liability policy established by the payment system operator, as it is explained in Section 7.1.3.

The EMV™ terminals at the point of service must be adapted such that the additional ICC-related data elements are transferred in the authorization/financial messages exchanged between the terminal and the AH, and vice-versa. This implies the modification of the existing terminal to the AH interface. The AH has to be modified to support the processing determined by the presence of the ICC-related data in the payment messages received from terminals.

The acquirer must also comply with fallback requirements, which state that an EMV™ compatible terminal must be equipped with a magnetic stripe reader. The magnetic stripe reader should allow the capturing of the card's financial data from its magnetic stripe, in case the card does not contain a chip or the chip is not functional.

7.1.3 Security politics

Security politics are part of the EMV™ regulatory framework defined by the payment system operator. They include guidelines for both issuers and acquirers concerning the choice of the most appropriate CAM and CVM to be implemented in chip cards and terminals in order to counter both counterfeit and fraudulent transactions. A counterfeit transaction is a transaction performed with a card that is not genuine, which is also referred to as a counterfeit card. A fraudulent transaction is a transaction involving a different user of the card than the legitimate cardholder to whom the card was issued. The guidelines concerning the choice of the appropriate CAM/CVM depend on the type of service implemented in a chip card application, and they also depend on the type of terminal and the type of card application that is actually used at the point of service.

The security politics further determine the security policies adopted by both issuers and acquirers in terms of controlling risk and reducing fraud while increasing the availability of the financial service for the cardholder and reducing the costs of the transactions through off-line completion. Security policies pertain to both the card and the terminal in terms of multi-application support policies, CAM policies, CVM policies, and risk management policies, to name only the most representative.

An important chapter of the security politics is the distribution of liabilities between issuers and acquirers in case disputes are generated by fraudulent and counterfeit transactions. In general, within the boundaries of an EMV™ payment system, the politic is to hold liable for both fraudulent and counterfeit transactions that party (issuer or acquirer) that did not complete the EMV™ chip migration. It is also common practice to hold liable for counterfeit/fraudulent transactions the party that fails to process an EMV™ transaction correctly. Thus, an acquirer is responsible for his terminals when they provide incorrect data and processing decisions to the chip card. In the same way, the issuer is responsible for the value of the personalization parameters and processing options available in a chip card.

The liability distribution in case of counterfeit transactions can be based on some of the following principles:

▸ An acquirer is liable for the counterfeit transactions authorized on-line using the financial data stored on the magnetic stripe of a card, in case the card contained an EMV™ chip and the terminal is not EMV™ compatible. This encourages the acquirer to accelerate the replacement of all the terminals with EMV™ compatible terminals that have obtained the Terminal Type approval level 1 and 2.

▸ The acquirer is responsible for all the counterfeit transactions authorized off-line for transaction amounts below the Terminal Floor Limit when the terminal is not EMV™ compatible and the card contains a chip. The same liability rule can be enforced when the terminal is EMV™ compatible, the card contains a chip, the reading of the chip data failed, and the terminal did not forward the transaction for authorization to the issuer.

▸ An acquirer is responsible for counterfeit transactions authorized on-line, in case both the terminal is EMV™ compatible and the card is an EMV™ chip card, but the Application Cryptogram (ARQC) of the card could have not been included in the authorization/financial request towards the issuer. This liability decision could encourage the acquirer to upgrade his network to provide full chip support.

▸ An issuer is liable for any counterfeit transactions authorized on-line whenever the terminal is EMV™ compatible but the financial data of the card was captured from the magnetic stripe of the card. This can happen either when the card contains no chip or when it contains a chip that is not functioning properly. This encourages the issuer to migrate to EMV™ chip cards that have obtained appropriate card type approval.

▸ An issuer is responsible for all the counterfeit transactions authorized off-line for transaction amounts below the Terminal Floor Limit when the terminal is EMV™ compatible and the card does not contain a chip.

The liability distribution in case of fraudulent transactions can be based on some of the following principles:

▸ An acquirer is responsible for any fraudulent transaction held in the following circumstances. The card contains a chip, and the CVM List indicates the preference of the issuer for either an off-line or on-line PIN verification. The terminal is either not equipped with a chip reading device or it is equipped with a chip reading device but its PIN pad does not conform to the minimal terminal requirements.

▸ An acquirer is responsible for fraudulent transactions completed off-line whenever the CVM chosen by the terminal is neither among those listed in the CVM List of the chip card nor the off-line PIN verification.

▸ The issuer is liable for any fraudulent transactions, even if the respective cards where blacklisted to terminals, whenever they are conducted on EMV™-compatible terminals equipped with secure PIN pad but the card does not contain a chip with an appropriate card application. This is encouraging the issuer to migrate to EMV™ chip cards that have obtained the card type approval.

> • The issuer is responsible for any fraudulent EMV™ transaction completed off-line, whenever the following conditions are simultaneously observed. The terminal chooses correctly the off-line completion of an EMV™ transaction according to the decision of the terminal risk management procedure. This decision is based on transaction amounts lower than the Terminal Floor Limit. The identity of the cardholder is verified with a CVM that is indicated in the CVM List personalized by the issuer or with an off-line PIN verification.

While the reduction of interchange fees can encourage acquirers to complete the partial chip upgrading of their networks, the liability politics can encourage both the chip migration of the issuer and the full chip upgrading of the acquirer's network. This is mainly due to the reduction of losses when processing counterfeit transactions and when disputes arise with the cardholder due to fraudulent transactions.

7.2   Deriving ICC specifications by issuers

This section begins to discuss some of the card design issues. First, we describe the process of defining the ICC functional requirements and ICC specifications by an issuer. Figure 7.1 illustrates this process.

We assume that the issuer is using the services provided by a certain payment system, whose payment network is managed either by a card association or a payment system operator.

In order to facilitate the implementation by issuers of one of his EMV™ card application brands, the payment system may first elaborate a set of minimal card requirements derived from the *EMV 2000* specifications, taking into account specific business objectives of the payment system. All the issuers that are interested in issuing cards displaying the corresponding brand must observe the minimal card requirements [5]. The payment system may further elaborate a set of proprietary ICC specifications, which customize the general EMV™ specifications to the needs of the payment system regarding the card design, within the limits imposed by the minimal card requirements [6]. Note that several ICC profiles can be derived. They answer various levels of security strength and performance for different prices (e.g., a $3 ICC profile). It is important to note that the payment system can directly elaborate the proprietary ICC specifications without establishing a set of minimal card requirements [7].

Figure 7.1
Definition of
the issuer ICC
specification.

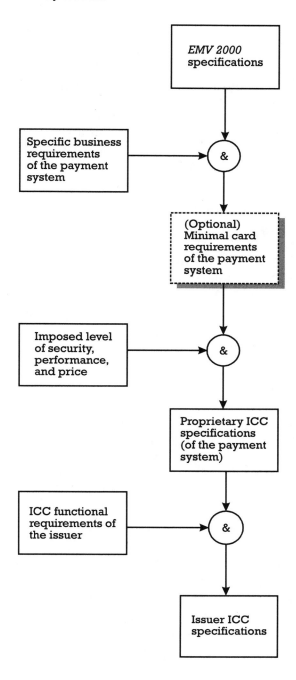

Taking into account its own business requirements, the issuer defines
the ICC functional requirements within the boundaries outlined in the

minimal card requirements imposed by the payment system, if any. Considering the ICC functional requirements and the proprietary ICC specification of the payment system, the issuer defines its own issuer ICC specifications, which answer its particular business needs in the framework regulated by the payment system.

Some of the topics the issuer's designer has to address in the definition of the ICC functional requirements are:

- Type of ICC architecture;

- Type of cryptographic support needed and its impact on the hardware/software platform of the ICC;

- Multiapplication support;

- ICC file system organization;

- ICC functions support;

- EMV™ application support for cardholder verification, card authentication, issuer authentication, issuer scripts processing, and card risk management.

The issuer ICC specification defines the requirements concerning:

- Data elements and files for application selection;

- Identification of the card common data objects, which are available for all the applications accommodated in the card;

- Identification of the application specific data objects and their organization in AEF(s);

- Definition of some application data objects, among which the most important are:

    - The content of the PDOL list whenever the ICC implements adaptable transaction profiles, variable AEF organizations, and card risk management depending on the particularities of the business environment at the point of service;

    - The AIP and AFL;

    - The content of the data object lists used for card risk management, namely CDOL1 and CDOL2;

- The content of the DDOL in case the DDA is chosen as a CAM;

- CVM codes appropriate for an application depending on the services it provides;

- Processing restriction parameters (e.g., application usage control, effective date, expiration date);

- The Issuer Action Code Denial/On-line/Default data objects, which can influence the terminal action analysis based on the status of the TVR.

- Definition of the card risk management and the proprietary data objects in connection with it;

- Requirements concerning the implementation of the EMV™ commands, with an emphasis on the GET PROCESSING OPTIONS, VERIFY, INTERNAL AUTHENTICATE, EXTERNAL AUTHENTICATE, and GENERATE AC;

- Requirements concerning the commands accepted in post-issuance and their processing by the card: identification of proprietary post-issuance commands for data updating, secret keys updating, and the corresponding security mechanisms.

7.3 Selection criteria of the ICC architecture

The ICC architecture refers to both the hardware organization and the software platform of the chip. In Section 3.2.1 we briefly presented a typical hardware organization of a chip and possible types of chip software platforms. In this section we first analyze the needs of the chip in terms of hardware resources according to the processing requirements of the EMV™ application. Second, we discuss selection criteria for choosing an appropriate type of ICC software platform, according to the business needs of the issuer.

7.3.1 ICC hardware resources

The choice of the ICC hardware architecture mainly depends on the processing needs of the EMV™ card application running in the chip. The dimension of the data and cryptographic parameters used by the card application determines the size of the EEPROM space needed in the card. The dimension of the application code itself can influence the size of the EEPROM, in case the application code is downloaded in the EEPROM and is not hard coded in the ROM mask of the chip.

If the card application must implement the CAM with the DDA mechanism or must implement the CVM as an enciphered PIN verified off-line by the ICC, then the chip must perform an RSA operation. This operation is needed either for producing a digital signature (DDA) or for decrypting the RSA digital envelope containing the PIN of the cardholder. The processing of the RSA operation is time consuming if it is implemented in software. This would infringe upon the business requirement of the issuer that the time allowed for the completion of an EMV™ transaction should be comparable to the time needed for completing the transaction with magnetic stripe. Therefore, the hardware structure of the ICC has to include a coprocessor specialized in performing arithmetic operations with long integers (of at least 768 bits), which are necessary to perform the RSA operation. This coprocessor is referred to as a cryptographic coprocessor. Certainly, the presence of the cryptographic coprocessor in the hardware architecture of the ICC increases the price of the chip. The price of the chip further varies depending on the bit length of the RSA modulus that can be processed by the cryptographic coprocessor, in the sense that the bigger the length of the modulus the higher the price. Currently, the bit length of the modulus is 1,024 bits [8–10], but there are chips on the market that can work with a bit length of 2,048 bits [8]. The issuer might be interested in generating the ICC private key and ICC public key pair used for DDA and/or generating the ICC PIN encipherment private key and ICC PIN encipherment public key pair by the chip during the personalization of the card application. Note that the generation in the chip of these key pairs does not influence the price of the chip.

The cost of the chip is influenced by the size of the EEPROM. The bigger the EEPROM size the higher the price of the chip. Chip cards with EEPROM in the range of 2 to 32 kilobytes are currently available [8], while cards with 64 kilobytes of EEPROM are expected soon. The type of ICC software platform heavily influences the size of the EEPROM. Thus, an ICC software platform allowing application download, like a Java platform [11] or a MULTOS platform [12], requires a considerable amount of EEPROM space for the application code itself. Moreover, since an EMV application uses public key cryptography for implementing the SDA, the DDA, or the enciphered PIN verified off-line by the ICC, EEPROM space has to be reserved for storing various certified public keys in the card, as well as the corresponding private keys. Therefore, one can see that the size of the EEPROM memory is an important factor to consider in the design of the ICC by the issuer, since it impacts on the price of the chip.

7.3.2 ICC software platform

When the issuer chooses to implement the EMV™ card application on an ICC with a proprietary software platform (see Section 3.2.1), the intrinsic price of the chip is low. Since there is no separation between the application code and the lower level native functions, then the operating system of the ICC is compact and can completely reside in the ROM. In this case there is no separation between the card manufacturer and the card application provider, since the card manufacturer writes the entire software of the ICC.

However, while the initial price of the card is low, there are other inconveniences that can increase the issuer's card costs during the lifetime of the card application.

> ‣ Since the functionality of the card application is fixed at the time of the card manufacturing, the issuer has limited possibilities of changing this functionality once the card has been produced. This means that the issuer has to spend a considerable budget for testing the card application before the card production is started, since the possibilities of subsequent repairing are limited. The repairing is only feasible for those chip operating systems allowing for patch loading.

> ‣ After the issuance of the card, the issuer has limited possibilities for adding new applications to the card, determined mainly by the available EEPROM and the adequate commands of the operating system. These applications could broaden the range of services the issuer can offer to cardholders—for example, loyalty applications, or e-purse applications. In this way the issuer could make his service more attractive for the cardholder and could better follow the trends of the market. Any new service involves the issuance of other cards, which determines comparable development efforts.

> ‣ The issuer may choose to order cards with several card producers, to be independent of possible production bottlenecks and delivery delays of any one of the card producers. This means that the testing effort for each new card producer has to be supported separately. If the issuers choose from a variety of ready EMV™ products from card vendors, then no extra development costs are involved. However, those issuers who have special functional requirements might find that the card vendors expect to be paid for the development effort.

When the issuer chooses to implement the EMV™ card application on a Java card, the intrinsic price of the chip is higher. However, the flexibility of the card justifies and can pay back this initial investment.

▪ The roles of the card manufacturer and application provider can be played by different organizations. Therefore, the issuer can more easily organize the card production process. Thus, the issuer is not compelled to pay separate development costs to each card manufacturer, since the Java card platform is standardized [11]. The development costs for the card application are lower, since the Java language is accessible to more programmers than the particular programming language of each proprietary ICC platform. Moreover, once the card application is written it can be easily ported to different Java cards from different manufacturers or from the same manufacturer when cards with more EEPROM memory are available. Thus, whenever card production reasons require multiple Java card vendors, the Java card application is not rewritten each time.

▪ The card issuers can more easily follow the trends of the market, in the sense that they can add new applications to the card during its lifetime. This is possible because applications can be downloaded to the card even after the card is issued. It is also important to note that Java cards can accommodate multiple applications while guaranteeing a high degree of security [13].

▪ The testing of the card application to be downloaded in Java cards is not so critical as in the case for proprietary ICC platforms. If errors are detected during a trial period, repairs can be easily made, since the applet can be rewritten and downloaded to the card, without going through a new manufacturing and issuance process.

7.4   Multiapplication ICC

A cardholder requires the issuer to have full availability of his or her money anytime and anywhere, through a range of appropriate payment instruments, as far as there is enough money in the account and the credit history records no abuses.

To answer this requirement optimally, the issuer should provide a range of card applications that answer various payment behaviors, (e.g., credit, debit, and stored value), both within the boundaries of a country (domestic environment) and internationally. The payment service delivered by each card application can be implemented by another payment system.

The issuer could issue a separate ICC to the cardholder for each card application it offers. This approach has the advantage of simplicity of the application management in the card and of the personalization process, but it involves separate costs for the issuance of each card.

Alternatively, the issuer may chose to implement multiple applications on the same ICC. This would reduce the cost ratio ICC/card application, but would increase the application management and personalization costs. With the advance of the Java cards, however, these costs tend to decrease, making accessible the "one chip multiple applications" approach [14].

In this section we analyze some aspects of issuing multiapplication cards. First, we discuss design principles regarding the choice of a set of card applications that can be simultaneously accommodated in the same ICC. Then, we address design principles for the definition of a card layout, considering both the file structure and the functionality of a multiapplication card.

7.4.1 Choice of a set of card applications

If the issuer chooses the multiapplication approach, a set of card applications that can be accommodated by the ICC must be defined. Several elements are simultaneously considered when defining this set:

▸ The types of retail financial services to be provided to a cardholder (e.g., ATM cash withdrawal, manual cash disbursement in a branch office of a bank, POS payments for goods and/or services with or without cashback possibility). Other services can be provided—for example, a loyalty scheme, in case the issuer has established a suitable agreement with a chain of merchants.

▸ The type of environment, domestic or international, where each service is available to the cardholder.

▸ The payment behavior with which the service is associated (i.e., debit, credit, stored value).

The issuer maps card applications to triples (service, payment behavior, environment), such that there are no card applications offering the same type of service, for the same type of payment behavior, in the same environment. This design restriction guarantees the minimal cost of the overall ICC implementation. To this end the issuer can build allocation tables of the kind shown in Figure 7.2.

Figure 7.2
Allocation
tables for card
applications.

Domestic environment		Service type		
		ATM	POS	Loyalty
Payment behavior	Debit	**CA1** YES	YES	NO
	Credit	NO	**CA2** YES	NO
	Stored value	NO	**CA3** YES	**CA4** YES

International environment		Service type		
		ATM	POS	Loyalty
Payment behavior	Debit	**CA5** YES	NO	NO
	Credit	YES	**CA2** YES	NO
	Stored value	NO	NO	NO

In the example described in Figure 7.2, the issuer provides the cardholder with an ICC containing a set of five applications allocated as follows:

1. Card application CA1 is a debit product available only in the domestic environment, providing ATM and POS payment services. CA1
   implements the EMV™ debit/credit functionality as defined in Book
   3 of the *EMV 2000* specifications.

2. Card application CA2 is a credit product available both in the domestic and international environments. At home the cardholder can use
   it only for payments at a POS, while abroad it can be used for
   ATM cash advance and POS payments. CA2 implements the EMV™
   debit/credit functionality.

3. Card application CA3 is a domestic electronic purse. CA3 implements a different functionality than EMV™ debit/credit, but it is EMV™ compliant in the sense that the organization of the data objects of the card application and its visibility to the EMV™ application selection mechanism complies with Book 1 of the *EMV 2000* specifications (see also Chapter 4).

4. Card application CA4 is a domestic loyalty scheme for a chain of merchants having adequate agreements with the issuer. CA4 implements non-EMV™ functionality and it is not EMV™ compliant in the sense that the terminal must apply a proprietary selection mechanism to execute this card application.

5. Card application CA5 is an international debit product for ATM cash withdrawal. CA5 implements the EMV™ debit/credit functionality.

For the same example, the ownership of the brands behind each card application is as follows:

▸ CA1 and CA3 are brands belonging to the national payment system operator of the country where the issuer is located.

▸ CA2 and CA5 are brands belonging to an international card association.

▸ Both the issuer and the chain of merchants own CA4, from which the cardholder accumulates points from payment transactions effected with any of the card applications from CA1 to CA3.

The issuer has to fulfill the following business conditions in order to be able to accommodate in his ICC the card applications mentioned above:

▸ The issuer is a subscriber to the services offered by the national payment system operator.

▸ The issuer is a member of the international card association.

▸ The issuer and the chain of merchants have established a bilateral business agreement concerning their participation in the loyalty program.

Not only must the issuer fulfill these business conditions but he must also observe the explicit rules of each payment system concerning the issuing of ICC cards including their brands. Therefore, the issuer has to take some restrictions into account:

▶ An ICC should not accommodate card applications coming from two different electronic payment system operators or card associations, which do not mutually support their brands. The coexistence of brands on the same card has to make the object of bilateral agreements. As an example, if either the card association or the national payment system operator states that their brands cannot coexist with another operator's brands on the same card, then the issuer is compelled to store (CA1, CA3) on a different card than (CA2, CA5).

▶ If explicitly stated by any of the payment systems, an ICC should not carry both debit and credit applications. For example, if the card association explicitly states this restriction, then CA2 cannot be included in the same set of card applications with any other debit card application, regardless of whether it is branded by the card association itself or any another payment system operator.

▶ An ICC should not carry applications of the same payment system for which the coexistence of brands is not explicitly allowed. Let us assume that there is another international debit card application provided by the same card association, referred to as CA5', offering both the ATM and the POS service. Then, the card association could explicitly rule out the coexistence of both CA5 and CA5' in the same ICC, since CA5' covers the functionality of CA5.

▶ In an open and interoperable environment, a registered AID, according to ISO 7816-5 [15], uniquely identifies a card application brand. If the issuer agrees to include in the ICC a card application belonging to a domestic electronic payment system that does not register its AID according to ISO 7816-5, then the issuer has to fulfill a supplementary condition. The issuer should take all the provisions of loading this card application with an AID different from any other AID coming from international payment system operators or card associations, without conflicting with these cross-border applications.

7.4.2 Card layout definition

In the definition of the card layout, the issuer has to define requirements both on the card's functionality and on the transaction files and data.

The issuer has to decide whether the ICC will accommodate only card applications implementing the EMV™ debit/credit functionality or card applications implementing other functionality than EMV™. Considering the example discussed in Section 7.4.1, in the former case the ICC can only include the card applications CA1, CA2, and CA5, while in the latter case all five applications can be hosted in the ICC. In Figure 7.3, we present the card's layout in the latter case.

Considering the fact that the EMV™ functionality is used by several applications, the issuer may define a sharable applet, whose set of method signatures represents the API accessible to CA1, CA2, and CA5. The methods of the sharable applet implement the generation of the application cryptogram, the DDA, the enciphered PIN verified off-line by the ICC, the

Figure 7.3
Card layout with EMV™ debit/credit and other functionality.

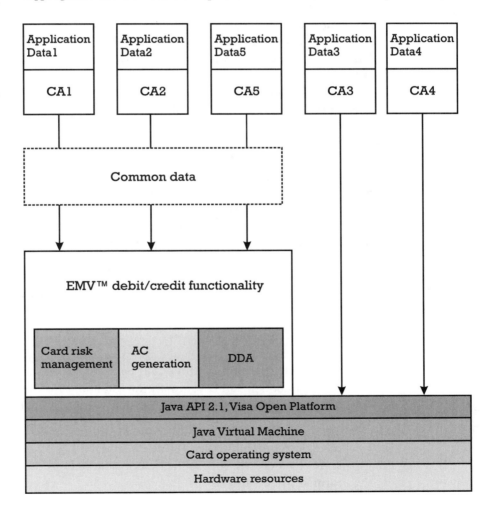

card risk management, and so on. This choice avoids repeating code for implementing EMV™ functionality in each separate applet CA1, CA2, and CA5, which can lead to saving EEPROM space.

Since only the application CA3 uses the functionality needed for processing stored value transactions, which is different than the EMV™ debit/credit functionality, then the issuer may require that all this functionality is implemented directly at the level of the applet CA3. The same observation applies to CA4.

In the remainder of the section we concentrate only on the management of files and data for the EMV™ debit/credit applications CA1, CA2, and CA5.

The issuer can define data objects that can be used in common by several EMV™ applications. These objects are referred to as card data objects. The objects that are accessible only to one application are referred to as application data objects. In Figure 7.3, application data 1 groups all the application data objects accessible to CA1, application data 2 groups all the application data objects accessible to CA2, and so on, while common data groups all the card data objects.

Among the card data objects and application data objects, one can distinguish between EMV™ defined objects and proprietary-defined objects.

EMV™ Defined Data Objects

Possible examples of EMV™ defined card data objects are the cardholder's name, track 2 equivalent data, and track 3 equivalent data. If DDA and/or enciphered PIN verified off-line by the ICC are implemented (for economy reasons of the EEPROM space), the issuer may decide—if the regulatory framework of each payment system represented in the card does not rule out this possibility—to keep the following cryptographic parameters as card data objects:

- The ICC private key used for computing the card's signature in the DDA: This is a card secret data object accessible only to the processing performed by the applets.

- The corresponding ICC Public Key Certificate, signed by the issuer, together with the other RSA public parameters—namely, the ICC Public Key Exponent, and eventually the ICC Public Key Remainder. This is a card public data object that is accessible to the terminal application.

- The ICC PIN encipherment private key, used for decrypting the RSA envelope containing the off-line enciphered PIN, could also be a card secret data object. This object is accessible only to the processing performed by the applets.

‣ The corresponding ICC PIN Encipherment Public Key Certificate, signed by the issuer, together with the other RSA public parameters—namely, the ICC PIN Encipherment Public Key Exponent, and eventually the ICC PIN Encipherment Public Key Remainder. This is a card public data object that is accessible to the terminal application.

Even though it is a good security practice to keep different cryptographic parameters for different security services, the issuer can decide for the reason of EEPROM economy that the same set of parameters can be commonly used by the DDA and the enciphered PIN verified off-line by the ICC.

Some examples of EMV™ defined application data objects are those related to the financial data, like the Application PAN, Application PAN Sequence Number, Application Expiration/Effective Date, Application Currency Code, Application Usage Control, and Application Version Number. Some security-related data objects like the Issuer Action Code–Denial/On-line/Default, Card Risk Management Data Object Lists (CDOL1 and CDOL2), CVM List(s), and the Signed Static Application Data are also EMV™-defined application data objects.

Proprietary-Defined Data Objects

The proprietary-defined card data objects are those objects defined by the issuer in connection with his specifically defined processing—for example, the card risk management (see Section 7.10.3):

‣ *Card period (specify: day/month) accumulator*, which represents the total amount spent by the cardholder with any of the applications hosted in the card, during a certain period;

‣ *Card last transaction day and the card last transaction month*, which represent the date when the last transaction with any of the applications hosted in the card was effected.

Proprietary-defined application data objects can include specific data objects needed by the card risk management in relation to each application, like the application period (specify: day/month) accumulator, application last transaction day and the application last transaction month. The following proprietary-defined application cryptographic data objects can be included here as well: the cryptogram version number, key index, MAC keys and encryption keys for secure messaging in connection with issuer script processing, and the application PIN. Note that all the keys and PIN data objects are secret objects accessible only to the appropriate processing performed by the applet.

In addition to card and application data objects, the issuer might define sharable data objects, which are objects accessible only to a well-defined subset of applications. Included in this category are cryptographic parameters in relation to the SDA mechanism. To explain this we again use the multiapplication example presented in Section 7.4.1. The issuer must obtain two Issuer Public Key Certificates relative to the same pair issuer private key/issuer public key (modulus and public key exponent):

▸ The national payment system operator signs one Issuer Public Key Certificate for the use of the application CA1 and for the use of any other EMV™ application of this operator that may eventually be loaded in the future in the ICC. In the set of sharable objects for CA1, the issuer includes, besides this certificate, the Certification Authority Public Key Index corresponding to the national payment system operator, the issuer public key exponent, and eventually the issuer public key remainder. The presence of the last object is dependent on the byte length of the modulus used by the payment system operator.

▸ The card association will sign another certificate for the use of the applications CA2 and CA5, and for any other EMV™ application of the card association that may eventually be loaded in the future in the ICC. In the set of sharable data objects for CA2 and CA5, the issuer includes, besides this certificate, the Certification Authority Public Key Index corresponding to the card association, the issuer public key exponent, and eventually the issuer public key remainder. This object may have a different value than that corresponding to the national payment system operator, in case the two organizations use RSA modulus of different length for signing certificates. The presence of this object is dependent on the byte length of the modulus used by the card association.

The issuer also has to decide whether the EMV™ applications in the card, namely CA1, CA2, and CA5, are visible from a payment system environment or this structure is not implemented. If the PSE is implemented, the issuer should appropriately define the AEF that keeps the PSE directory, the FCI of the PSE, and the FCI of each card application, observing the restrictions discussed in Section 4.3.1 and Section 4.3.4.

Considering the card layout presented above, a possible mapping of the card/application/sharable data objects into the card's file structure, which is publicly accessible to EMV™ terminals, is presented in Figure 7.4.

The directory file of the PSE is organized in the AEF01. The SFI of this file is indicated in the FCI of the PSE. The application elementary files AEF02 and AEF03 store the card data objects. These two files must be visible to all the card applications in the PSE. Each application in the PSE has its own application data objects mapped as follows:

▸ The application data objects of CA1 are mapped to the application elementary files AEF11 and AEF12. The visibility of these files is limited only to CA1.

▸ The application data objects of CA2 are mapped to the application elementary files AEF21 and AEF22. The visibility of these files is limited only to CA2.

▸ The application data objects of CA5 are mapped to the application elementary files AEF51 and AEF52. The visibility of these files is limited only to CA5.

Concerning the sharable data objects among applications, these are mapped as follows:

▸ The sharable data objects of the applications managed by the national payment system operator (e.g., CA1 and any other application of this operator that can be loaded in the future) are grouped in the application elementary file denoted AEFsh1(CA1). The visibility of this file is limited to CA1.

▸ The sharable data objects of the applications managed by the card association (e.g., CA2, CA5, and any other application of the card association that can be loaded in the future) are grouped in the application elementary files denoted AEFsh1(CA2, CA5) and AEFsh2(CA2, CA5). The visibility of these files is limited to CA2 and CA5.

The issuer reflects the visibility of these application elementary files in the AFL associated with each application, as follows:

▸ The AFL of the CA1 includes AEF02, AEF03, AEF11, AEF12, and AEFsh1(CA1).

Figure 7.4
Card file
structure
corresponding
to the proposed
layout.

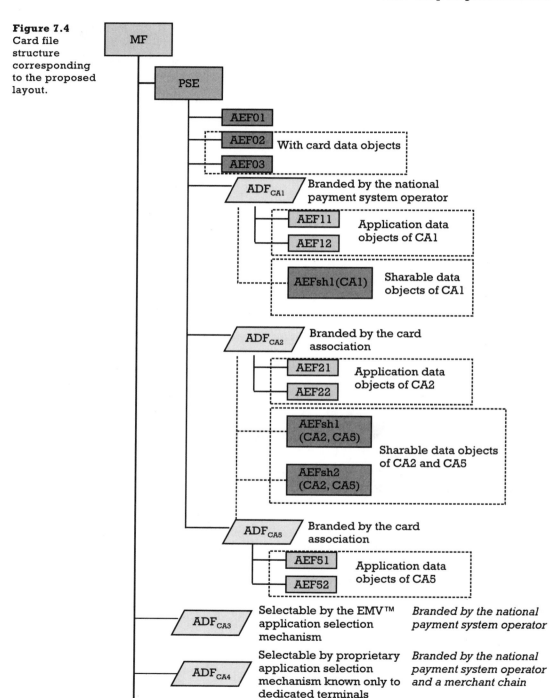

- The AFL of the CA2 includes AEF02, AEF03, AEF21, AEF22, AEFsh1 (CA2,CA5), and AEFsh2(CA2,CA5).

- The AFL of the CA5 includes AEF02, AEF03, AEF51, AEF52, AEFsh1 (CA2,CA5), and AEFsh2(CA2,CA5).

If the card layout is set up in this way, the READ RECORD command must be implemented following some supplementary requirements. Thus, whenever the SFI of an AEF is not in the realm of the currently selected ADF, the card must check whether there is an AEF with this SFI one level above in the card file structure. If this AEF is not found there, the card must check whether the current ADF has sharable files associated with it. In the affirmative case, the SFI of the AEF is searched among the sharable files associated to the current ADF.

7.5 Issuer's business case

The issuer's business case regarding the definition of an EMV™ card application can be described as a compromise between three rather contradictory requirements:

1. Availability of the financial service to the cardholder;

2. Security against counterfeit and fraudulent transactions;

3. Reduced operational costs when using chip cards.

7.5.1 Availability of the financial service

The issuer would like to provide his cardholders with highly reliable and easy-to-use financial services, whose availability is not vulnerable to the technical degrading of the payment system's components and devices, to the limitations of the terminal's capabilities, or to the timing restrictions of the transaction processing. Below, we list some possible availability policies of the issuer:

- A transaction should be completed off-line in case a failure of the acquirer's network or a failure of the payment system's network has occurred.

- A transaction should be completed with the financial information carried out by the magnetic stripe of the card in case the chip fails.

- The behavior of the card application should be adaptable to the particularities of the business environment at the point of service and to the terminal's capabilities. In Section 7.6 we outline the design of an adaptable card application. During the initiate application processing, the card provides different AFL(s) to the terminal in response to the GET PROCESSING OPTIONS command, depending on the type of terminal at the point of service, the amount involved in the transaction, and the merchant category code. This design approach increases the availability of the payment service. For example, whenever the card is involved in a payment transaction at a tollgate on the highway, it presents an AFL pointing to a fast CVM List then the default CVM List. The fast CVM List allows the completion of the transaction without the cardholder's verification. This facility increases the availability of the payment service to the detriment of security in order to answer the time constraint of completing the transaction in the shortest time possible to avoid the creation of traffic jams.

The issuer must also define the processing restrictions of each card application. This definition takes into account the prescriptions of the payment brand corresponding to the card application. Section 7.9 analyzes the definition of the processing restrictions by the issuer, such that a large variety of payment services are available to the cardholder, while no overlap should exist between card applications in offering the same service.

7.5.2 Improved security

The issuer would like to minimize its loss due to counterfeit and fraudulent transactions. This requires a strengthening of the card application's security, namely, of the CAM and the CVM. It is important to note that a design that addresses this requirement could negatively impact the availability of the financial service (the first requirement of the issuer) and the operational costs of the ICC (the third requirement).

For example, one way to reduce the number of counterfeit transactions is to ask for the on-line completion of all the transactions. In this case the on-line dynamic CAM reduces the risk of counterfeit cards, since the IH must verify each Application Cryptogram produced by the card. The communication costs increase, however, and could become unjustified in transactions involving a small amount (which infringes upon the third requirement of the issuer). Consequently, the profit of the issuer decreases, even though the reason is not the loss due to fraudulent transactions. Moreover, in the case of network degrading, this policy has a negative impact on the availability of the financial service (which was the first requirement of the issuer).

Another possibility for reducing the counterfeit transactions is to implement a dynamic off-line CAM through the DDA. This improves the availability, in case of network degrading, and decreases the communication costs. However, this increases the costs of the ICC since a cryptographic processor must be included in the ICC hardware platform. Considering the continuous improvements to technologies and the decreasing prices for an ICC including a cryptographic coprocessor in its configuration, this design solution could become preferable.

Section 7.7 presents design choices for CAM selection, and Section 7.8 presents design choices for CVM selection, while observing the trade-off between the issuer's requirements.

7.5.3 Reduced operational costs

The issuer would like to maximize its profit while operating the card application.

One way could be the minimization of communication costs through the off-line completion of transactions. Section 7.10 outlines the design of the card risk management such that the decision of the off-line completion of a transaction is taken after a careful evaluation of the risk.

Another way to increase the profitability of the card application is to spend little money on the ICC cards. We analyze the influence of the ICC costs on the choice of the CAM and CVM in Section 7.7 and 7.8, respectively.

The issuer's business case consists of establishing an appropriate trade-off between the availability of the financial service for the cardholder and the security on the one hand, and the communication costs and the implementation costs of the ICC on the other hand. In the following sections we analyze how this trade-off impacts the design of the processing performed by the ICC: the initialization of the EMV™ card application, the card authentication method, the cardholder verification method, the processing restrictions, and the card risk management.

7.6 Adaptive initiate application processing

Following a successful selection of an EMV™ application in the ICC, the terminal checks whether the PDOL is included or not in the FCI of the selected ADF. The issuer distinguishes between two cases:

1. The PDOL is not included in the FCI or it is included but is empty. In this case the GET PROCESSING OPTIONS command received from the terminal does not include any data from the business environment at the point of service. Therefore, the card has no input data to process with the GET PROCESSING OPTIONS command.

2. The PDOL is included in the FCI and is not empty. The card application indicates to the terminal a list of data objects from the business environment, which it would need to receive as input data to the GET PROCESSING OPTIONS command. This is the data the card needs to process in order to initiate the transaction.

In the first case the result of the processing performed by the card, consisting at least of the AIP and AFL, is always the same. The card has no way to adapt its behavior to a certain business environment or another, since no appropriate information is sent from the terminal.

In the second case, the result of the processing performed by the ICC can be made dependent on the content of the data objects required in the PDOL, which is provided by the terminal according to the existing situation at the point of service. Consequently, the ICC can adapt the EMV™ transaction profile, through the content of the AIP and AFL, to be the most appropriate from the point of view of the service availability.

In the remainder of this section we consider a design example of an adaptable card application, for which the following items are included in the PDOL:

▸ Terminal Type (tag 9F35): This indicates the environment of the terminal (attended/unattended), its communication capabilities (on-line only/off-line with on-line possibility/off-line only), and its operational control (financial institution/merchant/cardholder).

▸ Amount, Authorized (Binary) (tag 81).

▸ Merchant Category Code (tag 9F15).

For simplicity reasons, we assume a domestic debit/credit scheme where there are no problems linked to different currencies used by the card and terminal.

We will take a closer look at the way the issuer can specify the GET PROCESSING OPTIONS. Thus, the response elaborated by the card application will include a different AFL depending on the communication capabilities of the terminal, the amount involved in the transaction, and the type of merchant at the point of service.

After receiving the GET PROCESSING OPTIONS C-APDU, the card application checks whether the flow conditions needed to process this command are fulfilled.

> First, it checks that there is currently an application selected in the card.

> Second, the card checks that this is the first time in the current card session that the terminal issues the GET PROCESSING OPTIONS command.

If any of these conditions are not respected, the card responds with SW1SW2 = 6985, "Command not allowed; conditions of use not satisfied" (see Table I-4 in Book 3 of the *EMV 2000* specifications), and the initiate application processing is aborted.

The card application proceeds with verifying that the length of the data field received in the C-APDU corresponds to the expected length according to the length of the data elements included in the PDOL. If this verification does not pass, the card responds with the checking error code SW1SW2 = 6700, corresponding to "Wrong length." The card also positions a flag *PDOL Processing with Error*, which is used by the processing performed by the risk management of the card (see Section 7.10.3). The Application Transaction Counter (tag 9F36) in the card is incremented.

The card parses the byte string received in the value field of the data object with tag 83, according to the tag-length indicators contained in the PDOL. It stores the corresponding value fields of each tag-length indicator, obtaining the complete BER-TLV encoding of the data objects required from the terminal. In case the value field of any required data object is zero, the flag PDOL Processing with Error is set in the card with the meaning "Data element required in the PDOL is not provided." The card risk management process will consider this flag. If a higher resolution is needed during the card risk management processing, the card application can manage a separate flag for each data object present in the PDOL: "Terminal Type required in PDOL and not provided," "Amount, Authorized required in PDOL and not available," and so on. Once these data objects from the point of service are obtained, the card can determine the AFL that is appropriate in the given conditions.

The issuer defines two business contexts as follows:

Context 1

> The value fields of the corresponding data objects required in the PDOL are not provided in the data field of the GET PROCESSING OPTIONS command.

OR

▸ The required value fields are provided. The value field of the Terminal Type is an eligible value different than 13, while the Amount, Authorized is above the floor limit. The Terminal Type 13 corresponds to a terminal that has no on-line connection to a financial institution (off-line only), that is working in an environment attended by a shop assistant, and that is being controlled by a financial institution (see Annex A1 in Book 4 of the *EMV 2000* specifications).

OR

▸ The Merchant Category Code is different than the code associated with a tollgate operator for highway tax collection.

Within this business context, the issuer associates a default CVM List, which includes three CVRs. For each CVR, the corresponding CVM condition code is set to "Always" (00). Thus, the floor amount X and amount Y, which are associated with this CVM List, are null. Regarding the CVM code of these three rules, these are "Enciphered PIN verified on-line," "Plaintext PIN verification performed by ICC," and "Signature paper," respectively.

Context 2

▸ The required value fields in PDOL are provided. The value field of the Terminal Type is 13.

AND

▸ The Amount, Authorized is below a floor limit accepted as low risk by both the issuer and the acquirer.

AND

▸ The Merchant Category Code corresponds to a tollgate operator for highway tax collection.

This business context can be found at a tollgate on a highway, where the amounts are small and the cardholder has no opportunity to either type in a PIN or to sign the sales slip, unless he or she spends an amount of time that can lead to an unacceptable transaction time.

For this business context the issuer defines the fast CVM List, for which the amount X encodes the floor limit and the amount Y is zero. It contains only one CVR, for which the CVM condition code is 06, "If transaction is in application currency and is under X value," and the CVM code is "No CVM required."

Then, the issuer can organize the public information in the AEF(s) such that all the data elements common to both business contexts are arranged in the AEF(s) with the SFI equal to 1 and 2. The AEF with the SFI equal to 3 includes (besides other data elements specific to the first context) the default CVM List, while the AEF with the SFI equal to 4 includes (besides other data elements specific to the second context) the fast CVM List. Correspondingly, the application will keep two application file locators:

- AFL1 includes the list of file entries corresponding to the AEF(s) referred by the SFI 1, 2, and 3.

- AFL2 includes the list of file entries corresponding to the AEF(s) referred by the SFI 1, 2, and 4.

Thus, if during the processing performed by the card based on the value fields of the Terminal Type, Amount, Authorized, and Merchant Category Code the first business context is identified, then the card retrieves the AFL1. This AFL1 is included beside the AIP in the R-APDU. Otherwise, AFL2 is included in the R-APDU. When the card completes the processing successfully, the SW1 SW2 status words are set to 9000 and the R-APDU is sent to the terminal.

7.7 Design criteria for CAM selection

The EMV™ proposes the following three card authentication methods:

1. *Off-line static CAM:* This method is implemented with the SDA mechanism based on digital signatures. An overview of this mechanism is presented in Appendix D, Section D.6.2. More details concerning the specification of the SDA in the EMV™ are presented in Section 6.4.2.

2. *Off-line dynamic CAM:* This method is implemented with the DDA mechanism based on digital signatures. Appendix D, Section D.7.2, gives an overview of this mechanism. More details on the specification of the DDA in the EMV™ are presented in Section 6.4.3.

3. *On-line dynamic CAM:* This method is implemented with a MAC-based DDA as presented in Appendix D, Section D.7.1. Section 6.8.6

details the generation of the Application Cryptogram by the ICC for accomplishing the MAC-based DDA in the EMV™ specifications.

Table 7.1 presents a brief comparison of the necessary resources needed to support each of the CAMs presented above in terms of network resources, computational power of the ICC, and EEPROM space needs. The computational power and the EEPROM space will influence the ICC price.

7.7.1 On-line CAM

It can be seen from Table 7.1 that on-line CAM requires the lowest ICC resources, in terms of both computational power and storage space. The majority of the ICCs on the market support the computation of a triple DES operation with double length key, for producing the ARQC. The need for EEPROM space is reduced to the storage of a double length key of 16 bytes. This makes the lowest price for the ICC.

To implement the on-line CAM, the issuer must personalize in the ICC the CDOL1. CDOL1 is forwarded by the card application to the terminal during the execution of the transaction function read application data (see Section 6.3). CDOL1 is mandatory for inclusion in the content of the card application readable from the AFL. Some of the data objects that are recommended for inclusion in the CDOL1 are indicated in Section 6.8.6.1. Note that the implementation in the card of the GENERATE AC command, which computes the ARQC, is mandatory.

It is important to observe that the terminal is not involved in the on-line CAM, and therefore, it requires no computational resources, since the ARQC is sent over the acquirer's and payment system's networks and checked by the issuer during the authorization process performed by the IH.

Table 7.1
Resource Needs for CAM Support

	Network Resources	Computational Power of ICC	EEPROM Needs of ICC
On-line CAM	Full upgraded network	Triple DES with double length key	Double length DES Key (16 bytes)
Off-line static CAM	None	None	The byte-length of two RSA modulus (256 bytes for a bit-length of the modulus of 1,024 bits)
Off-line dynamic CAM	None	RSA operation	The byte-length of two RSA modulus (256 bytes for a bit-length of the modulus of 1,024 bits)

The necessary condition for implementing the on-line CAM is that the acquirer processing the card application in its terminal is connected to an EMV™ network offering full chip support. This network must transport the data package containing the ARQC generated by the ICC for card authentication, and the data objects used for producing it. This allows the IH to verify the correctness of the ARQC during the authorization process.

On-line CAM is the authentication method recommended for ATM services, which usually require on-line authorization and thus assume the existence of an EMV™ network offering full chip support.

7.7.2 Off-line static CAM

The second CAM, considering the resources required by the ICC, and implicitly its price, is the off-line static CAM. Note that the ICC performs no cryptographic operations for this type of CAM. However, the price of the ICC is higher than in the case of an ICC implementing the on-line dynamic CAM due to the EEPROM storage space required. The bigger the EEPROM needs the higher the price of the ICC. To implement the off-line static CAM in a card application, the ICC has to have enough EEPROM space to store the items listed below:

- Issuer Public Key Certificate (tag 90), which is the certified public key of the issuer by the certification authority. The length of this item is equal to the length of the RSA modulus used by the CA, which is denoted N_{CA}. At present, EMVCo has assigned expiration dates to the RSA modulus length used by the payment systems as follows: 768-bit ($|N_{CA}| = 96$ bytes) with expiration date in 12/2002, 896-bit ($|N_{CA}| = 112$ bytes) with expiration date in 12/2004, and 1,024-bit with expiration date in 12/2008. EMVCo reviews yearly the security of the RSA, according to the state of the art in cryptography, and makes adequate recommendations. The payment systems will introduce longer keys at the end of 2002, with a modulus of 1,152 bits ($|N_{CA}| = 144$ bytes), expiring in 2010 [16];

- Issuer Public Key Exponent (tag 9F32), which is represented on 1 or 3 bytes (corresponding to the values 3 or $2^{16} + 1$);

- Issuer Public Key Remainder (tag 92), on $N_I - N_{CA} + 36$ bytes;

- Certification Authority Public Key Index (tag 8F), on 1 byte, which points to the public key of the CA in the table kept with a terminal, in case a terminal knows several CAs;

- Signed Static Application Data (tag 93), with the length equal to the RSA modulus used by the issuer, and denoted N_I. The state of the art in cryptography recommends at least $| N_I | = 96$ bytes. The issuer computes this signature with his private key during the personalization of the card application. The issuer computes this signature on the content of the card that remains unmodified during its lifetime. Recommendations concerning the data objects to be included in the computation of the Signed Static Application Data are indicated in Sections 5.8 and 6.3.2. All these data objects must be included in the AEF(s) that are publicly readable and listed in the AFL.

The card industry offers a large choice of EMV™ platforms that support the off-line static CAM implemented with the SDA mechanism [17–19].

The terminal that verifies the authenticity of the card can be off-line, but it has to be able to verify the correctness of the static signed authentication data stored in the ICC by the issuer during personalization. This means that the terminal should be able to perform RSA operations. No network resources are required for performing the off-line static CAM.

7.7.3   Off-line dynamic CAM

The third CAM, considering the resources required by the ICC and implicitly its price, is the off-line dynamic CAM. The price of the ICC is higher than in the case of the off-line static CAM since an efficient computation of the RSA operation demands a cryptographic coprocessor in the chip's hardware architecture. Note, however, that the EEPROM requirements are sensibly equal to that of the off-line static CAM. In order to implement the off-line dynamic CAM in a card application, the ICC has to have enough EEPROM space to store the items listed below:

- All the data items mentioned in connection with the off-line static CAM, except for the Signed Static Application Data (tag 93);

- ICC Public Key Certificate (tag 9F46), which is the certified public key of the ICC by the issuer whose length is equal to the length of the RSA modulus used by the issuer, and denoted N_I;

- ICC Public Key Exponent (tag 9F47) that is represented on 1 or 3 bytes (corresponding to the values 3 or $2^{16} + 1$);

- ICC Public Key Remainder (tag 9F48), which is represented on $N_{IC} - N_I + 42$ bytes, where N_{IC} denotes the length in bytes of the RSA modulus used by the ICC. Since recent developments in factorization techniques show that factoring a modulus of 512 bits (64 bytes) is just a matter of motivation, it is recommend that N_{IC} be at least 768 bits (96 bytes).

The generation by the card of the digital signature on the data received from the terminal is triggered by the INTERNAL AUTHENTICATE command, which is mandatory for implementation in the ICC if the off-line dynamic CAM is chosen. This command has as a parameter the data to be signed by the card. The card must specify the structure of this data in the Dynamic Data Object List (DDOL), with tag 9F49, which has to be included in an AEF visible from the AFL. The following data objects are recommended in the DDOL:

- Unpredictable Number (tag 9F37);
- Terminal Identification (tag 9F1C);
- Terminal Country Code (tag 9F1A);
- Transaction Date (tag 9A).

7.7.4 Security considerations regarding CAM

On-line dynamic CAM is mandatory for implementation in all the EMV™ debit/credit card applications. It is performed during any on-line authorization with the issuer, provided that the acquirer managing the terminal at the point of service is connected to an EMV™ network offering full chip support. The successful completion of the on-line dynamic CAM with the issuer guarantees that the ICC at the point of service is genuine, unless a powerful attacker has succeeded in breaking into the chip and cloning the secret key used for computing the application cryptogram. Thus, the acquirer can fully guarantee the payment for the merchant for any authorized transaction by the issuer, since in case of a counterfeit card the issuer is held responsible for the failure of the tamper-resistance of the ICC. This provides a better level of security against counterfeit transactions to both the issuer and the acquirer compared to any on-line authorization performed with magnetic stripe cards, regardless of whether they use track 2 or track 3 for storing the financial information and the security protection measures (see Section 2.6.4).

Off-line static CAM is mandatory for implementation in all cards except for ATM-only cards, which are always authorized on-line. If a terminal is only operated off-line, the off-line static CAM is the minimal security level that must be implemented in the card. In this case it is recommended that the type of transaction be limited only to a retail POS service with small floor limits. Implementing the off-line static CAM with the SDA mechanism together with a sound terminal and card risk management decreases the risk of counterfeit off-line transactions performed with ICC when compared with counterfeit off-line transactions performed with magnetic stripe. However, the off-line static CAM does not rule out this risk. We briefly describe such an attack.

Step 1   The attacker builds a pseudoterminal, consisting of a PC equipped with an EMV™ card reader that knows to produce the appropriate sequence of commands corresponding to the EMV™ application selection mechanism, the initiate application processing, and the read application data. The pseudoterminal is instructed to record all the information in the FCI of the ADF containing the card application selected for attack, the AFL and AIP, and all the publicly readable information contained in the application elementary files visible from the AFL. This information includes the data items related to the off-line static CAM/SDA.

Step 2   A waiter attack is mounted as the one described in Section 2.6.1, using the kind of pseudoterminal described in step 1.

The attacker checks whether the Static Data Authentication Tag List (tag 9F4A) is among the data objects in the EMV™ data objects heap. If this is the case, this list should contain only the tag corresponding to the AIP. This is an indication that the AIP was considered in the static data to be authenticated, which was signed by the issuer. If this is the case, the attacker has no freedom in proposing a convenient AIP for his purpose other than the one in the genuine card. The attacker checks whether the genuine card supports DDA or combined DDA/GENERATE AC. If this is the case, the attacker is not able to create an appropriate emulator, without the risk that a terminal at the point of service could ask for an active DDA computation that would reveal off-line that the card is not genuine. Therefore, the attacker has to search for another ICC, which is not able to perform any form of DDA. The attack is restarted from step 1.

Step 3   If the attacker succeeds in recording the data from a card supporting only SDA, he can build an ICC emulator, containing an ADF that replicates the FCI, AFL, and the content of the publicly readable AEF(s) corresponding to the ADF in the genuine card. The emulator completely implements an EMV™ debit/credit application, for which the initiate application processing is adaptable according to the business environment at the point of service. To this end the PDOL includes the tag-length identifier of the Terminal Type data object.

- Whenever the Terminal Type indicates an on-line-only terminal, the emulator aborts the EMV™ transaction. This is because, unless the attacker does not break the tamper-resistance of the genuine ICC, the emulator cannot bypass the verification of an Application Cryptogram by the IH while not having the appropriate secret key.

- Whenever the Terminal Type indicates an attended terminal, the emulator aborts the EMV™ transaction. The attacker is not willing to risk an attendant becoming suspicious because of the look of the card, which could reveal imperfect artwork, logos, holograms, and other visual authentication means.

- For any other type of terminal the emulator is instructed to mount the attack. If the AIP was not included in the static data to be authenticated, the attacker may propose an AIP convenient to his attack. This AIP requires SDA, it does not require DDA; it requires cardholder verification, it does not require terminal risk management; and it indicates that the card cannot perform combined DDA/GENERATE AC. Thus, the card supports the minimal requirement of the off-line static CAM for a transaction that is candidate for off-line completion, while it avoids any active computation that can reveal off-line that the card is not genuine. Asking that the terminal does not perform terminal risk management, the attacker hopes to maximize his gain out of the current attack. If the AIP was included in the static data to be authenticated (see Section 5.8.1), the attacker has to try the attack with the AIP proposed by the genuine card. In the latter case, if the terminal risk management is required in the AIP, the attacker is compelled to a transaction amount below the terminal floor limit.

The ICC emulator is instructed to verify positively any VERIFY command that proposes either a plaintext PIN or an enciphered PIN. The card risk management of the emulator is also instructed to rule out any proposal of the terminal other than denial or transaction accepted off-line. If the terminal proposes a denial, the GENERATE AC should end with an error code, such that the issuer has no AAC revealing that a counterfeit transaction was denied, in case the terminal records also denied transactions in batch fails forwarded to clearing. If the terminal proposes an off-line acceptance of the transaction, the TC computed in the response to the GENERATE AC is bogus, since the emulator does not have the appropriate secret key to compute a correct cryptogram.

Step 4   The emulator is used at a point of service. If the business environment is appropriate for mounting the attack, the emulator will continue the transaction. When the data of the emulator is correctly set up, then SDA should be successful. The emulator reports success in the verification of any PIN submitted from the terminal. If the amount of the transaction is below the terminal floor limit, there is a good probability that the terminal action analysis will recommend the off-line completion of the transaction with GENERATE AC with TC, which is accepted by the card risk management of the emulator. The emulator produces the required TC and returns a success status word. The terminal records the payment message corresponding to the transaction, including the bogus TC produced by the emulator.

When this payment message is cleared with the issuer, the verification failure of the TC will allow the issuer to become aware of the counterfeit transaction. This could lead to the blacklisting of the corresponding card. This could impede the operation of the emulator with any "off-line with on-line possibility" terminal, which has the blacklisting facility. However, there is room for successful operation of the emulator on "off-line only" terminals, for which the updating of the blacklist, if any, takes a longer time.

From the description of this attack, it is clear that the complexity of mounting this scenario is significantly higher than copying and replicating the content of a magnetic stripe. Moreover, the return of the attacker is low, since the attack can be successfully mounted only on candy bar-like vending machines.

If there is a need to provide the user with a retail POS service with higher floor limits, at a terminal that has no on-line connection to the issuer, the off-line dynamic CAM is the appropriate security level to be implemented in the card.

When choosing between implementing the off-line static CAM or the off-line dynamic CAM, the issuer has to perform a risk analysis that evaluates the expected loss from counterfeit transactions against the supplementary costs implied by the off-line dynamic CAM with DDA. Since the trend in the chip card industry over the last 2 years shows that the price of chips including a cryptographic coprocessor in the architecture is decreasing, one can expect that more and more EMV™ debit/credit card applications will implement the off-line dynamic CAM with DDA. The card producers, however, are still offering DDA as an option rather than a series product.

When both off-line CAM methods are implemented in the card, the terminal should prefer the off-line dynamic CAM to the off-line static CAM.

7.8 Design criteria for CVM

This section outlines the impact on the ICC architecture of the following CVM: enciphered PIN verified on-line, plaintext PIN verification performed by ICC, and enciphered PIN verification performed by ICC. We analyze the computational and EEPROM requirements for each of these CVM(s), which could impact on the ICC price, and consequently on the choice of a CVM for an EMV™ card application. We also present principles concerning the definition by the issuer of a CVM List in the card application, depending on the type of financial service and the type of payment product (debit or credit).

7.8.1 Enciphered PIN verified on-line

The ICC is not involved in the implementation of an "Enciphered PIN verified on-line" CVM. It is the IH that verifies the correctness of the PIN introduced by the cardholder at the terminal. The secure keyboard of the terminal encrypts the PIN, and the corresponding cryptogram is included in the authorization message sent on-line to the issuer. In order to support this CVM, the acquirer has to guarantee two conditions:

1. The on-line connection of the terminal to the AH, and through the payment system network to the IH;

2. The management of the cryptographic material for transporting the PIN cryptogram along the path between the terminal and the AH and from this host to the corresponding node allocated to the acquirer in the payment system's network.

If the CVM fails, the issuer is the one that decides the response code sent back to the terminal in the authorization response message, and the management of the remaining PIN trails of the cardholder. The PIN Try Counter in the ICC is not modified, either in case of failure or in case of success.

The cardholder should not be aware whether a PIN is validated on-line or off-line or whether the ICC or the magnetic stripe technology is used for this validation. Therefore, the issuer should make the necessary provisions to guarantee that the same PIN applies for the same application regardless of the type of environment and the type of technology used to perform a transaction for a certain financial service.

7.8.2 Plaintext/enciphered PIN verification by ICC

In case the card application adopts as the CVM either the "plaintext PIN verification performed by ICC" or "enciphered PIN verification performed by ICC," the issuer must implement the following functionality in the card:

- The VERIFY command is mandatory for implementation in the ICC.

- The management of the PIN Try Counter (PTC), consisting of several actions:

  - Each consecutive unsuccessful trial of the PIN must decrease the value of the PTC.

  - Reaching the threshold of 0 for the PTC must block the PIN and the card will answer the VERIFY command with an error code.

  - The reset of the PTC to the value indicated by the parameter PIN try limit (which usually has a value of 3) can be explicitly performed by the issuer during an on-line transaction via an issuer script, when PTC = 0, or through a successful verification of the PIN before PTC = 0.

- In case "enciphered PIN verification performed by ICC" is implemented as CVM, the VERIFY command transports the RSA envelope containing the enciphered PIN. The terminal computes this envelope with the public key contained in the ICC PIN Encipherment Public Key Certificate. This certificate is produced with the issuer private key. The corresponding public key of the issuer can be retrieved from the issuer public key certificate, produced by the CA. Consequently, the ICC must store both these certificates in the publicly readable application elementary files listed in the AFL.

The operating system of the ICC must enforce an appropriate access control mechanism such that it must be impossible to access the reference PIN from outside the ICC, unless the tamper-resistance of the chip is broken.

7.8.3   Requirements for the implementation of various CVM

Table 7.2 compares the resources needed by the ICC to support enciphered PIN verified on-line, plaintext PIN verification performed by ICC, and enciphered PIN verification performed by ICC, in terms of network resources, computational power, and EEPROM space. The computational power and the EEPROM space have an impact on the ICC price.

It is important to note that if the "enciphered PIN verification performed by ICC" CVM is implemented in a card already implementing off-line static CAM, then that card has to provide supplementary EEPROM space only for the storage of the ICC PIN Encipherment Public Key Certificate. The certificate of the CA on the public key of the issuer is the same as that for the off-line static CAM. In this case, however, the ICC has to have a cryptographic coprocessor in its architecture for decrypting the RSA envelopes transporting the enciphered PIN.

If an ICC card accepts off-line dynamic CAM and if the RSA primitive is suitably chosen, then the same ICC key pair for performing digital signatures within DDA can be used for decrypting RSA envelopes containing the PIN. In this case no supplementary EEPROM space is needed for the "enciphered PIN verification performed by ICC" CVM. Otherwise, the EEPROM space has to be supplemented with the length N_I of the RSA modulus used to generate the ICC PIN Encipherment Public Key Certificate. Usually, an ICC implementing off-line dynamic CAM also implements the "enciphered PIN verification performed by ICC" CVM. This CVM guarantees the protection of the PIN's confidentiality on the interface between the terminal and the ICC.

Table 7.2
Resources Needed for the CVM Support

	Network Resources	Computational Power	EEPROM Needs
Enciphered PIN verified on-line	Network connection to the issuer, with symmetric key management.	None	None
Plaintext PIN verification performed by ICC	None	None	Space for the PIN block (8 bytes)
Enciphered PIN verification performed by ICC	None	The possibility of performing RSA operations with a cryptographic coprocessor	The byte length of two RSA modulus (256 bytes for a bit length of the modulus of 1,024 bits) Space for the PIN block (8 bytes)

Note that the "plaintext PIN verification performed by ICC" CVM is sensitive to eavesdropping attacks, even when the terminal is equipped with a secure keyboard, since the PIN leaves the terminal in clear. The task of the attacker is to tap in to the communication between the ICC and the terminal. In practice, however, this threat is difficult to mount, unless a terminal is appropriately modified to allow the attacker to insert a logger on the communication interface between the ICC and the terminal, without this modification being visible.

7.8.4 Criteria for the definition of the CVM List

The issuer considers several criteria when defining the CVM List in the card.

- The type of financial service for which the application is issued;

- The type of card application product and its eventual affiliation to a certain brand, which has its own recommendations regarding the list of acceptable CVM;

- The technological possibilities of the chip in terms of computing power and EEPROM space.

Considering the criteria listed above, the definition of the CVM List may take into account the guidelines contained in Table 7.3.

Table 7.3
Guidelines for the CVM List Definition

Card Product	Financial Service	List of Possible CVM
ATM—only debit card	ATM	*Enciphered PIN verified on-line*—mandatory
		Plaintext PIN verification performed by ICC—optional (ICC without computation power)
		Enciphered PIN verification performed by ICC—optional (ICC needs an RSA coprocessor)
Debit	ATM, POS	*Enciphered PIN verified on-line*—mandatory
		Plaintext PIN verification performed by ICC—mandatory
		Enciphered PIN verification performed by ICC—optional.
Credit	POS	*Plaintext PIN verification performed by ICC*—mandatory
		Enciphered PIN verification performed by ICC—optional
		Hand signature—mandatory for backwards compatibility with existing products and certain legislation
		No CVM—mandatory

7.9 Processing restrictions

The decisions of the issuer concern the policies regarding:

- The management of the Application Version Number (ICC, tag 9F08);

- The management of the type of transaction to be carried out by the ICC—Application Usage Control (ICC, tag 9F07);

- Application effective/expiration dates management.

7.9.1 Application usage control

This data object with tag 9F07 in the card is mandatory to be listed in the AFL. It establishes the type of environment and the range of services for which the card is issued:

- *Type of environment*: domestic or international;

- *Range of services*: goods, services, and ATM cash withdrawal.

If the issuer has subscribed to a card brand offered by a financial organization, then the structure and content of the Application Usage Control is defined for each brand.

Otherwise, the issuer has to define this parameter. Let us assume that the issuer offers a credit card product to be used in the following way:

- The credit card can be used for ATM cash withdrawal or for manual cash disbursement in a bank office in the international environment.

- The credit card can be used for paying for goods and services in both the domestic environment and the international environment.

- The credit card can be used for obtaining cashback at any POS in the domestic environment.

In this case the Application Usage Control bytes could be set up as follows.

Byte 1

- Bit 8 = 0: Invalid for domestic cash transactions;

- Bit 7 = 1: Valid for international cash transactions;

- Bit 6 = 1: Valid for domestic goods;

- Bit 5 = 1: Valid for international goods;

- Bit 4 = 1: Valid for domestic services;

- Bit 3 = 1: Valid for international services;

- Bit 2 = 1: Valid at ATMs;

- Bit 1 = 1: Valid at terminals other than ATMs;

Byte 2

- Bit 8 = 1: Domestic cashback is allowed;

- Bit 7 = 0: International cashback is not allowed;

- Bit 6–1 = RFU.

7.9.2   Application Version Number

The Application Version Number in the card (ICC, tag 9F08) is intended for the management of the backward compatibility between a card application and a terminal application.

Terminal applications will be backward compatible and will normally support all current version numbers. If the terminal identifies a card application in the ICC with a version number that is obsolete, the TVR bit will be set (bit 7, byte 2 of TVR). Contrarily, if the terminal identifies an ICC storing an application with a version number higher than its own most recent version, then the bit "ICC and terminal have different application versions" (bit 8, byte 2 of TVR) will be set. In both cases the issuer and acquirer policies, as defined in the terminal and Issuer Action Codes, are considered in order to continue or to stop the processing of the current transaction.

7.9.3   Application effective/expiration dates

The Application Expiration Date (tag 5F24 in the ICC) in the format YYMMDD must be set up by the issuer. This expiration date must be consistent with other information stored on the card:

- The two digits DD for the expiration day must be the same as the last day of the expiration month embossed/laser engraved on the card.

‣ The date in tag 5F24 must be consistent with the data on the magnetic stripe, if any, for fallback compatibility between the data in the ICC and data on the magnetic stripe.

It is not mandatory for the Application Effective Date (tag 5F25 in the ICC) to be stored in the card.

7.10 Card risk management

In order to determine the type of Application Cryptogram (i.e., TC, ARQC, or AAC) computed by the card application in response to the terminal's first and second GENERATE AC command, the card must run its own risk management.

Card risk management is not specified in the *EMV 2000* specifications, since it does not impact on interoperability. This is why the payment system has to define its own card risk management in the proprietary ICC specifications (see Section 7.2). The issuer can further refine this definition according to its own business case, considering the trade-off between the availability degree of the financial service and the level of risk willing to be accepted.

The aim of this section is to identify which are the components that participate in the definition of the card risk management (CRM) system. This analysis is carried out in a top-down approach, from general principles towards the necessary proprietary data objects that must be foreseen in the file structure of the card. We have chosen this approach believing that an understanding of the general picture helps the designer both in the analysis of a particular CRM solution proposed by a proprietary ICC specification and in tuning it according to its own needs. For a complete design example of the CRM, we refer to [7].

7.10.1 CRM Components

Figure 7.5 outlines an input/output perspective of the CRM system. This system can be seen as a set of CRM functions. It takes the CRM data as input and runs each and every CRM function that is included in the set. This is also true when the terminal asks for the transaction's denial (i.e., GENERATE AC with AAC), or when the card decides to answer with AAC following the execution of any CRM function in the set. Since each and every CRM function in the set must be executed, the order of execution of these functions is not necessary to be defined. After the processing of the CRM data, the CRM system produces the CRM results, which logically consists of two items:

Figure 7.5
CRM system
from the
input/output
perspective.

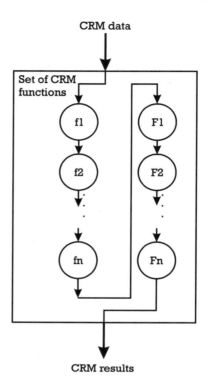

1. The type of Application Cryptogram the card agrees to compute in response to the GENERATE AC command;

2. The complete status of the card application, reflected in the CVR register. This register witnesses the processing of the EMV™ transaction from the card application's perspective. Therefore, its meaning is similar to that of the TVR and complements it. Each CRM function positions dedicated bits in the Card Verification Results Register (CVRR).

In the following sections, we present some possible types of CRM functions, the data objects that can be included in the CRM data, and several examples that define the CRM functions.

7.10.2   The set of CRM functions

The CRM functions effectively perform the risk evaluation during each EMV™ transaction. Depending on the nature of the identified security risks, the CRM functions can be grouped into several categories:

- CRM functions that evaluate the risks resulting from errors in the processing of the EMV™ transaction or from an incorrect EMV™ transaction flow;

- CRM functions that evaluate the financial risks due to overspending. (In the example considered below, we make a simplifying assumption that the card application(s) in the ICC is (are) used only for providing a financial service domestically);

- CRM functions that evaluate the financial risks due to frequent use of the card in off-line transactions.

In the first category one can define the following CRM functions—listed in the order of the EMV™ transaction stage where the processing error is considered:

- *PDOL processing error in the current transaction:* This CRM function is conditionally included in the set of CRM functions. Indeed, any time the PDOL is present in the FCI of the ADF corresponding to the card application, this CRM function is included in the CRM system. It indicates the actions to be taken by the card application in case the terminal does not provide the value filed of a data object indicated in the PDOL. This CRM function is associated with a processing error in the card application occurring in the current EMV™ transaction.

- *SDA processing error in the last transaction:* This CRM function is conditionally included in the set of CRM functions. The condition that must be fulfilled is that the SDA is foreseen in the transaction profile defined by the AIP of the card application. This means that bit 7 of byte 1 of the AIP, "Off-line SDA is supported," is set. It could be that the terminal does not correctly verify the signed static application data. This could lead the terminal to ask for the off-line denial of the transaction, which consists of computing the AAC in response to the GENERATE AC command. Usually, the card does not ask the terminal to generate an advice message to inform the issuer about the declined transactions unless the PIN try limit is exceeded. Therefore, the goal of this function is to identify whether SDA failed in the last transaction and whether the transaction was declined off-line, for informing the issuer during the current transaction about this incident. This CRM function is associated with a processing error in the terminal application.

- *DDA processing error in the last transaction:* This CRM function is conditionally included in the set of CRM functions, depending on whether the DDA is foreseen in the transaction profile defined by the AIP of the card application. This means that bit 6 of byte 1 of the AIP, "Off-line DDA is supported," is set. The motivation for the inclusion of this function in the CRM set is similar to the motivation given in the case of SDA. The goal of this function is to identify whether DDA failed in the last transaction and the transaction was declined off-line, for informing the issuer during the current transaction about this incident. This CRM function is associated with a processing error in the terminal application.

- *PIN Try Limit exceeded in the last transaction:* This CRM function is conditionally included in the set of CRM functions. Three conditions must be simultaneously fulfilled: (1) the cardholder verification is included in the transaction profile (AIP, byte 1, bit 5 = 1), (2) "Plaintext/Enciphered PIN verification performed by ICC" method is included in the CVM List, and (3) the VERIFY command was not issued in the current transaction. The function checks whether the PIN try limit in the card application was exceeded in the previous transaction.

- *On-line authorization not completed in the last transaction:* This CRM function is always included in the set of CRM functions. If the issuer must check the conditions of an EMV™ transaction, an on-line authorization is required. To this end, the card application computes an ARQC, which is sent in an authorization request message to the IH. After processing the authorization request, the IH computes an authorization response message, which is sent back to the terminal. Based on this authorization response message, the terminal computes the Authorization Response Code to be forwarded to the card. This CRM function checks whether during the previous transaction the card was removed from the terminal after computing the ARQC, but before receiving the Authorization Response Code.

- *Issuer authentication error in the last transaction:* This CRM function is conditionally included in the set of CRM functions, whenever the card application supports issuer authentication through the EXTERNAL AUTHENTICATE command in the transaction profile (AIP, byte 1, bit 3 = 1). The function checks whether during the previous transaction the ARPC was received from the IH in an authorization response message and whether the ARPC correctly authenticated the issuer to the card application.

> *Issuer script processing error in the last transaction:* This CRM function is unconditionally included in the set of CRM functions. The function checks whether during the previous transaction the card application failed to process issuer scripts received from the IH. The function also informs how many of the issuer scripts were successfully executed.

The CRM functions that evaluate the financial risks due to overspending include the following:

> *Overspending in a (specify: day/month) period by the application:* This type of CRM function is conditionally present in the CRM system, depending on whether the issuer personalizes the Application Currency Code in the card application. It protects the issuer against overspending by the cardholder above a threshold amount, expressed in the application currency code. The amount currently spent by the cardholder is monitored during a specified period of time. There could be several such CRM functions, for daily checking and/or monthly checking, depending on the type of card product, the payment behavior, and the type of financial service. The amount currently spent is monitored both in transactions completed off-line and in transactions completed on-line.

> *Overspending in consecutive off-line transactions by the application:* This type of CRM function is conditionally present in the CRM system. It protects the issuer against overspending, but the amount currently spent is monitored only in consecutive transactions completed off-line, regardless of the period of time.

> *Overspending in a (specify: day/month) period by the card:* This CRM function is included in the CRM system only for multiapplication cards hosting more than one EMV™ debit/credit card application. This function is subjected to the same conditions as the similar CRM function for an application, except for the fact that the amount currently spent is monitored in transactions completed by any EMV™ debit/credit card application present in the ICC.

> *Overspending in consecutive off-line transactions by the card:* This CRM function is included in the CRM system only for multiapplication cards hosting more than one EMV™ debit/credit card application. This function is subjected to the same conditions as the similar CRM function for an application. The difference is that the amount currently

spent is monitored in consecutive transactions completed off-line by any EMV™ debit/credit card application present in the ICC.

Of the CRM functions that evaluate the financial risks due to frequent use of the card in off-line transactions, one is the CRM function of the type "Frequent off-line use of the application." This type of CRM function is optionally included in the CRM system. It protects the issuer against excessive use of a card application only in transactions completed off-line. This would prevent the issuer from controlling time to time on a card application during an on-line authorization.

7.10.3   CRM data

The CRM functions take their input values from the set of CRM data. For the actual set of CRM functions proposed in Section 7.10.2, two groups of CRM data objects can be identified.

First, one can consider the group of CRM external data objects, which are requested by the card application from the business environment at the point of service. The tag-length identifiers of these objects are listed in CDOL1 and CDOL2. The terminal provides these data objects, which represent the input data to the first and second GENERATE AC command, respectively. They allow the card to update its internal state, to figure out the actual conditions in which the transaction is held, and to determine accordingly the level of risk. For example, when considering the CRM functions that evaluate the financial risks due to overspending as explained in Section 7.10.2, the data objects required from the point of service are the Amount, Authorized, the Amount, Other, the transaction date, and the Transaction Currency Code. When considering the CRM functions that deal with errors identified during the processing of the EMV™ transaction, the card also requires the TVR. Two bits of the TVR are relevant to this goal: the "Off-line static data authentication failed" (bit 7 in byte 1 of TVR) and the "Off-line dynamic data authentication failed" (bit 4 in byte 1 of TVR). They provide to the CRM system of the card the appropriate information as to whether the terminal has correctly completed the SDA or the DDA.

Second, the CRM data includes a set of CRM internal data objects. The data objects in this group represent a subset of the internal state of the card application. They allow the card to keep a history of the EMV™ transactions already processed, which could impact on the decision of completion elaborated in the current transaction. For the concrete set of CRM functions exemplified in Section 7.10.2, several categories of data objects can be identified (e.g., transaction flow flags, processing counters/counter limit parameters, and financial accumulators/accumulator limit parameters).

Transaction flow flags   The data objects in this category witness the correct or erroneous completion of a certain processing stage in the card application or in the terminal application. One flag is foreseen for the completion of every stage monitored for errors by the CRM functions. Every flag has only two possible values: 1 for error occurring during the monitored stage, and 0 for the correct completion of that stage. For the example we discuss, the following set of flags is relevant:

> *PDOL Processing with Error:* This flag is reset after the successful selection of the card application by the terminal. This flag is positioned by the card application after the processing of the data objects received in the data input of the GET PROCESSING OPTIONS. If the terminal fails to correctly provide the card with all the data required in the PDOL, this flag is set. Otherwise, the status of the flag does not change.

> *SDA Processing with Error:* This flag is reset after a successful authentication of the issuer following an on-line authorization of an EMV™ transaction by the issuer. The card application positions this flag after the completion of the card action analysis for the current transaction. The flag is set if the card action analysis decides that the current transaction is declined off-line and bit 7, "Off-line static data authentication failed," in byte 1 of the TVR is set. Otherwise, the status of the flag does not change.

> *DDA Processing with Error:* This flag is reset after a successful authentication of the issuer following an on-line authorization of an EMV™ transaction by the issuer. The card application positions this flag after the completion of the card action analysis for the current transaction. The flag is set if the card action analysis decides that the current transaction is declined off-line and bit 4, "Off-line dynamic data authentication failed," in byte 1 of the TVR is set. Otherwise, the status of the flag does not change.

> *On-Line Completion with Error:* This flag is reset following the receipt by the card of the issuer authentication information—namely, the ARPC. The receipt of this data item indicates the successful completion of the on-line authorization by the issuer, regardless of the value of the response code indicated in the authorization response message, and the

correctness of ARPC. The card application positions this flag after the completion of the card action analysis for the current transaction. The flag is set if the card action analysis decides that the card responds with an ARQC to the first GENERATE AC, which means that the current transaction is recommended for on-line monitoring by the issuer.

▸ *Issuer Authentication with Error:* The card application positions this flag during the issuer authentication stage, which is triggered by an EXTERNAL AUTHENTICATE command following an on-line authorization request. The flag is reset whenever the ARPC, received in the authorization response, verifies correctly. If the ARPC does not verify correctly, then the flag is set. If the issuer authentication is mandatory to be performed, following an on-line authorization by the issuer, but the second GENERATE AC is required before the EXTERNAL AUTHENTICATE, the flag is also set. In any other case the status of the flag does not change.

▸ *Issuer Script Processing with Error:* This flag is reset after each successful authentication of the issuer, following an on-line authorization of a transaction by the issuer. The flag is set if the card fails to correctly execute any of the scripts forwarded by the issuer.

The set of the transaction flow flags is kept in a proprietary data object, which is accessible only to the appropriate card application.

Processing counters and counter limit parameters   The data objects in this category keep track of the number of repetitive processing performed in the card application. Sometimes, a processing counter is associated with a counter limit parameter, which determines the card application to perform a predefined action when the counter reaches that limit.

▸ *PIN Try Counter* (PTC, tag 9F17): This counter maintains the number of possible PIN trials that are still available for the cardholder. This counter is associated with a counter limit parameter referred to as the PIN try limit, which is personalized by the issuer in the card application. This limit prevents the exhaustive search by an attacker of the correct PIN. The higher this limit the lower the security against fraudulent transactions but the better the availability of the card application for the legitimate cardholder who incorrectly types in a PIN or forgets the PIN. The PTC is counted down with each wrong PIN submission to the card. Its value is reset to the value of the PIN try limit after a successful verification of the PIN by the card application or following an appropriate issuer script command sent by the issuer and executed by the card.

▸ *Application Transaction Counter* (ATC, tag 9F36) and *last on-line ATC Register* (tag 9F13): These two counters maintain the total number of transactions performed by the card application and the number of the last transaction that was sent for on-line authorization to the issuer, respectively. Following any card action analysis recommending the ARQC as an outcome of the first GENERATE AC, the last on-line ATC Register is updated to the value of the ATC. The difference between these two parameters, which gives the number of consecutive off-line transactions performed by the card, is associated with a counter limit parameter referred to as the velocity limit, which is personalized by the issuer in the card application. The higher this limit the lower the control of the issuer on the card application but the better the availability of the financial service for the legitimate cardholder in situations where there are no POS terminals with the possibility of on-line authorization (remote villages, remote resort and vacation sites).

▸ *Issuer Script Counter:* This parameter keeps track of the number of issuer scripts successfully executed by the card. This counter is not associated with a counter limit parameter. When the issuer is informed about the value of this counter, it can appreciate the effect of the issuer scripts on the internal state of the card. The issuer script counter is a proprietary data object accessible directly only to the card application.

Financial accumulators and accumulator limit parameters   These are proprietary data objects accessible only from a card application. One category of accumulators keeps track of the cumulative value of the transactions performed both on-line and off-line in a period of time (e.g., 1 day or 1 month). Another type of accumulator keeps track of the cumulative value of the consecutive transactions performed off-line.

CRM data objects of the accumulator type are always associated with accumulator limit parameters, which are security thresholds that limit the tendency of overspending by the cardholder. The accumulator limit parameters are proprietary data objects personalized by the issuer according to the desired trade-off between security against overspending and the availability of the financial service. Thus, the higher the value of the accumulator limits, the higher the risk of overspending. However, the higher the value of the accumulator limits, the better the availability of the payment service for the cardholder.

Financial accumulators and their corresponding accumulator limit parameters can be associated with one card application or can be globally associated with the entire card, when at least two EMV™ debit/credit applications coexist in the same multiapplication card.

Several examples of such parameters, serving as input data to the CRM functions that evaluate the financial risks due to overspending (see Section 7.10.2), are listed below:

- *Application period (specify: day /month) accumulator:* Any accumulator in this category is updated with every transaction performed by a card application, regardless of whether it is completed off-line or on-line, if the following two conditions are observed. First, the Transaction Currency Code, as reported by the terminal, is the same as the application currency code, as personalized by the issuer in the card application. Second, the current date when the transaction is performed, as reported by the terminal in the transaction date, fits in the period considered for monitoring against overspending (i.e., the current day and/or the current month). The amount added to the accumulator consists of the Amount, Authorized and Amount, Other (if any). The accumulator is reset whenever the current date is outside the monitored period. This also updates the application last transaction day and application last transaction month. For every accumulator in this category, the issuer must define the appropriate application period (specify: day/month) accumulator limit. The issuer specifies both application period accumulators and the corresponding limits as proprietary application data objects (see Section 7.4.2).

- *Card period (specify: day/month) accumulator:* This accumulator is updated with every transaction performed by *any* of the EMV™ debit/credit applications existing in the card. The same two conditions as those explained for the application period (specify: day/month) accumulator are observed. For every defined card accumulator, the issuer must define the appropriate card period (specify: day/month) accumulator limit. All the card accumulators and their limits must be visible from all the concerned card applications participating in the monitoring of the global overspending risk. Therefore, the issuer specifies both card period accumulators and the corresponding limits as proprietary card data objects (see Section 7.4.2).

‣ *Application off-line accumulator:* This accumulator is updated with every off-line transaction performed by a card application, if the following two conditions are observed. First, the Transaction Currency Code, as reported by the terminal, is the same as the application currency code, as personalized by the issuer in the card application. Second, the card action analysis performed in the current transaction decides for the off-line approval of the transaction (TC computed in response to the first GENERATE AC). Corresponding to this accumulator the issuer defines the application off-line accumulator limit. The issuer specifies both the application off-line accumulator and the corresponding limit as proprietary application data objects.

‣ *Card off-line accumulator:* This accumulator is updated with every off-line transaction performed by *any* of the EMV™ debit/credit card applications existing in the card. The same two conditions as those explained for the application off-line accumulator are observed. Corresponding to this accumulator, the issuer defines the appropriate card off-line accumulator limit. The card off-line accumulator and its limit must be visible from all the concerned card applications participating in the monitoring of the global overspending risk. Therefore, the issuer specifies them as proprietary card data objects.

7.10.4 CRM function definitions

The execution of any CRM function processes one or several CRM data objects (as identified in Section 7.10.3) which represent the input data. The execution of each CRM function can be further parameterized with a set of issuer result flags. This allows the issuer to define one single general purpose CRM function, the result of which can be finer tuned, depending on the type of card application, the type of service, and the type of payment behavior. In the remainder of this section we examine the definition of two CRM functions, one of each of the first two categories of CRM functions as identified in Section 7.10.2. The other functions can be defined following the same methodology.

Issuer authentication error in the last transaction   This function belongs to the first category of CRM functions, which evaluate the risks resulting from errors in the processing of the EMV™ transaction. The Issuer Authentication with Error flag represents the input data to this function.

The set of issuer result flags that parameterize this function consists of only 1 bit, whose values have the following meaning: 1—if issuer authentication failed in the last transaction, submit the current transaction on-line; 0—if issuer authentication failed in the last transaction, continue with the next function in the set of CRM functions.

The processing of the function is formalized as follows:

> • If "Issuer authentication with error" is 0, the CRM system considers the next function in the set of CRM functions.

> • If "Issuer authentication with error" is 1, the CRM performs the following processing:

>> • The CRM system signals this anomaly, setting 1 bit allocated in the CVRR, which has the meaning "Issuer authentication with error in the last transaction."

>> • If the issuer result flag is personalized to 1, the function votes for the on-line transmission of the transaction to the issuer, proposing the computation of the ARQC in response to the first GENERATE AC.

>> • If the issuer result flag is personalized to 0, the function does not participate in the decision of what kind of completion is recommended for the current transaction, and the execution is transferred to the next function in the CRM system.

Overspending in a (Specify: Day) period by the application   This function belongs to the second category of CRM functions, which evaluate the financial risks due to overspending. The monitored period with which the function is concerned is 1 day.

> • The following CRM internal data objects are considered as input for this function:

>> • Application period (specify: day) accumulator;

>> • Application period (specify: day) accumulator limit;

>> • Application currency code;

>> • Application last transaction day;

>> • Application last transaction month.

If any of the objects mentioned above are not present in the card application, the execution is transferred to the next function in the CRM system.

- The following CRM external data objects are considered as input for this function:

  - Amount, Authorized;

  - Amount, Other;

  - Transaction Currency Code;

  - Transaction date.

If the terminal does not provide any of the objects mentioned above, the execution is transferred to the next function in the CRM system.

- This function is not parameterized through a set of issuer result flags.

- The processing of the function is formalized as follows:

  - If the Application Currency Code is different than the Transaction Currency Code, the CRM system considers the next function in the set.

  - If either the day or the month in the Transaction Date is different from either the application last transaction day or the application last transaction month, then the CRM internal data objects are updated as follows:

    - The application period (specify: day) accumulator is reset.

    - The application last transaction day and the application last transaction month are set to the corresponding values read from the transaction date.

  - If the day and month in the Transaction Date are the same as the application last transaction day and the application last transaction month in the card application, then the CRM internal data objects are updated as follows:

    - The value of the Amount, Authorized and the value of the Amount, Other (if any) are added to the application period (specify: day) accumulator.

▸ If the value of this accumulator is smaller than the associated application period (specify: day) accumulator limit, the CRM system considers the next function in the set.

▸ If the value of this accumulator is larger than the associated application period (specify: day) accumulator limit, the CRM system signals this anomaly by setting 1 bit allocated in the CVRR, which has the meaning "Accumulator limit overflow." The function votes for the on-line transmission of the transaction to the issuer, proposing the computation of the ARQC in response to the first GENERATE AC.

References

[1] Visa, "Chip Card: Testing and Approval Requirements," version 6.0, November 2001, http://www.international.visa.com/fb/vendors/industryserv/pdfs/Chip_Card_Testing_and_Approval_Requirements_Version_6.0.pdf.

[2] EMVCo, "Type Approval Terminal, Level 1: Administrative Procedures/Requirements/Test Cases," http://www.emvco.com/.

[3] EMVCo, "Type Approval Terminal, Level 2: Administrative Procedures/Requirements/Test Cases," http://www.emvco.com/.

[4] Visa, "VISA EU Smart Payment Product Principles," http://www.visaeu.com/for_business/for_industry_suppliers/about_smartcards.html.

[5] MasterCard, "Minimum Card Requirements for Debit and Credit," http://www.mastercardintl.com/newtechnology/smartcards/emv/emvspecs01_02.html.

[6] MasterCard, "M/Chip Lite," http://www.mastercardintl.com/newtechnology/smartcards/emv/emvspecs01_02.html.

[7] Visa, "VIS Specifications, version 1.4.0," http://www.international.visa.com/fb/paytech/smartcard/vsmartspecs/visspec.jsp.

[8] Schlumberger Sema, "Cryptoflex—Cards 16K," http://www.cryptoflex.com/Products/Cryptoflex_16K/cryptoflex_16k.html.

[9] Giesecke and Devrient, "Starcos SPK 2.3," http://www.gdm.de/eng/products/03/index.php4?product_id=348.

[10] Gemplus, "GPK (Gemplus Public Key) Cards," http://www.gemplus.com/products/microprocessor/gpk.htm.

[11] Sun, Java Card 2.1.1, Platform specifications, http://java.sun.com/products/javacard.

[12] Maosco Ltd., "Multos Overview," http://www.multos.com/multpres.ihtml.

[13] Sun, "Secure Computing with Java: Now and the Future (a White Paper),"
http://java.sun.com/marketing/collateral/security.html.

[14] Java Card Forum Task Force, "Java Card Management Specification," http://
www.javacardforum.org/Documents/Jcms10.PDF.

[15] ISO/IEC 7816-5, "Identification Cards—Integrated Circuit(s) Cards with
Contacts—Part 5: Numbering System and Registration Procedure for
Application Identifiers," 1994.

[16] EMVCo, "Frequently Asked Questions—Security," http://www.emvco.com/.

[17] Giesecke and Devrient, "Star Debit/Credit—The Secure Solution
for Your Chip Migration," http://www.gdm.de/eng/products/03/
index.php4?product_id=331.

[18] Schlumberger Sema, "Banking & Retail—EMV™ Migration," http://
www1.slb.com/smartcards/banking/emv.html.

[19] Gemplus, "GemVision Smart," http://www.gemplus.com/products/
microprocessor/gemvisionsmart.htm.

PART

III

Remote Debit and Credit with EMV™

CHAPTER

8

Contents

Remote Card Payments and EMV™

Consumers are using a growing number of access devices for participating in the e-/m-commerce framework, including home and office PCs, mobile phone handsets, personal digital assistants (PDAs), TV set top boxes, and mobile Internet access devices. Consequently, consumers would like to extend their actual payment experience with credit and debit cards to make remote payments, using the aforementioned access devices, as they would use the payment cards in face-to-face transactions. This requires the provision of an acceptable security level for remote card payments: authenticating consumers and their cards, authenticating merchants, protecting the card's financial data while conveyed from the cardholder access device to the merchant access device, and providing enough identification means for the transactions that would impede attackers to replicate them. These business requirements are the impetus for the addition of Annex D in Book 3 of the *EMV 2000* specifications, which defines the *Transaction Processing for Chip Electronic Commerce*. This framework allows the use of EMV™ debit and credit cards not only for paying in face-to-face transactions, as they were initially designed, but also for paying in remote transactions. This solution leverages the EMV™ payment function with the SET specification to provide the foundation for secure, portable, and cost-effective ICC-based transactions over the Internet [1].

This chapter concentrates on three objectives. First, we present two competing remote payment card methods: the TLS-based payment method and the SET. We analyze TLS and

SET from the viewpoint of security and convenience of use. This analysis shows the security limitations of the TLS-based solution compared with SET. The analysis also shows the advantages of the TLS-based solution over SET in terms of ease of operation. This is reflected by a greater acceptability of the TLS-based solution by cardholders and merchants. Second, we look at the possibilities of using the EMV™ chip cards for both increasing the security of the TLS-based remote card payments and increasing the acceptance of the SET payment method. Third, we present the transaction processing for chip electronic commerce. This framework allows issuers to better exploit their EMV™ chip migration effort, offering their clients the possibility of using the EMV™ chip cards not only in face-to-face transactions but also in remote transactions carried out on various channels.

The rest of the chapter is organized as follows. Section 8.1 proposes a model for remote card payments and the channels of interaction between cardholders and merchants. Section 8.2 uses this model to identify possible security threats in conjunction with remote transactions and the appropriate security services that counteract them. We present the structure of the Internet communication protocol stack. We also analyze the possibilities for the realization of these security services at various levels of this stack. This analysis leads to the discussion of the general purpose transport layer security protocol TLS, which can also be used for implementing a remote card payment, and the SET, which is an application layer security protocol dedicated to remote card payments. Section 8.3 describes the possibility of implementing remote card payments based on TLS. We identify the limits of the TLS-based solution in terms of security services opposed to specific threats in remote card payments. In Section 8.4 we discuss the SET solution in the original "software only" implementation. Section 8.5 discuses the pros and cons of the TLS-based solution versus SET. The analysis stresses the superiority of SET in terms of security and identifies its drawbacks regarding the ease of operation by cardholders and merchants. First, we show that the secure implementation of the on-line card authentication and the cardholder verification services, using an EMV™ chip card in the configuration of the cardholder access device, can improve the security of the TLS-based solution. Second, we make a resource analysis that shows that it is not practical to entirely base the management of the SET payment system functionality at the level of the cardholder access device, transforming it into a *thick* client. We outline that delegating some of the functionality of the cardholder access device to a remote wallet server run by the issuer decreases the operational requirements of the cardholder access device, which can be implemented as a *thin* client. Then we describe the integration of the EMV™ chip card in the configuration of the cardholder access device. In

Section 8.6 we present the transaction processing of the EMV™ chip cards for e-commerce, focusing on Annex D of Book 3 in the *EMV 2000* specification. This presentation includes the message flow between the various components of the cardholder access device, as well as the message flow between the cardholder access device and the computers of other participants in the payment system.

8.1 A model for remote card payments

Section 2.2 presented a model for the payment card processing in face-to-face transactions. In this section we present a possible extension of this model for supporting payment card processing in remote transactions. An overview of this model is presented in Figure 8.1.

The model aims at offering a unified framework of the payment card processing in remote transactions, both for the e-commerce and the

Figure 8.1
Payment card
processing in
remote
transactions.

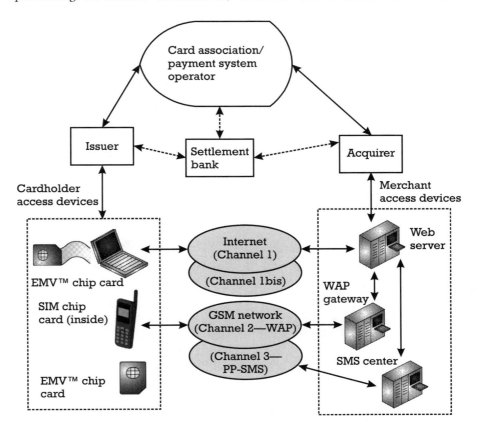

m-commerce scenarios. In both cases, the interaction between the card-holder and the merchant is carried out on open networks.

This interaction can be divided in two logical phases: the browsing/ordering phase and the payment phase. The two phases can be carried out using the same channel in the same open network, using different channels in the same open network, or using different channels in different open networks.

Browsing/ordering phase   For decades, distance selling has been a well-established commercial practice. Instead of physically visiting the shops, the consumer browses the commercial offer using some conventional channels provided by merchants, like printed catalogs or specialized television broadcast stations. After the consumer makes his or her choice, merchants provide the consumer with the facility of ordering the goods and services through mail order and/or telephone order (MO/TO). The merchant's operator dispatches the order received from the consumer and delivers the purchase to the address indicated in the order.

- E-commerce is a case of distance selling, where the browsing/ordering phase is carried out on an Internet channel. In the remainder of the book we assume only TCP/IP channels over the Internet.

- M-commerce is a case of distance selling, where the browsing/ordering phase is carried out on a wireless application protocol (WAP) channel over the GSM network (see Appendix G, Sections G.1 and G.2, for terminology).

Payment phase   In the payment phase, one can distinguish between:

- Payments carried out on conventional channels like those that were used in distance selling for MO/TO;

- Payments carried out on channels established over open networks.

At present, a considerable number of payment methods for e-commerce orders are still carried out *outside* any open network channel. The payment phase is completed in a session subsequent to the browsing/ordering phase, using a conventional channel. Checks and direct money transfers, or cash at delivery, which were used for MO/TO, are still widely used for paying in a domestic e-commerce environment. These methods provide the consumer with a considerable level of control regarding the whole transaction process [2], which can explain their use in the e-commerce framework. While these payment methods can be used for tangible goods, they are totally inappropriate for digital goods and services. These payment methods are not studied in this book.

For the scope of this book, we are only interested in remote card payments. The payment card data is conveyed between the cardholder and the merchant using an open network channel. This channel can be:

> A TCP/IP channel over the Internet;

> A WAP channel over the GSM network (see Appendix G, Section G.2, for explanations on WAP and PP-SMS);

> A PP-SMS channel over the GSM network.

There are various types of cardholder access devices (for details see Appendix G, Section G.3):

> *Unique Internet channel device* (channel 1 only): Both the browsing/ordering and the payment phases are carried out on a TCP/IP channel (channel 1) in one single session.

> *Unique WAP channel device* (channel 2 only): Both the browsing/ordering and the payment phases are carried out on a WAP channel (channel 2) in one single session.

> *Dual Internet channel device* (channel 1 and channel 1bis): The browsing/ordering phase (channel 1) and the payment phase (channel 1bis) are carried out on different TCP/IP channels, in different sessions.

> *Dual channel/dual network device* (channel 1 and channel 3): The browsing/ordering phase is completed on a TCP/IP channel (channel 1), while the payment phase is carried out on a PP-SMS channel (channel 3), in different sessions.

> *Dual mobile channel device* (channel 2 and channel 3): The browsing/ordering phase is completed on a WAP channel (channel 2), while the payment phase is carried out on a PP-SMS channel (channel 3), in different sessions.

8.2 Security aspects of remote card payments

The e-/m-commerce is a risky business environment. This is the consequence of the inherent lack of security of the networks sustaining the remote interaction between cardholders and merchants: no confidentiality of the transmitted data, no authentication of the sender or receiver, and no integrity of the transmitted data. Moreover, in a remote card payment neither the cardholder nor the card is present. Since there is no physical proximity of the cardholder and merchant or of the card and the terminal, like in a face-to-face transaction, card and cardholder impersonation is easy.

In this section we identify possible threats associated with remote transactions carried out on open networks. The analysis concentrates on the cardholder-merchant interface, which is most vulnerable to attacks. We determine appropriate security services that can counteract these threats. We show that the use of an EMV™ chip card in the configuration of the cardholder access device can improve the implementation of the card authentication and cardholder authentication services, as well as the non-repudiation service. Then, we review the structure of a communication protocol stack, and the possibilities for the realization of these security services at various levels of this stack.

8.2.1 Threats environment

The cardholder-merchant interface can be conventionally divided into three distinct security domains: the cardholder access device, the merchant access device, and their communication channel(s) [3]. We now look to some security threats in connection with remote transactions that characterize each domain.

8.2.1.1 Communication channel

Considering that many network technologies broadcast information to every computer located on a local area network or over an air interface, the threat analysis assumes that an attacker can intercept every message.

Sniffing or *eavesdropping* (see Appendix B) is the most obvious threat on the communication channel. Referring to Figure 8.1, the channels that are the most exposed to sniffing are channel 1 and channel 2, when they are used for both browsing/ordering and paying (i.e., the payment information of the card is included in the order forms).

> ‣ T1: The attacker sniffs the browsing/ordering channel. The goal is to obtain as much information as possible about the consumer's commercial habits. Sometimes, the term "snooping" is used to refer to gathering consumer's habits on the Internet [4]. The attacker can derive consumers' profiles, which he can then sell to shopkeepers.

These attempts not only attack the cardholder's privacy but also render him or her vulnerable to excessive and targeted advertising campaigns, which expose the cardholder to the risk of high consumption. Consumers associations have become more and more aware about this side effect of e-commerce. This kind of threat has received a lot of attention in the media.

• T2: The attacker sniffs the payment channel. He tries to filter out financial data in connection with credit and debit cards. The attacker can use this information for performing fraudulent transactions (see Section 2.6.2). This is an "electronic" waiter attack. While an investigation could have traced fraud back to the physical waiter, the electronic waiter is unnoticed and untraceable, because he was not directly involved in the transaction. Since the liability of the cardholder is limited, the issuer and the merchant dispute the loss generated by the fraudulent transactions. The merchant has limited payment guarantee, similar to the transactions performed in distance selling with MO/TO. Cardholders, even though they are not exposed to financial loss, feel a great inconvenience in having fraudulent payments linked to their cards. Consequently, the sniffing of the payment channel greatly concerns payment system operators and card associations. They see that their clients, cardholders, merchants, and financial institutions are reluctant to use payment cards in the e-/m-commerce environment due to the high rate of disputes.

Another important threat is *data modification* by an active attacker (see Appendix B), which mounts, for example, a man-in-the-middle attack (see Appendix D, Section D.4.1).

• T3: The attacker intercepts the browsing/ordering channel and modifies the order sent by the consumer to the merchant. The merchant delivers wrong items to his customer, who will refuse the reception. Besides the direct loss determined by the shipping costs, this attack degrades the quality of the service provided by the merchant, as perceived by his customers. The consequence is that the merchant can lose his customers.

• T4: The attacker intercepts the browsing/ordering channel and modifies the content of the merchant's Web/WAP page, with a twofold purpose.

1. The most obvious purpose for doing so is to modify the merchant's offer, such that a competitor of the merchant gains advantage of misinforming the consumer.

2. Another reason for modifying the merchant's content is less obvious. The attacker inserts in the modified page a Trojan horse, which is an executable program. The attacker instructs this program that once downloaded in the cardholder's browser and running in the cardholder access device, it tries to identify sensitive information and transmit it back to the attacker. The most sensitive information searched for is represented by cryptographic parameters (e.g., secret keys and private keys) used by other payment channels, like the channel 1bis in Figure 8.1, facilitating a SET payment protocol.

▸ T5: The attacker intercepts the payment channel and modifies the payment card data sent by the cardholder to the merchant. With high probability, false card data will lead to the rejection of the transaction by the issuer, which will treat it as an attempt of counterfeit transaction. Consequently, the service that is provided by the payment system operator or card association disappoints the cardholder. The cardholder may stop using the payment card in remote transactions, which is a loss to the payment system operator or card association.

Impersonating (see Appendix B) is easy in a remote transaction carried out on open networks. Any crook can pretend to be a famous mall. The crook displays the electronic decals of many credit cards, as icons inserted in his Web page. The consumer has no suspicion about this impersonation and forwards card details to the crook. Symmetrically, the use of a stolen credit card or of an invalid branded payment card account number raises no suspicion to the shopkeeper. The attacker cannot betray his nervous behavior on the wires.

▸ T6: The attacker impersonates the electronic decal of a payment card brand. The attacker runs a Web server that presents besides the commercial offer the icons of many credit cards, which his imaginary shop accepts for paying. Each icon can be assimilated with an electronic decal in the virtual window of this shop. The attacker collects the payment card data from as many cardholders as possible, mounting a massive electronic waiter attack. The attacker can sell the collection of card data to a malicious organization, which can subsequently attempt a large number of fraudulent transactions.

- T7: An attacker impersonates a valid payment card on a payment channel. The attacker hopes that the electronic shopper will authorize the counterfeit transaction and deliver the goods before the counterfeit card is recognized by the payment system.

- T8: A thief impersonates the legitimate cardholder on a payment channel. The attacker makes a payment with a stolen, lost, or card-not-received card, whose payment card account number is correctly branded. This attack leads to fraudulent transactions.

If the consumer changes his or her mind after ordering the purchases and effecting the corresponding payment, she tries to repudiate the transaction with the hope that she will recover her money.

- T9: Although a valid branded payment card account number is used by the legitimate cardholder, he or she may latter deny his or her participation in a remote transaction with the merchant. This leads to a dispute and loss by the merchant due to supplementary shipping costs. In case the merchant sells entertainment on demand, the cardholder attempts to enjoy the service without paying.

While the aforementioned threats are related to security, the *denial-of-service* attack attempts to deny the availability of a communication channel between the cardholder access device and the merchant access device.

- T10: The attack consists of flooding the merchant's access device with false requests coming from an automated bogus cardholder access device. This attack discourages a real cardholder from buying from the unavailable merchant, which leads to financial loss for the latter.

8.2.1.2   Cardholder access device

There are many possible penetration attacks depending on the nature of the access device and of its access control system. For the purpose of our analysis, however, we are concerned only with the Trojan horse threat described below.

- T11: The browser running in the cardholder access device interprets the content of a Web/WAP page, which might also contain executable programs. The downloaded program can be a Trojan horse that tries to take advantage of some security weaknesses of the browser (see also threat T4, number 2). If the attack succeeds, the program may identify secret cryptographic parameters stored in the cardholder access device, which can serve for implementing security services used by other payment applications.

8.2.1.3 Merchant access device

The threat we are concerned with here is a massive waiter attack as described below.

▸ T12: The attacker succeeds in breaking into the logical access control system of the merchant access device. The goal is to obtain the card financial data of as many cards as possible, which can be used in mounting a large number of fraudulent transactions. This attack can produce a high loss to the merchant, which can be held liable for the fraudulent transactions.

As can be seen, the threats of using payment cards in the e-/m-commerce environment are not new compared with face-to-face transactions, but they are easier to mount on open networks. The successful mounting of the corresponding attacks can lead to high volume and automated fraud, which unacceptably increases the loss of various participants in the e-/m-commerce business.

8.2.2 Security services for remote transactions

Security, or the perceived lack of it, is often mentioned as a reason of holding back on e-/m-commerce. This is the number one concern stated by consumers for hesitating to use their credit cards to make purchases over the Internet or GSM networks. In this section we identify appropriate security services that are able to counteract the threats identified in Section 8.2.1. A detailed definition of the security services is given in Appendix C, Section C.1.

Surfing the Web does not seem to endanger the consumer's privacy. The consumer feels anonymous while browsing the Web, like listening to the radio or browsing in a bookstore. In fact, Web surfers leave identifiable tracks at every Web site they visit [4].

▸ AnS1—Anonymity: This is the security service that addresses the protection of the consumer while browsing various shops' Web sites. Sometimes, visiting a certain Web site reveals some of the consumer preferences, even if the consumer does not order anything in that shop. The tool used for rendering the browsing anonymous is sometimes referred to as an anonymizer [4]. This service addresses threat T1.

Confidentiality services (CS) are intended to counteract the sniffing threats.

> • CS1—Confidentiality of the ordering phase: This confidentiality service is essential for impeding attackers from deriving consumers' profiles. It should be implemented by the browsing/ordering channel, and it should be provided regardless of the type of channel used to perform the payment itself. This security service addresses threat T1.

> • CS2—Secure messaging for confidentiality: This confidentiality service concerns the financial messages "on the fly" from the cardholder to the merchant, transmitted on the payment channel for completing the payment phase of a remote transaction. A financial message includes the payment card data, as the credit card number, the account number to which a debit card is linked, and the expiration date. This security service addresses threat T2.

> • CS3—Confidentiality of stored card data: This service refers to the confidentiality of the card data while it is stored in the permanent storage space of the merchant access device, prior to being submitted to the acquirer for clearing and settlement. This security service addresses threat T12.

Data authentication services (AS), which provide both data origin authentication and data integrity, are intended to counteract simultaneously the impersonation and data modification threats on a communication channel (see Appendix C, Section C.1).

> • AS1—Data authentication of the exchanged messages: This security service refers to the authentication and integrity of the transaction messages exchanged between the cardholder and the merchant. This security service is implemented on both the browsing/ordering channel and on the payment channel. The transaction messages protected by this service are:

> > • The message that includes the order sent by the consumer to the merchant on the browsing/ordering channel. This counters threat T3;

- ▸ The message that includes the offer provided by the merchant to the consumer. This counters threat T4;

- ▸ The message that includes the payment card data sent by the cardholder to the merchant. This counters threat T5.

- ▸ AS2—Authenticode: This security service refers to providing enough evidence about the authenticity and integrity of an executable program that is downloaded from a Web page. Even though it does not prevent the potential hostile actions of the executable program, it guarantees its linkage to the content of a Web page, and thus it offers accountability in case hostile actions are identified. This service protects against threats T4 and T11.

Entity authentication (ES) allows for the identification of the entities participating in a remote transaction.

- ▸ ES1—Server authentication: Cardholders need to identify merchants with whom they can securely conduct e-commerce. Server authentication is a security service that allows a Web server to produce enough evidence to any WEB browser that is a genuine server on the WEB, with which secure remote transactions can be carried out. This evidence is guaranteed by a third party, which is trusted by both the consumer and the merchant. The trusted third party (TTP) can be a certification authority broadly accepted on the Internet (e.g., VeriSign [5]). This service counters threat T4.

- ▸ ES2—Client authentication: This security service is similar to the server authentication but it concerns the client side. This service counters threats T3 and T5.

- ▸ ES3—Merchant authentication: This security service confirms that a merchant has a relationship with a financial institution, allowing the merchant to accept payment cards of a certain brand. This service provides the authenticity of the electronic brand decal displayed in the "virtual window" of an electronic shop. The service is intended to counter the impersonation attack T6.

- ▸ ES4—Cardholder account authentication: This security service ensures that the cardholder uses a valid branded payment card account number for completing the payment phase. This security service is intended to counter counterfeit transactions, which is threat T7.

▸ ES5—Cardholder authentication: This security service ensures the merchant that for each remote transaction the person providing the data of the payment card in the remote transaction is the legitimate cardholder of that card. The successful implementation of this service annihilates threat T8, which decreases the number of fraudulent transactions.

The implementation of the cardholder account authentication can rely on a set of verifiable secret card data, which is brand specific and is stored in the cardholder access device. One could say that proving the knowledge of this secret card data provides enough evidence for the cardholder authentication too. However, this is not true. To support this statement, we observe that a successful execution of a Trojan horse (see threats T4, 2 and T11) on the target cardholder access device reveals to the attacker the secret card data, which he can fraudulently use. This is the reason why the security services ES4 and ES5 are separately identified. Thus, there is no physical proof that the *legitimate* cardholder is interacting with the merchant while probating the authenticity of the cardholder account.

▸ TS1: A supplementary level of trust for cardholder authentication can be provided in case the set of verifiable secret card data is provided to the legitimate cardholder in a tamper-resistant token, working in combination with the cardholder access device. This token can be an EMV™ chip card, which is uniquely linked to the cardholder. Therefore, the tamper-resistance security service can be used to provide a physical proof of the cardholder's identity. If this physical proof is combined with something the legitimate cardholder knows, like a PIN, then this combination is accepted as sufficient to prove the presence of the cardholder in the remote transaction. The tamper-resistance security service directly counters threat T11 and helps enforce the cardholder authentication service (ES5).

Non-repudiation of the origin (see Appendix C, Section C.1) is the security service that counters the threat of denying the participation in a transaction by the initiator of the remote transaction.

▸ NS1—Cardholder non-repudiation: This security service ensures the merchant that for each remote transaction the cardholder cannot deny his or her participation in the transaction. The successful implementation of this service annihilates threat T9, which can lead to a decreasing number of disputes between the merchant and the cardholder.

Note that the implementation of the cardholder non-repudiation service also relies on a set of secret card data, which is uniquely linked to the cardholder. The cardholder access device uses this secret data to produce a non-repudiation proof verifiable by the merchant access device or by a third party. Therefore, the irrefutability of this proof depends on the secure storage of the cardholder's secret data. A solution could be that an EMV™ chip card hosts this secret data and produces the non-repudiation proof. The EMV™ chip card is part of the hardware configuration of the cardholder access device.

Alternatively, the cardholder's secret data is kept in a secure wallet server run by the issuer, which computes the non-repudiation proof on behalf of the cardholder. This computation is triggered by a successful authentication of the cardholder (see Section 8.5.3).

By using the EMV™ chip cards, an issuer leverages its investment in the EMV™ chip migration by providing a reliable and trusted mechanism for remote card and cardholder authentication [6].

8.2.3 Security services realization

Networks are typically specified in layers [7]. Each layer defines protocols for communication between peers at the same level. The Internet protocol suite is a four-layer system, as shown in Figure 8.2, where the communication subsystem (see Appendix C, Section C.2) consists of the link layer, the network layer, and the transport layer.

Figure 8.2
Internet protocol suite.

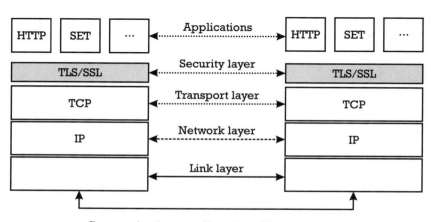

Communications medium (e.g., Ethernet cable)

The meaning of each layer and the representative protocols are listed below [8]:

- The link layer provides the physical interfacing with the communication medium (e.g., the Ethernet cable).

- The network layer handles the movement of packets around the network. The Internet protocol (IP) provides unreliable data transmission between nodes. It also defines the basis for the Internet addressing.

- The transport layer assures the data flow between two hosts, for the communication of the peer applications, one layer above. Most Internet applications use the transport control protocol (TCP), which is a connection-oriented data flow that provides transmission reliability. Multicast applications use a connectionless data flow that provides no reliability, called the user datagram protocol (UDP).

- The most common applications implemented on the TCP/IP stack are the Telnet for remote login, file transfer protocol (ftp), the simple mail transfer protocol (SMTP), and the HTTP.

The realization of security services protecting remote transactions and remote card payments can be achieved at various levels of the Internet protocol stack (see also Appendix C, Section C.2).

8.2.3.1 Security for the Internet Protocol

The IP security architecture [9] describes security mechanisms for the IP version 4 (IPv4) and IP version 6 (IPv6). It defines two specific security headers. The first is called the Authentication Header, which provides integrity and authentication [10]. The second is called the Encapsulating Security Payload (ESP), which provides confidentiality, and may also provide integrity and authentication [11].

8.2.3.2 Transport layer security protocols

There are several security protocols for adding security services to TCP. The most known representatives of the transport layer security protocols are Netscape's SSL, Microsoft's Private Communication Technology (PCT), and the TLS, elaborated by the Internet Engineering Task Force (IETF), which is the standardization organization of the Internet. The advantage of the transport layer security protocols is that they are application protocol independent. Used for remote e-commerce transactions and remote payments, a transport layer security protocol establishes a secure channel on the Internet (see Appendix C, Section C.2) between the access devices of a cardholder and a merchant, which can protect the card data on transit from one to another. Section 8.3 presents a payment method based on TLS.

8.2.3.3 Application layer security protocols

The most cited example of an application layer security protocol is the Secure HTTP (S-HTTP), which is a message-oriented communication protocol for securing messages that are transmitted using the HTTP. S-HTTP provides security services for confidentiality, data integrity, and non-repudiation of origin.

There are many proposals for secure payment applications, like First Virtual, CyberCash, NetBill, NetCheque, to name only a few. Each of these payment applications proposes its own registration procedures for participants and its secure payment protocol. However, none of these Internet payment applications have achieved widespread acceptance. One possible reason is their limited scalability. We will not go into further detail on any of them in this book. The interested reader can find a comprehensive overview of these Internet payment applications and protocols in [12]. Rather, we are interested in the SET secure payment application [13–15]. SET proposes a standardized, industry-wide secure payment protocol at the level of the application layer, which establishes a secure communication over an insecure channel (see Appendix C, Section C.2). Visa and MasterCard elaborated the SET standard with collaboration from a consortium of leading technology companies including Microsoft, Netscape, VeriSign, RSA, to name only a few. The SET designers overtook and developed a number of principles previously proposed by other payment and security standards, among which are the Internet Keyed Payment Protocols (iKP) [16]. Section 8.4 presents the payment method based on SET.

8.3   Remote payment method based on TLS

The SSL protocol [17] was specified by Netscape Communications, and is actually at version 3.0. The current TLS protocol [18], version 1.0, is elaborated by the IETF, and is based on the SSL version 3.0. Like SSL, TLS is composed of two layers: the handshake protocol and the record protocol. In the remainder of the section we refer only to the TLS protocol and its use for remote payments.

TLS-based solutions are suitable for implementation on unique Internet channel devices, where both the browsing/ordering phase and the payment phase are completed during the same session on the same channel. These solutions are suitable for small transaction amounts, considering the security limitations of the TLS protocol, as described in Section 8.3.3.

8.3.1   TLS handshake protocol

The TLS handshake protocol allows the server and (optionally) the client to authenticate each other. It also allows the negotiation of a symmetric encryption algorithm, with the corresponding cryptographic keys. The negotiated keys are made available to the record protocol operation for any connection established during a secure session between the browser and the server. The handshake protocol is described below, and is schematized in Figure 8.3. We use the notations and terminology explained in Appendix D, Sections D.1 and D.3.

The client forwards a set of CipherSuite proposals and a random number R_c to the server. Each CipherSuite includes the types of cryptographic algorithms together with the length of their parameters. These algorithms refer to key establishment, symmetric encryption, and the type of MDC used for deriving a keyed MAC (see Appendix D, Section D.2.2). In the remainder of

Figure 8.3
Overview of the
TLS handshake
protocol.

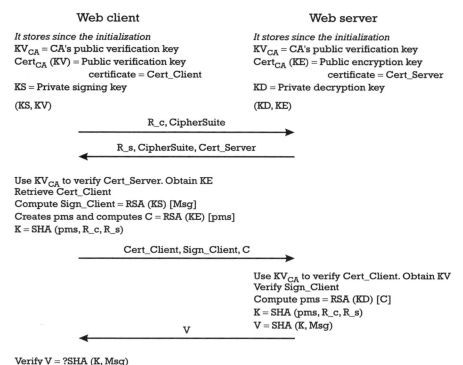

Web client

It stores since the initialization
KV_{CA} = CA's public verification key
$Cert_{CA}$ (KV) = Public verification key
        certificate = Cert_Client
KS = Private signing key

(KS, KV)

Web server

It stores since the initialization
KV_{CA} = CA's public verification key
$Cert_{CA}$ (KE) = Public encryption key
        certificate = Cert_Server
KD = Private decryption key

(KD, KE)

R_c, CipherSuite →

← R_s, CipherSuite, Cert_Server

Use KV_{CA} to verify Cert_Server. Obtain KE
Retrieve Cert_Client
Compute Sign_Client = RSA (KS) [Msg]
Creates pms and computes C = RSA (KE) [pms]
K = SHA (pms, R_c, R_s)

Cert_Client, Sign_Client, C →

Use KV_{CA} to verify Cert_Client. Obtain KV
Verify Sign_Client
Compute pms = RSA (KD) [C]
K = SHA (pms, R_c, R_s)
V = SHA (K, Msg)

← V

Verify V = ?SHA (K, Msg)

the protocol we assume that RSA is used for key establishment. Note that Diffie-Hellman is a possible alternative algorithm for key establishment, which is accepted by the TLS.

The server answers with its own set of preferred cipher suites, and a random number generated by itself, denoted R_s. The server also includes an RSA certificate $Cert\_Server = Cert_{CA}(KE)$ on its public encryption key, denoted KE. A certification authority accepted as a TTP by both the client and the server signs this certificate.

Using the public verification key KV_{CA} of the CA, the client verifies $Cert\_Server$ and retrieves the server's authentic KE. It is assumed that KV_{CA} is installed in both the client and the server.

If the server requires the authentication of the client, which is optional, the client has to retrieve the public key certificate $Cert\_Client = Cert_{CA}(KV)$, issued by the same CA, on the client's public verification key KV. The client uses the corresponding private signing key KS to generate a signature of the client, $Sign\_Client = RSA(KS)[Msg]$ on a message Msg that includes the random numbers created by both the server (R_s) and the client (R_c).

The client generates the so-called premaster secret, denoted pms, and creates an RSA digital envelope that wraps it, $C = RSA(KE)[pms]$. The premaster secret is used together with R_s and R_c to compute the master secret key $K = SHA(pms, R\_c, R\_s)$.

The client forwards $Cert\_Client$, $Sign\_Client$, and C to the server.

The server verifies the $Cert\_Client$, using the public verification key KV_{CA} of the CA, and retrieves the client's authentic KV. The server uses it to verify the signature produced by the client $Sign\_Client$, and if the verification is correct it accepts the authenticity of the client.

Using its private decryption key KD, the server unwraps the RSA digital envelope containing the premaster secret, i.e., $pms = RSA(KD)[C]$. The premaster secret is used in the same way as explained for the client to compute the master secret key K. The key K together with R_s and R_c are provided to the TLS record protocol of the server for the duration of a session.

The server also computes a key confirmation value V as the result of a one-way function (e.g., SHA), on the recovered master secret key and the message Msg [i.e., $V = SHA(K, Msg)$]. The server forwards this value to the client.

The client verifies the key confirmation value, and if this verification passes, it accepts the authenticity of the server, since only it would have been able to compute the premaster key from the RSA digital envelope. The key K together with R_s and R_c are provided to the TLS record protocol of the client for the duration of a session.

8.3.2   TLS record protocol

The TLS record protocol takes a message of arbitrary size to be transmitted, fragments it into appropriate blocks, optionally compresses the data, computes a MAC, enciphers, and transmits the result. A sequence number is also inserted for countering attempts to replay blocks or alter the order of the transmitted blocks. From the master secret key K, together with R_s and R_c, which are provided by the TLS handshake protocol, the TLS record protocol generates keys, initialization vectors for the CBC mode of the block cipher, and secrets for the keyed MAC computation. These cryptographic parameters are subsequently used for symmetric encryption, implementing the secure messaging for confidentiality service (CS2), and MAC computation, implementing the data authentication of exchanged messages (AS1). When the data authentication service is implemented with a MAC, the service is often referred to as secure messaging for integrity and authentication.

The messages that are effectively secured at the level of the TLS record protocol are the content request of the cardholder's browser, specifying the URL of the concerned merchant's Web page, and the commercial offer of the merchant returned in the content response of his Web server. The commercial offer can include the order form. After decryption by the cardholder's browser, the cardholder fills in the order form and the appropriate payment information, which is again encrypted and sent to the merchant's Web server.

8.3.3   Security limitations of the TLS protocol

In terms of security services, as introduced in Section 8.2.2, the TLS handshake protocol provides server authentication (ES1), and optionally, client authentication (ES2).

- The client authentication is based on a digital signature–based DDA mechanism (as explained in Appendix D, Section D.7.2). The client computes the digital signature $Sign\_Client = RSA(KS)[Msg]$ on a view of the messages exchanged with the server, using the client's private signing key KS. A CA accepted on the Internet issues the certificate $Cert\_Client = Cert_{CA}(KV)$ of the corresponding public verification key KV of the client.

- The server authentication is based on a MAC-based DDA mechanism (as explained in Appendix D, Section D7.1) with the master secret key K, derived from a premaster secret key proposed by the client. The premaster secret key is forwarded to the server in a digital envelope created with the server's public encryption key, *KE*, which is certified by the same CA on the Internet.

▸ This key establishment mechanism for the master secret key *K* is essential for the implementation by the TLS record protocol of the confidentiality of the ordering phase, of the secure messaging for confidentiality (CS2), and of the secure messaging for integrity and authentication (AS1). These services successfully counteract threats generated by external attackers, but they are powerless against attacks mounted by the entities involved in the remote transaction.

The fact that a CA on the Internet authenticates a merchant's server does not provide any security against attempts of impersonating the electronic decal of a payment card brand (T6). Similarly, the client's certificate provides no protection against attempts to use invalid payment cards (T7) or against fraudulent transactions (T8). This is mainly because the CA that issues the server and client certificates has no connection with the financial institutions either issuing payment cards or acquiring transactions performed with them. The certificates refer only to the fact that the Web server and/or the Web client can legitimately be connected on the Web, but it does not legitimate the two entities to participate in a certain application, whether it is payment or not.

The TLS provides neither the non-repudiation service (NS1) nor the confidentiality of the financial data of the cards after it is stored on the merchant's computer (CS3). This makes this solution rather sensitive to fraud both by the cardholder, who may deny having performed a transaction (T9), and by the merchant who can abuse the financial information of cards stored on his Web server (T12).

8.4   SET-based solutions

We saw in the previous section that the TLS protocol can provide enough trust that the cardholder's Web browser and the merchant's Web server are legitimate Internet users. The TLS also allows the establishment of a confidential channel between them. Thus, TLS is suitable for the secure completion of the browsing/ordering phase of a remote transaction, protecting the consumer against outsiders' sniffing or against merchant's Web server impersonation. When it comes to securing the payment phase, however, the TLS-based solutions rely on the assumption that the cardholder and the merchant know and trust each other.

SET does not really compete with TLS, since it secures the payment phase of the transaction. It provides enough assurance that a merchant and, optionally, a cardholder have a valid relationship with a payment card brand, via their acquirer and issuer, respectively. All the parties are validated via their SET digital certificates, which are issued under the trust hierarchy established by the payment card brand. Moreover, the payment card data (credit card number, expiration date) are encrypted such that the merchant's server never sees them in clear. Within the boundaries of some limitations, cardholder authentication and non-repudiation of the transaction are also provided.

8.4.1 SET model

The SET payment model can be obtained from the model of remote payment card processing presented in Figure 8.1. In the SET model, the cardholder has a dual Internet channel device (e.g., a PC running a TLS-enabled Web browser for completing the browsing/ordering phase and the SET payment application). SET can be regarded as a helper for the Web browser, which is used for the completion of the payment phase. The cardholder's PC talks to the merchant's server. This server further communicates with the payment gateway. This gateway can be seen as a dual port computer, which on one hand acts as an e-commerce terminal for the acquirer network and on the other as an AH for the merchant server. The SET model is schematized in Figure 8.4.

8.4.2 Setup of the SET payment scheme

In the framework of the SET payment system, the cardholder, the merchant, and the payment gateway, need cryptographic material to participate in a SET payment transaction.

- The cardholder has a signature key pair, which consists of a private signing key and the corresponding public verification key (cKS, cKV).

- The merchant has both a signature key pair (mKS, mKV) and a key-exchange key pair, which is composed of a private decryption key and a public encryption key (mKD, mKE).

- The payment gateway has also a signature key pair (pKS, pKV) and a key-exchange key pair (pKD, pKE).

Figure 8.4
SET model for
remote card
payments.

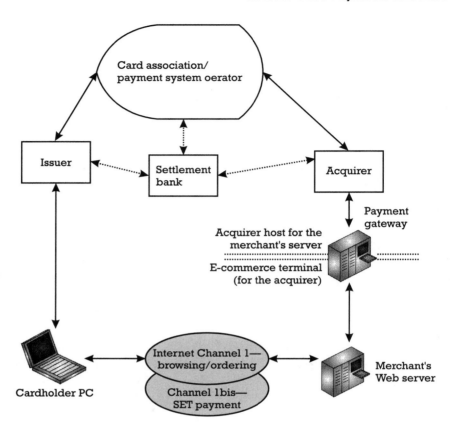

8.4.2.1 Public key certificates

Each aforementioned entity uses its private signing key *eKS* to produce a
digital signature, which anyone can verify using the corresponding public
verification key *eKV*. The digital signature mechanism requires a CA to guarantee the authenticity of the entity's public verification key with a signature
public key certificate (see Appendix D, Section D.4). The certificate itself is
a digital signature with the CA's private signing key, on the entity's public verification key *eKV* and other data characterizing each entity (i.e.,
Cert_eKV = Cert(caKS)[eKV, entity_data]). Note that *"e"* abbreviates the type
of entity: *"c"* stands for the cardholder, *"m"* stands for the merchant, and *"p"*
stands for the payment gateway.

The correct verification of an entity's signature public key certificate
vouches that:

‣ The CA guarantees that the *entity_data* included in the certificate is
data that characterizes the entity. Any attempt at modifying these
characteristics leads to an incorrect verification of the certificate.

▸ The public verification key of the entity is genuine and can be further involved in the verification of any digital signature produced by that entity.

Any sender can create a digital envelope with the receiver's public encryption key *eKE*. Only the receiver that has the corresponding private decryption key *eKD* can open the digital envelope. The digital envelope contains a secret session key *SSK* proposed by the sender to receiver, which can implement a confidential channel between them, where bulk data can be encrypted. If the receiver is the merchant, the sender uses *mKE* as the public encryption key; if the receiver is the payment gateway, the sender uses *pKE* as the public encryption key. To avoid a man-in-the-middle attack (see Appendix D, Section D.4.1), a CA must guarantee the authenticity of the receiver's public verification key with a key-exchange public key certificate (see Appendix D, Section D.4). The certificate itself is a digital signature with the CA's private signing key, on the receiver's public encryption key *eKE* and other data characterizing each entity (i.e., *Cert_eKE* = *Cert*(*caKS*)[*eKE*, entity_data]). Note that "*e*" abbreviates the type of entity: "*m*" stands for merchant, and "*p*" stands for the payment gateway.

The correct verification of an entity's key-exchange public key certificate vouches that:

▸ The CA guarantees that the *entity_data* included in the certificate is data that characterizes the entity.

▸ The public encryption key of the receiving entity is genuine and can be further involved in producing digital envelopes destined to the receiving entity.

8.4.2.2 SET certification hierarchy

In the SET model, the cardholder, the merchant, and the payment gateway are situated in different security domains. The cardholder recognizes the cardholder CA (CCA), the merchant recognizes the merchant CA (MCA), while the payment gateway trusts the payment gateway CA (PCA). It is common that an issuer plays the role of the CCA for its cardholders, while an acquirer plays the role of both an MCA and a PCA for its merchants and their associated payment gateways.

▸ The CCA uses its private signing key *ccaKS* to compute the *Cert_cKV* for cardholders. Anyone can use the CCA's corresponding public verification key *ccaKV* to verify *Cert_cKV* and to obtain an authentic copy of *cKV*.

‣ The MCA uses its private signing key *mcaKS* to compute the *Cert_mKV* and *Cert_mKE* for merchants. Anyone can use the MCA's corresponding public verification key *mcaKV* to verify *Cert_mKV* and *Cert_mKE*, to obtain an authentic copy of *mKV* and *mKE*, respectively.

‣ The PCA uses its private signing key *pcaKS* to compute the *Cert_pKV* and *Cert_pKE* for payment gateways. Anyone can use the PCA's corresponding public verification key *pcaKV* to verify *Cert_pKV* and *Cert_pKE*, to obtain an authentic copy of *pKV* and *pKE*, respectively. Note that *entity_data* included in the *Cert_pKE* may contain information about the supplementary processing facilities offered by the payment gateway, like support for on-line PIN and chip related data (see Section 8.6.2).

In order to enforce trust among entities in different security domains, a certification hierarchy is needed that allows entities in one security domain to verify certificates issued in another domain. A card brand can play the role of a brand CA, which is recognized and trusted by the cardholder CA, merchant CA, and payment gateway CA. This is a natural organization since issuers and acquirers respectively issuing and accepting cards of a certain brand are both clients of the same card association that promotes the respective card brand. Each brand CA has its own signature key pair (*bKS*, *bKV*), whose private signing key *bKS* is used to compute signature public key certificates for the public verification keys of all the subordinated organizations (i.e., *Cert_ccaKV*, *Cert_mcaKV*, and *Cert_pcaKV*, respectively).

The SET certification hierarchy could have at its root a SET industry CA, which can be a certification authority run by the SET consortium. This is the highest CA that is recognized and trusted by all the card brands adopting the SET payment standard. Each card brand certifies its public verification key *bKV* with the SET industry CA, which uses its signing private key *rootKS* to compute the *Cert_bKV*. The corresponding public verification key *rootKV* is widely known and is embedded in any SET application software. The SET certification hierarchy is schematized in Figure 8.5.

We define the CCA certification chain as the set of certificates *Cert_ccaKV* and *Cert_bKV*, the MCA certification chain as the set of certificates *Cert_mcaKV* and *Cert_bKV*, and the PCA certification chain as the set of certificates *Cert_pcaKV* and *Cert_bKV*.

In order to obtain an authentic copy of the public verification key of any of the entities CCA, MCA, or PCA, someone *traverses* the corresponding certification chain according to the following algorithm:

Figure 8.5
SET certification
hierarchy.

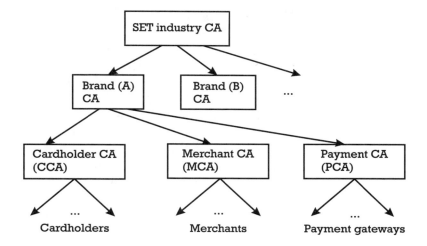

- Use *rootKV*, which is available to any SET software implementation, to check *Cert_bKV*. Obtain an authentic copy of the brand CA's public verification key *bKV*.

- Use the previously obtained *bKV* to check:

  - (*CCA certification chain*) *Cert_ccaKV*. Obtain an authentic copy of the CCA's public verification key *ccaKV*.

  - (*MCA certification chain*) *Cert_mcaKV*. Obtain an authentic copy of the MCA's public verification key *mcaKV*.

  - (*PCA certification chain*) *Cert_pcaKV*. Obtain an authentic copy of the PCA's public verification key *pcaKV*.

8.4.3 Registration of participants

Before being able to participate in any SET payment transaction, cardholders, merchants, and payment gateways must certify their public verification keys and public encryption keys with the appropriate CA. To this end, a certificate requesting entity and the CA run a registration protocol. Since the involvement of an EMV™ chip card in the SET payment transaction changes neither the cardholder registration nor the merchant registration procedures, we do not detail the corresponding protocols. We stress the security significance of the cardholder's certificate and merchant's certificates.

8.4.3.1 Cardholder registration

The cardholder's SET software generates the signature key pair (*cKS, cKV*) and transmits to the CCA the *cKV* item. The CCA uses *ccaKS* to compute *Cert_cKV* = *Cert*(*ccaKS*)[*cKV card_data*] on *cKV* and on some data items that characterize the cardholder's account, referred to as *card_data*. This certificate, together with the CCA certification chain, is returned to the cardholder access device, which securely stores them for further use.

The cardholder's signature public key certificate *Cert_cKV* is the electronic representation of the payment card. This certificate is issued such that *card_data* contains neither the card's account number (PAN) nor its expiration date (*CardExpiry*) in clear, but rather it contains the hash value of these two items concatenated with a secret value known only to the cardholder's software *PANSecret*. This secret value prevents guessing attacks on the PAN in the *Cert_cKV*.

Upon receipt and verification of the certificate, the merchant is assured at a minimum that the issuer, playing the role of the CCA, has validated the cardholder's account number—but the merchant cannot derive any information about the card data. The cardholder's signature public key certificate implements the cardholder account authentication (ES4) and the confidentiality of stored card data in the merchant's Web server (CS3). If the account number, expiration date, and the secret value are known, the link to the certificate can be proven. Within SET, the cardholder provides the account information and the secret value to the payment gateway where the link is verified.

8.4.3.2 Merchant registration

The merchant's SET software generates the signature key pair (*mKS, mKV*) and the key-exchange key pair (*mKD, mKE*) and transmits to the MCA the public items *mKV* and *mKE*. The MCA uses *mcaKS* to compute the signature public key certificate *Cert_mKV* = *Cert*(*mcaKS*)[*mKV merchant_data*] on *mKV* and on some data items that characterize the merchant's account, referred to as *merchant_data*. Among these data items, there is the merchant country code item. Similarly, the MCA computes the key-exchange public key certificate *Cert_mKE* = *Cert*(*mcaKS*)[*mKE merchant_data*] on *mKE* and *merchant_data*. Both certificates *Cert_mKV* and *Cert_mKE* together with the MCA certification chain are returned to the merchant access device, which securely stores them for further use.

The merchant's signature/key-exchange public key certificates function as the electronic substitute of the payment brand decal, which guarantees the relationship between the merchant and the acquirer concerning the acceptance of the payment card brand. These certificates implement the merchant authentication (ES3).

8.4.4 Secure SET channel over insecure networks

SET creates a secure channel over the insecure Internet, referred to as a SET channel. This channel offers the following features: data authentication (data integrity and origin authentication), entity authentication, non-repudiation, and confidentiality.

8.4.4.1 Establishment of a SET authentic and/or confidential channel

The SET channel is established between a proving entity and a verifying entity, belonging to separate security domains, guaranteed by CA1 and CA2, respectively. Both certification authorities are hierarchically subordinated to the same brand CA and have appropriate certification chains to the SET industry CA. Both the proving and the verifying entity run the SET software, which has an authentic copy of the *rootKV*. The proving entity has a signature key pair (*eKS, eKV*) and a signature public key certificate signed by CA1 (i.e., *Cert1_eKV = Cert(ca1KS)[eKV,$_{proving}$entity_data]*). The verifying entity has a key-exchange key pair (*eKD, eKE*) and the corresponding certificate from CA2 (i.e., *Cert2_eKE = Cert(ca2KS)[eKE,$_{receiving}$entity_data]*). The proving entity sends a message *M*, which is part of the SET payment transaction processing, to the verifying entity. The SET makes sure that there are no messages in the SET payment transaction processing that are identical, so that replay attacks are not possible. The protocol for establishing the SET channel between the two parties is as follows:

▸ The verifying entity retrieves the *Cert2_eKE* and the CA2 certification chain. It sends both items to the proving entity.

▸ The proving entity performs the following processing to establish the SET channel, which consists of the superposition of a certificate validation channel, an authentic channel, and a confidential channel:

1. Use the *rootKV* to traverse the CA2 certification chain. An authentic copy of the CA2's public verification key (*ca2KV*) is obtained.

2. Use *ca2KV* to verify the key-exchange public key certificate *Cert2_eKE*. An authentic copy of the public encryption key *eKE* of the verifying entity is obtained.

3. Create a digital signature on the SET transaction data *M*.

   ▸ Compute the hash value of the message *M* through the collision-resistant hash function H [i.e., $h = \mathrm{H}(M)$].

- Retrieve the private signing key *eKS* and call the RSA function to compute the digital signature $S = \text{RSA}(eKS)[h]$. Since the messages in any SET transaction are different than the messages in any other transaction, the digital signature can be assimilated with a dynamic authenticator produced by a digital-based DDA mechanism (see Appendix D, Section D.7.2).

- Retrieve the signature public key certificate *Cert1_eKV* and the CA1 certification chain.

4.   Create a confidential channel with the verifying entity.

- Generate at random a session secret key *SSK* to be used in connection with the DES block cipher.

- Use the previously generated key to compute $C' = \text{DES}(SSK)$ [*bulk_data*], where the bulk data is composed of the transaction data (*M*), the digital signature *S* on it, the signature public key certificate *Cert1_eKV*, and the CA1 certification chain. The cryptogram C' protects the confidentiality of the transaction data and guarantees that an external attacker cannot exploit any information he could obtain by verifying the digital signature *S*, the signature public key certificate *Cert_eKE*, or any other certificates in the chain of CA1.

- Use the authentic copy of the receiving entity's public encryption key *eKE* (obtained in step 2) to create an RSA digital envelope *C* containing the session secret key, $C = \text{RSA}(eKE)[SSK]$.

5.   Send C' and *C* to the verifying entity.

- The verifying entity performs the following processing:

6.   Use the private decryption key *eKD* to decrypt the digital envelope *C*, to obtain the session secret key, $SSK = \text{RSA}(eKD)[C]$.

7.   Use *SSK* to decrypt the cryptogram C' and to obtain the bulk data (i.e., $bulk\_data = \text{DES}^{-1}(SSK)[\,C']$).

8.   Parse the bulk data in the transaction data (*M*), the digital signature *S* on it, the signature public key certificate *Cert1_eKV*, and the CA1 certification chain.

9. Use the *rootKV* to traverse the CA1 certification chain. An authentic copy of the CA1's public verification key (*ca1KV*) is obtained.

10. Use *ca1KV* to verify the signature public key certificate *Cert1_eKV*. An authentic copy of the public verification key *eKV* of the proving entity is obtained.

11. Use *eKV* to call the RSA function on the digital signature received from the proving entity and to obtain the witness hash value *h* of the message *M*, *h* = RSA (*eKV*) [*S*].

12. Compute the hash value *h'* on the transaction data *M* as obtained from the parsing of the bulk data. Accept the authenticity of the proving entity if *h'* = *h*.

Figure 8.6 outlines the establishment of a SET channel between two parties.

Figure 8.6
Establishment
of a SET
channel.

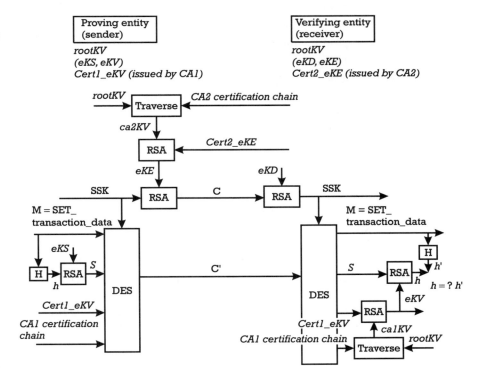

8.4.4.2 Data authentication

The data integrity and data origin authentication of the message M is provided. Indeed, the use of a collision-resistant hash function H for formatting the messages to be signed guarantees that any modification of M will lead to a different hash value computed by the verifying entity, which will not pass the verification predicate. The data origin authentication is related to the impossibility that a third party that does not know the private signing key can create a digital signature that passes the verification predicate. This service guarantees the data authentication of exchanged messages (AS1).

8.4.4.3 Entity authentication

SET authenticates the entities participating in a remote transaction:

- Cardholder to merchant (optional);

- Cardholder to payment gateway (optional);

- Merchant to cardholder;

- Mutual authentication between merchant and payment gateway.

To this end, each proving entity computes a digital signature. The successful verification of this signature proves to the verifying entity that only the *holder* of the private signing key could have signed the message, which includes a freshly generated challenge. However, someone could question the degree of assurance that the holder of the signing private key is one and the same as the legitimate entity to which the corresponding signature public key certificate was issued during registration (Section 8.4.3). Therefore, public key signature mechanisms are critically dependent on the security of the generation and storage of the private signing keys. Merchants' servers and payment gateway computers should employ cryptographic modules to perform cryptographic functions and to generate and store signing private keys and decryption private keys.

The degree of assurance whether SET provides the cardholder authentication service (ES5) depends on the evaluator's belief about the possibility of mounting Trojan horse attacks (threat T11) or about the effectiveness of the Authenticode security service (see AS2). The involvement of an EMV™ chip card in the architecture of the cardholder access device enforces the tamper-resistance security service (TS1), which would eliminate the suspicion about both the card authentication and cardholder verification (see Section 8.5.3).

8.4.4.4 Non-repudiation

A digital signature produced by the cardholder access device on a message *M* including enough details about the conditions of the remote transaction could also serve to provide the cardholder non-repudiation service (NS1). Since only the cardholder could compute that value, he or she cannot later deny her participation in the transaction. Similarly to the entity authentication service, the question is whether a court would accept the possibility that someone else than the legitimate cardholder has triggered the computation of the digital signature on behalf of the cardholder, or whether a skilled attacker could have cloned the cardholder's signing private key.

8.4.5 SET dual signatures

The provision of the confidentiality of the stored card data in the merchant's server (CS3) requires some precautions in the design of the cryptographic protocols.

First, we have already stressed in Section 8.4.3 that the cardholder's signature public key certificate is issued such that it contains neither the card's account number nor its expiration date in clear.

Second, during a payment transaction with SET, the cardholder has to produce a signature with his or her private signing key on the transaction data, which serves as a simultaneous dynamic authenticator for the cardholder authentication both towards the merchant and towards the payment gateway. This data includes two items—namely, the order instruction and the payment instruction.

- The order instruction (*OIData*) contains the details about the products or services to be purchased.

- The payment instruction (*PIData*) contains details about the cardholder's account (credit card number, expiration date) to which the public verification key was linked, through the cardholder's signature public key certificate.

To implement the confidentiality of the stored card data (CS3), the merchant should not see the payment instruction. At the same time, the privacy of the cardholder would be better protected if the payment gateway does not see the order instruction, admitting that banks would be interested about how their clients spend money. At the same time, the payment instruction and the order instruction must be linked, such that the payment is transferred to the merchant only if the cardholder accepts the offer. In order to fulfill all these goals, the SET uses the dual signature mechanism. The principle of this mechanism and details on how it is used in the SET payment transaction processing are presented in the next section.

8.4.6 SET payment method

An overview of a remote transaction, the payment phase of which is completed with the SET payment method, is presented in Figure 8.7.

8.4.6.1 Overview of a remote transaction with SET payment

During the browsing/ordering phase, the cardholder accesses the Web server of a merchant, browsing the offered products or services. The cardholder fills in an order form, specifying his or her choice and indicating the credit card brand chosen for payment. Although SET does not specify the information, a Web server has to send to the cardholder's SET payment software, following the completion of the browsing/ordering phase, some data items that are recommended in the SET initiation message [19]:

▸ Order description (*OD*): This item describes the product and/or services acknowledged by the cardholder in his or her order form.

Figure 8.7
Remote transaction with SET payment method.

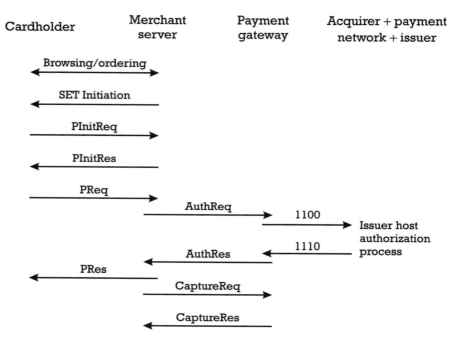

▶ Purchase Amount (*PurchAmt*): This data item indicates both an amount and its currency code. The amount represents the total price to be paid for the selected products and services, to which handling and shipping costs are added.

▶ The acceptable payment brands for the merchant: The brand identifiers can be directly included in the SET initiation message. Supplementary, the URL in the *SET-Brand* header, which is included in the initiation message, references the directory on the merchant server where the cardholder system can access the file containing the acceptable brands for the merchant.

SET specifies only the protocol of the payment phase in a remote transaction. The protocol can be split into three logical stages:

1. *Purchase processing* is the stage in which the cardholder confirms the order and supplies the payment instruction, which is inaccessible to the merchant and is further tunneled to the payment gateway. The step is accomplished through the exchange of the Purchase Initiate Request and Purchase Initiate Response (PinitReq/PinitRes) messages, and of the purchase request and purchase response (PReq/PRes) messages.

2. *Payment authorization* is the stage in which the merchant accepting the order of the cardholder creates an authorization request (AuthReq) message, tunneling the cardholder's payment instruction, and forwarding it the to the payment gateway. The payment gateway creates an authorization request message (1100) and forwards it to the appropriate bankcard network, which treats it similarly to the case of face-to-face transactions. After the appropriate issuer decides upon the approval or the rejection of a guarantee of funds, it elaborates an authorization request response message (1110). This message is returned to the payment gateway, which further elaborates an authorization response (AuthRes) towards the merchant. If the issuer approves the transaction, the merchant ships the goods or performs the services indicated in the order.

3. *Payment capture* is the stage in which the merchant triggers the payment from the payment gateway, of a transaction that was previously authorized. The payment gateway translates a capture request message into funds transfer to the merchant's account. At the end

the merchant is informed about the way the capturing stage is completed, through the capture response message.

The following sections describe the purchase processing and payment authorization stages. The level of detail is one that we believed will allow the reader to understand the extension of the SET protocol to support the transport of EMV™ related data. We briefly explain the payment capture phase.

8.4.6.2 Purchase processing

PinitReq   The purchase processing stage of the SET payment starts with the cardholder device sending the purchase initiate request (PInitReq) message to the merchant. The PInitReq message specifies the context of a transaction, including:

> • Identifier of the credit card brand to be used (*BrandID*);
>
> • Bank identification number (*BIN*) from the cardholder's account number (first six digits);
>
> • Cardholder's preferred language;
>
> • *RRPID* identifier of the PInitReq/PInitRes pair;
>
> • Challenge r_c to guarantee the freshness of the merchant's signature.
>
> • Information about the certificates already available in the cardholder device.

PinitRes   The merchant receives the PInitReq message and elaborates the payment initiate response (PInitRes):

> • Create the response data PInitResData, including the same *RRPID* as for the request, a transaction identifier (*TransID*) specifying the current date (PReqDate), the cardholder's challenge r_c, and a fresh challenge of the merchant r_m for the subsequent signature produced by the cardholder.
>
> • Compute $S1 = RSA(mKS)[H(\text{PInitResData})]$, which establishes a SET channel providing only authenticity without confidentiality (Step 3, first two bullets, in Section 8.4.4.1).
>
> • Search in PInitReq the information about the certificates the cardholder already stored in his or her device. It could be that the certificates of the

merchant and/or payment gateway are already available in the card-holder device. If this is not the case, retrieve the merchant's signature public key certificate $Cert\_mKV = Cert(mcaKS)[mKV\ merchant\_data]$ with the MCA certification chain and/or the payment gateway's key-exchange public key certificate $Cert\_pKE = Cert(pcaKS)[pKE,\ payment\_gateway\_data]$ with the PCA certification chain.

▸ Compose PInitRes from PInitResData, and $S1$. Depending on the certificates already existing with the cardholder, add the appropriate items among the following $Cert\_mKV$, MCA certification chain, $Cert\_pKE$, PCA certification chain.

▸ Send PInitRes to the cardholder.

PReq After receiving the PInitRes, the cardholder first verifies this response and elaborates a purchase request (PReq) message, as follows.

▸ Verify the authenticity of the merchant and the integrity of the information received.

  ▸ Check the authenticity of the merchant's electronic brand decal. Traverse the MCA certification chain from the $rootKV$ to obtain an authentic copy of $mcaKV$. Use this key to validate $Cert\_mKV$ and obtain an authentic copy of the merchant's public verification key mKV.

  ▸ Use mKV to dynamically authenticate the merchant and to check the integrity of his response. Compute $h = RSA(mKV)[S1]$ and compare it with the hash value $h' = H(PInitResData)$ computed locally by the cardholder. If they are equal, the cardholder is assured about the authenticity of the merchant and the integrity of PInitRes.

▸ Traverse the PCA certification chain from the $rootKV$ to obtain an authentic copy of $pcaKV$. Use this key to validate $Cert\_pKE$ and obtain an authentic copy of the payment gateway's public encryption key pKE.

▸ Generate the order instruction part of the PReq message, $OIData$, using the information obtained in the SET initiation message. It includes the transaction identifier ($TransID$), the identifier of the card's brand (BrandID), the BIN of the issuer of the card, the hash value HOD of a byte string $HODInput$, and the merchant's challenge r_m, which guarantees the uniqueness of the SET transaction data. The *HODInput* includes the *OD* and the purchase amount (*PurchAmt*). Thus, the *OIData* does not contain the *OD* or *PurchAmt* in clear, since *OIData* is not transmitted on a confidential channel to the merchant.

- Generate the payment instruction part of the PReq message, *PIData*. It consists of the *PIHead* and *PANData* items. The *PIHead* includes:

    - *TransID:* This allows the payment gateway to link the *OIData* and *PIData*, coming from two different sources (the merchant and the cardholder, respectively) in a unique purchase request message.

    - *HOD, PurchAmt*, merchant's identifier.

    - A keyed MAC (HMAC) of the identifier of the transaction record in the merchant's database *XID* with the secret generated by the cardholder software during the registration protocol with the CCA, *PANSecret*.
      The *PANData* encompasses the credit card number (PAN), the expiration date (*CardExpiry*), *PANSecret*, and *EXNonce*, which is a fresh random.

- Produce a dual signature *DS*. To this end, compute H(*OIData*) and H(*PIData*), concatenate them, and compute another hash value on the result [i.e., H(H(*OIData*) ∥ H(*PIData*))]. Compute $DS = RSA(cKS)$ (H(H(*OIData*) ∥ H(*PIData*))).

- Create a SET authentic channel *M* with the merchant, composed of H(*PIData*), *OIData*, *DS*, *Cert_cKV*, and the CCA certification chain.

- Create a SET authentic and confidential channel *P* with the payment gateway.

    - Compute the *payment_message* from the payment instruction *PIData*, *DS*, and H(*OIData*).

    - Generate *SSK* to compute the encrypted payment message $C' = DES$ (SSK) (*PIData* ∥ *DS* ∥ H(*OIData*)).

    - Using the authentic copy of the payment gateway's public encryption key *pKE*, create a digital envelope including the *SSK* and the *PAN* of the cardholder (i.e., $C = RSA$ (*pKE*) [*SSK* ∥ *PAN*]).

    - *P* consists of *C'* and *C*.

- Compute PReq as a superposition of M and P, where only M is intended for the merchant, while P is just tunneled by the merchant to the payment gateway. Send PReq to the merchant.

PRes   After receiving the PReq, the merchant first verifies the authenticity of the cardholder. Then, the merchant elaborates an authorization request (AuthReq) for the payment gateway, which allows the matching of an order instruction coming from the merchant with a payment instruction coming from the cardholder. The merchant computes a purchase response (PRes), without necessarily waiting for the authorization response (AuthRes) of the payment gateway.

- Verify the authenticity of the cardholder and the integrity of the information received in the part M of the PReq.

  - Check the authenticity of the electronic representation of the payment card. Traverse the CCA certification chain from the *rootKV* to obtain an authentic copy of *ccaKV*. Use this key to validate *Cert_cKV* and obtain an authentic copy of the cardholder's public verification key *cKV*.

  - Use *cKV* to dynamically authenticate the cardholder and the integrity of her purchase request. Compute the H(*OIData*), concatenate it with H(*PIData*), and apply once again H. Compare the result H(H(OIData) ‖ H (PIData)) computed locally with the witness value computed by the verification of the dual signature DS (i.e., RSA(*cKV*)[*DS*]). If they are equal, the merchant is assured about the authenticity of the cardholder and the integrity of the part M in PReq, and consequently of the *OD*.

- The merchant processes the *OD*.

- The merchant includes the part P of the PReq, consisting of the encrypted payment message C' and the digital envelope C, together with the cardholder's signature public key certificate *Cert_cKV* and the CCA certification chain, in the AuthReq addressed to the payment gateway.

- The merchant is not compelled to wait for the AuthRes to his AuthReq before computing the PRes message and sending back to the cardholder.

    To this end the PResData is formatted, including enough identification information (*TransID*, RRPID), the current session challenge r_c

of the cardholder, and the PResPayLoad item. This last item indicates the conditions of completion of the current purchase processing. Thus, when the payment gateway has not yet answered, then a completion code cc = *orderReceived* is included in the PResPayLoad. If the payment gateway rejects the transaction then cc = *orderRejected*, and the PRes- PayLoad could also include the *AcqCardMsg* (eventually received in AuthRes), explaining a reason for the rejection in *Auth-Code*. When the payment gateway has authorized the payment, then the completion code is cc = *authPerformed* and the *AcqCardMsg* could indicate the authorization date (AuthDate), a ratio of how much of the purchase amount was actually authorized (whether the whole amount is authorized or a smaller amount).

The merchant's software signs the PResData, computing $S2$ = RSA (mKS) [H (PResData)]. Both the PResData and $S2$ are sent to the cardholder, for verification, together with the merchant's signature public key certificate *Cert_mKV* and the MCA certification chain.

- The cardholder's software verifies the authenticity and integrity of the payment response PRes received from the merchant.

  - Retrieve the authentic copy of the merchant's public verification key *mKV*. If this copy cannot be retrieved, traverse the MCA certification chain from the *rootKV* to obtain an authentic copy of *mcaKV*. Use this key to validate *Cert_mKV* and obtain an authentic copy of the *mKV*.

  - Use *mKV* to compute h = RSA(mKV)[$S2$] and compare it with the hash value h' = H(PResData) computed locally by the cardholder. If they are equal, the cardholder is assured about the authenticity of the merchant's response PRes.

  - If the payment gateway did not send the status of the transaction, an order inquiry can be subsequently sent to the merchant to find out the final result of the SET payment.

8.4.6.3 Payment authorization

AuthReq   The payment authorization stage of the SET payment starts with the merchant sending the AuthReq message to the payment gateway. It consists of two parts: the payment instruction related message P, which was originally sent by the cardholder inside PReq and destined to the payment gateway, and an authorization message in relation to the order instruction created and signed by the merchant. When the payment gateway receives AuthReq, it checks the consistency between the two parts of the request, independently elaborated by the cardholder and merchant, but which are linked together, using the dual signature and the transaction identifier (*TransID*).

▸ The merchant creates an authentic and confidential channel (Section 8.4.4.1) with the payment gateway.

 ▸ Create AuthReqData specifying the conditions of the transaction to be authorized, including the purchase amount (*PurchAmt*), the *TransID* from the order instruction, a locally generated hash value of the *OIData*, and other information related to the current transaction.

 ▸ Sign it with the *mKS* and compute $S3 = \text{RSA}\ (mKS)[\text{H}\ (\text{AuthReqData})]$.

 ▸ Generate at random the symmetric key *SSK1* and compute $C'1 = \text{DES}(SSK1)[\text{AuthReqData}\ \|\ S3]$.

 ▸ Use an authentic copy of the payment gateway's public encryption key *pKE* to produce a digital envelope *C1* containing *SSK1* (i.e., $C1 = \text{RSA}(pKE)[SSK1]$).

▸ The merchant tunnels the authentic and confidential channel established between the cardholder and the payment gateway during the payment processing stage. To this end, the AuthReq includes the payment message $P = (C, C')$ received from the cardholder within PReq, the cardholder's signature public key certificate *Cert_cKV*, and the CCA certification chain.

▸ The merchant includes in the AuthReq his own cryptogram, $C'1$, of the authorization data and the corresponding digital envelope, C1. If the payment gateway has no authentic copies of the merchant's public verification key (*mKV*) and public encryption key (*mKE*), the AuthReq includes also the *Cert_mKV* and *Cert_mKE*, together with the MCA certification chain.

▸ The merchant sends AuthReq to the payment gateway.

AuthRes The payment gateway receives AuthReq from the merchant and checks it. If the verification passes, the payment gateway formats an authorization request (1100) message according to the requirements of the bankcard association network that connects to the IH and forwards the 1100 message. After processing this authorization request, the IH elaborates an authorization request response (1110) message, which is sent back to the payment gateway. This message consists of two parts: the issuer's response, concerning the approval or rejection of the current transaction, and a capture token. The merchant software uses this token to complete the payment capture stage, which is the last stage of the SET payment.

> The payment gateway parses the AuthReq received from the merchant and checks the consistency between the order instruction and payment instruction, coming on independent channels, from the merchant and cardholder, respectively.

> > Traverse the MCA certification chain from the *rootKV* to obtain an authentic copy of *mcaKV*. Use this key to validate *Cert_mKV* and *Cert_mKE*, and obtain an authentic copy of the merchant's public verification key *mKV* and public encryption key *mKE*.

> > Use the payment gateway's private decryption key *pKD* to open the digital envelope *C*1 and to obtain the symmetric key *SSK*1 (i.e., $SSK1 = \text{RSA}(pKD)[C1]$).

> > Use *SSK*1 to decrypt *C′*1 and obtain the authorization data of the transaction AuthReqData together with the signature *S*3 of the merchant on this data.

> > Use the authentic copy of the merchant's public verification key *mKV* to check the signature *S*3. To this end, compute $h = \text{RSA}(mKV)[S3]$ and compare it with $h' = \text{H}(\text{AuthReqData})$, computed locally. If the verification passes, accept the authenticity and integrity of the authorization data, including the order instruction as presented by the merchant $h2 = \text{H}(OIData)$ and the transaction identifier *TransID*.

> > Traverse the CCA certification chain from the *rootKV* to obtain an authentic copy of *ccaKV*. Use this key to validate *Cert_cKV* and obtain an authentic copy of the cardholder's public verification key *cKV*.

> > Use the payment gateway's private decryption key *pKD* to open the digital envelope *C* originated by the cardholder and tunneled by the merchant. Obtain the symmetric key *SSK* and the cardholder's account information (i.e., $SSK \parallel \text{PAN} = \text{RSA}(pKD)[C]$).

- Use *SSK* to decrypt *C'* and to obtain the payment message, *PIData* || *DS* || H(*OIData*) = DES^{-1} (SSK) [*C'*].

- Compute the hash value $h1$ = H(*PIData*) of the payment instruction *PIData* recovered from the cardholder's cryptogram and concatenate it with the order instruction as presented by the merchant $h2$ = H(*OIData*). Compute locally the hash value h' = H(h1 || h2).

- Verify the dual signature *DS*. To achieve this, compute h = RSA (*cKV*)[*DS*] and compare it with h' obtained above. If the verification passes, the payment gateway has the guarantee that the order instruction presented by the merchant is the order instruction on which the cardholder agrees. The payment gateway also checks that the *TransID* from the order instruction is one and the same value with that present in the payment instruction.

- The payment gateway has all the elements to compute the message 1100 and to send it to the issuer. After receiving the corresponding 1110 response from the IH, the payment gateway elaborates the authorization response AuthRes to the merchant. This message contains the following:

- Information about the approval or rejection of the transaction (AuthResPayload), from which the merchant server can further compose the PResPayLoad included in the PRes. The AuthCode gives the error code in case of rejection;

- The AcqCardMsg, providing supplementary information from the IH for the cardholder software, which is also included in the PRes;

- The capture token, which is subsequently used in the payment capture stage.

    The message is sent to the merchant using an authentic and confidential channel.

8.4.6.4 Payments capture

The merchant initiates this stage in order to get paid for a transaction that was already authorized and for which the delivery of purchases or services was already completed. The merchant composes and sends to the payment gateway a capture request message (CapReq), including the amount involved in the previously authorized transaction and the capture token. The payment gateway receives the request and sends to the issuer for clearing, using the same bankcard network as for authorization stage. The payment gateway sends a capture response (CapRes) to the merchant, who will store it for reconciliation with the payment received from the acquirer. This closes the SET payment.

8.5   TLS versus SET or wallet servers and EMV™ cards

For the scope of remote card payments in the e-commerce environment, at the moment there are two competing trends. Those who are partisans of decreasing fraud at the cost of enforcing security prefer SET, while those who are aiming at a faster increase of the e-commerce volume at the cost of accepting a higher business risk prefer TLS. In fact, the use of a wallet server architecture and the integration of an EMV™ chip card in the configuration of the cardholder access device increase the competitiveness of both methods, improving the security of TLS-based solutions and decreasing the operational overhead of SET. This architecture leads in fact to a unified framework for remote transactions.

8.5.1   Security makes the difference

In Section 8.3.3 we show that TLS does not provide appropriate authentication services for payment: merchant authentication (ES3), cardholder account authentication (ES4), and cardholder authentication (ES5). Therefore, using TLS-based payment card methods in remote transactions may still generate a high number of disputes. Electronic waiter attacks are also more likely to appear, since there is no cryptographic protection of the card data stored in the merchant access device (CS3). Not only is the level of fraud a concern, but also the prestige of the payment card brand, considering that fraud on the Internet is intensively publicized.

Therefore, SET appears to be a reasonable alternative for increasing the security of the remote card payments. SET appropriately implements the cardholder account authentication (ES4), the cardholder authentication (ES5), the cardholder non-repudiation (NS1), the merchant authentication (ES3), and the confidentiality of the card data in the merchant access device (CS3). We mentioned in Section 8.4.4 that the successful implementation of the cardholder authentication and cardholder non-repudiation services is dependent on the degree to which the cardholder's private signing key is securely generated and stored in the cardholder access device. Table 8.1 comparatively presents the range of security services offered by the TLS-based methods and the SET method.

Table 8.1
Comparison of the Security Services Offered by TLS and SET

Security Service	Phase	Threats	TLS	SET
AnS1—Anonymity	Browsing/ordering (B/O)	T1	No	No
CS1—Confidentiality of the ordering phase	B/O	T1	Yes	No
CS2—Secure messaging for confidentiality	Payment	T2	Yes	Yes
CS3—Confidentiality of stored card data with the merchant	Payment	T12	No	Yes
AS1—Data authentication of exchanged messages	B/O	T3, T4	Yes	No
	Payment	T5	Yes	Yes
AS2—Authenticode	B/O	T4, T11	No	No
ES1—Server authentication	B/O	T4	Yes	No
ES2—Client authentication	B/O	T3	Yes	No
	Payment	T5	Yes	Yes
ES3—Merchant authentication	Payment	T6	No	Yes
ES4—Cardholder account authentication	Payment	T7	No	Yes
ES5—Cardholder authentication	Payment	T8	No	Yes
NS1—Cardholder non-repudiation	Payment	T9	No	Yes
TS1—Tamper-resistance security service	Payment	T11	No	No

By analyzing Table 8.1, it can be seen that SET better addresses the security of the payment phase than TLS. This is the premise on which payment card brands can guarantee the payment of the authorized transactions for SET-enabled merchants. This is a considerable advantage compared to the TLS payment method, which still complies with the same rules and regulations as the MO/TO transactions.

Since SET addresses only security issues during the payment phase, it cannot counter threats during the browsing/ordering phase, for which the cardholder access device and the merchant access device must establish a TLS channel.

8.5.2 Acceptability is a main concern

When it comes to the acceptability of e-commerce, the payment method plays an important role. Cardholders are naturally attracted by the payment method providing the easiest way of using their credit cards or debit cards for remote payments on the Internet. Both the cardholder and the merchant are also attracted by a payment method that does not require investments in software and hardware, or high operational costs. The participation of either the cardholder or the merchant in any complex decision-making process, especially related to the enrollment of participants in the payment method, increases the reluctance of even experienced Internet users.

Thus, those who prefer the TLS-based payment card solutions, despite their security limitations, invoke their high acceptability from both cardholders and merchants. Their main argument is that this transport layer security protocol is user friendly and does not require deployment efforts, since they are implemented in the majority of browsers and servers interacting through the HTTP on the Web. Thus, neither cardholders nor merchants are compelled to buy supplementary software for payment applications. The involvement of these network protocols in transactions is transparent to cardholders. Moreover, participants do not undergo complicate registration procedures.

Compared with TLS, installing, registering, and running SET is more difficult. After buying the specialized SET software, a cardholder must install it on his or her machine, connect to the appropriate CCA (e.g., the card's issuing bank), and request a certificate. Before a certificate is issued, the cardholder has to prove his or her identity to the CCA, according to a procedure that is not specified by SET but is established by each payment card brand. Added to these registration-related inconveniences are the differences a cardholder perceives related to the browsing/ordering phase and the choice of the payment method. The SET does not specify the way a cardholder connects to the merchant's Web site, selects the goods to purchase, makes the choice about the payment option, and how the cardholder's SET application is invoked by the merchant. Therefore, someone can expect that the use of a SET package will appear different for cardholders, depending on the software provider offering the SET integrated solution and on the specific registration procedure of each card brand. Moreover, since the digital certificates are at the core of the SET security solution, each cardholder has to take care about renewing his or her certificate after its expiration date. These could be some of the reasons why the acceptance of SET is still poor among both cardholders and merchants. This is at least the case for the *thick wallet* configuration of the SET software.

In the remainder of this section we refer to the thick wallet configuration. The SET application running in the cardholder's PC is sometimes referred to as a SET wallet, or simply a wallet. In the "software only" case, this wallet consists of four functional components that are presented in Figure 8.8.

The cardholder interface and I/O device is responsible for the system input/output, such as the keyboard, screen, and graphic user interface. The cardholder database is responsible for the management of the cardholder's payment-related data, like the signature public key certificate and card data (e.g., the PAN and the expiration date), but also for personal data of the cardholder, like delivery address and telephone number. The cardholder database must be stored such that the confidentiality and integrity of the data is ensured. The SET private key manager is responsible for the secure storage and use of the cardholder's private signing key. The integrity and confidentiality of this key has to be guaranteed to enforce the cardholder authentication and non-repudiation services. The SET message manager deals with the interaction between the cardholder's PC and the merchant's Web server during a payment transaction and between the cardholder's PC and the CCA server during a certificate issuing transaction, according to the SET protocols. The SET private key manager in conjunction with the SET message manager must process the generation of the cardholder's signature key pair, signature public key certificate request, and purchase request signing operations in a manner that assures the security of the private key.

In a thick wallet configuration, all the aforementioned functional components are installed and run in the cardholder's PC. In this case the cardholder is responsible for the management of all these components, according to their required level of security. This operational overhead appears to be a barrier against the acceptance of the SET payment method, at least by the cardholders.

Figure 8.8
SET functional
components.

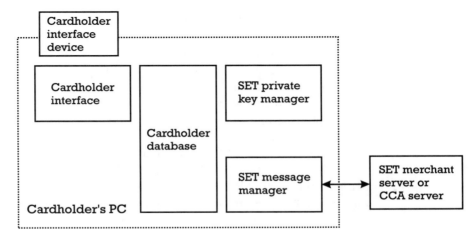

8.5.3 Improved solutions with wallet servers and EMV™ cards

Acknowledging the wide acceptability of the TLS-based payment method, but recognizing its security weaknesses, the first trend is to improve its security to answer the high demands of remote card payments, especially considering card and cardholder authentication. At present, the most cited example is the Visa initiative 3-D Secure™ [20]. This solution provides authentication of participants in remote card payments, besides the confidentiality and integrity of the payment information. It is important to note that 3-D Secure can be implemented without requiring specialized cardholder software or hardware. A similar proposal by MasterCard is called the Secure Payment Application (SPA™) [21].

Since basing the management of the SET payment system entirely on the cardholder access device (e.g., the thick wallet approach) determines serious acceptability barriers, the second trend is the adoption of "simplified" SET solutions. When we refer to "simplified" SET, the meaning is that this should be the perception of the cardholder. An example of such a solution is the Visa initiative 3-D SET™ [22], which is a major evolution of the original SET within the distributed structure of the Three Domain Model. Within this model, the cardholder and her bank form the issuer domain, the merchant and his bank form the acquirer domain, while the cardholder's bank and the acquirer's bank are interacting in the interoperability domain.

The competitiveness of both TLS-based solutions and SET can be improved, admitting that there is no way to base the management of a payment method entirely on the cardholder access device. The issuer, or a payment system operator acting on behalf of the issuer, must establish a remote wallet server at an intermediate level between the cardholder device and the issuer. On the one hand, the wallet server talks to the cardholder access device for the cardholder authentication, and on the other hand the wallet server talks to the merchant access device for the completion of a payment method. The payment management is now based on the combination cardholder access device and wallet server. This architecture also confers the advantage that the cardholder can use the same type of payment experience, regardless of the type of access device (i.e., whether it is a PC or a mobile phone), and the type of interconnection channel. In this case, the initial model of the payment card processing in remote transactions, which is presented in Figure 8.1, is modified as shown in Figure 8.9.

In this model the ordering/browsing phase is still carried out directly between the cardholder and the merchant. However, the wallet server, acting on behalf of the cardholder, completes the payment phase with the merchant access device. The wallet server triggers the payment phase only

Figure 8.9
Wallet server
in remote
payment card
processing.

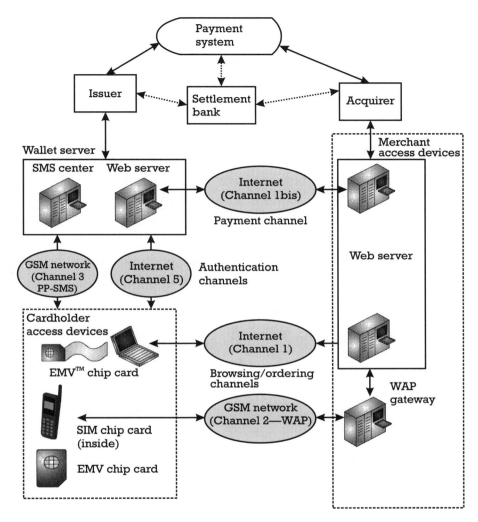

following a successful authentication of the cardholder. Thus, the remote transaction is carried out in three distinct phases, browsing/ordering, cardholder authentication, and payment, which are completed in different sessions. The interaction between the wallet server and the merchant to complete the payment phase is carried out on a TCP/IP channel on the Internet (channel 1bis). The types of channels used for the interaction between the cardholder and the merchant access devices for completing the browsing/ordering phase, and between the cardholder access device and the wallet server for completing the cardholder authentication depend on the type of the cardholder access device:

- Dual Internet channel device (channel 1 and channel 5): The browsing/ordering phase (channel 1) and the cardholder authentication phase (channel 5) are carried out on different TCP/IP channels.

- Dual channel/dual network device (channel 1 and channel 3): The browsing/ordering phase is completed on a TCP/IP channel (channel 1), while the cardholder authentication phase is carried out on a PP-SMS channel (channel 3).

- Dual mobile channel device (channel 2 and channel 3): The browsing/ordering phase is completed on a WAP channel (channel 2), while the cardholder authentication phase is carried out on a PP-SMS channel (channel 3).

In the remainder of this section, we present the thin client architecture for the SET payment method [1]. It is derived from the wallet server architecture presented in Figure 8.9 in the following way. The implementation and operation of the SET functional components presented in Figure 8.8 (except for the cardholder interface) are transferred from the cardholder access device, which can be regarded as a client, to the wallet server. This can facilitate the update and management of a large number of cardholder access devices by the issuer or its delegated payment system operator, since their major SET functionality is concentrated on the server. Since the installation of the remaining SET components on the cardholder access device is less complex, we can assume that the acceptability of cardholders will increase. In the thin client architecture, the cardholder access device can be implemented with lower software and hardware resources (e.g., a mobile phone).

The thin client running on the cardholder access device consists of the SET cardholder interface component and a software/hardware component, for the cardholder authentication to the wallet server. In the simplest case, the cardholder's authentication mechanism can be implemented with a user ID and a password. The identification information of the cardholder is transmitted on a confidential and authentic channel from the issuer to the cardholder during the setup of the system. The cardholder presents the identification information to the wallet server during the authentication phase of each remote transaction, assuming also that the authentication channel (channel 3 or 5 in Figure 8.9) is confidential. There is also the possibility of using a one-time password scheme, which would confer the dynamic dimension of the cardholder authentication mechanism, while still remaining in the software only domain.

Concerning the transaction flow of the SET payment method in the thin client configuration, this is overviewed in Figure 8.10, only for that part of the transaction flow that is modified compared to the original SET transaction flow as presented in Figure 8.7.

After the completion of the browsing/ordering phase, the merchant server sends to the cardholder access device the SET Initiation message (1), describing the conditions of the transaction (see Section 8.4.6.1). The cardholder forwards this description of the purchase together with enough identification information to the wallet server (2). The wallet server conducts the cardholder authentication either locally, if the issuer delegated to it the necessary identification information of cardholders, or through an out of band mechanism that is connected directly to the issuer. If the wallet server correctly identifies the cardholder, it will trigger a SET payment phase with the merchant on behalf of the cardholder. To this end, the wallet server and the merchant exchange their certificates and realize the purchase transaction initialization with the pair of messages PInitReq(3)/PinitRes(4). Then, the wallet server produces the transaction dual signature on behalf of the cardholder and forwards the PReq (5) message to the merchant. The

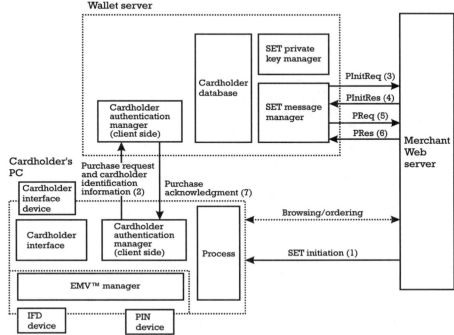

Figure 8.10
SET transaction flow in the thin client architecture.

merchant authorizes the transaction with the payment gateway (AuthReq). The payment gateway inquires of the appropriate issuer (1100 message) and receives the appropriate response (1110 message), based on which it elaborates the authorization response (AuthRes) towards the merchant. The merchant finally transmits the PRes (6) to the wallet server, which further informs the cardholder about the status of the transaction with a purchase acknowledgment message (7).

In the password mechanisms mentioned above, the authenticity of the cardholder is reduced to a set of data in his or her possession, which can be easily copied or stolen. There is no *physical proof* that the legitimate cardholder is interacting with the wallet server. A better level of confidence can be provided with verifiable secret data from a cardholder specific token. This token is uniquely linked to the cardholder. The EMV™ chip card can serve as such a token, since its tamper-resistance impedes attackers from easily counterfeiting it or copying its secret data. The AC produced by the EMV™ chip can serve as an on-line CAM, which can prove without any doubt that the card is not counterfeit (ES4). If the production of the AC is combined with a DDA, the signature produced by the card can be used as an irrefutable proof of the cardholder's participation in a certain transaction. This provides an optimal implementation of the cardholder non-repudiation service (NS1). Moreover, when the computation of the combined AC/DDA is conditioned by the correct verification of a PIN, then the physical presence of the cardholder in the remote transaction is assured, which implements the cardholder authentication (ES5).

The cost paid for these security improvements is the need to integrate the EMV™ message manager component in the structure of the SET thin client, coordinating both the ICC interface device and, optionally, the (secure) PIN entry device. If the PIN entry is not included in the configuration, then once again the cardholder authentication is linked to the on-line CAM, which does not really prove the physical presence of the cardholder in the remote transaction. Only the combination between something the cardholder has (the EMV™ chip card) and something the cardholder knows (PIN) is accepted to prove the physical presence of the cardholder.

8.6 Transaction processing for chip e-commerce

The transaction processing for chip electronic commerce is presented in Annex D of Book 3 in the *EMV 2000* specifications [1]. It extends the SET specification by including an EMV™ chip card in the configuration of the cardholder access device. The EMV™ chip card allows both on-line card authentication, through the generation of an Application Cryptogram by the card, and cardholder verification, through the use of an optional cardholder PIN. The transaction flow of the chip electronic commerce is presented in Figure 8.11.

This transaction flow abstracts the cardholder access device to the interaction between the cardholder system and an EMV™ chip card. It does not, however, consider the internal communication between the components of the cardholder system. In Section 8.5.3 we considered the case when the cardholder system consists of two components: a thin client and a remote wallet server.

Figure 8.11
Transaction flow of the chip electronic commerce.

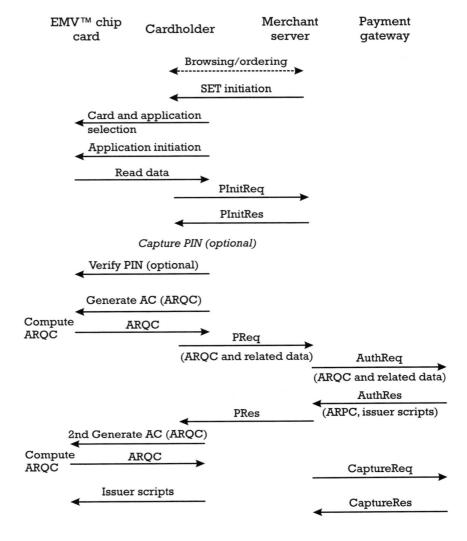

8.6.1 EMV™ application context in the cardholder system

Following the browsing/ordering phase, the merchant server has all the necessary data to start the payment phase. To this end, it creates the SET Initiation message (see Section 8.4.6.1) and invokes the cardholder system. This initiation message includes data about the transaction details (like the order description, purchase amount, and transaction currency code), the list containing the identifiers (BrandID1, BrandID2, ..., BrandIDn) of all the acceptable card payment brands for the merchant, and the URL referencing the file that contains the corresponding electronic decals of the acceptable payment brands for the merchant. Once this file is downloaded from the merchant server, the cardholder system can also display the corresponding decals of the acceptable brands. The cardholder system presents to the cardholder all the payment options available at the merchant site.

8.6.1.1 Account selection and card selection

The cardholder system asks the cardholder to perform the account selection and card selection stage. The cardholder is offered the possibility of selecting the preferred payment brand, and indicating the appropriate payment account and the corresponding card. If this card is an EMV™ chip card, the cardholder is prompted to insert the chip card in the ICC interface device. The chip card should not be removed from the ICC interface device until the cardholder system explicitly asks the cardholder to do so.

8.6.1.2 EMV™ transaction profile

At present, the EMV™ message manager overtakes the processing in the cardholder system. It performs a restricted EMV™ transaction, the profile of which is limited to the following stages:

- Application selection (see Section 4.4);
- Initiate application processing (see Section 6.2);
- Read application data (see Section 6.3);
- Cardholder verification (see Section 6.6);
- Terminal action analysis (see Section 6.8);
- Issuer script processing and completion (see Section 6.10).

Considering that the authorization of a transaction in the e-commerce environment is always performed on-line by the issuer, the cardholder system skips the processing corresponding to the off-line data authentication (see Section 6.4), the processing restrictions (see Section 6.5), and the terminal risk management (see Section 6.7) stages.

During the interaction between the cardholder system and the EMV™ chip card, the cardholder system can be seen as a terminal that runs an EMV™ terminal application. This terminal application is setup with the following parameters:

- The Terminal Type (tag 9F35) indicates the cardholder system's environment, its communication capabilities, and its operational control (see Section 6.5.2). In the chip electronic commerce framework, the cardholder system behaves as an unattended terminal, which is connected on-line to the issuer and is under the control of the cardholder. This corresponds to the Terminal Type = 34 (Annex A1 of Book 4 in the *EMV 2000* specifications).

- The type of financial transaction performed by the cardholder system with a remote merchant server limits to the purchase of goods and services. This means that the value field of the Transaction Type (tag 9C) data object is always 00.

- The processing performed by the cardholder system is dynamically reflected in only a few bits of the TVR, the rest being statically set, since the corresponding stages of the EMV™ transaction are skipped.

  - In the first byte of the TVR only bit 6, "IC Card Data missing," is dynamically set, following the evaluation of the mandatory card data objects received from the EMV™ card. Since the off-line data authentication is not included in the transaction profile, bit 8, "Off-line data authentication was not performed," is set to 1, while all the other bits in byte 1 of the TVR are statically set to 0.

  - The bits in the second byte of the TVR, reflecting the results of the processing restrictions, and the bits of the fourth byte of the TVR, corresponding to the terminal risk management, are statically set to 0 since these stages are not performed in the chip e-commerce EMV™ transaction. Only bit 8 in byte 4, "Transaction exceeds floor limit," is statically set to 1 to indicate that all the transactions must be forced on-line, regardless of the amount authorized.

  - The bits in the third byte of the TVR, corresponding to the results of the cardholder verification processing, and the bits in the fifth byte corresponding to the issuer script processing, are dynamically set following the status of the processing performed by the cardholder system.

8.6.1.3 Application selection

First, the cardholder system builds the list of applications supported by the merchant (see Section 4.4), taking every BrandID included in the SET initiation message and searching for an equivalent AID in the BrandID-AID table. The content of this equivalence table is regularly updated by the cardholder system, which downloads it from a dedicated server on the Internet.

Second, using the list of applications supported by the merchant, the cardholder system performs the application selection mechanism. The result of this mechanism is the application candidate list.

> ‣ If the candidate list is empty, the cardholder system either automatically updates the BrandID-AID table or it prompts the cardholder to confirm that the correct EMV™ chip card is used.
>
> > ‣ If this confirmation is provided, the cardholder system updates the BrandID-AID table. If, after the update, a mutually supported application cannot be found, the cardholder system requests that the card be removed from the interface device, and the card selection phase is repeated.
> >
> > ‣ Otherwise, the cardholder system requests that the card be removed from the interface device, and the card selection phase is repeated.
>
> ‣ If there is one or several common applications in the candidate list, the cardholder system displays them, allowing the cardholder to participate in the final application selection (see Section 4.4.3).
>
> > ‣ If an Application Preferred Name (tag 9F12) is provided in the FCI of a common ADF (see Section 4.3.1.1), the cardholder system must display the name of the application according to this string. To this end, the cardholder system uses the Issuer Code Table Index (tag 9F11), which must be present in the FCI, to choose the appropriate alphabet code table. This table allows displaying the characters in the alphanumeric string application preferred name. Therefore, the cardholder system has to keep the ISO 8859 code tables, which allow the correct decoding of alphanumeric strings in various alphabets.

- ▸ If there is no Application Preferred Name in the FCI of a common ADF, the cardholder system will use the Application Label (tag 50), which is mandatory for inclusion in an FCI to display the common application.

- ▸ If the FCI of an ADF includes the FCI Issuer Discretionary Data template, the cardholder system will retrieve the Issuer URL (tag 5F50) data object from this template. The value field of this data object references the visual image of the brand logo associated with the ADF on the payment system operator's server. This logo file is then brought into and displayed on the cardholder system, besides either the Application Preferred Name or the Application Label.

After the final application selection is performed, the cardholder system obtains the FCI of the ADF that hosts the selected EMV™ card application. The cardholder system stores, for future use, the following data objects: the AID of the selected application (tag 4F or tag 84), the Language Preference (tag 5F2D), and the PDOL (tag 9F38), if the last two data objects were personalized in the FCI.

8.6.1.4   Initiate application processing and read application data

During the initiate application processing, the selected EMV™ card application may require in the PDOL (see Section 6.2.2) a number of data objects from the cardholder system. These data objects describe the transaction details that are relevant for the EMV™ card application, as they are known to the cardholder system after receiving the SET initiation message from the merchant server. The cardholder system sends the GET PROCESSING OPTIONS command to the card application, including the values of the required data objects. Taking into account the transaction details received from the cardholder system, the EMV™ card application can adapt its strategy to best suit the business environment (see Section 7.6). Consequently, the EMV™ card application informs the cardholder system through the AIP (see Section 6.2.3) about the transaction profile it supports, and particularly whether it supports the cardholder verification phase or not. The EMV™ card application also informs the cardholder system about the content and organization of its public data, through the AFL (see Section 6.2.3).

During the read application data (see Section 6.3), the cardholder system retrieves the publicly available content of the card application, following the indications it received in the AFL. The cardholder system checks whether the mandatory data objects are present (see Section 6.3.2): Application Expiration Date (tag 5F24), Application PAN (tag 5A), CDOL1 (tag 8C), and

CDOL2 (tag 8D). If the cardholder verification stage is supported by the card application (bit 5 = 1 in the first byte of AIP), the cardholder system must verify the presence in the card of the CVM List (tag 8E). The cardholder system stores the mandatory data objects, and eventually the CVM, for future use. It also checks whether the Application PAN Sequence Number (tag 5F34) and the track-2 equivalent data (tag 57) are personalized in the card. The IH could require the track-2 equivalent data for accomplishing an on-line PIN verification. If these two last data objects are personalized in the card, the cardholder system also stores them for further processing.

8.6.2 Purchase initialization (PInitReq/PInitRes)

After establishing the EMV™ transaction context, from the EMV™ card application and the order information received in the SET Initiation message, the cardholder system initiates the SET purchase transaction, through the PInitReq and PInitRes messages.

The cardholder system creates the PInitReq as described in Section 8.4.6.2, except that for the BrandID, BIN, and the cardholder's preferred language data items, the cardholder system uses appropriate data objects retrieved from the EMV™ card application. The following processing is performed by the cardholder system:

▸ The identifier of the card brand to be used *BrandID* is obtained from the AID of the selected card application (tag 4F or tag 84). To this end, search the AID in the BrandID-AID table and obtain the equivalent brand identifier BrandID corresponding to this AID.

▸ The bank identification number (*BIN*) is formed from the first 6 digits of the Application PAN (tag 5A) as retrieved from the EMV™ card application.

▸ The cardholder's preferred language is obtained from the Language Preference (tag 5F2D) data object retrieved from the FCI of the selected EMV™ card application.

The merchant server processes the PInitReq received from the cardholder system and elaborates the appropriate PInitRes towards the cardholder system in the same way as when no EMV™ chip card is involved.

After receiving PInitRes, the cardholder system performs the same processing as that described in Section 8.4.6.2. The cardholder system checks the existence of the private SET certificate extension SETExtensions in the *entity_data* of the key-exchange public key certificate *Cert_pKE* of the payment gateway (see Section 8.4.2.2). The SETExtensions lists the SET message extensions for payment instructions that the payment gateway supports. Each available SET message extension is indicated with an OID.

For the scope of the chip e-commerce framework there are two meaningful OIDs:

- id-set-PIN-Any-Source: This OID means that the payment gateway accepts the extending of the SET messages to allow the verification of an on-line PIN by the issuer. The cardholder's PIN can be entered via any device, including the normal keyboard of a PC [23].

- id-set-commonChip: This OID indicates that the payment gateway is able to transmit the minimum EMV™ data elements and the AC to the acquirer, which can forward them via the appropriate payment network to reach the issuing financial institution. The minimum EMV™ data elements allow the issuer to verify the cryptogram produced by the EMV™ card application during the terminal action analysis stage (first GENERATE AC). Thus, the issuer can implement the on-line card authentication method [24].

8.6.3   Cardholder verification

The cardholder system conditionally performs the cardholder verification stage:

- If bit 5 = 1 in the first byte of the AIP, the cardholder system performs the cardholder verification.

- Otherwise, the cardholder system directly processes the terminal action analysis stage of the EMV™ transaction.

During the cardholder verification stage, the cardholder system obtains enough information from the cardholder to allow identity verification, either directly presenting it to the EMV™ chip card or transmitting it on-line to the issuer for verification.

Regardless of the type of cardholder verification method negotiated between the cardholder system and the EMV™ card application, the common processing performed by the cardholder system is described in Section 6.6.3, where the cardholder system abstracts the terminal application.

In this stage of the processing, the cardholder system knows the OIDs of the SET message extensions supported by the payment gateway and the CVM List (tag 8E) from the EMV™ card application. Based on this information, the cardholder system decides whether the cardholder verification method can be off-line PIN verification by the EMV™ card application, on-line PIN verification by the issuer, or another proprietary method specified by the payment system. The decision process performed by the cardholder system is as follows:

- The cardholder system will prompt for off-line PIN entry if the following two conditions are simultaneously fulfilled:

  1. The CVR of the current method in the CVM List indicates that the cardholder verification is the off-line PIN verified by the card.

  2. The id-set-commonChip is among the OIDs of the SET message extensions supported by the payment gateway, as indicated in the key-exchange public key certificate *Cert_pKE*. If this OID is present, it indicates that the payment gateway can transport the ARQC to the issuer for on-line card authentication. If the card authentication is successful, the issuer also has a physical proof of the legitimate cardholder's participation in the transaction, since only a correct verification of the PIN by the card would have triggered the computation of the ARQC.

  In case both conditions are fulfilled the cardholder system continues the processing of the off-line PIN as presented in Section 6.6.4.

  If the second condition mentioned above is not fulfilled, the cardholder system will not prompt for off-line PIN entry, but shall attempt processing the next CVR in the CVM List.

- The cardholder system will prompt for on-line PIN entry if the following two conditions are simultaneously fulfilled:

  1. The CVR of the current method in the CVM List indicates that the cardholder verification is the on-line PIN verified by the issuer.

  2. The id-set-PIN-Any-Source is among the OIDs of the SET message extensions supported by the payment gateway, as indicated in the key-exchange public key certificate *Cert_pKE*. If this OID is present, it indicates that the payment gateway can transport

the PIN suitably encrypted to the issuer for on-line cardholder verification.

In case both conditions are fulfilled the cardholder system continues the processing of the on-line PIN as outlined in Section 6.6.5.

If the second condition mentioned above is not fulfilled, the cardholder system will not prompt for on-line PIN entry, but shall attempt processing the next CVR in the CVM List.

8.6.4 Terminal action analysis

The cardholder system conditionally performs the terminal action analysis. This stage of the EMV™ transaction is performed only when the id-set-commonChip is among the OIDs of the SET message extensions supported by the payment gateway, as indicated in the key-exchange public key certificate *Cert_pKE*.

The cardholder system abstracts the terminal application in its interaction with the EMV™ card application, following the processing described in Section 6.8, with several exceptions mentioned below.

The cardholder system always asks for an ARQC as a reference control parameter of the GENERATE AC command, without comparing the TVR against the Issuer Action Codes, personalized in the card, or against the terminal action codes.

Concerning the data objects required by the EMV™ card application in the CDOL1, the cardholder system performs the following processing:

‣ The value field of the Amount, Authorized is obtained by extracting the amount component from the PurchAmt parameter as specified in the SET initiation message. Note that the value field of the Amount, Other is zero since there is no cashback in the e-commerce purchase transaction.

‣ The value field of the Transaction Currency Code is obtained by extracting the currency code component from the PurchAmt parameter as specified in the SET initiation message.

‣ The value field of the transaction date, in the format YYMMDD, is obtained from the PReqDate data item, delivered in the format YYYYMMDD in the PInitRes message, by striping the two leftmost YY digits.

- The value field of the Transaction Type is equal to 00, corresponding to the purchase of goods or services, representing a parameter of the cardholder system.

- The value field of the TVR is that one set up by the cardholder system, during the processing of the EMV™ transaction.

- The value field of the Terminal Country Code is obtained from the merchant country code data item included in the *merchant_data* characterizing the merchant. This data is retrievable from the merchant's signature public key certificate *Cert_mKV*, which is included in the PInitRes.

- The cardholder system does not create the value field of the Unpredictable Number at random, but diversifies it from the XID component of the *TransID* (which is included in the PInitRes). This allows the payment gateway to regenerate it following the same diversification algorithm.

In response to the GENERATE AC command, the EMV™ card application computes either the ARQC, as required by the cardholder system, or an AAC, if the card risk management decided to reject the transaction. This cryptogram is returned to the cardholder system together with the following data objects:

- Cryptogram Information Data (mandatory);

- Application Transaction Counter (ATC, mandatory);

- Issuer Application Data (IAD, optional).

If the terminal action analysis is accomplished with an AAC, as a result of the first GENERATE AC, then the cardholder system terminates the transaction and informs the cardholder that it is now permissible to withdraw the EMV™ card from the interface device.

8.6.5 Purchase request and response

The cardholder system creates the PReq, taking into account whether:

- The cardholder has a signature public key certificate *Cert_cKV*;

- The cardholder verification method is performed and which is its type (on-line/off-line);

‣ The terminal action analysis is performed and which is the type of its result cryptogram (ARQC or AAC).

The decision processing is described below.

If the cardholder has a signature public key certificate *Cert_cKV*, the cardholder system will compute the dual signature *DS*. Compared to the processing described in Section 8.4.6.2, the following modifications are enacted concerning the content of some data elements in OIData and PIData:

‣ In the PANData template of PIData:

  ‣ The PAN item consists of the value field of the PAN data object with tag 5A as it is read from the EMV™ card application.

  ‣ The *CardExpiry* data item, which is in the format YYYYMM, is obtained from the value field of the Application Expiration Date (tag 5F24), which is in the format YYMMDD, making the following format conversion. The cardholder system transforms the YY value from the Application Expiration Date into a four-digit year YYYY as prescribed by the EMV™ norms.

‣ In the OIData the items *BrandID*, *BIN*, and *Language* are filled in with the corresponding value fields of the data objects read from the EMV™ card, according to the processing and conversion rules already explained in conjunction with the PInitReq message (see Section 8.6.2).

If the cardholder verification method selected by the cardholder system is on-line PIN verified by the issuer, the following supplementary processing is required in conjunction with elaborating PReq:

‣ After the cardholder system captures the PIN, either via a functionally secure encrypting PIN entry device or via a PC keyboard entry with software encryption, the PIN is first transformed into a PIN field of 8 bytes. The PIN filed is submitted to an XOR operation with the account number field, also of 8 bytes, which is obtained from the PAN. The result of the XOR operation is a plaintext PIN block. In this way the PIN is bound to the PAN, preventing the swapping of PAN versus PIN, and assuring that enciphering the same PIN value under a given key shall not produce the same ciphertext for different accounts. Before including it into the digital envelope *C* (see

Section 8.4.6.2), which is currently used for wrapping the PAN and the session key SSK, the plaintext PIN block of 8 bytes is encrypted with SSK (i.e., ePINBlock = DES(SSK)[plaintext PIN block]). Thus, the digital envelope becomes $C = RSA(pKE)$ [$SSK \| PAN \| ePINBlock$]. This digital envelope is included in the confidential and authentic channel P established by the cardholder system with the payment gateway, which is transmitted in the PReq and is tunneled by the merchant server.

▸ The content of the PANData template is also modified to include besides the *PAN*, *CardExpiry*, *PANSecret*, and *EXNonce*, an extra data item: the plaintext PIN block.

If the terminal action analysis is accomplished with an ARQC, the cardholder system creates the commonChip extension in the PIHead portion of PIData. The following EMV™ data objects, in the TLV format, are included in any order in the emvData field of the commonChip extension:

▸ EMV™ data objects processed in relation with the CDOL1:

  ▸ Transaction details: Amount, Authorized (tag 9F02), Amount, Other (tag 9F03), Transaction Currency Code (tag 5F2A), Transaction Date (tag 9A), and Transaction Type (tag 9C);

  ▸ Terminal environment: Terminal Verification Results (tag 95), Terminal Country Code (tag 9F1A), and Unpredictable Number (tag 9F37).
    The sources from where the aforementioned data objects were obtained by the cardholder system, and the corresponding processing is presented in Section 8.6.4.

▸ Application Interchange Profile (tag 82), as it was obtained by the cardholder system in the response to the GET PROCESSING OPTIONS command (see Section 8.6.1.4);

▸ Application PAN Sequence Number (tag 5F34) as it was read from the EMV™ card application;

▸ Track-2 equivalent data (tag 57), as read from the EMV™ card application, whose PAN and expiration date fields are overwritten with 0;

▸ Data objects returned by the EMV™ card application in the response to the first GENERATE AC: Application Cryptogram (tag 9F26), Application Transaction Counter (tag 9F36), Cryptogram Information Data (tag 9F27), and Issuer Application Data (tag 9F10).

8.6.6   Authorization request/response

The payment gateway processes the AuthReq as described in Section 8.4.6.3, with the following modifications:

▸ Use the payment gateway's private decryption key pKD to open the digital envelope C originated by the cardholder and tunneled by the merchant. Obtain the symmetric key SSK and the cardholder's account information, and check whether the cryptogram of the PIN block is inside the envelope (i.e., $SSK \parallel$ PAN $\parallel$ ePINBlock = RSA (pKD) [C]). If the payment gateway supports on-line PIN processing, the rest of the processing described in this paragraph is performed inside a secure module. The ePINBlock cryptogram is decrypted with SSK to obtain the plaintext PIN block as $DES^{-1}(SSK)$ [ePINBlock]. The plaintext PIN block is submitted to an XOR operation with the account number field, which is obtained from the PAN, to recover the PIN field. Convert this PIN field to another PIN block format if needed, reencrypt it under symmetric encryption, and then pass the reencrypted PIN in the 1100 authorization request message (see also Section 6.6.6). This message is directed via the acquirer to the appropriate payment network and further to the issuer.

▸ Use SSK to decrypt C' and to obtain the payment message, $PIData \parallel DS \parallel$ H($OIData$) = $DES^{-1}(SSK)$ [C']. Check whether the commonChip extension is included in the $PIHead$ part of $PIData$. If so, recompute the Unpredictable Number using the same data and algorithm like those involved by the cardholder system. Compare the result with the value field of the data object with tag 9F37 as included in the emvData field of the commonChip extension. If the two values are different, proceed directly to elaborate an AuthRes with the error code piAuthMismatch in the AuthCode, with no need to format the 1100 authorization request message.

▸ Format the 1100 Authorization Request message and forward it to the acquirer. The acquirer delivers the message to the appropriate payment network, which forwards it to the card issuer. The issuer evaluates the 1100 Authorization Request and decides on the authorization or the rejection of the transaction, sending the adequate 1110 Authorization Request Response back to the payment gateway.

After receiving the 1110 authorization request response message from the issuer, via the payment network and acquirer, the payment gateway creates the AuthRes as outlined in Section 8.4.6.3, with the following additional processing:

- If either the Issuer Authentication Data with tag 91(see Section 6.8.6.1) or the issuer script(s) encoded either with tag 71 or 72 (see Section 6.10), or both, are included in the 1110 authorization request response, the payment gateway must transmit them to the merchant server. To this end, the payment gateway prepares the AuthRes that includes the AcqCardMsg. This data template is extended with acqCardExtensions, which transports whatever EMV™ data objects were received by the payment gateway from the issuer to be handed over to the merchant server. The merchant server forwards them to the cardholder system in the PResPayload field of the PRes message, which includes the AcqCardMsg with acqCardExtensions and AuthCode.

- If the merchant server supplies the data required to capture approved transactions either to the payment gateway or directly to the acquirer, then the merchant server must additionally provide the dataEMV™ field of the commonChip extension. This allows for the verification of the authenticity of the card involved in the transaction through the correctness of the cryptogram produced during the terminal action analysis. To be able to provide this additional data during the payment capturing stage, the merchant server has to obtain it from the payment gateway.

  - If the merchant server is allowed to capture a previously authorized transaction outside the SET, then the payment gateway must provide it with the emvData in clear, as an extension of the AuthResPayload field of the AuthRes.

  - If the merchant server captures the transaction as specified by SET, then it is sufficient if the payment gateway transmits to the merchant server the emvData through the TokenOpaque field of the capture token.

8.6.7 Completion of the EMV™ transaction

Whenever the cardholder system does not receive the PRes message in a timely manner, or if the PRes message is processed in due time but the AuthCode is one of the values listed below (with their corresponding meaning), the cardholder system shall perform a second GENERATE AC with the AAC as reference parameter and with the value field of the Authorization Response Code (tag 8A) set to Z3. The cardholder system informs the cardholder that the card can be removed from the interface device.

- orderReceived: PReq received by the merchant server and PRes sent back before the AuthRes is returned by the payment gateway.

- noReply: The issuer did not respond to the authorization request.

- piAuthMismatch: The data from the payment instruction elaborated by the cardholder does not match the order instruction elaborated by the merchant server or the Unpredictable Number recomputed by the payment gateway does not match the value field of the data object with tag 9F37 as included in the commonChip extension.

- systemError: The request could not be processed by an upstream system (acquirer, financial network, issuer, etc.) because data in the request is invalid.

Whenever the cardholder system receives the PRes message in a timely manner and the AuthCode does not indicate orderReceived, noReply, piAuthMismatch or systemError, it will perform the following processing:

- Examine the contents of the acqCardExtensions of the PRes to determine whether issuer scripts (tag 71 or 72) are present. If scripts are present, they are processed as outlined in Section 6.10.

- The cardholder system requires the completion of the EMV™ transaction with a second GENERATE AC. To this end, the cardholder system examines the AuthCode of PRes to determine which type of cryptogram it should request.

  - If the AuthCode indicates one of the error codes (declined, callIssuer, AmountError, expiredCard, invalidTransaction), the cardholder system shall request an AAC and will assign the value 05 to the Authorization Response Code (tag 8A).

▸ If the AuthCode indicates approved, the cardholder system shall request a TC and will assign the value 00 to the Authorization Response Code (tag 8A).

After receiving the card's response to the second GENERATE AC command and after the execution of all issuer scripts present, inform the cardholder that it is permissible to remove the card. The results of the second GENERATE AC are ignored, in the sense that they are not communicated through the capture request message to the payment gateway.

References

[1] EMVCo, *EMV 2000 Integrated Circuit Card Specification for Payment Systems, BOOK 3—Application Specification*, Version 4.0, December 2000, http://www.emvco.com/specifications.cfm.

[2] K. Boehle, "CashWorld 2001: Some Impressions and Lessons on the Future of Internet Payments," Internet draft, http://epso.jrc.ec.

[3] Garfinkel, S., and G. Spafford, *Web Security, Privacy & Commerce*, Second Edition, Sebastopol: O'Reilly & Associates, 2001.

[4] Boyan, J., "The Anonymizer—Protecting User Privacy on the Web," in *CMC Magazine*, September 1997, http://www.december.com/cmc/mag/1997/sep/boyan.html.

[5] VeriSign, "Securing Your Web Site for Business," http://www.verisign.com/products/site/index.html.

[6] MasterCard, "A White Paper: Using EMV for Remote Authentication," http://www.mastercardintl.com/newtechnology/smartcards/emv/RA_Entire_Manual.pdf.

[7] ISO 7498-1, "Information Processing—Open Systems Interconnection—Basic Reference Model—Part 1: The Basic Model," 1994.

[8] Fummy, W., "Internet Security Protocols," in B. Preneel and V. Rijmen (eds.), *State of the Art in Applied Cryptography*, Berlin, Germany: Springer LNCS 1528, 1998, pp. 186–208

[9] Atkinson, R., *Security Architecture for the Internet Protocol*, Request for Comments (RFC) 1825 (PS), August 1995.

[10] Atkinson, R., *IP Authentication Header*, Request for Comments (RFC) 1826 (PS), August 1995.

[11] Atkinson, R., *IP Encapsulating Security Payload (ESP)*, Request for Comments (RFC) 1827 (PS), August 1995.

[12] O'Mahony, V., M. Pierce, and H. Tewari, *Electronic Payment Systems for E-commerce*, Second Edition, Norwood, MA: Artech House, 2001.

[13] SETCo, "SET Secure Electronic Transaction 1.0 Specification—The Business Description," May 1997, http://www.setco.org/set_specifications.html.

[14] SETCo, "SET Secure Electronic Transaction 1.0 Specification—The Programmer's Guide," May 1997, http://www.setco.org/set_specifications.html.

[15] SETCo, "SET Secure Electronic Transaction 1.0 Specification—The Formal Protocol Definition," May 1997, http://www.setco.org/set_specifications.html.

[16] IBM Research, "iKP—A Family of Secure Electronic Payment Protocols," in *The First USENIX Workshop on Electronic Commerce*, New York, 1995.

[17] Freier, A. O., P. Karlton, and P. C. Kocher, *The SSL 3.0 Protocol*, Internet-Draft, November 1996.

[18] Dierks, T., and C. Allen, *The TLS Protocol—Version 1.0*, Internet-Draft, November 1997.

[19] SETCo, "External Interface Guide to SET Secure E-Commerce," http://www.setco.org/download.html.

[20] Visa, "Visa Authenticated Payment Program, 3-D Secure[TM]," http://www.international.visa.com/fb/paytech/secure/main.jsp.

[21] MasterCard, "Secure Payment Application (SPA[TM])," http://www.mastercardintl.com/newtechnology/ecommercesecurity/spa/.

[22] Visa EU E-Commerce, "3-D SET," http://www-s2.visa.com/pd/eu_shop/merchants/faqs/main.html.

[23] SETCo, "The On-line PIN Extensions to SET Secure Electronic Transaction[TM] Version 1.0," http://www.setco.org/extensions.html.

[24] SETCo, "The Common Chip Extension to SET Secure Electronic Transaction[TM] Version 1.0," http://www.setco.org/extensions.html.

Appendix A: Security Framework

This appendix describes a possible security framework. It facilitates the qualitative understanding of security issues encountered in the analysis and design of electronic payment systems. This process is schematized in Figure A.1.

A top-down approach can be used in the description of this security framework, following the steps listed below.

Step 1: Interface decomposition   Each electronic payment system is composed of a number of interfaces, with each interface opposing two parties. Generally, the main interfaces are cardholder-merchant, merchant-acquirer, acquirer-card association, card association-issuer, and issuer-cardholder. Depending on the particular features of each payment system, other interfaces could be identified.

Figure A.1
Definition of
a security
framework.

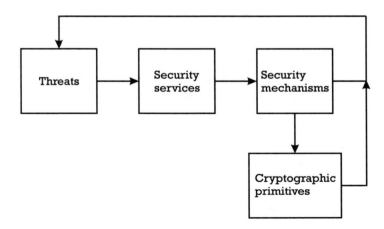

Step 2: Threat analysis   On each identified interface, the two parties have established a business relationship, which determines a set of transactions to be performed between them. For the completion of each transaction, messages are exchanged from one party to another according to a well-established protocol. The threat analysis identifies the consequences of possible protocol deviations on the business interests of each party. The parties participating in the protocol are first concerned about the threats generated by third parties, which are not eligible to participate in the protocol. If the two parties are mutually distrustful, they have to protect themselves from threats arising due to the misbehavior of each party during the participation in the protocol. Appendix B defines some of the security threats that can be identified in any interface between two communicating parties.

Step 3: Security services   Each threat can be countered by a security service, which is a generic solution towards reducing or eliminating the impact of a threat on the business interests of the parties. The definition of the security requirements is the second step in the construction of the security framework, mapping security services to threats. Appendix C describes the security services that can counter the identified threats: confidentiality, entity authentication, data origin authentication and integrity, timeliness, and non-repudiation.

Step 4: Security mechanisms   Each security service is implemented through an adequate security mechanism. The attribute adequate refers to the trade-off between providing the required level of security and the cost of implementing the corresponding security mechanism. This means that the choice of a security mechanism is biased by economical considerations: the level of strength of the security mechanism must be in accordance with the value of the assets to be protected by parties. Risk management is the process of selecting the security mechanism in a cost-effective way.

The main security mechanisms used in the design of the protocols underlying payment systems' functionality are described in Appendix D, including symmetric and asymmetric enciphering, cryptographic hash functions, digital signatures, public key certificates, cardholder verification mechanisms, static and DDA mechanisms.

Step 5: Cryptographic primitives   A security mechanism can be implemented with one or several cryptographic primitives. The choice of one cryptographic primitive or another is also determined by a trade-off, this time between the level of strength of the primitive against known classes of attacks and the costs determined by the implementation of the primitive. These costs are related to key management as well as software and hardware platforms needed to implement the primitive. In many cases, the choice of a cryptographic primitive is strongly influenced by subjective factors, among which are export regulations dictated by national security reasons, claimed intellectual rights protected by patents, and protectionist measures.

Appendix E is dedicated to block ciphers, their operating modes, and the main representatives. Appendix F presents a tutorial on the RSA public key encryption system and the RSA digital signature scheme. The interested reader can find more information on cryptographic primitives in [1].

Reference

[1]   Menezes, A. J., P. C. van Oorschot, and S. A. Vanstone, *Handbook of Applied Cryptography*, Boca Raton, FL: CRC Press, 1996.

Appendix B: Generic Security Threats

The most obvious threat to a communication established between two parties, the sender A(lice) and the receiver B(ob), is a third party E(ve), also called eavesdropper or attacker, who wiretaps the communication channel, as schematized in Figure B.1.

It can be argued that wiretapping is difficult, but, in fact, it is just a matter of cost. Tapping a telephone line is cheaper than tapping a communication held on a Bluetooth channel, an optical cable, or even a coaxial cable. Tapping an Internet connection is also much easier than penetrating the proprietary communication network of a card association. The attacker's determination to wiretap a communication line is motivated only by the potential gain, which should be higher than the cost of the technologies needed to break in. There are two major wiretapping possibilities. Passive wiretapping consists of listening in on the messages sent on the communication channel, which can result in unauthorized disclosure of information. Active wiretapping consists of intercepting, modifying, and then relaying the messages, which can result in the modification of the information

Figure B.1
Communication
channel
wiretapping.

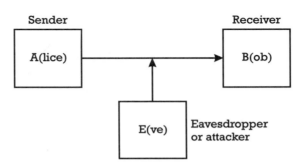

transmitted between parties. Active wiretapping is more difficult than passive wiretapping.

Other threats can be associated with the attempts of the communicating parties to misbehave during the protocols carried out between them, which can result in false statements of the sender or receiver. This category of threats is meaningful for the communication between two parties that are mutually distrustful and try to repudiate a transaction after its completion. As an example, the cardholder and the issuing bank can be considered parties that are mutually distrustful. On one hand the cardholder can deny a previous money withdrawal at an ATM, hoping that the evidence about this transaction provided by the bank to a judge, who is called to arbitrate the dispute, will be not enough to incriminate him or her. On the other hand, a bank can falsely claim that the cardholder withdrew money from her account, while, in fact, this transaction never happened. In the real world the second scenario is less probable then the first scenario. However, a threat analysis has to identify all the possible deviations by parties from the normal behavior. It is also worth noticing that it is not the *bank* that is mounting the attack (after all, the bank is a role that is played by an actor), but rather a dishonest employee abusing the prerogatives of his position with the bank.

In the remainder of this appendix some of the generic threats related to the communication between two parties are discussed.

› Attempting to intercept sensitive information exchanged between two parties is called eavesdropping or monitoring. In the case of electronic payment systems, the threat of eavesdropping consists of obtaining confidential financial information while it is being exchanged between the parties. The attacker can use this information in a variety of scenarios for obtaining material advantages.

› The impersonation threat consists of the false association between the entity involved in a transaction and the authorized entity, which is entitled to participate in that transaction. In the context of payment systems, the impersonation threat refers mainly to cardholder impersonation and issuer impersonation, since the business interests of these two roles are the most endangered when the attacks exploiting the impersonation threat succeed. Also, the terminal impersonation can lead to leakage of financial information stored by cards that can be further exploited by an attacker.

‣ The data modification threat targets both the data sent on the communication channel between two parties and the content of data stored in computers representing the parties during protocols. The data modification threat on the communication channel between parties assumes active wiretapping by the attacker who attempts to alter in an undetectable manner the transaction data sent between the parties. The undetectable alteration of the data content stored in the computers of parties participating in a protocol is another form of a data modification threat. When referring to electronic payment systems, the most frequent attack of this kind is the modification of a card content through a successful impersonation of the issuer.

‣ Somehow a paradoxical situation can appear where the sender and receiver have established a secure channel for their communication, protecting against eavesdropping, data origin impersonation, and data modification, but they did not consider the time coordinate in their security implementation. If the receiver has no means to distinguish between identical messages retransmitted at different moments in time, an attacker could use this weakness to mount a replay attack. The attacker taps the communication channel and copies both data and security information, which is replayed later. If the data represents a transaction proof, a dishonest receiver could claim more than one time the payment from the sender.

‣ When the parties participating in a protocol are mutually distrustful, the denial attack consists of false statements of the sender or receiver about their participation in the protocol. The sender could deny the fact that she sent a message to the receiver while the receiver could deny that he ever received the message claimed by the sender. This category of threats is meaningful for the communication between two parties that try to repudiate a transaction after its completion.

‣ The implementation of many security mechanisms involves secret cryptographic parameters, like secret keys for symmetric ciphers, private keys for asymmetric ciphers, and PIN codes for off-line cardholder verification. These secret parameters have to be stored in plaintext in the permanent memory of the device, during its personalization stage. Since cards and terminals are operated in an unprotected environment, there is the threat that an attacker tampers with the device in order to obtain the values of cryptographic parameters stored in the device or to modify sensitive data in the device. Two kinds of attempts can be mentioned: physical penetration and logical penetration. Physical penetration refers to the attempt of directly accessing the hardware resources of a device in order to read, modify, or delete sensitive information. Logical penetration of a device refers to obtaining or modifying sensitive information in a device only through eligible commands with suitably chosen parameters. These commands bring the device in a "sensitive state" that allows functions that are not normally permitted. Logical penetration is sometimes called data manipulation.

Appendix C: Security Services

The security services described in this appendix, data confidentiality, entity authentication, data authentication (data origin authentication and data integrity), non-repudiation, and timeliness, counter the possible consequences of the threats generated by passive and active wiretapping. The security services that prevent attackers from tampering with the device representing a participant to a protocol, either physically or logically, are generically called device integrity services.

C.1   Service description

The goal of *data confidentiality* is to protect against an unauthorized disclosure of information through eavesdropping (see Appendix B). Referring to Figure B.1, the sender wants to be reassured that whenever he or she sends a message to the receiver, even if the eavesdropper could passively wiretap the message he would not be able to get the content of the message. In the case of electronic payment systems, the confidentiality service concerning the financial messages exchanged between the communicating parties is often referred to as *secure messaging for confidentiality*.

Entity authentication is the security service that allows the verifying entity through the acquisition of corroborative evidence to check the identity of the proving entity. This service is intended to counter the impersonation threat (see Appendix B). In the case of electronic payment systems, entity authentication has specific variants, as listed below:

> ‣ If the proving entity is a cardholder, proving its identity either to the IH (on-line verification) or to a chip card (off-line verification) playing

the role of the verifying entity, then entity authentication is also referred to as *cardholder verification*. The cardholder verification establishes the link between the actual user of a card and the eligible cardholder.

> • If the proving entity is a card and the verifying entity is the IH, the entity authentication service is also referred to as *on-line card authentication*.

> • If the proving entity is a card and the verifying entity is a terminal, the entity authentication service is also referred to as *off-line card authentication*.

> • When the proving entity is the IH and the verifying entity is the card, the entity authentication service is also referred to as *issuer authentication*.

> • If the proving entity is the terminal and the verifying entity is the card, the entity authentication service is also called *terminal authentication*.

When a time variant is considered in the production of the corroborative evidence (i.e. when the timeliness service is considered), entity authentication allows the verifying entity to check that the proving entity was active at the time when the evidence was created or acquired. Thus, the verifying entity can check that the proving evidence is not replayed from a previous entity authentication. In case of either on-line or off-line card authentication, if the verification process considers a time variant for the proof production, then the process is referred to as *dynamic card authentication*. This requires the production of a new proof every time the card authentication is performed. Dynamic card authentication protects against the threat of card counterfeiting. This is true unless the attacker was able to clone the secret parameters used during the proof generation, following a successful device tampering attack.

If the verification process does not consider any time variant for the proof production, then the process is referred to as *static card authentication*. This service does not protect against the counterfeit card attack, since the static proof [e.g., the static authenticator (see Appendix D, Section D.6)], once wiretapped by the attacker, can be replayed many times. However, the service can check that data in the card has not changed since the issuer personalized the card, effectively countering the threat of manipulating the content of data stored in devices.

Data authentication is a security service consisting of two inseparable components [1]:

1. *Data origin authentication* provides enough evidence to the receiver whether or not the sender is really the one claiming to be.

2. *Data integrity* provides enough evidence to the receiver whether or not the content of the information changed compared to the initial content as intended by the sender.

The two components are inseparable, since it does not help the receiver to know that the received data has not been altered unless he has the confirmation that this data was sent by the right sender. When the data authentication service is enforced, the attacker can impersonate neither the sender nor manipulate the data (see Appendix B). In case of electronic payment systems, data authentication considers the authentication and integrity of financial messages exchanged between parties, and is often referred to as *secure messaging for integrity and authentication*.

Non-repudiation counters the threat of denying the participation in a transaction by one of the mutually distrustful entities involved in the communication (see Appendix B). Depending whether the sender or the receiver generates the denial threat, one can distinguish between two basic forms of this security service.

1. *Non-repudiation of origin* counters the false statements of the sender, which tries to repudiate having sent a message.

2. *Non-repudiation of delivery* protects against the attempts of the receiver to falsely deny that he received a message from the sender.

Timeliness is the security service that protects against reply attacks (see Appendix B). This security service relies on inserting a time variant component in the messages exchanged between the communicating parties, which makes any message exchange unique.

Tamper resistance is the generic security service that counters the threat of device tampering through physical penetration. The most common example of a tamper resistant device is an integrated circuit card, or chip card, the resources of which are protected from being directly accessed.

The security service that counters the logical penetration in a device is the *access control*. A successful logical penetration means, in fact, exploiting a security hole in the access control system of the device.

C.2 Realization of security services

Referring to a generic communication protocol stack, like the one outlined in Figure C.1, the realization of the security services can be localized at either of the two levels [2].

1. *Secure channel*: The communication subsystem provides the sender and receiver applications with the necessary means for information exchange. The choice of implementing security services into the communication subsystem leads to a solution where a secure communication channel is made available to the applications.

    ‣ This solution was adopted by the SIM Toolkit Application designers who foresaw the realization of confidentiality, data authentication, timeliness, and non-repudiation services at the level of the short message service point-to-point (SMS-PP) transportation layer [3, 4].

    ‣ A similar approach was adopted by Netscape Communications, which designed and proposed the SSL as a transport layer security protocol for the Internet [5]. This security layer is interleaved between the communicating applications and the TCP/IP protocol stack, which is used for the Internet connections. Starting from the SSL protocol, the IETF working group proposed the TLS [6]. The security services provided by this protocol are confidentiality, entity authentication, and key establishment [7].

2. *Secure communication over insecure channel*: Here the communication subsystem provides the sender/receiver applications with a communication link, which initially in itself is not secure. Realizing the

Figure C.1
Generic
communication
protocol stack.

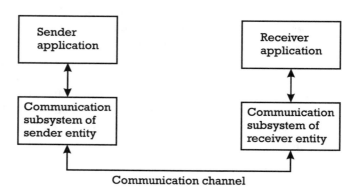

Communication channel

security services at the application level leads to the situation where the application itself builds a secure link over the insecure communication channel. The following payment standards implement security at the application level:

- EMV™ debit/credit application both in the chip card and card accepting device terminal [8–11], as detailed in Chapter 6.

- Common Electronic Purse Specification (CEPS) [12] application both in the chip card and card accepting purchase or loading device.

- SET [13] application in the consumer's PC, merchant's Web server, and payment gateway of the acquirer, as is outlined in Chapter 8.

References

[1]   ISO 7498-2, "Information Processing—Open Systems Interconnection—Basic Reference Model—Part 2: Security Architecture," 1989 (first edition).

[2]   Verschuren, J., "Security of Computer Networks," in B. Preneel and V. Rijmen (eds.), *State of the Art in Applied Cryptography*, Berlin, Germany: Springer LNCS 1528, 1998, pp. 163–185.

[3]   ETSI, Global System for Mobile Communication, *Digital Cellular Telecommunications System (Phase 2+); Technical Realization of the Short Message Service (SMS) Point-to-Point (PP)*, GSM 03.40, Version 7.4.0, Release 1998.

[4]   ETSI, Global System for Mobile Communication, *Digital Cellular Telecommunications System (Phase 2+); Security Mechanisms for the SIM Application Toolkit; Stage 2*, GSM 03.48, Version 8.3.0, Release 1999.

[5]   Freier, A. O., P. Karlton, and P. C. Kocher, *The SSL 3.0 Protocol*, Internet-Draft, November 1996.

[6]   Dierks, T., and C. Allen, *The TLS Protocol—Version 1.0*, Internet-Draft, November 1997.

[7]   Fummy, W., "Internet Security Protocols," in B. Preneel and V. Rijmen (eds.), *State of the Art in Applied Cryptography*, Springer LNCS 1528, 1998, pp. 186–208.

[8]   EMVCo, *EMV 2000 Integrated Circuit Card Specification for Payment Systems, BOOK 1—Application Independent ICC to Terminal Interface Requirements*, Version 4.0, December 2000, http://www.emvco.com/specifications.cfm.

[9]   EMVCo, *EMV 2000 Integrated Circuit Card Specification for Payment Systems, BOOK 2—Security and Key Management*, Version 4.0, December 2000, http://www.emvco.com/specifications.cfm.

[10] EMVCo, *EMV 2000 Integrated Circuit Card Specification for Payment Systems, BOOK 3—Application Specification*, Version 4.0, December 2000, http://www.emvco.com/specifications.cfm.

[11] EMVCo, *EMV 2000 Integrated Circuit Card Specification for Payment Systems, BOOK 4—Cardholder, Attendant, and Acquirer Interface Requirements*, Version 4.0, December 2000, http://www.emvco.com/specifications.cfm.

[12] CEPSCo, *Common Electronic Purse Specification, Functional Requirements*, Version 6.3, September 1999, http://www.cepsco.com.

[13] SETCo, *SET Secure Electronic Transaction 1.0 Specification*, May 1997, http://www.setco.org/set_specifications.html.

Appendix D: Security Mechanisms

Security services are implemented through security mechanisms. This appendix outlines some of the basic security mechanisms needed in the design of electronic payment systems: encryption, cryptographic hash functions, digital signatures, cardholder verification mechanisms, and SDA and DDA mechanisms.

D.1 Encryption

Encryption is the security mechanism that implements the confidentiality service. Encryption can be implemented in two categories of schemes. The first group contains symmetric or conventional cipher systems; the second group includes asymmetric or public key cipher systems. Figure D.1 presents a unified model for an encrypted channel, incorporating both symmetric and asymmetric systems [1].

The goal of the sender is to transmit the plaintext P to the receiver such that even if an attacker is able to wiretap the channel the plaintext cannot be retrieved. The sender transforms the plaintext P into the cryptogram or ciphertext C, applying a mathematical transformation referred to as the encryption algorithm E, the specification of which is publicly known. An encryption key KE parameterizes the encryption algorithm. After receiving the cryptogram C, the receiver applies the decryption algorithm D, the specification of which is also publicly known. Similarly to the encryption algorithm, a decryption key KD, which is related to the encryption key KE, parameterizes the decryption algorithm. The relation established between KE and KD is different for symmetric than for asymmetric encryption systems. The key distribution center (KDC) generates and distributes the

Figure D.1
Unified model
for symmetric
and asymmetric
encryption
systems.

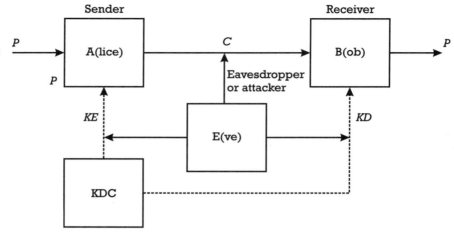

encryption/decryption key pairs (KE, KD) in the system. Secure channels have to be established for the distribution of these keys to both the sender and the receiver. The security requirements of the distribution channels, however, are different for the sender and receiver in case of symmetric and asymmetric cipher systems. The attacker has access to the specification of the encryption and decryption algorithms (E, D). The attacker can also capture the cryptogram C. There are some exceptions concerning the public availability of the algorithms. The most notable examples are the algorithms A3, A5, and A8 used by the security services implemented in the GSM network [2].

D.1.1   Symmetric encryption

In the case of symmetric ciphers, $KE = KD = K$. The distribution channels towards the sender and receiver have to provide both confidentiality and data authentication services. Knowledge of E, D, and C does not allow the attacker to derive P nor the key K.

A symmetric cipher (E, D) is the best-suited mechanism for implementing the confidentiality service on a communication channel connecting two entities that already share a common key.

The following example shows the use of symmetric encryption for implementing the secure updating of parameters in a chip card. This operation allows the issuer to update the parameters of an application running in a chip card even after the card is already issued to the cardholder and is now in its utilization stage. The sequence of commands sent by the issuer that performs the updating of parameters is sometimes called issuer scripts [3].

The issuer has stored in the card a special secret key that parameterizes a symmetric cipher, which is used to implement the secure messaging for confidentiality that protects against the eavesdropping of issuer scripts. This key is referred to as the issuer script key (*ISK*). Anytime a secret parameter is updated in the card, the issuer sends it encrypted with *ISK* from the issuer host through the payment network to the terminal where the card to be updated is inserted. Since only the card knows this key, the confidentiality of the cryptographic parameters sent through issuer scripts is protected.

D.1.2 Asymmetric encryption

In the case of asymmetric ciphers, *KE* is different from *KD*. The encryption key *KE* is made public by the KDC, and thus the distribution channel to the sender has to provide only data authentication (see Section D.4) and not confidentiality. The distribution channel towards the receiver has to provide both confidentiality and data authentication services. After receiving *KD*, the receiver has to make provisions for protecting the confidentiality of this key, which is therefore referred to as the private decryption key. On one hand, knowledge of *E*, *D*, and *C* does not allow the attacker to derive the plaintext *P*. On the other hand, knowledge of the public encryption key *KE* does not allow the attacker to derive the secret decryption key *KD*.

A well-known class of mathematical functions that achieves these features is the class of trapdoor one-way functions. A function *E* parameterized through *KE* is said to be one-way if giving the argument *P* and the parameter *KE* is easy to compute the image $C = E(KE)[P]$. However, giving *C* is computationally unfeasible to obtain $P = D(KD)[C]$ without knowledge of the parameter *KD*, where *D* is the inverse function of *E* in the sense that $P = D(KD)[E(KE)[P]]$. A one-way function is said to be a trapdoor if the computation of *P* is easily performed from *C* at the moment when the parameter *KD* is provided as a trapdoor information. A well-known trapdoor one-way function is the RSA function, as it will be presented in Appendix F.

The asymmetric ciphers are relatively slow when compared with the symmetric ciphers. This low performance is mainly due to the nature of the algorithms implementing trapdoor one-way functions, implying arithmetic computations with long integers with lengths greater than 300 digits. Contrarily, the algorithms specifying symmetric ciphers are based on Boolean functions, implying bit-wise operations more suited to the machine architecture running the algorithm. The performances of asymmetric algorithms can be improved through the use of a cryptographic coprocessor, which is a dedicated computational architecture specialized in the arithmetic with long integer numbers. This coprocessor, however, increases the cost of the devices, making asymmetric encryption more expensive when compared with the symmetric encryption.

An asymmetric cipher is the most suited mechanism for implementing the confidentiality service on a communication channel connecting two entities that have not exchanged keys on beforehand, and thus they cannot use symmetric cipher systems.

The length of a message to be encrypted using an asymmetric cipher is limited, usually by the length of the public encryption key (see Appendix F). Thus, encrypting a long message means the repeated use of the asymmetric algorithm, which certainly degrades the performance level of the system. Therefore, a session secret key is generated at random by the sender A and is encrypted with the public encryption key of the receiver B, namely KE_B, resulting in the cryptogram $C = E(KE_B)[SSK]$. This process is sometimes referred to as a key transport mechanism or key wrapping. After receiving the cryptogram C, which is sometimes called a digital envelope, the receiver decrypts it to obtain the session secret key SSK (i.e., $SSK = D(KD_B)[C]$). From now on, the sender can use the session secret key with a symmetric cipher (E', D') to encrypt bulk data $C' = E'(SSK)[Bulk data]$. "Bulk data" is sometimes the term used for longer messages. Correspondingly, the receiver can use the transported SSK to decrypt the bulk encrypted data C' (i.e., $Bulk data = D'(SSK)[C']$). The process is schematized in Figure D.2.

D.2 Cryptographic hash functions

Hash functions were first introduced in connection with database management systems for easy searching of records in big tables. To achieve this goal, the information in a record is compressed to a quantity of fixed length,

Figure D.2
Secret key
wrapping.

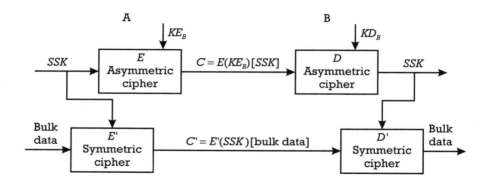

which is called a hash code, that serves as an identification label of a record. As will be outlined below, using hash functions for cryptographic purposes implies supplementary design requirements, which adds the attribute *cryptographic* to the term "hash function." Because only *cryptographic hash functions* are considered in this book, they will be simply referred to as *hash functions*.

A hash function maps an input of arbitrary length to a hash code of fixed length, *n* bits. Two categories of hash functions can be distinguished:

1. Unkeyed hash functions, which are generally referred to as message digest codes (MDC);

2. Keyed hash functions, which are generally referred to as MACs.

Hash functions are security mechanisms used for implementing the data authentication service (see Appendix C). The basic idea of using a hash function for implementing the data authentication service is to transfer the authenticity of an arbitrary long message to the authenticity of its hash code. The MDC is an essential security mechanism for implementing other security services (e.g., entity authentication and non-repudiation). Thus, the MDC is a basic building block for an efficient implementation of digital signature schemes. A unified and comprehensive treatment of the analysis and design of cryptographic hash functions can be found in [1].

Even though an MDC is an unkeyed hash function, generally the payment system literature uses the term "hash function" to refer to an MDC. Even though we do not agree with this terminology abuse, we conform to it so as not to confuse the reader. Therefore, in the remainder of this appendix the term "hash function" is used to designate only an MDC. Note that rigorously speaking the MAC is also a hash function, which is parameterized by a secret key, but for the goals of this book the terms "hash function" and "MAC" are disjunctively used.

D.2.1   Hash function

The following requirements are imposed on a hash function.

- First, the hash function must be a one-way function, in the sense that given the input x is easy to compute $H(x)$, while for all the images h in the range of H it is computationally unfeasible to derive an input x such that $h = H(x)$, a feature that is sometimes called *first preimage resistance*. The description of H is publicly known.

- Second, even though there are arguments $x \neq x'$ for which $H(x) = H(x')$, giving a pair $(x, H(x))$, it is computationally unfeasible to find x' such that $H(x) = H(x')$, a feature that is called *second pre-image resistance*. This feature is enough for providing an adequate level of security against external attackers, which can only observe the pairs $(x, H(x))$ but have no way to influence the choice of x. However, in order to provide protection against inside attackers, consisting of one of the communicating parties, a supplementary condition must be fulfilled. It must be computationally unfeasible to find *any* arguments $x \neq x'$ for which $H(x) = H(x')$, a case for which the hash function is said to be collision resistant.

Over the years many hash function candidates were proposed.

- In the first generation of hash functions, the fixed bit-length of the hash code was 128 bits. Among the most popular cryptographic primitives used as hash functions in this category are the algorithms MD4 [4] and MD5 [5], which were proposed by the RSA Laboratories, and the RIPEMD algorithm, proposed by the research project RACE-R1040 financed by the European Commission [6]. Some successful attacks, however, have revealed that these cryptographic primitives were not collision resistant. These attacks showed that providing the collision resistance feature for a hash function required that the length of the hash code be at least 160 bits.

- A second generation of hash functions, with the length of the hash code of 160 bits, contains the SHA-1 algorithm, the Secure Hash Algorithm that is proposed by the National Institute of Standards and Technologies (NIST) in the United States [7]. The European equivalent is the RIPREMD-160 [8], proposed by Dobbertin, Bosselaers, and Preneel as a collision-resistant hash function improving on the original RIPEMD proposal.

Since no secret key is involved in the computation of a hash function, there is no overhead involved by the key management. In this case, however, a supplementary authentication channel is needed for every hash code. To better understand this, assume that a hash code is intended to protect the authenticity of a public encryption key used by a bank to receive encrypted messages from clients. To this end, the bank sends its client a letter containing a tamper evident part, which, when it is opened, reveals the verification hash code of the public encryption key. The public encryption key itself is sent in clear over the Internet, with no protection. After receiving it, the customer applies the indicated hash function to the message consisting of this key, and if it matches the verification hash code received by mail, the public encryption key sent over the Internet can be accepted as authentic. In this case the classic mail service provides the authentication channel for protecting the authenticity of the verification hash code.

D.2.2 MAC

The MAC is a suitable mechanism implementing secure messaging for integrity and authentication on the communication channel established between the sender and the receiver. In the case of a MAC, the authenticity of data relies on the secrecy and authenticity of a secret key K, which guarantees the origin of data. Assume that the sender and receiver have exchanged the secret key K in the framework of a key management scheme. Then, in order to provide the data authentication service for a message M, the sender has to compute the MAC value on M using the secret key K. The sender transmits both the message M and the MAC value to the receiver. After receiving the message M, the receiver computes using the same secret key K the MAC verification value on M and compares it with the received MAC value. If the computed MAC and the received MAC are equal, the receiver has the confirmation that the origin of data is that claimed, and that data was not modified during its transmission. If a unique time-variant sequence is included in the message M, the replay threat can also be countered, as explained in Section D.7. The secure messaging for integrity and authentication implemented with a MAC is schematized in Figure D.3.

Technically, a MAC is a hash function H that is parameterized by the secret key K. Given an input x of arbitrary length and the secret key K, the

Figure D.3
Data
authentication
using a MAC.

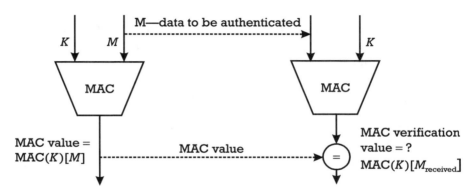

MAC value of the input x is computed as $MACvalue = H(x, K)$. The length of the MAC value is fixed, n bits, with $n \geq 32...64$. The description of H is publicly known. Given the value of the input x and of the secret key K, the computation of $H(x, K)$ must be easy. However, giving *only* x it is computationally unfeasible for an attacker that does not know K to determine $H(x, K)$ with a better probability than $1/2^n$, which is, in fact, the probability of guessing the MAC value. Moreover, the history of sequences $\{x_i, H(x_i, K)\}$ obtained from previous computations of the MAC on input values x_i that can be chosen by the attacker does not help to determine the key K nor the image $H(x', K)$ for *any* new input value x'.

One category of MAC primitives is that derived from the corresponding MDC primitives, appending the secret key K to the data to be authenticated. They are referred to as keyed MAC. The secret key K can be appended in front of the data to be authenticated as a prefix [i.e., $MAC(K)[x] = MDC(K\|x)$]. The secret key can be also appended at the end of the data to be authenticated as a suffix [i.e., $MAC(K)[x] = MDC(x\|K)$]. There is also the possibility that the secret key envelopes the data to be authenticated, being appended both in front and at the end of the data to be authenticated [i.e., $MAC(K)[x] = MDC(K \| x \| K)$]. Even though a MAC constructed from an MDC offers a high throughput, there is the suspicion of a certification weakness concerning this type of construction [9]. A second category of MAC primitives is based on block ciphers, and their construction will be discussed in Appendix E, Section E.4.

D.3   Digital signature schemes

A digital signature of a message is a string of bits dependent on some secret information known only to the originating entity and on the content of the message being signed. A digital signature associates a message with an originating entity, named the signer. A digital signature scheme is a suitable security mechanism for enforcing data authentication (data origin authentication and data integrity), entity authentication, and non-repudiation security services.

In the communication framework presented in Figure B.1, the sender of a message is the signer, while the receiver of a pair message/digital signature is the verifier of the signature.

A digital signature scheme consists of the following items:

> ‣ A *key generation algorithm KG*, which generates a pair of a public verification key and private signing key (KV, KS) for the signer;

> ‣ A *signature generation algorithm Sign(KS)[M]*, which is a method for producing a digital signature *S* on a suitably formatted message *M* using the private signing key *KS*;

> ‣ A *signature verification algorithm Verify(KV)[S, M']* ?= "True," which is a method that allows the receiver to verify a signature *S* on the formatted message *M* using the public verification key of the signer. The output of the verification algorithm yields either *true* or *false*.

A *signing procedure* consists of a method for formatting data into formatted messages that can be signed, a signature generation algorithm, and a *signing protocol* between the signer and the verifier. A verification procedure consists of a signature verification algorithm and a method for recovering data from the message.

The *ordinary signing protocol* between the signer and the verifier, which is needed for establishing a signing procedure, is a one-step protocol where the signer computes $S = Sign(KS)[M]$ using his or her private signing key *KS* on the message *M*. She sends to the receiver the signature *S*, eventually together with the message *M* in case it cannot be recovered from *S*. After receiving it, the receiver verifies the signature *S* on the message *M* using the public verification key *KV* of the signer. If the verification predicate *Verify(KV)[S, M]* yields *true*, the originating entity is considered authentic, the integrity of the message is accepted, and the receiver has an irrefutable proof in case the sender later repudiates having sent the message *M*. The protocol is schematized in Figure D.4.

A digital signature scheme must fulfill the following requirements:

> ‣ Each signer (Alice) can efficiently generate signatures on messages of her choice, using her private signing key KS.

Figure D.4
Ordinary
signing
protocol.

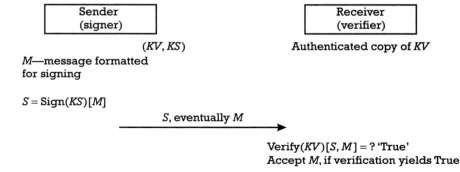

▸ Each verifier (Bob) can efficiently check the validity of a signature generated by a signer, using his public verification key KV.

▸ An attacker, which knows only the public verification key of the signer and has recorded a finite sequence of pairs message/signature $(M_i, Sign(KS)[M_i])$, cannot efficiently generate signatures on behalf of the signer on new messages that she did not previously sign.

For the purposes of this book, only two types of attacks are considered in connection with digital signature schemes: the no-message attack and the adaptively chosen message attack. In both cases, the attacker has a limited computational power. In the no-message attack, the attacker only knows the signer's public verification key. In the adaptively chosen message attack, the attacker can dynamically ask the legitimate signer to sign any message, using her as a kind of oracle. At a first glance, the second type of attack seems only theoretical. The following example proves the contrary. Assume the attacker controls a card acceptor device and the signer is a chip card that implements an RSA signature scheme. Then, the attacker can format messages and send them to be signed by the card. With the supplementary knowledge the attacker accumulates from the pairs $(M_i, Sign(KS)[M_i])$, where the messages are chosen by herself, the chance to derive a signature on a new message that was never signed by the signer increases. This is the strongest attack on digital signature schemes.

Digital signature schemes can be grouped into signature schemes with appendix and signature schemes with recovery.

D.3.1   Signature scheme with appendix

A signature scheme with appendix requires the entire message M as an input to the verification algorithm. Thus, in this case $M' = M$ and the signer has to transmit the entire message M to the verifier for completing the verification algorithm. The verification predicate becomes $Verify(KV)[S, M]$?= "True."

Examples of signature schemes with appendix are RSA with PKCS#1 [10, 11] and DSA [12].

When the signer has to produce a signature on a message of variable length, or with a length that is much larger than the bit length of the formatted message accepted in the signature generation algorithm, then a signature scheme with appendix is the suitable mechanism. This approach is adopted on a communication channel between a mobile phone implementing a payment token and a wallet server implementing a payment mechanism. In this case the wallet server needs a non-repudiation guarantee for the payment order sent from the mobile phone of the customer.

The method of formatting messages to be signed from the message set into messages that can be signed, which form the signing set, uses a collision-resistant hash function H, which is applied to the message set.

D.3.2 Signature scheme with recovery

A signature scheme with recovery does not require a priori knowledge of the entire message M for performing the verification algorithm. In this case the verifier can recover a part M_R of M from S, such that the signer has to send only M' separately to the verifier (i.e., $M = M_R \| M'$). There are situations when the entire message M can be recovered from S, the case for which M' is empty and $M = M_R$. Since the verification algorithm recovers part of the formatted message, the verification predicate is referred to as the recovery predicate and is denoted $Recover(KV)[S,M'] = \{?\text{"True,"} M_R\}$.

The ISO 9796-2 [13] standard describes signature schemes with recovery and illustrates the use of the RSA for implementing them.

Most signature schemes with message recovery are applied to messages of fixed length. As it will be presented in Section D.4, a public key certificate is a digital signature produced by a certification authority on the public encryption key or on the public verifying key of a participant in an electronic payment system. The length of such a public key is fixed and limited by a security parameter, like the bit length of the key. If the length of the formatted messages accepted in the signature algorithm is greater than the bit length of the key to be certified (plus some redundancy needed in the verification algorithm), then the signature scheme with recovery is the suitable mechanism for certification.

The method of formatting messages to be signed from the message set into messages that can be signed, which form the signing set, applies a redundancy function to the message set. A well-known example of a redundancy function is given in ISO 9796-2 [13].

The two types of schemes are not mutually exclusive. Specifically, any scheme giving message recovery can be used for provision of digital signatures with appendix. For example, in EMV™ [14] producing the signature consists of applying the scheme to a hash value of the message. If the message is short enough, then the verification algorithm recovers the entire message and the hash value from the signature (as will be described in Appendix F, Section F.3). Otherwise, the verification algorithm recovers only a part of the message in addition to the hash value.

D.4   Public key certificates

Section D.1 stated that in case of asymmetric ciphers the distribution channel used for transmitting the public encryption key KE of the receiver B
from the KDC to the sender A, even though it does not require data confidentiality, must implement the data authentication service.

D.4.1   Authenticity of public keys

Indeed, imagine that this channel is not being protected against the impersonation threat. In this case an active attacker can mount a "man-in-the
middle attack," whose scenario is described below. In this case an attacker
E(ve) could interpret the encrypted messages sent by A and intended for B
without breaking into the asymmetric cipher. The attacker E intercepts the
distribution channel from the KDC to A and learns the public encryption key
of B, referred to as KE. The attacker also produces a key pair consisting of a
public encryption key and a private decryption key (KE', KD'), using the
same key generation algorithm as the KDC. She sends KE' to A pretending
that it is sent by the KDC as the public encryption key of B. Since there is no
protection against the impersonation threat, A does not have any suspicions.
The sender A uses the key KE' to encrypt sensitive information, which is
intended for B. The attacker intercepts the cryptogram produced with KE'
and uses the corresponding private decryption key KD' to decipher this
cryptogram. After learning the sensitive information, the attacker encrypts
the data with the public encryption key KE, which really belongs to B. Neither A nor B realizes that its communication was disclosed. This is the reason
why A must be convinced that she is encrypting under the authentic public
encryption key of B. Public key certificates are the most used security
mechanism to authenticate public keys in a system.

In order to implement public key certificates, both the sender A and the
receiver B hire the services of a TTP, which is assumed to be honest and fair.
Each party could delegate the generation of its private key/public key pair to
the TTP, or it could produce this pair itself. In any case, the TTP produces the
public key certificate on the public key of this pair for each participant, the
reason for which the TTP is also called the certification authority. In the
framework of electronic payment systems, the role of the CA is often played
by an issuer when it generates public key certificates for public keys of chip
cards, or rather is played by a card association or a payment system operator
when it generates public key certificates for public keys of issuers.

D.4.2   Public key certificate generation

The CA must take appropriate measures for verifying the identity of *B* before generating a public key certificate for this entity. For example, when the entity *B* is a chip card, its public encryption key has to be certified by the issuer, which plays the role of the CA. During the personalization stage, the chip card can generate a pair consisting of a public encryption key and a private decryption key, or the issuer can generate this pair on behalf of the card and securely download the private decryption key in the chip. Only the chip card knows the private decryption key. The personalization terminal of the issuer further processes the card's public encryption key. To this end, the terminal computes the public key certificate associated with the card and downloads it in the chip in a protected production environment, which provides authentication. The issuer can keep a certificate revocation list with the public key certificates of all the compromised chip cards in the system.

To produce a public key certificate, the CA can use a digital signature scheme with recovery. The pair consisting of the public verification key and the private signing key used by the CA is denoted (KV_{CA}, KS_{CA}). To generate a public key certificate, the CA signs a formatted message *M*, which has a fixed length and is composed of several items [14]:

- The *certificate format* distinguishes between various types of certificates—for example, public key certificates for public encryption keys or public key certificates for public verification keys.

- The *CA identification number* is the identifier that differentiates between several CAs that can coexist in a complex system.

- The *certificate expiration date* is the time limit until a certificate is considered valid. After this date the verifier rejects the certificate even if the recover predicate of the CA's signature holds true.

- The *certificate serial number* is an identifier that distinguishes among the certificates generated by a CA.

- Identification means of the hash algorithm used for formatting messages, in case the signature scheme with recovery is applied to a hash code of the message to be signed.

- Identification means of the algorithm used by the signature scheme with recovery.

- The length of the public key to be certified and the public key itself.

A public key certificate generated by CA on the public key of an entity PK_B is denoted $Cert_{CA}(PK_B)$. It consists of the concatenation of the signature part and the data part. The signature part is computed as $Sign(KS_{CA})[M]$, where $M = M_R \| M'$ and PK_B is included in M besides items like the certificate format, the CA identification number, and the other items listed above. The formatted message M consists of two parts, M_R and M', where M_R is the part that can be directly recovered by the verifier from the signature part of the public key certificate. M' represents the data part of the public key certificate that has to be separately transmitted to the verifier such that the *Recover* predicate can be evaluated. Note that the data part can be empty whenever the whole message M can be recovered from the signature part. Thus, one can consider that $Cert_{CA}(PK_B) = \{Sign(KS_{CA})[M], M'\}$.

D.4.3 Public key certificate verification

The entity A can verify the authenticity of the public key of the entity B, if A has an authentic copy of the public verification key KV_{CA} of the CA.

If the CA is the highest organization in a certification hierarchy, then there is no means to provide the authenticity of the key KV_{CA} in a cryptographic way. For example, this is the case when the CA is a card association. All the parties in the system know this key from a broadcast channel like a newspaper, or through normal mail sent by the CA to all the parties, the authenticity of which is provided by other means than cryptography.

However, if the CA is subordinated hierarchically to another organization CA' then KV_{CA} has to be further certified by CA'. As an example, if the CA is an issuer that certifies the public keys of the chip cards issued to its clients, then CA' is the card association where the issuer subscribed.

The entity A can verify the authenticity of the public key certificate of B as follows:

‣ Retrieve the public key certificate $Cert_{CA}(PK_B) = \{Sign(KS_{CA})[M], M'\}$ of B from the entity itself or from a central database.

‣ Retrieve the public verification key KV_{CA} of the CA that generated the certificate either directly, when the CA is the highest organization in the certification hierarchy, or through the verification of a chain of certificates when the KV_{CA} is certified by another certification authority CA' at a higher level.

‣ Use KV_{CA} to compute the predicate $Recover(KV_{CA})[\ Cert_{CA}(PK_B)] = \{?"True," M_R\}$. If the verification holds true, compute the formatted message $M = M_R \parallel M'$, from which the entity A can retrieve the public key PK_B of the entity B.

D.5   Cardholder verification mechanisms

The cardholder verification mechanism implements the entity authentication service when the proving entity is the cardholder. A cardholder verification mechanism is intended to prove the link between the actual user of a card (or, generally, the user of a payment token) and the legitimate cardholder to which the card was issued.

D.5.1   Manual signature

Manual signature is the only cardholder verification mechanism the result of which can be assessed by a human operator, like, for example, the attendant of a POS terminal. The POS attendant asks the actual user of the card to perform a manual signature on a receipt stating the conditions of the current transaction. The attendant compares the signature of the actual user of the card against the witness signature of the cardholder written on the tamper-evident stripe added on the back side of the card. The verification is passed if the two signatures *resemble*. Even though this method is simple, it is always biased by the graphological skills of the attendant. The false acceptation rate (FAR), which represents the probability that a false signature passes as adequately resembling the witness signature, is greater than zero. The manual signature is still widely in use for credit cards implemented with magnetic stripe. Note that EMV™ allows defining the manual signature as the preferred or even the only allowed cardholder verification method for a card product [3]. However, since the FAR of the manual signature is high and since other cardholder verification methods have gained ground, the manual signature will gradually become a fallback method used for the cases when the chip, terminal, or issuer host functionality is degraded.

D.5.2   Enciphered PIN verified on-line

On-line PIN verification is the cardholder verification mechanism performed directly by the issuer host, based on the PIN typed in the terminal at the point of service during the current transaction. This mechanism is based on the comparison between the *PIN image control value*, which is produced from the PIN actually captured by the terminal, with the *PIN image stored value*, corresponding to the cardholder that is stored in the cardholders' database managed by the issuer host. The PIN image is produced with a one-way function, which can be implemented with a MAC. This CVM is suitable if there is an on-line connection between the point of service and the issuer.

The user of a payment card types the PIN into the PIN pad of an ATM or POS terminal. This PIN is transmitted from the terminal to the issuer. During its transmission, the confidentiality service is implemented with a symmetric encryption mechanism. First, the PIN pad encrypts the PIN using the transportation key *TK1* known to the tamper resistant device of the terminal, which is also referred to as a SAM. After receiving this cryptogram, the SAM uses the transportation key *TK1* to decrypt the PIN. Then, the SAM encrypts the PIN under a different transportation secret key *TK2*. If between the acquirer, which is responsible for managing cryptographic parameters in the SAM, and the issuer of the card there is a bilateral agreement, then *TK2* is accessible to the issuer's host. In this case the cryptogram containing the PIN is tunneled to the issuer's host via the acquirer's host and the card association payment network without any other conversion. Otherwise, for each different security domain the communicating parties share a separate transportation key. The cryptogram containing the PIN is decrypted and encrypted again under a different transportation key for each separate security domain it traverses: from the SAM to the AH, from the AH to the network processor of the card association, and finally from the network processor to the issuer host. Once the secure module of the issuer host decrypts the actual PIN captured at the point of service, it can produce the PIN image control value, which is compared against the PIN image stored value corresponding to the presumed cardholder, as it is stored in the cardholder database.

Appropriate key management procedures must be adopted in order to provide the suitable secret keys needed by the communicating parties. The on-line PIN cardholder verification method is widely used for magnetic stripe debit/credit payment cards operated at unattended terminals that can establish an on-line connection to the issuer host. The method is also operable with debit/credit payment cards implemented with chip cards [3].

D.5.3 Plaintext PIN verification performed by the chip card

Plaintext PIN verification is the cardholder verification mechanism based on the direct comparison between the PIN captured at the terminal with the witness PIN corresponding to the cardholder that is stored in the chip of a card [3, 15]. This cardholder verification method is suited in case the card has a chip with tamper-resistant EEPROM where the witness PIN is stored by the issuer during the personalization stage. The method is widely applied when there is no on-line connection between the point of service and the issuer—the reason for which it is sometimes referred to as off-line PIN verification.

If the terminal environment is secure enough against eavesdropping, the terminal submits the PIN to the chip card as plaintext. After receiving it, the chip compares it with the witness PIN stored in it. If the comparison is positive, the chip card has successfully identified the cardholder, and the payment application is activated.

If the terminal environment is susceptible to eavesdropping, the terminal first encrypts the PIN and sends the corresponding cryptogram to the chip card. This cardholder verification method is referred to as off-line encrypted PIN verification. Depending on the encryption mechanism used, this cardholder verification method can have two different implementations, as explained in the following sections.

D.5.4 Symmetric enciphered PIN verification

If the terminal has a SAM where a secret PIN encryption key *PEK* was stored by the acquirer in agreement with the issuer, then the PIN can be securely transmitted to the card using a symmetric encryption mechanism, following the procedure described below.

Since the personalization stage, the issuer has already stored in the chip card the key *PEK*. When a symmetric enciphered PIN verification is performed, the card generates a random number r intended to counter replay attacks, which is transmitted to the terminal. With the participation of the SAM, the terminal encrypts the PIN with the encryption algorithm E parameterized by the key *PEK* (i.e., $Out1 = E(PEK)$ [*PIN*]). The terminal performs an XOR operation between r and *Out1*, and the result is once again encrypted with the same algorithm parameterized by the same secret key *PEK* (i.e., $C = E(PEK)[r \text{ XOR } Out1]$). The cryptogram C is sent to the card undergoing the cardholder verification process. After receiving C, the card decrypts it with the decryption algorithm D parameterized by *PEK*, obtaining $C1 = D(PEK)[C]$. An XOR operation is performed between the result $C1$ and the random r (i.e., $C2 = r \text{ XOR } C1$). Finally, the card applies once more D parameterized by *PEK* to $C2$ in order to obtain $PIN = D(PEK)[C2]$. This value of the decrypted PIN is compared to the witness PIN stored in the chip, and if the comparison holds "True," the user of the card is the legitimate cardholder.

D.5.5 Asymmetric enciphered PIN verification

If the acquirer managing the terminal has not established an agreement with the issuer of the card, then the PIN can be securely transmitted from the terminal to the card following the procedure described below.

Referring to Figure D.1, assume that the sender is a payment terminal and the receiver is a chip card. The cardholder types in the PIN using the PIN-pad of the terminal, which has to transmit it to the chip card for performing locally the cardholder verification. Since the issuer of the card and the acquirer responsible for the management of the terminal did not establish a business relationship beforehand, there is no symmetric key stored in the terminal that has a correspondent in the chip card. But the issuer has generated in connection with the card a pair public encryption key/private decryption key, (KE_{card}, KD_{card}), and has certified the public encryption key KE_{card} with a CA, recognized as a TTP by both the issuer and the acquirer. This certificate $Cert_{CA}(KE_{card})$ provides the authenticity of the public encryption key KE_{card} and the fact that it is linked to the card. (Note that certification is discussed in Section D.4.) The issuer has downloaded the key pair and the corresponding certificate in the card during the personalization stage. The issuer does not trust the environment where the terminal is installed and assumes the eavesdropping threat, requiring the encryption of the PIN during its transmission from the terminal to the card. Moreover, the replay threat is also considered, since an attacker could register the cryptogram containing the PIN and later retransmit it to the card. In this case the following steps describe the protocol established between the card and the terminal, which is schematized in Figure D.5:

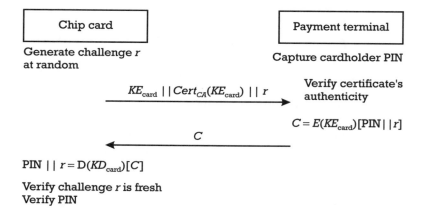

Figure D.5
PIN encrypted with a public key cryptosystem.

▸ The chip card generates a random number r, called a challenge, and transmits it together with the public encryption key of the card KE_{card} and its certificate $Cert_{CA}(KE_{card})$ to the terminal.

▸ The cardholder types in his or her secret PIN using the PIN-pad of the terminal. The terminal verifies the authenticity of the certificate $Cert_{CA}(KE_{card})$. If the verification passes, the terminal uses the key KE_{card} for the encryption of a message consisting of the concatenation of the PIN, the confidentiality of which is to be protected, and the challenge r, which guarantees that each execution of the protocol is unique, countering eventual replay attacks. The inclusion of the random r in the cryptogram also protects against mounting a dictionary attack, since the PIN is chosen from a restricted domain and the cryptogram is produced with a public key. It results in the cryptogram $C = E(KE_{card})$ [PIN $\|$ r], which is sent to the chip card.

▸ Using the private decryption key KD_{card}, the chip card computes $M = D(KD_{card})[C]$. The last significant part of M is compared against r to check that the received cryptogram is not replayed from a previous execution of the protocol. The most significant part of M is compared against the PIN stored in the card since the personalization stage. If the comparison is positive, the cardholder is considered legitimate by the card's payment application.

D.5.6 Cardholder verification based on biometrics

Biometrics represents another possible cardholder verification mechanism. Instead of using a PIN to locally identify the cardholder at the point of service, the cardholder's biometrics can be used instead, through comparing the biometrics captured at the terminal with the corresponding digitized witness stored in the card since the personalization stage. Suitable biometrics include fingerprints, hand geometry, retina diffraction features, voice recognition, and face recognition. An important advantage is that biometrics cannot be forgotten, stolen, or forged. The FAR, however, representing the probability that an attacker is accepted as the legitimate cardholder, and the false rejection rate (FRR), representing the probability that the legitimate cardholder is rejected, are greater than zero. (In this context it is worth noticing that the FAR and the FRR for the plaintext/enciphered PIN verified either off-line or on-line are also grater than zero, even though they have the smallest false rates among the cardholder verification mechanisms.)

When this disadvantage is combined with the high price of terminals including a biometrics reader, one can see why, at present, there is no encouraging business case for biometrics, at least in electronic payment systems. It is also important to mention that an attacker that successfully recorded the biometrics captured by a terminal during its transmission to the chip card for comparison can mount any attack as those described for a wiretapped PIN. In order to avoid this attack, several projects were launched for adapting the biometrics reader directly on the card. This is actually the case for fingerprints, which becomes the favorite biometrics for this type of cardholder verification mechanism.

D.6 SDA mechanisms

The SDA mechanisms provide the authenticity and integrity of critical financial data stored in the card or generally in a payment token, identifying unauthorized alterations of this data after the personalization stage. An SDA mechanism, however, does not detect counterfeit cards, since the same precomputed authentication value remains unchanged for any transaction.

D.6.1 MAC-based SDA mechanism

In the case of magnetic stripe cards, the issuer computes during the personalization stage a static authenticator ($Static\_Auth_i$), which is stored on the magnetic stripe. This value is computed as a MAC on financial data that is specific to the card, $financial\_data_i$, with a secret key SK_i unique for each card (i.e., $Static\_Auth_i = MAC(SK_i)[financial\_data_i]$). The issuer computes SK_i applying a MAC on the PAN of the card PAN_i, parameterized with the master key MK of the issuer (i.e., $SK_i = MAC(MK)[PAN_i]$).

During a transaction performed at a terminal, the static authenticator $Static\_Auth_i$ captured from the magnetic stripe of the card is sent in the authorization request to the issuer. Based on the information in the authorization request, the issuer recomputes the $Static\_Auth_i$ according to the same algorithm as that used during personalization. The issuer compares the received $Static\_Auth_i$ against the recomputed $Static\_Auth_i$, and if the verification passes, the information of the card is accepted as authentic.

The $Static\_Auth_i$ does not prevent counterfeiting, since a successful attacker that has cloned the content of a magnetic stripe card has also obtained the $Static\_Auth_i$, which is a precomputed value that remains unchanged for all transactions.

D.6.2   Signature-based SDA mechanism

In the case of chip cards, the issuer computes a digital signature during the personalization stage, referred to as the static authenticator $Static\_Auth_i$, on the financial data stored in the card, $financial\_data_i$. This signature is produced with the private signing key KS_{ISS} of the issuer (i.e., $Static\_Auth_i = Sign(KS_{ISS})[financial\_data_i]$). Since only the issuer is able to generate this signature and the verification of the signature is passed only if the content of the financial data did not change, the authenticity and integrity of the data stored in the chip card is guaranteed (see Section D.3). Both the financial data and the static authenticator are stored in the tamper-resistant EEPROM of the chip card. The use of a digital signature has the advantage that it can be checked by anyone having the public verification key KV_{ISS} of the issuer.

If one assumes that the terminal has an authentic copy of KV_{ISS}, then the terminal can check off-line the authenticity of the chip card (i.e., $Verify(KV_{ISS})[Static\_Auth_i, financial\_data_i]$?= $True$). This is the case when there is a business agreement between the acquirer managing the terminal and the card issuer, such that the authentic copy of KV_{ISS} is stored in the tamper-resistant EEPROM of the terminal. In an interoperable environment, where there is no business relationship between the acquirer and issuer, the public verification keys of issuers are not stored in the terminal. Rather, the key KV_{ISS} is stored in the EEPROM of the chip card, since the personalization stage, together with a certificate released by a certification authority on this key, $Cert\_KV_{ISS} = Cert(KS_{CA})[KV_{ISS}]$, which establishes its authenticity. The card association can play the role of the CA. The only business constraint is that both the acquirer (which manages the terminal) and the issuer (which is responsible for the card) are members of this card association. The acquirer has to make provisions that an authentic copy of the public verification key of the CA, denoted KV_{CA}, is loaded in all the terminals.

In order to authenticate to the terminal, the chip card retrieves from its EEPROM the certificate $Cert\_KV_{ISS} = Cert(KS_{CA})[KV_{ISS}]$, the static authenticator $Static\_Auth_i$, and the financial data $financial\_data_i$ of the chip card and sends them to the terminal. After reception, the terminal uses KV_{CA} and verifies the certificate $Cert\_KV_{ISS}$ (i.e., $Verify(KV_{CA})[Cert\_KV_{ISS}, KV_{ISS}]$?= $True$). If the certificate is authentic, the terminal recovers the public verification key of the issuer KV_{ISS}. Using this key, the terminal verifies the correctness of the static authenticator and assesses the authenticity of the financial data stored in the chip card.

Since in the protocol described above there is no time variant pattern that can counter a replay attack, card counterfeiting cannot be prevented if an attacker wiretaps the interface between the chip card and the terminal.

D.7 DDA mechanisms

One possibility of implementing DDA is by using a challenge-response mechanism. For every new execution of the DDA protocol, the verifying entity generates a "fresh" challenge, which is sent to the proving entity. The proving entity applies a cryptographic transformation parameterized by a specific key on the received challenge to elaborate a response, which is sent back to the verifying entity. After assessing the correctness of the response with respect to both the challenge and the cryptographic material, the verifying entity decides whether the proving entity is the one claiming to be. The mechanism prevents replay attacks, since the value of the response is always different for a new challenge, being suitable for implementing the timeliness security service (see Appendix C, Section C.1).

If the proving entity is a chip card, the mechanism precludes the counterfeiting of the card, since only the card that stores the appropriate cryptographic key can compute a correct response to each new challenge. Moreover, the response can prove the legitimacy of critical data stored in the card, covering in this way the functionality of SDA mechanisms, if this critical data is included in the computation of the response.

D.7.1 MAC-based DDA

DDA can be implemented with a MAC primitive (see Section D.2) that uses a session key SSK mutually shared by the proving entity and the verifying entity.

When the proving entity is the chip card (which is operated by the terminal at the point of service) and the verifying entity is the issuer host, the mechanism is also called on-line DDA or even on-line card authentication. The session key SSK is derived for each transaction with respect to a transaction counter TC that changes for each execution of the protocol. The SSK key is derived from a common secret key SK_i associated by the issuer with the card since the personalization stage, and which is stored in the tamper-resistant EEPROM of the card.

The protocol of the DDA based on a MAC is as follows. The terminal submits to the card the data describing the conditions of a transaction at the point of service, $transaction\_data$, concatenated with a challenge r that is generated at random for every new transaction. To the information sent by the terminal, the card appends the transaction counter TC, and also some financial data $financial\_data_i$ specific to the card, which also contains the card identifier. The card computes the dynamic authenticator $Dynamic\_Auth_i$ $= MAC(SSK)[transaction\_data \parallel r \parallel TC \parallel financial\_data_i]$ and returns it to the terminal. The terminal forwards to the issuer the authorization request $auth\_req = transaction\_data \parallel r \parallel TC \parallel financial\_data_i$ together with the authenticator $Dynamic\_Auth_i$. After receiving the authorization request, the issuer uses the card identifier in the $financial\_data_i$ and retrieves the secret key of the card SK_i. Using this key, the issuer recomputes the session key SSK corresponding to the transaction counter TC. The issuer computes the *authenticator verification value* $AVV = MAC(SSK)[auth\_req]$. The card is considered genuine (not counterfeit) and its critical data authentic if the authenticator verification value computed by the issuer equals the dynamic authenticator sent by the card (i.e., $Dynamic\_Auth_i = AVV$).

Note that in the case when the acquirer and the card issuer have previously established a business relationship, the computation of the authenticator verification value AVV can be delegated by the issuer to a SAM plugged in the terminal. This is the case when the card is an e-purse and the verifying entity is the POS or ATM terminal at the point of service.

D.7.2 Digital signature–based DDA

If the terminal where the transaction is performed has no possibility of online communication with the issuer and the acquirer responsible for the terminal has no business relationship with the card issuer, a MAC-based DDA is technically not possible. In this case DDA can be implemented with a digital signature scheme.

To this end, the chip card has a hardware architecture that includes a cryptographic coprocessor, which is able to efficiently perform a digital signature. Assume for simplicity that during the personalization stage the issuer generates at random a pair of a private signing key and a public verification key (KS_{card}, KV_{card}) that are uniquely linked to the card. The issuer uses its private signing key KS_{ISS} to generate a certificate on the public verification key of the card, $Cert\_KV_{card} = Cert(KS_{ISS})[KV_{card}]$. This certificate proves the authenticity of the key KV_{card} and its link to the card. However, since there is no business agreement between the acquirer and card issuer, the terminal has no authentic copy of the public verification key KV_{ISS} of the issuer, and thus it cannot assess the certificate $Cert\_KV_{card}$. Therefore, the issuer has to obtain a certificate on its own public verification key KV_{ISS} from a certification authority, $Cert\_KV_{ISS} = Cert(KS_{CA})[KV_{ISS}]$, which establishes the authenticity of KV_{ISS}. The card association can play the role of the CA. The only business constraint is that both the acquirer (which manages the terminal) and the issuer (which is responsible for the card) are members of this card association. The acquirer has to make provisions that an authentic copy of the public verification key of the CA, denoted KV_{CA}, is loaded in all the terminals.

During the personalization stage, the issuer securely loads in the tamper-resistant EEPROM of the chip card the key pair (KS_{card}, KV_{card}) together with the certificates needed for assessing the authenticity of KV_{card} (i.e., $Cert\_KV_{card}$ and $Cert\_KV_{ISS}$).

The protocol of the DDA based on a digital signature is as follows. The terminal submits to the card the data describing the environment of a transaction at the point of service, *environment_data*, concatenated with a challenge r that is generated at random for every new transaction. To the information sent by the terminal, the card appends the financial data *financial_data$_i$* specific to the card, the integrity of which has to be checked. The card computes the dynamic authenticator as a digital signature with its private signing key KS_{card} on the message M = *environment_data* $\|$ r $\|$ *financial_data$_i$* (i.e., $Dynamic\_Auth_i$ = $Sign(KS_{card})[M]$). The card forwards the terminal with the dynamic authenticator $Dynamic\_Auth_i$ together with KV_{card}, $Cert\_KV_{card}$ and $Cert\_KV_{ISS}$. The terminal verifies the dynamic authenticator as follows:

▸ Using the public verification key KV_{CA} of the certification authority, recover from the certificate $Cert\_KV_{ISS}$ the public verification key KV_{ISS} of the issuer, which can be now accepted as authentic.

▸ Using the public verification key KV_{ISS} of the issuer, recover from the certificate $Cert\_KV_{card}$ the public verification key KV_{card} of the card, which can be now accepted as authentic.

▸ Using the public verification key KV_{card} of the card, check the dynamic authenticator produced by the card, $Verify(KV_{card})[Dynamic\_Auth_i, M]$?= *True*. If the verification is passed, the card is considered genuine (not counterfeit) and its critical financial data is accepted as unaltered.

D.7.3 One-time passwords

Another possibility for implementing DDA in devices that do not have cryptographic capabilities is the use of one-time passwords. The limitation of this mechanism, however, is that the verifying entity has to have a business agreement with the issuer of the device implementing the proving entity.

When personalizing the device of the proving entity, the issuer generates an *initial seed* X_0, and starting from this value it recurrently applies a hash function H to compute the sequence $X_i = H(X_{i-1})$, with $i = 1, \ldots, n$. The sequence of arguments $\{X_i\}_{i=0,\ldots,n-1}$ is stored in the permanent memory of the device implementing the proving entity, which is tamper resistant protected. The issuer transfers to the verifying entity the first hash code $X_1 = H(X_0)$, from which the verifying entity can compute the sequence of hash codes $\{H(X_{i-1})\}_{i=2,\ldots,n}$. In this setup, the personalization sequence suffices for n executions of the protocol.

The first time the proving entity authenticates to the verifying entity, it will send X_{n-1}. The verifying entity applies the hash function H on X_{n-1} and compares it with $X_n = H(X_{n-1})$ from the sequence of hash codes it computed itself. If the verification holds true, the authentication is successful and both entities delete from the list of passwords X_{n-1} and $X_n = H(X_{n-1})$, respectively. In the next authentication, the proving entity uses X_{n-2}, while the verifying entity uses $X_{n-1} = H(X_{n-2})$. The process can be repeated n times until the proving entity uses X_0 while the verifying entity uses $X_1 = H(X_0)$.

References

[1]   Preneel, B., "Analysis and Design of Cryptographic Hash Functions," Doctoral Dissertation, KU Leuven, March 1993.

[2]   Vedder, K., "GSM: Security, Services and the SIM," in B. Preneel and V. Rijmen, (eds.), *State of the Art in Applied Cryptography*, Springer LNCS 1528, 1998, pp. 224–240.

[3]   EMVCo, *EMV 2000 Integrated Circuit Card Specification for Payment Systems, BOOK 3—Application Specification*, Version 4.0, December 2000, http://www.emvco.com/specifications.cfm.

[4]   Rivest, R. L., *The MD4 Message-Digest Algorithm*, Request for Comments (RFC) 1320, Internet Activities Board, Internet Privacy Task Force, April 1992.

[5]   Rivest, R. L. *The MD5 Message-Digest Algorithm*, Request for Comments (RFC) 1321, Internet Activities Board, Internet Privacy Task Force, April 1992.

[6]   RIPE Integrity Primitives, *RIPEMD, Final Report of RACE Integrity Primitives Evaluation* (R1040), June 1992.

[7]   NIST FIPS PUB 180-1, *Secure Hash Standard*, April 1995.

[8]   Dobbertin, H., A. Bosselaers, and B. Preneel, "RIPEMD-160: A Strengthened Version of RIPEMD," *Fast Software Encryption, Third International Workshop*, Springer LNCS 1039, 1996, pp. 53–69.

[9]   Preneel, B., and P. C. van Oorschot, "MDx-MAC and Building Fast MACs from Hash Functions," *Proc. CRYPTO '95*, 1995, Berlin, Germany: Springer LNCS 963, pp. 19–32.

[10] Rivest, R. L., A. Shamir, and L. Adleman, "A Method for Obtaining Digital Signatures and Public-Key Cryptosystems," *Communications of the ACM*, No. 21, 1978, pp. 120–126.

[11] RSA Laboratories, *PKCS#1: RSA Encryption Standard*, version 1.5, November 1993.

[12] NIST FIPS PUB 186, *Digital Signature Standard*, May 1994.

[13] ISO/IEC 9796, "Information Technology—Security Techniques—Part 1: Digital Signature Scheme Giving Message Recovery," 1991; "Part 2: Mechanisms Using a Hash-Function," 1997.

[14] EMVCo, *EMV 2000 Integrated Circuit Card Specification for Payment Systems, BOOK 2—Security and Key Management*, Version 4.0, December 2000, http://www.emvco.com/specifications.cfm.

[15] CEPSCo, *Common Electronic Purse Specification, Functional Requirements*, Version 6.3, September 1999, http://www.cepsco.com.

Appendix E: Block Ciphers

A block cipher is a cryptographic primitive that can be used for implementing symmetric encryption mechanisms. It can be also used in the construction of other security mechanisms, including the MAC schemes.

The cryptographic literature provides many examples of block ciphers; the most used are the Data Encryption Standard (DES) [1], IDEA, RC-5, and Blowfish.

E.1 Definition and parameters

A block cipher is an encryption algorithm E described by a one-to-one invertible function parameterized by a secret key K of k bits, which maps plaintext blocks P_i of n bits to ciphertext blocks C_i of the same bit-length, $C_i = E(K)[P_i]$. The decryption algorithm D is the inverse mapping of the function E, $D = E^{-1}$, which computes the plaintext block P_i from the ciphertext block C_i using the same secret key K as a parameter, $P_i = E^{-1}(K)[D_i]$.

When encrypting a message M of arbitrary bit-length l using a block cipher, a padding operation could be applied to the message M before splitting it into blocks of appropriate bit-length.

> • When the length l of the message M is a multiple of n, the message can be directly split into a number of t blocks, such that $l = t * n$. There are padding schemes, like that proposed in EMV™ [2], that can add one single block with a predefined structure at the end of the given message, such that the bit-length l' of the padded message M' becomes $l' = (t + 1)* n$.

▸ When the length of the message M is not divisible by n, the message M is first padded with a number of bits such that the length l' of the padded message M' is divisible by n. Depending on the padding scheme, the number of resulting blocks is $t = \lceil l/n \rceil$ or $t = \lceil l/n \rceil + 1$, where $\lceil l/n \rceil$ denotes the smallest positive integer greater than the result of the division l/n. In this case the length of the padded message is $l' = t * n$.

After appropriately padding, the plaintext message M is divided into a number of i plaintext blocks of the fixed bit-length n, $P_1, ..., P_i$. For plaintext messages exceeding one block in length, various modes of operations for block ciphers can be used, as described in Section E.2.

The block size (n) impacts on the security of a block cipher. The larger the block size, the better its security (see the CBC operation mode in Section E.2). The block size also influences the complexity of the block cipher, for which a larger block size reflects in a more complex algorithm and in a more costly implementation. The block size can also affect performance, when padding is required.

The key size (k) defines an upper bound on the security of a block cipher by considering the brute force attack, which consists of the exhaustive search of the secret key K: the attacker tries all possible keys. The attacker only needs a single matching pair plaintext block, ciphertext block produced with that key. Longer keys increase the efforts of the attackers performing exhaustive key search. Longer keys, however, involve additional operational costs determined by the generation, transmission, and storage of these keys.

The values of the block size and key size parameters are given for several well-known block ciphers. The block cipher DES operates on blocks of $n = 64$ bits with a key of $k = 56$ bits. The block cipher IDEA uses a key of $k = 128$ bits to encrypt blocks of $n = 64$ bits. Rijndael, which has recently been chosen as the block cipher of the Advanced Encryption Standard (AES) [3], is designed with the goal of accepting various key sizes of $k = 128$, 192, 256 bits, while the block size is $n = 128$. The Rijndael, designed by Daemen and Rijmen was chosen in October 2000 by the NIST in United States as the DES replacement.

E.2   Modes of operation

When using a block cipher, it is not recommended to split the data into blocks and encrypt every block separately. Depending on the application, several modes of operations were proposed [4], namely the electronic code-book mode (ECB), the cipher block chaining mode (CBC), the cipher feed-back chaining mode (CFB), and the output feedback chaining mode (OFB). For the purpose of this book, we describe only the first two operation modes.

In ECB each block of plaintext is encrypted independently of the other blocks that form a message, $C_i = E(K)[P_i]$, $i = 1, ..., t$. The decryption is also carried out independently and is described by the relation $P_i = E^{-1}(K)[C_i]$, $i = 1, ..., t$. The following remarks apply to the ECB mode:

▸ Reordering the ciphertext blocks will result in the reordering of the plaintext blocks. This fact allows an attacker the possibility of com-puting a ciphertext message corresponding to an eligible plaintext message without the need of K, but relying only on a given set of cryptograms.

▸ For the same key K, the same plaintext block is always transformed in the same ciphertext block, a fact that can be exploited in a dictionary attack.

▸ The errors do not propagate, in the sense that a simple or multiple bit error within a ciphertext block will only affect the decryption of the block in which the error appears.

▸ The ECB mode is suitable for encrypting messages with a length that is smaller than or equal to the block size. The ECB mode is useful for the key derivation process, where the derived key equals the length of the block size (see Section E.5).

In the CBC mode the encryption operation on the current plaintext block is chained with the ciphertext block of the previous encryption opera-tion. The first encryption operation is chained to an initial vector IV, since there is no previous operation, $C_1 = E(K)[P_1 \text{ XOR } IV]$. The other ciphertext blocks are computed as $C_i = E(K)[P_i \text{ XOR } C_{i-1}]$, $i = 2, ..., t$. The decryp-tion process of the first ciphertext block is computed with the formula $P_1 = E^{-1}(K)[C_1] \text{ XOR } IV$. The other ciphertext blocks are computed as $P_i = E^{-1}(K)[C_i] \text{ XOR } C_{i-1}$, $i = 2, ..., t$. The following properties characterize the CBC mode:

▸ The chaining operation makes the ciphertext blocks dependent on all preceding blocks, which counter the reordering of ciphertext blocks.

- Using different values of the initial vector IV prevents the same plaintext encrypting to the same ciphertext.

- Due to the chaining, the errors propagate, in the sense that a simple or multiple bit error within a ciphertext block will affect the decryption of the block in which the error appears and that of the succeeding ciphertext block.

- If it happens that two ciphertext blocks created with a block cipher in the CBC mode under the same key are equal, then it is easy to compute the bit-wise XOR of the two corresponding plaintext blocks. In other words, if this happens, then information about plaintext leaks. Indeed, if one looks to the output C_i, then after $2^{n/2}$ outputs one can expect a match $C_i = C_j$ with a high probability. This is the reason why the block size influences the security of the block cipher. Then P_i XOR $C_{i-1} = P_j$ XOR C_{j-1}, which further leads to P_i XOR $P_j = C_{i-1}$ XOR C_{j-1}. Note that this is not due to any weakness of the underlying block cipher, but is rather a consequence of the way the CBC mode is constructed.

E.3   DES, Triple-DES, and AES

This appendix does not detail the block ciphers DES, Triple-DES, and AES. The reader can find information on these subjects in the cryptographic literature [5] and in the AES draft [3]. This presentation discusses the shortcomings of DES, its evolution to Triple-DES, and finally their replacement by the AES. Furthermore, the use of DES and Triple-DES algorithms for symmetric encryption is presented in the ECB and CBC mode, as it is actually used for the EMV™ implementations [2].

   DES is the most used block cipher and is, in fact, the de facto standard for symmetric encryption worldwide. Despite many years of research, no method has been published that breaks a DES encrypted message substantially faster than exhaustive key search, which consists of trying all the 2^{56} different keys on a pair plaintext block and ciphertext block that is known to the attacker. Theoretical attacks were proposed that break DES using a significantly smaller number of encryption operations than 2^{56}, but these required supplementary conditions that are not realizable in practice. For example, the differential cryptanalysis attack requires that the legitimate entity perform a huge number of operations for the attacker, providing 2^{43} pairs of plaintext/ciphertext. In the majority of applications, however, DES keys would not be used for such an intensive operation during their entire lifetime. This theoretical threat is the motivation why the design of payment systems recommends the use of session keys, which are operated only a few times during one single session.

Nevertheless, nowadays the DES is not considered to be sufficiently secure. In 1997 a DES key was successfully retrieved by a network of computers cooperating over the Internet after a search of approximately 4 months. However, using special purpose hardware, like the machine built in 1998 for a price of $130,000, the expected searching time decreases to 112 hours [6].

Using multiple encryption can counter the threat of brute force attacks on the 56-bit key of DES. The practice of encrypting twice under different DES keys was not resistant to a man-in-the-middle attack. This fact established the encryption-decryption-encryption (E-D-E) Triple-DES with double-length key, simply referred to as Triple-DES, as the effective modality for increasing the resistance against the exhaustive key searching from 2^{56} to 2^{112}. In this case the key K consists of two (single-length) DES keys, often called the left key K_L and the right key K_R, such that $K = K_L \parallel K_R$. The cryptogram is computed as $C_i = \mathrm{DES}(K_L)[\mathrm{DES}^{-1}(K_R)\ [\mathrm{DES}(K_L)[P_i]]]$. The plaintext block is computed from the ciphertext block as $P_i = \mathrm{DES}^{-1}(K_L)[\mathrm{DES}(K_R)$ $[\mathrm{DES}^{-1}(K_L)[C_i]]]$. It is not known, however, whether there are some weaknesses using Triple-DES, which leads security experts to the conclusion that it is better to have a block cipher that is designed from the beginning with the goal of larger keys.

With both DES and Triple-DES the block size remains 64 bits. As it was explained in Section E.2, this means that in the CBC mode, after 2^{32} DES operations, one can find with a good probability two identical cryptograms, which can lead to plaintext leakage.

The AES block cipher [3] corrects both the problem of larger key sizes and block sizes at a reasonable level of performance compared to Triple-DES. Thus, with a key of 128 bits, which is the smallest accepted by the cipher, the number of operations that have to be performed for exhaustive key search amounts to the astronomical figure of 2^{128}, which is foreseen to be protective at least for the next 20 years. The block size was adjusted to 128 bits, which increases to 2^{64} the number of CBC operations after which two cryptograms match, which is again considered highly secure. It is expected that systems relying on Triple-DES for symmetric encryption will gradually migrate to AES.

For the purpose of this book, however, only the DES and Triple-DES will be considered, since the majority of the standards describing payment systems, like EMV™, CEPS, and SET, have not yet updated to AES.

The specific use of DES and Triple-DES in the ECB and CBC modes will be considered according to the EMV™ standard [2]. Thus, the encryption algorithm E is either DES or Triple-DES.

The padding is performed according to the following rules:

1. If the initial message M has a byte-length that is not a multiple of 8 bytes (64 bits), perform padding. Add in the rightmost position of M the byte 80h, followed by the smallest number of bytes 00h such that the length of the padded message $M' = M \parallel 80 \parallel 00 \parallel \ldots \parallel 00$ is a multiple of 8 bytes.

2. If the initial message M has a byte-length that is a multiple of 8 bytes, two cases can be distinguished, depending on predefined rules adopted in the design. It can be that the padding is not performed and the message M' equals the initial message M. It can be that the message M is padded with a block of 8 bytes, $80 \parallel 00 \parallel \ldots \parallel 00$, in the rightmost position in order to obtain M'.

After the padding is performed, the message M' is divided in t blocks, P_i, $i = 1, \ldots, t$, which can be submitted to the cryptogram computation algorithm. This algorithm uses a session key K_s of 8 bytes (see Section E.5) if E is DES, or a key $K_s = K_{SL} \parallel K_{SR}$ of 16 bytes if E is Triple-DES.

In the ECB mode, each plaintext block P_i of 8 bytes is encrypted independently of the other blocks that form a message in a cryptogram of 8 bytes, $C_i = E(K_s)[P_i]$, $i = 1, \ldots, t$. The decryption is also carried out independently and is described by the relation $P_i = E^{-1}(K_s)[C_i]$, $i = 1, \ldots, t$.

In the CBC mode, each ciphertext block of 8 bytes is computed as $C_i = E(K_s)[P_i \text{ XOR } C_{i-1}]$, $i = 1, \ldots, t$. The initial vector IV is equal to $C_0 = \text{'00'} \parallel \text{'00'} \parallel \text{'00'} \parallel \text{'00'} \parallel \text{'00'} \parallel \text{'00'} \parallel \text{'00'} \parallel \text{'00'}$. The decryption process is described by the formula $P_i = E^{-1}(K_s)[C_i] \text{ XOR } C_{i-1}$, $i = 1, \ldots, t$, where the initial vector IV is equal to $C_0 = \text{'00'} \parallel \text{'00'} \parallel \text{'00'} \parallel \text{'00'} \parallel \text{'00'} \parallel \text{'00'} \parallel \text{'00'} \parallel \text{'00'}$.

E.4   MAC using a 64 bit-length block cipher

This appendix presents the computation of an s-byte MAC, with $4 \leq s \leq 8$, according to ISO 9797 [7], using a 64 bit-length block cipher E, which can be DES. The following steps describe the computation of the MAC [2]:

1. Pad the message M on which the MAC is computed according to method 2 of the ISO 9797. To this end add the mandatory byte 80h in

the rightmost position of M. Then add the smallest number of bytes 00h, which makes the length of the padded message $M' = M \parallel \text{'80'} \parallel \text{'00'} \parallel \ldots \parallel \text{'00'}$ a multiple of 8 bytes. The message M' is then divided in t blocks P_i, $i = 1, \ldots, t$.

2. The MAC session key K_s consists of only a leftmost key of 8 bytes $K_s = K_{SL}$, or of the concatenation of a leftmost key K_{SL} and a rightmost key K_{SR}, such that $K_s = K_{SL} \parallel K_{SR}$, which is 16 bytes in total.

3. Use the 64 bit-length block cipher DES with the key K_{SL} in the CBC mode on the blocks P_i, $i = 1, \ldots, t$ to obtain H_i, $i = 1, \ldots, t$ as $H_i = \text{DES}(K_{SL})[P_i \text{XOR} H_{i-1}]$, $i = 1, \ldots, t$. The initial vector IV is equal to $H_0 = \text{'00'} \parallel \text{'00'} \parallel \text{'00'} \parallel \text{'00'} \parallel \text{'00'} \parallel \text{'00'} \parallel \text{'00'} \parallel \text{'00'}$.

4. Compute an 8-byte final block H_{t+1} either according to the main process of ISO/IEC 9797 (i.e., $H_{t+1} = H_t$), or according to the Optional Process 1 of ISO/IEC 9797 (i.e., $H_{t+1} = \text{DES}(K_{SL})[\text{DES}^{-1}(K_{SR}) [H_t]]$).

5. The MAC is then computed as the most significant s bytes of H_{t+1}.

E.5 Key derivation

This appendix deals with the process of key derivation, which is useful at least in the following two situations, which are typical for the design of electronic payment systems.

1. Since tamper-resistant devices cannot be completely trusted, the issuer stores in the EEPROM of the device cryptographic material that is unique to the device but is derived from some master key of the issuer. Thus, the secret key that is specific to the device is derived as $K_d = F_1(MK)[Diversification\_Info]$. According to its key management policies, the issuer establishes the content of the diversification information $Diversification\_Info$. It may contain items like the serial number of the device, the identifier of the master key used for key derivation, and/or other information specific either to the device or to the issuer. The specific form of the derivation function F_1 and the features of the master key MK are also particular choices of the issuer.

2. Since the repeated use of one single key for performing CBC encryption can lead to the leakage of information about the plaintext (see Section E.2), it is highly recommended that the confidentiality

service for each communication session be implemented with a session key. The value of the session key K_s is derived from the same permanent key K_p, which is known to both parties, using as diversification information a time-variant byte sequence, like a random number or the value of a counter, which is incremented for each new transaction performed. Thus, the session key is computed as $K_s = F_2(K_p)$ [*time_variant*]. The communicating parties jointly convene the algorithm describing the function F_2 and the features of the permanent key K_p.

Specific details on these algorithms are provided in the descriptions of some business cases presented in the book.

References

[1]   NIST FIPS PUB 46, *Data Encryption Standard*, January 1977 (revised as FIPS PUB 46-1:1988 and FIPS PUB 46-2:1993).

[2]   EMVCo, *EMV 2000 Integrated Circuit Card Specification for Payment Systems, BOOK 2—Security and Key Management*, Version 4.0, December 2000, http://www.emvco.com/specifications.cfm.

[3]   NIST FIPS PUB Draft, *Advanced Encryption Standard*, http://csrc/nist/gov/publications/drafts/dfips-AES.pdf.

[4]   NIST FIPS PUB 81, *DES Modes of Operation*, December 1980.

[5]   Menezes, A. J., P. C. van Oorschot, and S. A. Vanstone, *Handbook of Applied Cryptography*, Boca Raton, FL: CRC Press, 1996.

[6]   Kocher, P. C., "Breaking DES," *RSA Laboratories' Cryptobytes*, Vol. 5, No. 2, 1999, also at http://www.rsa.com/rsalabs/pubs/crypto.

[7]   ISO/IEC 9797, "Information Technology—Data Cryptographic Techniques—Data Integrity Mechanisms Using a Cryptographic Check Function Employing a Block Cipher Algorithm," 1994.

Appendix F: RSA Encryption and Signature Scheme

The name RSA is derived from the inventors of the algorithm, Rivest, Shamir, and Adleman who presented the algorithm in [1]. RSA is an asymmetric system as described in Appendix D, Section D.1, where each user has a private key known only to him. Corresponding to this key is a public one, accessible to anyone. Data processed with one key can be recovered using the other key. At the same time there is no way that an attacker could recover the private key from the public key, a feature that is based on the difficulty of factoring large numbers. Using various operation modes, RSA can be used as an asymmetric encryption algorithm for secret key distribution or as a digital signature scheme.

F.1 Key generation

Each entity creates an RSA public key and the corresponding private key according to the following key generation algorithm:

1. Generate at random two distinct large prime numbers p and q, of approximately the same size.

2. Compute the modulus as the product of these two primes, $n = p * q$. Compute the Euler function of the modulus $\varphi(n) = (p-1) * (q-1)$.

3. Choose the public exponent e, $1 < e < \varphi(n)$, such that the greatest common divisor (*gcd*) of e and $\varphi(n)$ is 1 [i.e., $gcd(e, \varphi(n)) = 1$].

4. Use the extended Euclidian algorithm to compute the unique integer d, referred to as the secret exponent, $1 < d < \varphi(n)$, such that $e * d = 1 \mod \varphi(n)$.

5. The private key of the entity consists of the pair (n, d) and optionally the pair (p, q); while the public key of the entity consists of the pair (n, e).

Note that the computation of d can be performed with the universal exponent of n, which equals the least common multiple (*lcm*) of $p - 1$ and $q - 1$ denoted $\lambda(n) = lcm \ (p - 1, q - 1) = \varphi(n) / \gcd(p - 1, q - 1)$, using the formula $e * d = 1 \mod \lambda(n)$. The advantage is that the resulting d is smaller than in the case when d is computed with respect to $\varphi(n)$. Since p and q were generated at random, however, it is expected that $\gcd(p - 1, q - 1)$ is small, and correspondingly, the values of the secret exponent computed either way are approximately the same size.

In the key generation algorithm it was euphemistically stated that the primes p and q should be *large*. Their size is usually correlated to the state of the art in the factorization problem. The factorization of the modulus n implies breaking RSA. Indeed, someone who can successfully factor the modulus n in the primes p and q can easily compute $\varphi(n)$, and then applying the extended Euclidian algorithm can compute d from e and $\varphi(n)$. The largest published factorization, using the General Number Field Sieve algorithm is that of a 512-bit modulus (about 155 digits), reported in August 1999. Therefore, the bit-length of n is required to be minimum 768 bits, but for a system designed to work for several years a bit-length of at least 1,024 bits is highly recommended. Certainly, the bit-length of the modulus impacts on the performance: the bigger the modulus the slower the RSA operation. When the execution time is a functional constraint, the increase of the modulus' length reflects in a more expensive hardware/software platform of the device performing the RSA operation. If the device performing the RSA operation is a chip card, the presence in the hardware architecture of the chip of a cryptographic coprocessor specialized in long arithmetic operations is a must, which slightly increases the cost of the cards.

It was never proved that breaking RSA necessarily implies factoring the modulus, but there is good evidence that this implication does not hold if the public exponent is small. Some popular values of a few years ago, of a public exponent of value 3 or 17, are no longer recommended. Based on recent results in the area of RSA cryptanalysis [2, 3] the public exponent for RSA must be sufficiently large. The commonly used value $2^{16} + 1$ is still acceptable, but for a higher level of assurance the value of the public exponent should be generated at random on 32 bits or even 64 bits, with odd values.

F.2   Public and secret RSA operations

The public and secret RSA operations can take any integer number m as input, which satisfies the condition $0 \leq m \leq n - 1$. The results produced by any of the operations remain in the same range as m.

- The public RSA operation is computed with the public key (n, e) on the number m, using the formula $P(n,e)[m] = m^e \bmod n$. The sign "$^{\wedge}$" stands for a modular exponentiation.

- The secret RSA operation is computed with the private key (n, d) on the number m, using the formula $S(n,d)[m] = m^d \bmod n$.

It is shown in [1] that the two operations are inverse of each other (i.e., $P(n,e)[\ S(n,d)[m]] = m)$, for all the numbers m in the range $[0, n - 1]$.

Using various operation modes, RSA can be used as an asymmetric encryption algorithm for secret key distribution (see Appendix D, Section D.1) or as a digital signature scheme (see Appendix D, Section D.3). When referring to the communicating parties A and B in Figure B.1, assume that:

- A is the sender of an encrypted message to the receiver B. To this end B has generated the RSA key pair consisting of a private decryption key $KD_B = (n_E, d_E)$ and the corresponding public encryption key $KE_B = (n_E, e_E)$. A has an authentic copy of this public encryption key, which could have been delivered as a public key certificate by a CA, which is accepted by both A and B (see Appendix D, Section D.4).

- A is the signer of a message while B is the verifier of the signature generated by A on that message. To this end A has generated the RSA key pair consisting of a private signing key $KS_A = (n_S, d_S)$ and the corresponding public verification key $KV_A = (n_S, e_S)$. B has an authentic copy of this public verification key, which could have been delivered as a public key certificate by a CA, which is accepted by both A and B.

The public RSA operation represents an encryption when the public exponent e and the modulus n are the components of the public encryption key $KE_B = (n_E, e_E)$ of the receiver B, and the number m represents confidential information, like a secret session key. In this case $E(KE_B)[m] = P(n_E, e_E)[m] = m^\wedge(e_E) \bmod n_E$.

The public RSA operation represents a signature verification when the public exponent e and the modulus n are the components of the public verification key $KV_A = (n_S, e_S)$ of the signer A. The number S represents the signature with appendix on a message M, which has to be verified. In this case $Verify(KV_A)[S, M] = P(n_S, e_S)[S] = S^\wedge(e_S) \bmod n_S ?= R(M)$, where R is a suitable redundancy function. If the signature scheme offers message recovery, then $Recover(KV_A)[S, M'] = P(n_S, e_S)[S] = S^\wedge(e_S) \bmod n_S ?= R(M_R \parallel M')$, where R is a suitable redundancy function, M_R is the part of the message M that can be recovered from S, and M' is the part of M that has to be explicitly sent by A to B such that the recover function is computable.

The secret RSA operation represents a decryption when the secret exponent d and the modulus n are the components of the private decryption key $KD_B = (n_E, d_E)$ of the receiver B, and the number m represents a cryptogram, like a digital envelope wrapping a secret session key. In this case, $D(KD_B)[m] = S(n_E, d_E)[m] = m^\wedge(d_E) \bmod n_E$.

The secret RSA operation represents a signature generation when the secret exponent d and the modulus n are the components of the private signing key $KS_A = (n_S, d_S)$ of the signer A, and the number m represents the message M to be signed with some redundancy. In this case, $Sign(KS_A)[M] = S(n_S, d_S)[m] = m^\wedge(d_S) \bmod n_S$.

F.3 Digital signature giving message recovery

This appendix outlines the digital signature scheme with message recovery using a hash function as described in the EMV™ specification for security [4], which is further adapted from the standard ISO/IEC 9796-2 as follows:

> • The signature generation and signature verification functions are performed only with the secret and public RSA operations with odd exponents. This is because the Rabin variant of RSA, using even exponents, and in particular a public exponent equal to 2, was proven insecure. When the attacker can persuade the signer to produce signatures on a few particular messages chosen by the attacker, the attacker can actually compute the signer's private signing key [2]. This is the reason way the Rabin variant was removed from the list of approved cryptographic algorithms for asymmetric cryptography in the *EMV 2000* specifications [4].

▸ The redundancy function is implemented with a hash function, like the SHA-1 with a hash code of 160 bits (see Appendix D, Section D.2), which avoids some of the recent attacks on the standard ISO/IEC 9796-1 [5–8]. In the RSA case with odd exponents, the details of the attack vary depending on the particularities of the methods for padding and adding redundancy to the data string before applying the RSA secret operation. In all cases the attack requires the construction of a large set of chosen data strings with special mathematical properties, which are not meaningful for specific applications. However, none of these attacks would succeed if a hash code is always signed rather than any other redundancy-built message.

▸ Add a header and trailer byte to obtain a unique recovery procedure.

F.3.1   Signature generation

The signature is computed by the signer on a message $M = M_R \parallel M'$, where M_R is the part recoverable from the signature and M' is the part that must be separately sent by the signer. The byte-length of the message M is L. The secret RSA operation is performed with respect to the modulus n_s of byte-length N and the secret exponent d_s. In this setup the signature generation algorithm takes place in the following way.

Case 1: Message M entirely recoverable from S   In this case $M = M_R$ and M' is empty, which is equivalent to $L \leq N - 22$.

1. Compute the hash code of M through the SHA-1 algorithm and store the result of 20 bytes in H.

2. When $L = N - 22$, define $B = 4A$. Otherwise, define block B as a byte string of $N - 21 - L$ bytes, $B = (4B \parallel BB \parallel ... \parallel BB \parallel BA)$.

3. Define $E = BC$.

4. Define the N-byte block X as the concatenation of B, M, H, and E (i.e., $X = B \parallel M \parallel H \parallel E$).

5. Compute the RSA secret operation on X corresponding to the signature generation mode and obtain the signature $S = Sign(KS_A)[X] = S(n_s, d_s)[X] = X^\wedge(d_s) \bmod n_s$.

Case 2: Message *M* is not entirely recoverable from *S*   In this case $M = M_R \parallel$ *M'*, where M_R is $N - 22$ bytes and *M'* is $L - N + 22$ bytes.

1.   Compute the hash code of *M* through the SHA-1 algorithm and store the result of 20 bytes in *H*.

2.   Split $M = M_R \parallel M'$, where M_R is $N - 22$ bytes and *M'* is $L - N + 22$ bytes.

3.   Define $B = 6A$.

4.   Define $E = BC$.

5.   Define the *N*-byte block *X* as the concatenation of *B*, M_R, *H*, and *E* (i.e., $X = B \parallel M_R \parallel H \parallel E$).

6.   Compute the RSA secret operation on *X* corresponding to the signature generation mode and obtain the signature $S = Sign(KS_A)[X]$ $= S(n_s, d_s)[X] = X^\wedge(d_s) \bmod n_s$.

F.3.2 Signature verification

The verifier performs the signature verification on the signature *S*. If the message *M* is bigger than $N - 22$ bytes, then the part *M'* of the message that can not be retrieved from *S* is also an input to the recover predicate. The public RSA operation is performed with respect to the modulus n_s of byte-length *N* and the public exponent e_s. In this setup the signature verification algorithm takes place in the following way.

Case 1: Message *M* entirely recoverable from *S*   In this case $M = M_R$ and *M'* is empty, which is equivalent to $L \leq N - 22$.

1.   Check that the byte-length of *S* is *N*.

2.   Retrieve the *N* byte number *X* from the digital signature *S* with the formula $X = Recover(KV_A)[S, M' = empty] = P(n_s, e_s)[S] = S^\wedge(e_s) \bmod n_s$.

3.   Check the redundancy of *X*. To this end *X* is first split in $X = B \parallel M \parallel H \parallel$ *E*, where:

   ▸ *B* = '4A' or *B* is a leading byte string of the form $B = (4B \parallel BB \parallel \ldots \parallel BB \parallel BA)$.

> • H is 20 bytes long.

> • E is 1 byte long.

> • $M = M_R$ consists of the remaining bytes.

4.   Check whether the byte E is equal to BC.

5.   Check whether SHA-1(M) ?= H.

If and only if all the checks from steps 3 to 5 are passed, is the signature accepted as genuine.

Case 2: Message M is not entirely recoverable from S.   In this case $M = M_R \parallel M'$, where M_R is $N - 22$ bytes and can be recovered from the signature. The part M' is $L - N + 22$ bytes and has to be separately sent to the verifier.

1.   Check that the byte-length of S is N.

2.   Retrieve the N byte number X from the digital signature S with the formula $X = Recover(KV_A)[S, M'] = P(n_s, e_s)[S] = S^{\wedge}(e_s) \bmod n_s$.

3.   Check the redundancy of X. To this end X is first split in $X = B \parallel M_R \parallel H \parallel E$, where:

> • B is 1 byte long.

> • H is 20 bytes long.

> • E is 1 byte long.

> • M_R consists of the remaining $N - 22$ bytes.

4.   Check whether the byte B is equal to 6A.

5.   Check whether the byte E is equal to BC.

6.   Concatenate the part M_R recovered from X with the part sent separately by the signer M' (i.e., compute $M = M_R \parallel M'$). Check whether SHA-1$(M) = H$.

If and only if all the checks from steps 3 to 6 are passed is the signature accepted as genuine.

F.4   Digital signature and encryption with PKCS#1

This section outlines the digital signature scheme as described in the PKCS#1 standard [9]. Note that the same standard specifies the encryption/decryption of a data block that can transport symmetric keys.

Data formatting   Both the encryption and the digital signature use the same data formatting: the *encryption block EB* submitted to either the public RSA operation (encryption) or secret RSA operation (digital signature) has the format $EB = 00 \parallel BT \parallel PS \parallel 00 \parallel D$, representing a byte-string.

- The block type BT equals 00 or 01 for a digital signature, but for the scope of this book only $BT = 01$ is considered, which improves the parsing of EB and eliminates some potential attacks on the signature mechanism. The block type BT equals 02 for encryption.

- The data D represents either the secret keys to be wrapped in the digital envelope (encryption) or the hash-code of the message to be signed. The byte-length of D, denoted $|D|$, must be smaller or at most equal to $N - 11$, where N represents the byte-length of the modulus n of the RSA operation.

- The padding string PS consists of $N - 3 - |D|$ bytes. If $BT = 01$, all the bytes of PS are FF; while if $BT = 02$, each byte of PS is generated at random.

Signature generation with PKCS#1

1.   The message M to be signed is hashed with the selected *MDC* algorithm, obtaining the hash code H.

2.   The hash code H and the *MDC* algorithm identifier are combined in an ASN.1 (abstract syntax notation) value, which is further BER-encoded (basic encoding rules) to give an octet data string D.

3.   Compute the encryption block EB as explained in the "Data Formatting" section, with $BT = 01$.

4.   Interpret the byte-string EB as an integer m, which is always smaller than the modulus n_s.

5. Perform the secret RSA operation on m corresponding to the signature generation mode and obtain the signature $S = Sign(KS_A)[m] = S(n_s, d_s)[m] = m^\wedge(d_s) \bmod n_s$.

6. Interpret S as a byte-string, which is forwarded together with the message to the verifier.

Signature verification with PKCS#1

1. The byte-string S received from the signer is rejected if the bit-length of S is not a multiple of 8, or if the corresponding integer value is bigger than the value of the modulus n_s.

2. Perform the public RSA operation on S corresponding to the signature verification mode and obtain the integer $m = Verify(KV_A)[S, M] = P(n_s, e_s)[S] = S^\wedge(e_s)\bmod n_s$.

3. Interpret the integer m as a byte-string EB of length N bytes.

4. Parse EB into a block type BT, a padding string PS, and the data D. Reject the signature if BT does not equal 01, or if the byte-length of PS is less than 8 bytes or the bytes in PS are different than FF.

5. BER-decode D to obtain a hash code H and an MDC algorithm identifier. Reject the signature if the MDC algorithm identifier is not in the set of accepted MDC algorithms.

6. Using the MDC algorithm identifier, select the appropriate MDC and compute the hash code H' on the message M, sent by the signer as a mandatory item for the verification process. If the computed H' is different than the hash code H retrieved from D, reject the signature. Otherwise the signature on M is accepted as valid.

Encryption–key wrapping with PKCS#1

1. The sender computes at random a double-length DES key of 16 bytes for a Triple-DES algorithm. The data D consists of this double-length DES key. This is just an example, but any secret cryptographic parameter(s) with a byte-length smaller than $N - 11$ bytes can be encrypted.

2. Compute the encryption block EB as explained in the "Data Formatting" section, with $BT = 02$. The padding string contains a number of $N - 3 - |D|$ random bytes.

3. Interpret the byte-string EB as an integer m, which is always smaller than the modulus n_E.

4. Perform the public RSA operation on m corresponding to the encryption mode and obtain the digital envelope $c = E(KE_B)[m] = P(n_E, e_E)[m] = m^\wedge(e_E) \bmod n_E$.

5. Interpret c as a byte-string, which is forwarded to the receiver.

Decryption–key unwrapping with PKCS#1

1. The byte-string c received from the sender is rejected if the corresponding integer value is greater than the value of the modulus n_E.

2. Perform the secret RSA operation on c corresponding to the decryption mode and obtain the number $m = D(KD_B)[c] = S(n_E, d_E)[c] = c^\wedge(d_E) \bmod n_E$.

3. Interpret the integer m as the byte-string EB of length N bytes.

4. Parse EB into a block type BT, a padding string PS, and the data D. Consider that the received digital envelope is not correct if BT does not equal 02, or the byte-length of PS is less than 8 bytes.

5. Retrieve the double-length DES key transported in D and store it for later use.

References

[1]   Rivest, R. L., A. Shamir, and L. Adleman, "A Method for Obtaining Digital Signatures and Public-Key Cryptosystems," *Communications of the ACM*, No. 21, 1978, pp. 120–126.

[2]   Coppersmith, D., et al., "Low-Exponent RSA with Related Messages," *Proc. Eurocrypt'96*, Berlin, Germany: Springer LNCS 1070, 1996, pp. 1–9.

[3]   Coppersmith, D., "Finding a Small Root of a Univariate Modular Equation," *Proc. Eurocrypt'96*, Berlin, Germany: Springer LNCS 1070, 1996, pp. 155–165.

[4] EMVCo, *EMV 2000 Integrated Circuit Card Specification for Payment Systems,*
     BOOK 2—Security and Key Management, Version 4.0, December 2000, http://
     www.emvco.com/specifications.cfm.

[5] Coron J.-S., D. Naccache, and J. P. Stern, "On the Security of RSA Padding,"
     Proc. Crypto'99, Berlin, Germany: Springer LNCS 1666, 1999, pp. 1–18.

[6] Coppersmith, D., S. Halevi, and C. Jutla, "ISO 9796 1 and the New Forgery
     Strategy," *Research contribution to P1363 (1999),* http://grouper.ieee.org/groups/
     1363/Research/cryptanalysis.html#attack9796.

[7] Grieu, F., "A Chosen Messages Attack on the ISO/IEC 9796-1 Signature
     Scheme," *Proc. Eurocrypt 2000,* Berlin, Germany: Springer LNCS 1807, 2000,
     pp. 70–80.

[8] Girault, M., and J.-F. Misarsky, "Cryptanalysis of Countermeasures Proposed
     for Repairing ISO 9796-1," *Proc. Eurocrypt 2000,* Berlin, Germany: Springer
     LNCS 1807, 2000, pp. 81–90.

[9] RSA Laboratories, *PKCS#1: RSA Encryption Standard,* version 1.5, November
     1993.

Appendix G: E-Commerce and M-Commerce Related Technologies

G.1 E-commerce and m-commerce

The use of the Internet continuously increases as more and more households become connected to the Internet. A growing number of people use the Internet for sending and receiving electronic mail, for finding and retrieving information on the World Wide Web (Web), and also for shopping and purchasing. Thus, the Web has become a huge virtual market, without borders, providing consumers with enormous offers and merchants with incredible opportunities for revenue. At present, many of the purchases made are of CDs, books, electronic components and computer hardware, software delivered on material support, airline tickets, hotel reservations, and also digital goods (e.g., information on demand, access to databases, and on-line software downloading). This business framework is commonly called electronic commerce, or simply e-commerce.

At the same or greater rate of increase as the Internet is the usage of wireless mobile networks, which allow subscribers to establish mobile voice communications, text, and data transfers. At present, an example of such a network is the Global System for Mobile Communications, commonly known as GSM. In the near future other wireless mobile networks will be implemented—namely, the General Packet Radio Service (GPRS) and the Universal Mobile Telecommunication System (UMTS). The UMTS is part of the third generation (3G) mobile communication system. 3G provides enhanced services compared to those offered today by the GSM network, together with a whole range of mobile Internet services. Mobile applications refer to added value services offered by the wireless mobile network operators to their subscribers in addition the basic service of voice communication. They allow clients to use the keypad and the display of their mobile phones or mobile Internet access devices to ask for services and to receive the appropriate responses. Mobile commerce, simply referred to as m-commerce, is such a service, which allows subscribers to order and purchase goods while they are roaming. Among the preferred purchases bought while roaming are on-line content (like entertainment and news), fast food, products from vending machines, and services like paying for parking or public transportation tickets. In this appendix, we outline some technologies in relation to the GSM network. This type of wireless mobile network will be used for exemplification purposes in our explanations.

G.2   SIM, STK, SMS, and WAP

The Subscriber Identity Module (SIM) [1] is a small-sized chip card plugged in the mobile phone. The main task of a SIM is to grant access to the GSM network services only to authorized persons. This is absolutely essential to operators for ensuring reliable billing. Apart from this primary function, the SIM also stores some additional data in connection with telecom services, such as abbreviated dialing numbers, the last dialed number, etc. To support mobile applications, the SIM must also implement the SIM Application Toolkit standard (STK) [2]. Unlike the SIM, which is regarded by the mobile phone as a server application that offers data storage and cryptographic functionality, the STK is an active element. Using it, the GSM operator can actually control the user interface of the mobile phone according to its own purposes. It becomes possible to change or add menus, send and receive short text messages with application data, display service information, and ask the user to select or enter data. Therefore, the STK is a powerful instrument when designing mobile applications. The code of the mobile application resides in the SIM.

The Point-to-Point Short Message Service (PP-SMS) [3] allows the subscriber to send short text messages or to receive short text messages from another subscriber or an SMS center, through a point-to-point channel. The subscriber selects the telephone number of the recipient, enters the short message via the keypad of the mobile phone, and sends it. Each mobile phone is also able to receive short messages. Mobile applications running in the SIM can also use the same mechanism of sending and receiving short messages to implement a protocol with a peer application. In this case the short messages are not edited by the subscriber but prepared by the application and sent to the SMS center. The information that is returned from the SMS center in a short message is not read as text but it is handled by the mobile application. Short messages are very well suited for supporting transaction type services (e.g., mobile banking, mobile fund transfer, and mobile payments for m-commerce). The mobile application server runs on a computer that is connected to the GSM network via an SMS center.

Another possibility of implementing mobile applications uses the WAP [4], which is an open, global standard for mobile solutions and for connecting mobile terminals to the Internet. WAP-based technology permits the design of interactive, real-time mobile services for mobile handsets, whether they are phones, PDAs, or other types of mobile access devices. The advantage of the WAP technology when compared to the STK/SMS is that it makes receiving and reacting to information on the mobile phone easy and user friendly. Some differences when compared to STK/SMS-based mobile applications are as follows:

› The mobile phone handset must be WAP enabled, (i.e., must implement the WAP protocol). At the moment the ratio of WAP enabled handsets is still small, while the penetration on the market increases below the initial expectations.

› The WAP server controls the interface of the mobile application provided to the subscriber. Correspondingly, the quality of this interface strongly depends on the display possibilities of the mobile handset (e.g., only if the display of the handset supports graphics, will the bitmaps and images be displayed).

› WAP applications are slower than the STK/SMS-based applications, since the user interface needs to be downloaded from a remote server.

Beginning with WAP 1.2, end-to-end security is supported. The Wireless Identity Module (WIM) is used for storing cryptographic parameters and executing cryptographic algorithms. The WIM can be plugged into a second socket in the mobile phone handset, different than the one reserved for the SIM, or the SIM can also accommodate the functionality of the WIM, in which case the SIM is referred to as the SWIM.

G.3   Access devices for remote card payments

This appendix analyzes the hardware and software configurations of the cardholder and merchant access devices that allow their interaction on the appropriate open network channels.

To support a browsing/ordering channel over the Internet, denoted channel 1 in Figure G.1, the cardholder access device runs a Web browser and the merchant access device runs a Web server. Both access devices must have the adequate hardware for establishing a network connection, together with the appropriate software implementing the TCP/IP protocol stack. Usually, the cardholder access device can be a personal computer or a workstation, while the merchant access device can be a small computer like a PC or workstation, if the number of Web accesses is small, or a powerful mainframe for frequently accessed commercial sites. Their interaction is schematized in Figure G.2.

In this scenario, the commercial offer of a merchant is represented as Web pages, which are stored on the merchant's Web server. The Web pages can be written with the hypertext markup language (HTML), or with the extended markup language (XML), and the Java Script scripting language. The cardholder's browser makes a content request using the uniform resource locator (URL) address of the concerned Web page. The Web server

Figure G.1
Payment card processing in remote transactions.

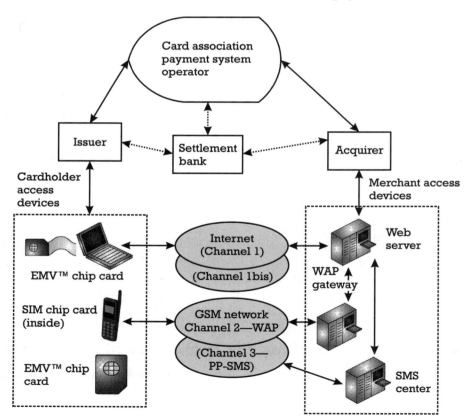

Figure G.2
Browsing/
ordering
channel over
the Internet.

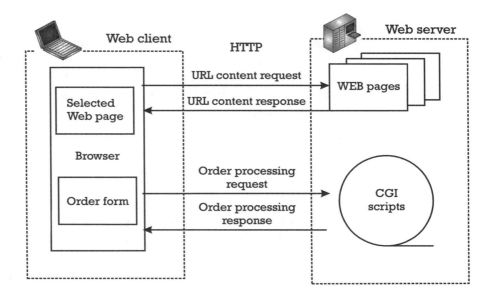

returns a response that includes the content of this Web page, which is displayed by the cardholder access device. The browser is a client that requests services to the Web server, which provides the appropriate responses, according to the rules of the htypertext transfer protocol (HTTP). Thus, the cardholder can retrieve and display the appropriate commercial offer of the merchant. Not only can the cardholder inform herself about the merchant's offer from the content of a Web page, but if this page also includes an ordering form she can also make her choice and order the desired purchases. To this end the cardholder's browser sends a processing request of the order form to the merchant's Web server. The server processes this request, using, for example, the common gate interface (CGI) technology, and elaborates a processing response informing the cardholder about the completion of her order, and eventually providing a receipt.

▸ Unique Internet channel device (channel 1 only): If the ordering form retrieved from the merchant's Web page requires information about the cardholder's payment card, the browsing/ordering Internet channel serves also as a payment channel. This is the case when both phases of the cardholder-merchant interaction can be completed using the same channel over the Internet. Both the browsing/ordering phase and the payment phase are completed in the same session. For this payment method, the Web server includes a script that captures the payment card data received from the Web browser and creates an authorization request that is forwarded to the appropriate acquirer, where the merchant is a client. The access devices of both the cardholder and the merchant do not need supplementary software or hardware resources. However, since the established channel must be secured, both the Web browser and the Web server must be cryptographically enabled.

▸ The ordering form retrieved from the merchant's Web page contains only the information needed for negotiating a common payment method between the consumer and the merchant. Two peer payment applications, running on the cardholder access device and on the merchant access device, respectively, interchange messages according to a dedicated protocol for completing the payment phase. The protocol, including the security measures considered appropriate for safeguarding the interests of the participants, is specific to each payment application. Thus, the two applications establish a secure communication over an insecure channel. We present two possibilities:

  ▸ Dual Internet channel device (channel 1 and channel 1bis): A separate TCP/IP channel over the Internet is established between the two peer payment applications (e.g., channel 1bis in Figure G.1). This is the case when each phase of the cardholder-merchant interaction is completed using a different channel over the same open network. The payment phase is completed in a different session than the browsing/ordering phase. The cardholder can use the same access device like the one used for ordering/browsing (e.g., a PC). The software configuration of the cardholder and merchant access devices must include the adequate software for running the peer payment application on each side. If the payment card is an EMV™ chip card, the hardware configuration of the cardholder access device includes a chip card reader, which is EMV level 1 compatible, together with the appropriate software driver.

  ▸ Dual channel/dual network device (channel 1 and channel 3): A separate PP-SMS channel over the GSM network is established between the two peer payment applications (e.g., channel 3 in Figure G.1). This is the case when each phase of the cardholder-merchant interaction is completed using a separate channel over different open networks. The payment phase is completed in a different session than the browsing/ordering phase. In this case the cardholder may have a separate access device, which can be a mobile phone that is different than the one used for browsing (e.g., a PC). The mobile phone is able to establish the PP-SMS channel and to run the mobile payment application. This mobile payment application can reside directly in the SIM or in a separate EMV™ chip card, read from the dual slot of the mobile phone. The dual slot is a chip card reader, which is also EMV level 1 compatible. In addition to the Web server, the merchant device also runs the peer payment application, which must be able to communicate with the SMS center. This center is able to establish an SMS channel with the cardholder mobile phone and to intermediate between the cardholder and merchant peer payment applications.

For supporting a browsing/ordering WAP channel, denoted channel 2 in Figure G.1, the cardholder access device is a mobile phone that runs a micro browser, which interprets WAP content referred by an URL and displays this content to the end user. The merchant access device runs an origin server, providing the WAP content. A WAP gateway provided by the GSM operator encodes the requests coming from the micro browser to the origin server and decodes the responses coming from the origin server to the micro browser. An overview of a typical WAP architecture is presented in Figure G.3.

The commercial offer of a merchant is represented as WAP pages, which are stored on the merchant's origin server. The WAP pages can be written with the wireless markup language (WML) and the wireless markup

Figure G.3
Browsing/
ordering WAP
channel over
the GSM
network.

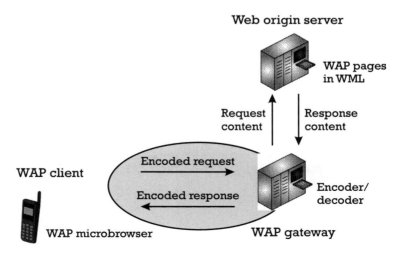

language script (WMLScript) scripting language. The cardholder's micro-browser makes a content request using the URL address of the concerned WAP page. The origin server returns a response that includes the content of this WAP page, which is displayed by the cardholder's mobile phone. The WAP page can also include an ordering form, where the cardholder can make her choice on the desired purchases.

- Unique WAP channel device (channel 2 only): If the ordering form retrieved from the merchant's WAP page requires the information about the cardholder's payment card, the browsing/ordering WAP channel (channel 2 in Figure G.1) also serves as a payment channel. This is the case when both the browsing/ordering phase and the payment phase can be completed using the same WAP channel over the GSM network. Both the browsing/ordering phase and the payment phase are completed in the same session. Since the established channel must be secured, the micro browser, the WAP gateway, and the origin server must be cryptographically enabled.

- Dual mobile channel device (channel 2 and channel 3): The ordering form retrieved from the merchant's WAP page contains only the information needed for negotiating a common card payment method between the cardholder and the merchant. Two peer mobile payment applications, running on the cardholder's mobile phone and on the merchant access device, respectively, interchange messages according to a dedicated protocol for completing the payment phase. A separate PP-SMS channel over the GSM network must be established between the two peer payment applications (e.g., channel 3 in Figure G.1). This is the case when each phase of the cardholder-merchant interaction is completed using a different channel over the same GSM network. The payment phase is completed in a different session than the browsing/ordering phase. The mobile payment application can reside directly in the (W)SIM or in a separate EMV™ chip card, read from the dual slot of the mobile phone.

G.4 WAP protocol suite compared to Internet

The WAP suite is compared to the Internet protocol suite as presented in Table G.1.

Table G.1
Comparison between the Internet and the WAP Protocol Suites

Internet	WAP
HTML and JavaScript	WML and WMLScript
HTTP	Wireless Session Protocol (WSP)
	Wireless Transaction Protocol (WTP)
TLS-SSL	Wireless Transport Layer Security (WTLS)
TCP/IP	Wireless Datagram Protocol (WDP)
UDP/IP	UDP

References

[1] ETSI, Global System for Mobile Communication, *Digital Cellular Telecommunication System (Phase 2+); Specification of the Subscriber Identity Module–Mobile Equipment (SIM-ME) Interface*, GSM 11.11, Version 8.3.0, Release 1999.

[2] ETSI, Global System for Mobile Communication, *Digital Cellular Telecommunications System (Phase 2+); Specification of the SIM Application Toolkit for the Subscriber Identity Module–Mobile Equipment (SIM-ME) Interface*, GSM 11.14, Version 8.3.0, Release 1999.

[3] ETSI, Global System for Mobile Communication, *Digital Cellular Telecommunications System (Phase 2+); Technical Realization of the Short Message Service (SMS) Point-to-Point (PP)*, GSM 03.40, Version 7.4.0, Release 1998.

[4] WAP Forum, *Wireless Application Protocol Architecture Specification*, WAP-210-WAPArch-20010712-a, http://www.wapforum.org/what/technical.htm.

About the Author

Cristian Radu was born on September 2, 1962, in Craiova, Romania. In 1981 he obtained his B.A. from the High School Of Mathematics and Physics Nicolae Balcescu of Craiova. In 1986 he graduated from the Automation and Control Faculty program at the Polytechnic University of Bucharest, Romania. He holds a Ph.D. in electrical engineering from the Catholic University of Leuven, Belgium.

After his graduation, Dr. Radu worked as an electrical engineer with the Automation Institute of Bucharest, Romania, until January 1990. From February 1990 through March 1993 he worked as an assistant professor with the Automation and Control Faculty at the Polytechnic University of Bucharest. In April 1993, he joined the Computer Security and Industrial Cryptography Group in the ESAT Department of the Catholic University of Leuven. Dr. Radu obtained two European Union research scholarships and participated in several European research projects related to the analysis and design of electronic payment schemes. In October 1997 he defended his Ph.D. dissertation, "Analysis and Design of Offline Electronic Payment Systems." From December 1997 through March 2002, he worked as a payment system consultant for Integri NV in Belgium. Since March 2002 he has worked as an independent consultant for payment system and telecom operators in Belgium.

Index

Practical Process Simulation Using Object-Oriented Techniques and C++,
 José Garrido

Risk-Based E-Business Testing, Paul Gerrard and Neil Thompson

Secure Messaging with PGP and S/MIME, Rolf Oppliger

Software Fault Tolerance Techniques and Implementation,
 Laura L. Pullum

*Software Verification and Validation for Practitioners and Managers,
 Second Edition,* Steven R. Rakitin

Strategic Software Production with Domain-Oriented Reuse, Paolo Predonzani,
 Giancarlo Succi, and Tullio Vernazza

Systems Modeling for Business Process Improvement, David Bustard,
 Peter Kawalek, and Mark Norris, editors

User-Centered Information Design for Improved Software Usability,
 Pradeep Henry

*Workflow Modeling: Tools for Process Improvement and Application
 Development,* Alec Sharp and Patrick McDermott

For further information on these and other Artech House titles,
including previously considered out-of-print books now available through our
In-Print-Forever® (IPF®) program, contact:

Artech House
685 Canton Street
Norwood, MA 02062
Phone: 781-769-9750
Fax: 781-769-6334
e-mail: artech@artechhouse.com

Artech House
46 Gillingham Street
London SW1V 1AH UK
Phone: +44 (0)20 7596-8750
Fax: +44 (0)20 7630-0166
e-mail: artech-uk@artechhouse.com

Find us on the World Wide Web at:
www.artechhouse.com